What the hell am I doing here?

*Travels with an
occasional war correspondent*

What the hell am I doing here?

*Travels with an
Occasional War Correspondent*

PAUL MOORCRAFT

Brassey's (UK) Ltd
London • Washington

First English Edition 1995

UK editorial offices: Brassey's, 33 John Street, London WC1N 2AT
UK orders: Marston Book Services, PO Box 87, Oxford OX2 0DT

North American Orders: Brassey's Inc.
PO Box 960, Herndon, VA 22070.

The Author has asserted his moral right to be identified as
the author of this work.

Library of Congress Cataloging in Publication Data
available

British Library Cataloguing in Publication Data
A catalogue record for this book is available from the British Library

ISBN 1 85753 121 3

Typeset by Solidus (Bristol) Ltd
Printed in Great Britain by
Bookcraft (Bath) Limited

To Jan,
who held my hand
and led me
through a minefield.

About the author

Paul Moorcraft, 46, calls himself a 'renegade academic turned journalist'. He has been, *inter alia*, an elected Welsh Nationalist politician, a Sandhurst instructor, university professor, policeman, film producer, occasionally on the dole and always a traveller. As a sideline, Dr Moorcraft has lectured (variously) in history, politics, international relations and social sciences, as well as journalism, at the universities of Rhodesia, Natal, Cape Town, the Witwatersrand, the Open University (UK), Cardiff, Bournemouth and Deakin (Australia). In 1992 he was Distinguished Visiting Radford Professor of Journalism at Baylor University, Texas.

More seriously, as a freelance he has covered most of the major wars of the last 20 years for BBC radio, major TV networks, and newspapers such as *Time*. His first satirical book, *A Short Thousand Years* (1979), was about Rhodesian Prime Minister Ian Smith's promise that black rule would take a millennium. His last book for Brassey's was surprisingly, and successfully, sober: *African Nemesis: War and Revolution in Southern Africa, 1945–2010* (1990). From 1993 he lived in Australia while writing a book on 'Oz culture'. In 1994, after covering South Africa's first non-racial elections, he left Australia to return to Wales, via Thailand and Bosnia.

Contents

Plates appear between pages 244 and 245

List of maps

Guns and poses

I can't tell you exactly what type of book this is because I don't know. Yes, it is mainly about war zones. Sure, it's about travel in exotic locations. It is about journalism. And there is, I hope, humour as well as adventure.

Perhaps I can explain *why* I wrote it. I have spent the best part of the last 20 years travelling and talking to unusual people in unusual places but it is *not* the war memoirs of a Welsh hack. My initial impulse to travel in and write about war zones was based on my frustrations as a Sandhurst instructor and, later, university academic. I didn't want just to talk about or research other countries, I wanted to *feel* them. Another reason was my objection to the type of journalism, especially American TV news, which suggests that reporting and film-making are based on synthetic travels in a bubble. At the other end of the scale, I objected just as vehemently to some TV stars' mock heroics, super-hyped on air. I wanted to explain what went on behind the scenes, particularly the cock-ups. Mostly *my* cock-ups.

I have struggled hard to be neutral about conflicts, without being afraid to call a spade a bloody shovel when necessary. So if you're looking for political correctness, don't read this book. Although I have sometimes used the dialogue style of a novel, the conversations are based upon my notes and video or audio recordings. In short, I have tried to make my account as accurate as possible.

Sometimes people say to me: 'I would do what you do if I didn't have a wife, kids and a mortgage.' For most of my travels I had a very large German shepherd, which often trotted faithfully behind me. For some of the time I had a wife and family and even, for a brief period, a large mortgage. The fact that now I have none of these suggests that you have to be a trifle eccentric to spend your life travelling and trying to write about it.

Nevertheless, I believe readers will identify with my travails – travels comes from the same word – as I walk to Kabul with a camel (and holy warriors) who hated me, get lost on a motorbike ride with psychopaths in central Mozambique, fall down drunk in a shebeen in Soweto or, like everyone else, become totally confused in Lebanon and ex-Yugoslavia by the craziness of politicians. Looking back, I don't know how I managed to wriggle out of some of the countries I visited, usually with a film, book or radio story in my bag. I am probably the world's clumsiest person: I make Mr Bean look like Nureyev. I hope you can sometimes smell not just the cordite but also the fear, usually mine.

I do occasionally talk about guns and battles but I am more concerned with colourful characters, the customs, politics and landscapes. Buildings interest me more than bullets. Some of the stories are about journeys from A to B via Z; others are about living for long periods in a country. Sometimes I write about specific events; in other stories I try to catch the mood of major upheavals, such as the collapse of communism in Eastern Europe. But it's not all depressing: I sometimes stretch the definition of conflict and write about nice places. There are some philosophical themes but they are very implicit – I am trying to recount stories, not lecture. Although I would be a fool and a liar if I said I wasn't influenced by other writers, I have tried to do something different with *What the hell am I doing here?* I still don't know what it is but, as I said, I have tried above all to tell a series of stories. I hope you enjoy reading them.

The photographs are my own, except where indicated otherwise. I have few acknowledgements, mainly because most of the people I met in this line of work did everything they could to hinder, discourage or, occasionally, shoot me. But I would like to thank Trish for accommodating me, Karen for pointing out my many lapses of good taste (all of which remain), Jane, my agent, and Jenny, my publisher. Mary, Cherry and Justine advised on the editing. Slavka and, later, Jo helped me survive Geelong. Three friends gave comfort through the lonely nights: 'caffeine, nicotine and Springsteen'. I salute Nick, who was killed in Kurdistan, and Al, who survives everything. Finally, Tim, thanks for covering, and kicking, my butt so often.

Paul Moorcraft
Geelong, Australia
July 1994

Introduction

The mountains encircling Kabul are savage, beautiful and sometimes treacherous – like the people who inhabit them. Death had stalked their valleys for five years, in the form of Soviet Hind helicopter gunships. These flying tanks were exquisitely armed: a 12.7mm cannon protruded from the nose, and the stub wings carried bombs and rockets. At first I wasn't too worried about them, as they had been swashbuckling across the clear Afghan skies for days, ignoring us as eagles scorn flies. The mountains seemed to provide protection: the guerrillas were blasé, and I too had become complacent.

That complacency was shattered at 7am on 21 July 1984: the gunships came calling. The Russians had launched a major offensive to clear the *Mujahedin* rebels from their positions around the capital. I was dozing in a mud hut, along with the rest of our five-man film team, when someone shouted 'Choppers!'.

Two fat Mi-24 Hinds were hovering above like expectant vultures. The cameraman, Chris, rushed to set up the equipment to film them. The 'Captain', a richly-moustachioed Afghan officer who had defected to the *Mujahedin*, screamed at us to take cover. He knew what was coming.

We grabbed our heavy rucksacks and some of the bulky film equipment. Our translator, 'Doc', shouted, 'Put your equipment in the cave.' We hastily shoved our kit away as the five-bladed helicopters drew closer. 'Take cover in there,' Doc ordered nervously. The tiny, exposed cave was full of ammunition – it seemed suicidal to hide there if high-explosive bombs started to crash down on us, so Chris and I ran into a small gully. There was no other cover on the stark hillside except a few trees and three decrepit mud huts about 100 yards away. As the only buildings in the area they would presumably be prime targets for the gunships' rockets. Crouching in the gully, we realised it was used as a latrine, but we didn't dare move. Better shit than shrapnel.

Four sleek MiG-23 aircraft arrived and performed a high-altitude turn above the valley; then swooped down and started to bomb the valley floor

1

half a mile from where we crouched. Two more MiGs joined the party. Framed against the clear sky, their deadly grace was almost bewitching.

The helicopters dropped altitude and hovered just above us. A guerrilla opened up with a 'Dasheka' anti-aircraft gun. If by some miracle the Hinds hadn't seen us before, they could hardly ignore us now. Pointlessly, I shouted, 'Shut up'. He was only 60 yards away but he couldn't have heard me above the gunfire, even if he had spoken any English. In vain, I searched my severely limited Pushtu vocabulary for a translation.

The MiGs blasted away. As they came out of their bombing runs they sometimes shot out anti-heat-seeking missile flares, which left a mosaic of cloud patterns against the deep blue sky. Chris was cursing like a banshee. Action all around, and from our gully we could not film properly. 'Bend over,' he shouted.

'Is this some last perverted wish, Chris?' I asked, with more bravado in my voice than I felt.

'No, you fool, I haven't got the tripod. Bend over and kiss your arse good-bye.'

'You forget the tripod, I have my face full of crap and my backside napalmed. Great holiday.'

Chris laughed. 'If it was easy everybody would be doing it.'

I bent over, nose into the shit, and Chris put the camera vertically on my back to film the gunships right above us. What a way to go, I thought, acting the human tripod as we filmed – in full colour – our own demise. Each long minute had an acute intensity, a strange purification. Despite the fear, there was a kind of unreality. I felt I was the subject, and also the observer, of a surreal Fellini movie. Above all, I pondered on the psychological role reversal acted out by our film crew.

We had seen lots of war recently in southern Africa. The other four members of the TV crew had all been professional soldiers before becoming film-makers; they were veterans of conflicts in Rhodesia, Angola, Namibia and Mozambique. I had covered these wars as a journalist. We had often flown in helicopters, chasing or filming black insurgents on the ground. Now the tables were turned.

We were indistinguishable from our scruffy companions. We, too, were dirty, smelly, frightened guerrillas, caught in the open by government gunships. After years of being on the 'other side' – the mechanised, 'death-from-the-air', safe side – the hunters had become the hunted. I understood a lot about Africa in those Afghan minutes.

Mujahedin tracers flecked past the heavily-armoured gunships as they dropped closer, seeming oblivious to the ground fire. Cowering in the gully we might stand a chance if the aircraft bombed us, but the choppers' napalm would devastate the whole mountainside, and us. Two MiGs flew low along the valley and turned in long, graceful arcs: real Second World War stuff. With the heavy Arriflex camera on my back, I craned my head around to stare straight up at the hovering Hinds. I could see their vast array of weaponry very clearly. Chris muttered: 'Right, they've finished bombing below us. It's our turn next.'

'What the hell am I doing in Afghanistan?' I asked myself.

1

Rhodesia – a short thousand years

Rhodesia

Tours of purgatory

I can't really explain how I started out on my long journey without maps.
I regarded most of the trips as holidays, not tours of purgatory, although
Afghanistan was an exception. Despite my deep roots in Wales, perhaps
I became addicted to exile, to always being a foreigner, a lone stranger
in an unfamiliar setting. Maybe I found wandering more stimulating than

belonging. To me, modern Britain has swapped roots for aerials.

I started off with all the keyboard courage of an academic. My degrees in politics and defence studies were of no practical use. True, I had been a senior civilian instructor teaching war studies at the Royal Military Academy, Sandhurst, where I played rugby, rode horses and did some shooting, all equally badly. I even showed some of the expected macho form by having a row with Princess Anne; I felt sorry for her then husband, my fellow instructor Captain Mark Phillips. But I was the proverbial round peg in a square hole. I half-liked the place, but it certainly didn't like me. The only time the commandant said a good word to me was on the rugby field. Just once he shouted 'Come on, Wales' instead of 'Come on, Sandhurst'. After two years the establishment, tired of indulging my working-class eccentricities and robust views on Welsh nationalism, was glad to see me go.

I had often felt as though I was the only sane man in a loony bin, recalling the old Sandhurst adage: 'From the roof of Old College you can see the panorama of an entire army career – first Sandhurst, then Aldershot, later Staff College, and finally Broadmoor lunatic asylum.' One of the politer names I was called in the officers' mess was 'rebel'. So moving to a rebel colony seemed appropriate: I wanted to experience war, not talk about it.

The lure of Africa

'Rhodesia is a well-armed suburb masquerading as a country.' The first sentence I ever wrote about the place just about summarised my initial political views on Rhodesia. How could the whites, outnumbered by blacks 25 to one and ostracised by the world, hang on to power for so long? How could they argue with arithmetic? And because of the political furore, Rhodesia and more especially South Africa had almost ceased to be geographical entities. To the outside world they were more a *condition*, a disease. South Africa was no longer a country but a map of the mind, in which anyone could find his own place.

What is more, as a boy I had been seduced by the African tales of writers such as Rider Haggard. As a student, and occasionally a man of substances, I had been touched by its apparent mysticism. Armed with conventional wisdom, curiosity and just a touch of romanticism, I set out for Africa in March 1976.

I had a cheap return ticket to Kenya because I couldn't afford the fare to Johannesburg. My only preparation was replying to an ad in *The Guardian* for a job lecturing at the University of Rhodesia – the country's sole university and exempt from UN sanctions because it was multiracial. I saw the ad by chance the week before I left and gave a forwarding address in Grahamstown, South Africa, where a friend of mine was a visiting lecturer – a long shot, because I didn't know whether I would even get that far.

My trip to Kenya had been prompted by a friend who taught in Nyeri. Over a beer in a dingy Welsh pub, he suggested a visit; within a month he was showing me around sunny Kenyan game parks. But despite his expansive hospitality I knew that I would find the white-ruled states more interesting, so I used the last of my money to buy a ticket to Johannesburg.

Andy Gancewicz met me at Jan Smuts airport: a big, aggressive, kind-hearted Pole with whom I had worked briefly on the *Western Mail* in Cardiff. Andy and his wife Lynn thought I was demented when I said I was thinking about travelling to Rhodesia. 'There are lots of jobs here in Jo'burg. Why go to a place where the Afs are knocking the hell out of the whites? There's a war on.'

'That's precisely why I want to go. To find out why.'

Andy showed me around Johannesburg, a downtown concrete jungle alleviated by opulent northern suburbs. It seemed so rich, powerful and organised after decaying, ex-colonial Nairobi: I didn't like Jo'burg and didn't want to work there. After five weeks I decided to find my Grahamstown friend, Alan Ward, another Sandhurst instructor. But he wasn't in Grahamstown, and the only response to my letter was a cryptic message: *In Lesotho. Get to Maseru. Then travel to Masieneking. Three bus stops due west proceed up a large hill to the left, turn right at the kraal, walk for a mile or so; there you will find me. Gone native.*

Alan was one of the most unadventurous and conventional Englishmen I had ever met. It was not the sort of message I expected. Intrigued, I set out to hitchhike to Lesotho. I thought it would take me a day; it took two. I had always found hitchhiking a useful way to meet people and find out about a country, and this long trip taught me a lot about white South African attitudes. On the bus out of Maseru, Lesotho's tiny, dusty capital, I also learned about African customs. A chicken perched on my head and a goat backed onto my lap. I disembarked with relief at Alan's hill and, carrying my small rucksack, started to walk in the blazing midday sun.

My white friends in Africa seemed suspicious and wary of Africans. They didn't travel on African buses or walk around African areas. Whites in Africa didn't walk at all; they drove. Walking through the scrub on a dirt path, I was therefore considered something of an oddity. I was greeted warmly by the locals, who seemed to materialise out of thin air and went out of their way to be helpful when I asked for directions. Their long, convoluted explanations, in broken but often fluent English, were confusing but more than friendly.

I gleaned the beginnings of two important truths on my brief safari to find Alan. One, African directions are unreliable; you are always told, out of politeness, what they think you want to hear. If it's ten miles and you look tired, you'll be told it's just a mile or so. As I usually looked exhausted on forays into the bush, over the years I always received the same encouraging directions. It also paid to ask one person: consulting a group produces a long debate in the local language which, when translated into English, ends up as gobbledygook. It was some time before I gave up *asking* directions and learned to request that I be *shown* the way. With rare exceptions, strangers would make long detours to accompany this oddball white. The tremendous bush skills of rural Africans were impressive – I later made long journeys with trackers and guerrillas who seemed to have a built-in compass even when travelling at night through virgin bush.

The second thing I learned was to distrust the white fear of Africans. 'Go in there and you'll get robbed or knifed.' Most whites lived cocooned in their own fears, hatreds and prejudices. Later, when I witnessed the mayhem in Soweto or the results of massacres in Rhodesia, I sometimes succumbed to the white siege mentality. At times, I carried a gun. Experience taught me to be cautious but my first instincts, based on naive curiosity, mostly prevailed.

I kept walking and asking directions. Yes, there were some whites working in a nearby village. Sweat poured from me. I got the inevitable encouragement: 'It's not far from here.' Eventually I came upon a small clearing with a few mud huts scattered around. In the middle of a group of African children was a thin Englishman with baggy shorts and a knotted handkerchief on his head. It had to be Alan.

I could not resist a cliché: 'Dr Livingstone, I presume.'

Alan was as pleased to see me as Livingstone was to encounter another Welshman, Henry Morton Stanley. I spent a week helping him build a schoolhouse, even though he was even less of a handyman than I. We slept in a mud hut, drank with the tarts in the local beer hall, learned bits of Sesotho, and played paternalistic white *bwanas*.

I stayed with Alan for another week in Grahamstown. He taught politics at Rhodes University, so I earned my keep by giving a few lectures on a recent trip to Israel. A letter arrived from the University of Rhodesia offering me an interview for a temporary post teaching politics. They included a return airfare. For the previous two weeks the road linking Rhodesia with South Africa had been closed because of guerrilla attacks.

'You must be mad to teach politics in the middle of a civil war,' Alan said. 'I hear that the last five white politics lecturers were deported.'

'If they want a lunatic, I have the right qualifications.'

I borrowed some money from Alan, caught an overnight train to Johannesburg and flew to Salisbury. On the plane I discovered that the man in the next seat was not only a Welshman from Corwen but also a lecturer at the University of Rhodesia. We landed in Salisbury at 10pm, and I asked Hywel: 'Should I adjust my watch?'

'Aye, put it back 20 years,' said my compatriot.

He gave me a lift into the deserted city centre and suggested I stay at the Ambassador Hotel. 'All the journalists go there. Try the Quill Club bar.'

The Quill Club – the press bar – became my regular haunt and the hub of political gossip during the last years of the war. The interview was for a four-month contract; but Rhodesia, later Zimbabwe, would be my base – my home – for five fascinating years. I went there to teach, but I was much more interested in the politics.

After a few drinks in the bar, I returned to my room and switched on the TV. *M.A.S.H.* came on the monochrome single-channel set. It was reassuringly familiar. Next morning I heard bands playing, and scampered into the street to see a parade of young girls, 'drummies', marching with elaborate uniforms, pom-poms and batons flying. It all looked so uncomfortably American, although I was standing next to a very English, red-painted box with the Royal Mail insignia.

I went by taxi to the university, about three miles from the city centre. Salisbury seemed orderly, with immaculate gutters and grass verges. Government buildings were cast in the high colonial style, schools in penal Victorian with the occasional Gothic touch, and some of the houses had a Cape Dutch flourish. The city seemed to be hosting a rally for vintage cars; then I realised what sanctions had done to Rhodesian motoring. We drove along wide roads lined with opulent jacarandas and bougainvillaea, through spacious suburbs with giddy mansions and beautifully tended gardens. By contrast the university looked run-down: low, cheap buildings in a sea of bush grass.

I found my way to the Department of Political Science and introduced myself to Beryl, the secretary. I was spellbound by her speech – recognisably English, but the clipped delivery and patois made it sound like another language. After a brisk interview with Hasu Patel, the head of department, I was offered a four-month contract teaching political theory and American government, of which I knew little. I would teach whatever I was asked, although I didn't have a book or a note in my meagre luggage. In the administration block friendly, tanned, English-colonial types sorted out formalities, took me for lunch and lent me $10.

I was given a room in the female hall of residence and left to my own devices.

Despite the war, Rhodesia was a very friendly place. In my years of travelling throughout the country both blacks and whites were almost always courteous and easygoing, with little of the sullen black resentment and white aloofness I had encountered in South Africa. The historian Lord Blake put it well: 'Apartheid south of the Limpopo is a religion, north of it a dubious and impractical expedient.'

I moved into a 'mess', a communal house, near the university, bought an ancient Morris Minor and started my classes. About 85 per cent of my students were black, the rest were whites in their early twenties. In one tutorial I had Prime Minister Ian Smith's errant son, Alec, plus two relatives of the black nationalist leaders Joshua Nkomo and Ndabaningi Sithole. Inevitably most academic political discussions reverted to local issues. It is difficult to discuss abstract political theory and engage students with Plato in the middle of a civil war. One student would refer to the guerrillas as 'terrorists', another would term them 'freedom-fighters' or the 'boys in the bush'. I was caught in the semantic cross-fire and struggled for a terminological compromise. 'Guerrilla' seemed the obvious choice, although some white students objected.

After a week in Rhodesia I had accommodation and a job. I needed to explore the place and, above all, get my head around the political complexities – especially if I were to avoid the fate of my five pre-decessors, although I didn't think there was much competition for my job. I soon had a pretty good idea why both blacks and whites were fighting, but I could never work out why the Rhodesian whites thought they could actually win. The same applied to South Africa. It just seemed to be delaying the inevitable: the longer the conflicts went on, the more radical and vengeful the black successor regime would be.

UDI – the Unilateral Declaration of Independence in 1965 – was both a bluff and a blunder. Except for a few hotheads, the Rhodesian armed forces would not have resisted a British military intervention but Harold Wilson, the Labour premier, didn't have the guts or a big enough parliamentary majority. And it was a blunder because the Rhodesians were essentially independent anyway. If Ian Smith had been half as cynical as some of the British politicians he dealt with, he could have secured Rhodesian independence and then torn up the agreement. So followed sanctions and war. Wilson threw away his best card by renouncing the use of force at the outset and opting for sanctions instead. Threatening to 'throw the book' at the Rhodesians, he simply flicked a few pages ... one at a time. Sanctions were a gesture, never a concerted policy. Until 1974 they boosted rather than undermined the rebel colony.

Britain kept supplying oil, making more than enough money to pay for a useless naval blockade supposedly to stop the oil getting there in the first place. It came via South Africa.

This led to the greatest paradox of the Rhodesian war. Rhodesia broke away from Britain to avoid black rule, but Ian Smith became totally dependent on a South African government which was even more determined than London to establish a moderate black leader in Salisbury. (For 'moderate' read 'pliable'.) Pretoria wanted to show that sanctions didn't work and couldn't be seen publicly to ditch a white ally.

Until 1976 Rhodesia's diplomatic history was a long melodrama punctuated by angry encounters on ships and trains, foolish estimates and silly superlatives. The country's fate would be decided largely on the battlefield. White Rhodesians were sucked into a war they were manifestly losing: if the 1979 Lancaster House talks had not intervened, military defeat was around the corner. I spent most of my five years there trying to understand why the whites couldn't see why they were bound to lose.

I stayed mainly in Salisbury, where roughly half the white population of around 240,000 lived. I did travel around the country on convoys, in helicopters, occasionally on horseback and very occasionally on foot, but it was a difficult war to get to grips with. Even when I switched to full-time writing few journalists were allowed near the actual fighting. There were few 'battles' and most of these were in cross-border raids into Mozambique and Zambia. The war was mainly one of fleeting skirmishes and death from the air by 'Fireforce' helicopters. Short of actually enlisting or accepting conscription, few hacks witnessed any real action.

So I hung around the press bar: falling off the high bar stools and risking the sandwiches were not entirely ignoble introductions to the Rhodesian art of war. And medals should have been awarded for drinking the local 'wine', said to be the only booze in the world from which you could catch bilharzia.

Salisbury, now Harare, is my favourite city in Africa. Like many writers based there I wrote books and articles full of righteous indignation about racial injustice; like them I lived well and enjoyed myself. Two friends who wrote for the most liberal British newspapers, *The Guardian* and the *Observer*, regularly thundered on about opulent white lifestyles while sitting comfortably surrounded by servants, a pool and a tennis court.

Like my more ostentatiously liberal colleagues, I became angry at the stupidity and cruelty of both black and white politicians and soldiers. I grieved at the death of friends and acquaintances. I was incensed by the murder of the white survivors of the Viscount aircraft shot down by Nkomo's guerrillas, the killings of black villagers in alleged 'cross-fire' and the massacre of missionaries, especially at Elim in 1978 because I was in the area at the time. When you see murder face to face the anger remains.

The university was intensely political, partly because some of the most prominent black nationalists taught there. Usually they were not harassed openly by the police. It was a little like Ulster, where Sinn Fein was legal and the IRA was banned. The guerrillas were shot or hanged, but leaders such as Ariston Chambati were normally allowed to teach. I learned a great deal from Ariston, who had an office next to mine. There was one attempt on his life and the university built a big fence around the campus; whether to keep insurgents out or academics in I never decided.

Salisbury – little white island

You could live in Salisbury and see very little of the war. The city was mesmerised by the killing in the countryside and yet paradoxically seemed entirely untouched by it. Salisbury was simultaneously remote, charming, claustrophobic and seductive. Notices everywhere proclaimed 'Loose talk costs lives', 'Think about national security, don't talk about it', and 'Big Ears is a Terrorist'. But every white dinner party and pub conversation tittle-tattled about the war. Everybody claimed to have inside information about secret deals with the guerrillas, cock-ups in the high command, new South African weapons ... The second major topic of conversation concerned who was screwing whom.

The conversation was often about the 'situation' – the war – but the ambience was of the colonial heydays of the 1950s: squash at the club, bridge and tennis parties, cocktails at the Reps theatre bar, racing at Borrowdale and endless dinner parties with servants to do the washing-up. Rugby and cricket were important even though South Africa was the only opponent. Which marriages were breaking up? 'Did you hear what she did when he was on call-up?' Petrol rationing was always a popular topic. Who was bringing in olives, pantyhose, Smarties, Marmite, whisky or car parts from South Africa? And all the foreign exchange fiddles. 'How on earth did he get an Irish passport?' Who was 'taking the gap' (emigrating) next?

Yet the polite 'business as usual' was often a deliberate act of temporary oblivion, especially for the men. By the end of the war the call-up extended to age 60. Some younger men spent 'six months in, six months out' of the army every year; some were on continuous call-ups. One-man businesses collapsed. Many urban wives concentrated on pottery and bridge, but the women on the farms lived with the everyday reality of mined roads, cattle-maiming, poisoned wells, attacks at night, the Agric-Alert security system warning of a guerrilla raid on the next-door farm, the crash of broken glass, the rattle of AKs, the rush of adrenalin and the dash for weapons beside the bed, shouting at the children to lie down in the corridor between the bedrooms, the smell of fear, cordite ... and eventually the awful sickly-sweet overpowering stench of death. It was on isolated farms, half-sleeping, listening, waiting for different sounds amidst the drumming of the cicadas, that I learned about bush war.

Sometimes Salisbury did feel the war. A bomb exploded at Woolworth's, killing 11 and maiming dozens. Guerrillas hit the main oil storage depot, destroying a quarter of the country's stocks. The smoke hung over the city for days. Your bags were searched in nearly every shop. At night you watched the TV news about Combined Operations headquarters' communiqués to find out if any of your friends had been killed. British foreign secretaries came and went. Everyone hated Dr David Owen – 'Dr Death'. Too smug by half. Peace seemed remote but the war could not be lost.

Whites in Salisbury would say things like 'Things will come right', 'The world will come to its senses' and 'Good ol' Smithy knows what he's doing'. Seventy-five per cent of whites voted for Smith during the UDI years and *after* independence. I spoke informally to him or interviewed him on a number of occasions, but I could never figure out how this sincere, narrow-minded man could generate such a blind following. Maybe he was just a typical Rhodesian; he accurately represented the worst and best of white society. I hesitate to use the word 'culture', but there was a culture of sorts based upon a siege mentality. UN harangues, the war and sanctions galvanised the spirit of white nationalism.

Rhodesian propaganda had little effect on blacks but it did work on the whites ... proof of the old adage that people believe what they want to believe. White society was vitiated with wishful thinking. The majority of white Rhodesians fell hook, line and sinker for the Rhodesian Broadcasting Corporation's view of the world. The guru of RBC, Harvey Ward, summed up its philosophy precisely: 'The Beatles, international finance groups and colonial freedom agitators are all agents of a communist plot to achieve world domination.' Often the London School of Economics, the KGB, CIA, BBC and *The Guardian* were thrown in for good measure. If you could believe that sort of guff, you could also keep voting for Smithy. As in most wars, patriotism displaced perception.

The TV and radio harped hypnotically on a few basic themes: the chaos in black states, disorders elsewhere in the world (especially in countries like Britain which attracted southern African émigrés), and the monolithic communist threat. Smith claimed to have 'the happiest blacks in the world', bar a few troublemakers misled by professional Moscow-trained agitators. Few whites could put themselves in the shoes of blacks and realise that they would fight too if they were deprived of an effective vote, given inferior schooling, medical services and land, and treated as second- or third-class citizens.

The censorship of news and the pitifully small holiday and emigration allowances made many whites captives rather than supporters of the RF government, although there were also many true believers. The negative portrayal of the outside world intensified the cancer of isolation in what was already a parochial society. Rhodesians seemed to understand little of the modern world and heartily disliked what they did understand. 'Well, after all, there are only three places in the world: Rhodesia, Down South [South Africa] and Overseas.'

Many whites believed they were sincerely battling against communism to preserve a civilised Christian order, not merely to protect a three-servants-two-cars-one-swimming-pool lifestyle. Although the whites did fight long and hard, and despite the ubiquitous weaponry and uniforms, Rhodesia was not a militaristic society. They much preferred beer and *braais* (barbecues) to military parades. Later, as black rule became imminent, the whites looked back with sorrow and resignation rather than anger; with a bruised pride in having survived so long against the odds. Few outsiders could doubt their courage, or their stupidity.

Most Rhodesians had come from Britain, and were expatriates as much as patriots. Many would have voted Liberal or Labour 'at home'. Crossing the equator did not suddenly turn them into racists. Many had seen the white refugees who fled the carnage in the Congo, Uganda and Mozambique. Once prosperous Zambia, formerly Rhodesia's partner in the Central African Federation, had turned into an economic basket-case after independence. Living conditions for whites and blacks were very favourable compared with most of Africa's ramshackle black states. Whites had good reason to fear for 'standards'. Rhodesia, it had to be admitted, was an extremely well-administered state, and not just for whites.

Salisbury seethed with intrigue, much of it concocted in the Quill Club. But there was another Salisbury away from foreign correspondents, sports clubs, broad streets, perfectly cultivated gardens and pedestrian malls. Over 600,000 people lived in 138 suburbs. About 500,000 blacks lived in 12 of these, known as townships. This was a different world. The little brick houses with tiny gardens were growing more and more overcrowded. Tens of thousands of blacks were fleeing the Tribal Trust Lands (TTLs), from a war that had destroyed their cattle, burnt their huts and killed their children, victims of both guerrillas and security forces. Frightened people huddled with their kinsfolk if they were lucky, or built shanties and scavenged where they could.

As I explored the inequality of life in Rhodesia, I began to understand the reasons for the war. In many ways Rhodesia was unsophisticated and behind the times – a living museum. Rhodesians tended to look back to the days when Britain was Great, before socialism, as they saw it, gutted the bulldog spirit. Like Victorians, white Rhodesia loved to commemorate everything with a monument. The early pioneers conquered the land by force, defeating the indigenous Shona and Ndebele peoples, and all the plaques and statues seemed to shout: 'We fought for this land, and by God we're going to keep it.' This was the kind of fierce patriotism Rider Haggard had written about. I had found what I came for, and began to admire it, despite its wrong-headedness.

I started to understand the Rhodesians' love affair with the land – the rolling hills of Inyanga, the majestic wildlife, the mysterious balancing rocks, the crystal-clear, champagne quality of the air, the invigorating climate, the sense of space, the sensual perfume of jasmine in the suburban gardens and the rugged wild aromas of the bush – but not with its native people. White Rhodesians paid more attention to their roses, their Currie Cup cricket, horses, dogs and the level of algae in their pools than to the black people whose land they shared in unequal proportions. Rhodesia may have appeared boundless to the white man because his five per cent of the population owned 50 per cent of the land and all the political power. It could not last.

I was befriended by the Rhodesian version of the Kennedys, Senator Sam Whaley and his family, despite their considering me a 'communist'; that is, someone who didn't worship Ian Smith. Sam was a close friend and adviser of Smithy, yet he regularly chatted to me in his study after offering me a Cuban cigar, and allowed his two charming daughters to take me on trips around the country. I couldn't stomach their politics most of the time but I couldn't help but like white Rhodesians, especially the Whaleys. On 24 September 1976, I sat with the whole family to watch Ian Smith on TV. The tired-looking premier's face seemed even more frozen than usual; half of his face was paralysed by his war injuries. He gave a solemn 21-minute address to the nation, uttering the unutterable. The Whaleys listened with equal solemnity. Smith talked about 'responsible' (not African) majority rule, adding: 'The alternatives to acceptance of the proposals were explained to us in the clearest of terms which left no room for misunderstanding.'

Trying to pin down Smith was like trying to nail jelly to a wall. A galaxy of British politicians had tried and failed. Only Dr Henry Kissinger, the US Secretary of State, had done it, using meat-axe diplomacy with the utmost charm. British politicians had the colonial albatross around their necks again. Kissinger handed them the management of the Geneva conference on Rhodesia which followed Smith's climb-down. The best headline came when the Reverend Canaan Banana left Bishop Muzorewa to join guerrilla leader Robert Mugabe: an irresistible banner reading 'BANANA SPLITS'. Geneva failed and Smith gave up trying to negotiate in a public forum with Mugabe and Joshua Nkomo, who had formed the Patriotic Front. Instead Smith would forge an 'internal settlement' with more pliant men such as Bishop Muzorewa. But the Patriotic Front controlled the guerrilla armies; the Bishop did not.

I left Salisbury to spend some time lecturing at the universities of Cape Town and Natal. On my return I needed to see what was happening out in the countryside. White Rhodesia had largely been a tale of two cities, one of which – Bulawayo – was semi-comatose, while Salisbury was a little white island cut off from the realities of the war.

Battlefield tour

I had already travelled around most of the country but somehow felt I should take in the beauty as well as the tragedies. The South Africans were preparing for a mass exodus of whites from Rhodesia. It might be my last chance to see the sights. As it happened, I was completely wrong but it gave extra impetus to my sightseeing.

I went south from Salisbury to the Zimbabwe Ruins, the impressive dry-stone remains of a great spiritual and trading centre of the twelfth to fourteenth centuries. The Rhodesian Front had always insisted it was built by Arabs or Phoenicians, even that it was the site of King Solomon's mines. It was erected by the indigenous precursors of the Shona people but it was hard for the whites, settled in the country for less than a hundred years, to admit that. I liked nearby Fort Victoria, with its shabby colonial feel. (This is now named Masvingo – I have used Rhodesian titles when describing events before 1980; many towns and streets were renamed after independence.)

The road from Fort Victoria to Chipinga ran through hostile territory. I had three companions in the car, all armed to the teeth. Normally I travelled without a weapon, especially on journalistic assignments, but we had missed the convoy and I knew the guerrillas opened fire without asking about press cards. As dusk approached every bend and *kopje* seemed ominous. Big signs warned against travelling after 3pm, especially without armed convoy escorts. We finally reached Chipinga, a mini Dodge City. Rifle racks in the hotel bar were stacked up with FNs. The locals seemed pleased that visitors had come to their town, just a few miles from the Mozambique border. The whole eastern border with Mozambique was full of crossing points for Mugabe's guerrillas.

Later I explored the Chimanimani mountains and the border town of Melsetter. The area has a distinct ecology: lush green slopes dotted with wild figs lead to remnants of dense evergreen forests hung with orchids and carpeted with ferns. On the upper slopes grew aloes and proteas. Despite the beauty, the nervousness of the local white farmers became contagious. Many had been driven off their land by Mugabe's men. The rich Eastern Highlands, with their tea and coffee plantations, were suffering the brunt of the war.

The main town in the east was Umtali, nestling in hills right next to the border and once a haunt of retired colonial public servants from India and Kenya. Perhaps the most durable relic of the old colonels and *memsahibs* was the Umtali Club. The juxtaposition of photographs of Cecil Rhodes, the Queen and Ian Smith never failed to amuse me. It was very stuffy and English, but even there the war was beginning to bite. The port had run out for the first time since 1896. Fewer visitors came to Umtali these days. I ventured into the Publicity Association office: 'Brave, beautiful city' was the last inscription in the visitor's book. Umtali had been mortared recently, and white schoolchildren had marched through the streets singing 'Rhodesians Never Die'.

To the south of Umtali was the Vumba, dangerous and lush. It had been the home of many retired folk who dabbled in a little farming. I used to stay regularly at the attractive Leopard's Rock Hotel, rather like a French chateau with its steeply-pitched roof capped by turrets, high up in the Vumba overlooking Mozambique, but it was closed after a mortar attack. I had worked in the area, helping to edit a book by a retired British officer, Major Tom Wigglesworth, who had been captured by Mugabe's guerrillas and endured a gruelling time. But he was full of sometimes complimentary insights about the insurgents, and scathing about the Rhodesian Front's propaganda. He was one of a handful of whites taken prisoner and released. The guerrillas made great propaganda play of their humanity in releasing white prisoners, while Smith's men hanged captives, but little was said of the many white civilians who were massacred or simply disappeared.

I also spent time in Inyanga, justifiably likened to the Scottish highlands. The whites enjoyed the cool mountain air, trout-fishing and pine forests which reminded some of home. For nostalgia I enjoyed the Troutbeck Inn, especially its big fires in the rooms.

Because Rhodesia was land-locked, the more affluent inhabitants of Salisbury kept boats on Lake Kariba. The lake, a man-made reservoir, was one of the largest in Africa – 169 miles long and 25 miles at its widest. It was the closest thing to a beach Rhodesia had. The hotels on the shore and the casino attracted lots of visitors until Nkomo's forces ended tourism by shooting down two Viscount passenger aircraft.

To be entirely cynical, there is something to be said for war-time travelling in countries which have good hotels. You meet the locals without being pestered by clicking cameras and high prices. The heightened alertness – for a while – is enjoyable and perhaps even therapeutic. I became angry at the deaths and the futility of it all, but it didn't usually put me off my steak. You'd go nuts if you let it get to you. So I spent a lot of time in excellent hotels and safari lodges in places like Kariba and Victoria Falls. It was a bit like being in Saigon; you could commute to the war, have a shower and drink, and then write up or file your story. And the phones worked.

Some of the islands on Kariba, as well as lonely promontories, hosted small bush camps. Bumi was perhaps the best. I planned a trip there at the height of the war with a South African girlfriend, and asked a colleague who knew the place well whether I should take anything special. 'Yes, a pair of trousers in case there's a fire.'

The idea of going to these lonely places was to get away from the war, although there were often 'troopies' (soldiers) on 'R and R' (rest and recreation). On official press tours soldiers and officers rarely talked; in remote locations such as Bumi, or overnighting on farms, I often dug up the real angst behind the RF propaganda, as well as enjoying the exquisite fauna and flora. There was nothing like sitting on the water's edge watching the lights of the boats fishing for kapenta (a sardine-like fish which, sun-dried, was a popular form of local nutrition), or listening to the eerie cry of the fish eagles which haunt Africa's wetlands. Buffaloes, elephants, impala, hippo and crocodiles – 'flat dogs' in Rhodesian parlance – were in abundance.

Rhodesia's most famous tourist attraction was the Victoria Falls, which managed to keep up a trickle of visitors during the worst excesses of the conflict. A statue of Livingstone, the first white to encounter this wonder in 1855, stands like some sodden hitchhiker abutting the falls as they cascade over a massive basalt shelf 1,700 yards wide and 100 yards deep. The spume of spray, 500 yards high, can be seen 30 miles away: the locals call it *mosi oa tunya* – the smoke that thunders. A spectacular steel bridge spans the gorge into Zambian territory. Trains crossed to take food to Zaire and Zambia, despite sanctions, but access on foot was forbidden during the war.

One of the first buildings in the area was the grand old Victoria Falls hotel, a classic colonial watering hole. Monkeys would boldly steal from the tables as guests sat in the courtyard surrounded by the strong, sweet smell of frangipani and syringa trees. Occasional gunfire from the erratic Zambian army did not deter the booze cruises above the falls. Fish eagles, gin and tonic, the roar of the falls and the incomparable fiery red of an African sunset ... all this and not an American baseball cap or a Japanese camera in sight.

South of the Victoria Falls was the Wankie game reserve, as big as Northern Ireland. When the rains came in late October or November the *sandveld* was verdant with grass and foliage; the gemsbok, hartebeest, wildebeest and giraffe of the dry savannah rubbed shoulders with waterbuck, reedbuck, buffalo, elephant and zebra. To the south-east lay Bulawayo, capital of Matabeleland, with streets designed to be wide enough to turn round a wagon with a team of 12 oxen. To the far south-east was Beitbridge and the Limpopo border with South Africa. On long drives through Matabeleland the granite castle *kopjes* set against the setting sun, the smooth trunks of the upside-down giant baobabs with their coppery sheen, the *mukwa* (bloodwood) trees with their round bristling pods hanging like medals, colourfully-dressed African women trudging along dusty tracks with massive bundles on their heads all convinced me that if I left Africa it would break my heart. Then I would read a newspaper and the idiocies of the politicians would almost convince me to bribe my way onto the first flight out.

Africa is about strong passions of love and hate. Europe breeds indifference; everything about Africa evokes emotion – the colours, the rains on the dry earth, the storms, the spontaneity of its peoples ... the sheer lack of conformity to nearly everything man-made. The whites tried to tame Africa in their own image. Wherever the British settled they planted trees and gardens, built churches with neat rows of pews, and ran lending libraries. In Rhodesia, throughout 1977 and early 1978, Ian Smith tried to design a very complicated and tidy constitutional settlement which would establish the kind of majority rule which whites were prepared to live with. In short, tame blacks.

In March 1978 Smith signed an agreement with Muzorewa, Reverend Sithole and Chief Chirau. An election based on one person, one vote would be held; meanwhile the leaders would form a transitional government. The Patriotic Front described the agreement as a 'phoney black UDI policed by whites'. In many ways it was. Smith, his security force commander, Peter Walls, and Ken Flower, the intelligence chief, were still running the war. Martial law was extended until, by the end of the fighting, 95 per cent of the country was included. Military aircraft used 'sky-shouts' to propagandise the peasantry. Even the spirit mediums were bribed to support the whites. Leaflets were issued on their behalf but the tribesmen were cynical: their ancestors had never resorted to printing presses before. Whatever the politicians spouted in Salisbury, the military had the final say, although many TTLs (Tribal Trust Lands) could be entered only in strength by the security forces. Thousands of guerrillas roamed the bush, trying to indoctrinate, educate or intimidate the 'masses'.

Rhodesian forces were stretched. Cross-border raids allowed some operational initiative, as did heliborne Fireforce operations inside Rhodesia, but mostly the strategy was containment via the protected villages, equivalents of Vietnam's 'strategic hamlets'. Both the Bishop and Sithole began to form their own armies, the so-called auxiliaries, supposedly comprising guerrillas who had accepted the internal settlement and come 'on-sides' although very few genuine insurgents joined up. They mainly scooped up supporters from the armies of the unemployed in the townships. The auxiliary commanders had great names, such as Comrade Mick Jagger, but their dreadlocks, bandoliers and black power salutes frightened the whites and did little to impress blacks.

Five separate armies now fought for the hearts and minds of the peasantry: Smith, Muzorewa, Sithole, Mugabe and Nkomo all had large forces. But hearts and minds live in bodies. The body counts escalated as many white officers regarded the transitional government as a convenient Africanisation of the war and got on with straightforward 'culling'. They adopted the Nixonian amendment: once you've got them by the balls, their hearts and minds would follow. One white officer told me: 'If we carry on like this, we'll end up with a white majority.' A government 'harmony' campaign to improve race relations was thrown out: troopies called bullets 'harmony pills'.

Dirty tricks on vultures

A racial Armageddon looked possible, so in trooped the 'vultures' of the foreign press corps. The run-up to the first election in April 1979 brought a wave of hacks. The 'Gang of Four' – Smith and Co. – wanted maximum publicity, so for once it was relatively easy to get press accreditation. It was a time of madness for Rhodesia: wild press parties were the order of the day. The hacks had lots of real money, US dollars and pounds, and liked a good time. Most of the indigenous white males were 'out in the bush slotting gooks', so the press corps attracted hordes of bored local females, many of them tanned, blonde Amazons. This did nothing to improve relations between the soldiers and the press.

Special Branch (SB) boosted its surveillance of journalists – and were not always friendly. A distinguished cameraman left his expensive camera gear for a very short time. It was blown up. 'Suspicious package, sir.'

You had to watch the black politicians as well. Jacques Clafin, the UPI bureau chief in Salisbury, thrust the microphone of his tape recorder deep into a limousine loaded with black delegates leaving the internal settlement talks, hoping to catch a comment or two. When the car drove off, he noticed his gold watch was missing. Nor did he get any comments.

One of the SB regulars in the Quill Club had his expense account increased to cover drinks with friendly journalists. Never had so many journalists shown so much affection in one place. Paul Ellman, a prominent British journalist, complained that he couldn't get a phone. 'How can you bug me if I don't have a phone?' he asked the permanent SB attachment to the Quill Club bar. His phone was installed the next day.

An SB man took me for a slap-up lunch. 'Of course we know who you're working for,' he said with few preliminaries. 'It doesn't matter – we're working with the British too.'

'I'm not working for anyone,' I protested.

'C'mon, it doesn't matter now. A Thatcher government will recognise us. You're ex-Sandhurst. You're always talking to the military. You're good friends with relatives of Ian Smith, Sam Whaley's daughters and you could hardly keep a secret of the fact that you spend a lot of time at Flower's place.'

Until he put it to me as baldly as that, I hadn't really connected everything. The Sandhurst tag – even though I had been a civilian instructor, and an eccentric one to boot – had always caused problems but I hadn't thought of the social connections before. I was indeed friendly with Ken Flower, a short, genial Cornishman and the longest-serving spymaster in the 'West', but the initial reason I went to his house was to play tennis on his superb grass court. Only once had he broached the question of confidentiality: 'You are a journalist and a family friend.' Just that. It was understood that I would never mix the two. He trusted me, even though we rarely had political discussions.

I told the SB man he was barking up the wrong tree. He asked me to keep an eye on one or two people he assured me were working 'for the other side'. KGB? CIA? Mugabe? I thought it politic not to ask. Then he offered me a temporary military commission so that I could be paid. I told him politely to bugger off. 'Besides,' I added, 'Welshmen don't normally get commissions.'

Lots of funny things started to happen. I have always subscribed to the cock-up rather than the conspiracy theory of history, so I didn't think they were related at the time, but in retrospect they might have been.

First my revolver disappeared from its locker, then reappeared a day later. I questioned my domestic worker – I would have said 'maid' in those days – in case she had noticed anything unusual. I had recently argued in the Quill Club that journalists shouldn't carry weapons on assignment, even though nearly all whites carried guns, especially outside the cities. Lord Richard Cecil, a squash partner, had just been killed, the only white journalist to die in the line of duty in Rhodesia. Ironically, not only was he a Salisbury, after whose forebear the city had been named, but also probably the most militarily experienced journalist in the country, having been a Guards officer before he became a film-maker. He was carrying an FN rifle (which he had accidentally made inoperative) while filming the war, and was shot at close range.

Then I received my call-up papers. Technically, male residents under 38 could be conscripted if they had lived for two years in the country; I had become a resident a few months before. In one respect I was quite keen to see the war from the inside, but on the other I could not fight for a lost cause I didn't believe in. Besides, I had just started stringing for *Time* magazine and been elected as vice-chairman of the Press Club. Many resident journalists did serve part-time in the police, but I told the call-up board I would leave the country. They said they would imprison me. 'Try it, ' I said. 'Great publicity just before your damn election.'

The next morning I received a letter which said a mistake had been made. I was given a year's deferment.

Then my phone started to play tricks on me. Like most journalists, I felt self-important enough to assume that my phone was tapped. (In South Africa I picked up my phone and heard one of my conversations played back to me.) Something really odd happened in the week that Smith turned down my request to interview him for *Time*. Normally there were few problems with the phone system, although it was beginning to creak with lack of maintenance due to the war. I picked up the receiver to call a female friend who lived a few doors away from Smithy and, before I dialled, I heard voices. I put it down and tried again. More voices, voices I recognised. I put the phone down; I had been well brought up.

I didn't ring my friend for a day or so, then tried her number again. I heard Janet Smith, the premier's wife, chatting. This time my journalistic curiosity got the better of my manners. To be fair, I rang my friend only when I wanted to talk to her, and if I got Smith's hotline, fair enough. I could hear a two-way conversation and they presumably couldn't hear me as long as I didn't make a noise. There was no click when I picked up my phone. Mind you, I was always afraid I would cough or someone would bang on my door. I made notes on some fairly inconsequential gossip and used one or two humorous quotes later.

'Where did you get that stuff?' one observant foreign hack asked.

'Have you got access to SB's taps on Smithy?' I couldn't bring myself to admit that I had been eavesdropping. 'Good sources.'

I had talked to Janet Smith once or twice informally at the Whaleys but they were my friends. If she had told me there that Ian was an habitual sheep-shagger I wouldn't have used the information for the same reasons that I wouldn't use anything I heard at the Flowers. It may surprise some readers to discover that journalists do have ethics. This must have been some stuff-up in the SB: they were tapping me and Smithy, and the little fish got caught up in the big fish's loop. When I stopped going out with Smith's neighbour I refrained from ever using that number again, although I was sorely tempted a little later when I was trying to work out if there was a military coup in the offing.

The funny things stopped happening. Good things happened. I started getting all sorts of military clearances and access to the war. I got into Combined Operations (ComOps) HQ regularly, was given lifts on the precious few helicopters, and senior army and intelligence officers started talking to me. I thought it was a late blossoming of my Celtic charm.

There were still some hiccups. I spent weeks trying to get the official censors at ComOps to pass a photograph I wanted to put on the front cover of a book. It was a lyrical shot of four distant helicopters flying over a landscape at sundown. They claimed that if the pic was magnified the crude heat-dispersal baffles – to deter heat-seeking missiles – could be seen, and I was given a firm no. That December ComOps sent me a Christmas card, with the very same picture on the front. No wonder the Rhodesians lost the war.

Election fever

The 'Gang of Four' thought they would win international recognition and thus the war with the first one-man, one-vote election in April 1979. The Patriotic Front refused to take part and vowed to blow the election booths away. Over 70,000 members of the security forces guarded the polls.

I criss-crossed the country on behalf of *Time* with Peter Jordan, a daredevil photographer. The Bishop was due to attend a mass rally in Que Que TTL, going by helicopter for security reasons. Peter and I were in a vehicle that could ford rivers and travel cross-country: a hire car. About 20 miles from the rally a police road-block stopped us. 'Hell, man. You can't go down this road. There's terrs [terrorists] all over the place. We wouldn't try it in our [mineproofed] vehicles. Go back.'

I thought that eminently sensible advice. Peter would have none of it. He argued and argued until the police, in exasperation, let us through. My map-reading skills were under par but I navigated along dirt tracks. Armed only with a big Press sign on the dash, we bumbled along until what I had been dreading for years while travelling in the bush finally happened. The barking stutter of AK fire shattered our over-confidence as we careened around a bend. Blue-denim-clad figures with AKs, about 20 men, came out of the bush a few hundred yards ahead. I flicked my eyes to the rear – similar figures were behind us.

'Oh shit,' said Peter, as I started waving the Press sign, not expecting it to do any good. We had no alternative but to stop the car. Since we couldn't escape, I reckoned it was good tactics to get out. Psychologists argue that you have far less chance of getting a speeding ticket if you chat to the traffic cops outside your own mobile piece of territory. Peter and I walked up to the advancing guerrillas and put on our best affable berk routines. Peter chatted away about working for the foreign press. He was told brusquely to shut up and turn around. To persuade us, AKs were shoved in our backs.

Normally guerrillas would simply open fire, not act like road-blocks. After a long search of our documents and gear, I took a chance and explained that we were on our way to speak to the Bishop. It was a hunch because I couldn't work out whether they were on-sides auxiliaries or real guerrillas. They seemed to relax a little when I implied that the good Bishop was practically waiting for us, and eventually let us go after scrounging some foreign cigarettes. I found out later that they were real 'gooks', some of the few who had accepted the amnesty and joined Muzorewa a few weeks before.

When we got to the rally, the Bishop hadn't arrived. Drums pounded; T-shirts bearing Muzorewa's slogan – 'We are the Winners' – were given out free, as were liberal amounts of goat and chicken. This was African-style politicking. Auxiliaries in their teens stood around, festooned in weaponry. A young boy who looked about ten stood guard over a mortar. The local commander, Comrade Enoch, looked far more formidable. He told me he had been committed to the armed struggle but now believed majority rule was at hand. 'The Bishop will bring peace.'

I wasn't prepared to argue with him but as Muzorewa's Rhodesian air force helicopter descended on the overawed villagers, I wondered about the little man who portrayed himself as the black Moses. If he had the support of the masses, why was it too dangerous for him to travel around by road and mix with his people? When I talked to him, he seemed fit and happy despite the long days of campaigning. He led Peter and me on a short jog. A decent man, but not too bright. Not ruthless enough.

The Bishop won 51 of the 72 seats reserved for blacks in the 100-seat parliament, becoming the first black premier of the awkwardly couched Zimbabwe–Rhodesia, a name which reflected the sham of the zebra-like supposed black state. But ComOps regarded the April election as its crowning success. Nearly two million people voted in a 64 per cent poll, with little Patriotic Front disruption. It proved that the external guerrillas were nowhere near 'imminent victory'. Never had a ruling minority done so much to hand over (apparent) power to a dominated majority. Few Rhodesians expected the election to work at all, thinking it would be like a British league soccer match: enjoyed only by the foolhardy, the fanatical and the well-armed.

Time magazine wanted to run the Bishop's victory on the front cover. I slaved with Bill McWhirter, the bureau chief, to prepare the copy. *Time* editors would ring from America in the middle of the night, asking stupid questions: 'Do you recall that bell on the mission church you mentioned in your story? Well, can you check out when and where it was made?' We had stuck our necks out to visit the mission in the first place, and by now it was probably crawling with guerrillas. I applauded the thoroughness and professionalism of the magazine, but there was little appreciation of the difficulties on the ground.

After all our efforts they cut the copy drastically and put Woody Allen on the cover. Bill mumbled something about President Carter's opposition to the internal settlement. We sent a cable suggesting a compromise – putting Woody in a dog's collar. Disgruntled, I went to a *braai* in the prime minister's mansion. 'Muz', as everyone called him, was holding a house-warming party. The sedate atmosphere had been transformed into a Mad Hatter's Tea Party. Black Africa was in the white citadel: African women were making pots of *sadza*, scruffy kids scampered around, surly bodyguards lurked with AKs. White advisers, the speech-writers and ad-men who had sold their man to the masses, were everywhere. I sensed the impermanence, and left early to do some shopping. In one department store, I fell into conversation with a white housewife who said: 'Before I buy something expensive, I ask myself, "Is it small enough to take with me?"'

The election brought no respite from the war. It escalated savagely, even though Muzorewa became defence minister as well as premier. No one recognised his government, not even South Africa. The vital factor was British recognition; it was still technically the British colony of Southern Rhodesia. Despite the fact that a Conservative observer group officially acknowledged the fairness of the April elections, Britain's prime minister, Margaret Thatcher, refused to accord diplomatic recognition to Muzorewa. It was his death knell, even though the Salisbury *Herald* raged:

'Is Mrs T a Labour prime minister in drag?'

The black–white coalition in Salisbury started to self-destruct. The white generals fell out and the Bishop's party split. Reverend Sithole, who had won a small number of seats, sniped away. Some of the middle-aged white police reservists guarding Muzorewa objected to protecting him. One told me: 'All the whites are called up. Who's protecting our homes? Why don't they call up blacks to look after their own leaders?' No one wanted to be the last white to die for Zimbabwe. A very small number of blacks had been conscripted for political reasons. There was no shortage of volunteers in a sea of desperate unemployment. Already about 80 per cent of the Rhodesian armed forces were black.

White morale slumped. One soldier who had been on continual call-up moaned: 'The First and Second World Wars were wars of honour. But what are we fighting for in the Rhodesian war? Just to keep squabbling kaffirs in parliament.' The constant use of a new phrase in the media upset the whites and prompted one European businessmen to quip: ' "Comrade" is the Russian word for kaffir.'

Muzorewa's failure to end the war exacerbated race relations. Whites had thought: put up with Muz in exchange for peace. It just hadn't happened. The economy was on its beam ends. As one prominent businessman observed: 'You're down to the die-hards now. You could call us the intrepid, the loyal or the financial prisoners.' It was difficult to start a new life in South Africa or Britain with just 1,000 Rhodesian dollars. Fiddling foreign exchange became a national pastime among the whites. Many foreign correspondents, with ready access to foreign money, made small fortunes on the black market. One even bought a farm in Britain with the proceeds.

Ian Smith was still in the Cabinet, as Minister without Portfolio, or 'Minister with all the Portfolios', as Nkomo dubbed him. Rhodesian Front hard-liners still insisted that the war could be won militarily. Under Muz the raids on neighbouring states were intensified but the war was being lost inside the country. Government infrastructure – schools, clinics, animal dip-tanks and local councils – had been wiped out in the more isolated TTLs, where most of the approximately six million Africans lived. The Marxist government in Mozambique fully backed Mugabe and sent in at least 500 regular troops to help his forces in Zimbabwe-Rhodesia. White power was being swamped by the sheer numbers of the guerrillas. As one member of the elite Selous Scouts said after a major raid into Mozambique in late 1979: 'We knew then that we could never beat them. They had so much equipment and there were so many of them. They would just keep coming with more and more.'

The security forces could not have survived for more than another year without massive South African military intervention. The 1979 Lancaster House conference saved the whites from defeat. White Rhodesia was on its knees, but so were the neighbouring states which harboured the guerrillas. Mozambique and Zambia forced Mugabe and Nkomo to compromise at the peace talks. After endless haggling and a firm hand by Lord Carrington, compromise was reached. A new constitution and a cease-fire were agreed. In December 1979 Lord Soames took over as governor: the first time in the long imperial recessional that a colonial official had replaced an African president.

New elections were scheduled for February 1980 and over 350 foreign correspondents flocked into Salisbury. As the local press club representative I tried to make them welcome, using the opportunity to plug my recent book on Rhodesia. I added an appendix to help foreigners comprehend the patois, military jargon, Shona words and agit-prop which passed for local political dialogue.

One of my best instructors in local patois was Pearl, a mixed-race woman officially designated as 'coloured', or a 'goffel' in crude slang. The coloureds traditionally defended their small community by erecting a linguistic barrier to exclude honkies from their conversation. They were supposedly honorary whites – they could vote and be conscripted – but were nonetheless treated as second-class citizens. Their linguistic defence mechanism was transformed into poor man's poetry.

'What's the time?' became 'bowl me the ages'. 'Let's go' translated as 'agitate the gravel'. A garage attendant might be asked to 'throw some sky into my rounds' (put air in my tyres). If a coloured dropped a bottle of beer he might say: 'My *Shumba*'s been slain by gravity.' If he wanted a lift into town he might ask: 'Man, can I have a charity glide into society?'

English-speaking Rhodesians were very rude about the Afrikaners who made up about 20 per cent of the white population. 'Hairybacks', 'rock-spiders' and 'ropes' (thick, twisted and hairy) were more polite sobriquets. Some Afrikaners were very uncomplimentary about blacks, describing them as 'oxygen-wasters'. The PF used colourful terms for whites but reserved their greatest venom for the 'blood-sucking black stooges' in the 'internal, infernal' settlement. Political correctness was not in vogue.

The 1,300 troops in the British-led Commonwealth monitoring force faced a mountain of problems in maintaining the cease-fire. The well-fleshed governor was sitting on a powder keg. The country was ravaged by five marauding armies. Around 30,000 had been killed, although less than 1,000 were white civilians and servicemen. This was, however, a high figure for a small, close-knit community. The whites were bitter, particularly in the security forces, and Soames had to rely upon them to run the country till independence. Soames was like the Pope; he had no divisions. And General Walls, the security forces' commander, knew it. Walls and Soames kept their cool while the country teetered again on the brink of a return to full-scale fighting. The Rhodesians were convinced that the Brits had cooked up the so-called 'ABM' option – Anybody But Mugabe. Pretoria was also certain that London wanted to patch together a coalition to keep the Marxist Mugabe out in the cold.

From the cease-fire in December until the election, the country was on edge. Hitching rides on armoured vehicles and helicopters I zoomed around Goromonzi, Banket and Sinoia in Mashonaland, little army outposts in Matabeleland and farms in the eastern districts. The security forces were itching to wipe out the thousands of guerrillas herded together in a dozen assembly points, each supervised by a clutch of nervous Commonwealth troops. The dirty tricks brigades bumbled everywhere, trying to knock off Mugabe or blowing up printing presses and churches. The Rhodesian SAS had arranged for bogus ballot boxes stuffed with pro-Bishop papers. Mugabe's guerrillas, many of whom had remained outside the assembly points, indulged in massive intimidation of the voters. Most of the British troops showed true grit but some of their senior officers were playing fast and loose with the Rhodesian women. In one case a very senior British officer was foolish enough to seduce the wife of an equally senior Rhodesian officer. If the Rhodesian had shot the Brit, as he intended, God knows what would have happened to the cease-fire.

Lots of whites were preparing for the 'Beitbridge 500', the distance in miles to the South African border, and I was not alone in starting to hoard petrol. 'Taking the gap' to the south was jokingly referred to as 'defecting to the West'. Rhodesian troops – and tanks, seen for the first time – took up positions around key installations. South African troops didn't even bother to pretend they were Rhodesians with thick Afrikaans accents.

Eventually 2,702,275 men and women, under the watchful eyes of 570 British bobbies standing by the polls, voted in the middle of February rainstorms. Everyone waited for the results on 4 March 1980. Would it be peace, or coup and all-out war in southern Africa?

Before the TV results came in I knew there had been an upset for the whites; I had been up most of the night talking to party organisers. But it was still a shock after years of listening to white propaganda. In a 93 per cent turnout, Muzorewa gained only three seats, fewer than the number of his campaign helicopters paid for by Pretoria. Mugabe won a stunning victory with 57 seats. Nkomo got the 20 seats everyone but Nkomo had predicted. As one top Nkomo aide told me: 'You give them one man, one vote and look what they do with it.' Rhodesian whites went into a state of catatonic shock.

We waited for the coup. It didn't come: Walls and the Brits calmed down the hotheads. Walls told his ComOps staff that Rhodesia 'will not copy the rest of Africa'. A rapid exodus of South African troops and equipment followed. Everyone shredded their files. The white PR manager of the Bishop's campaign was in tears. His shredding machine had jammed after someone tried to destroy some 'We are the Winners' T-shirts in it. Flower's powerful Central Intelligence Organisation burnt its files on details of trade with the Eastern bloc (which was larger than commerce with Western sanctions cheats like the French), and its links with the Vatican and British and French intelligence. Files on the CIO's extensive network of allies throughout black Africa were shoved in the incinerator of the local crematorium. Rhodesia had surprising black allies – most African politicians couldn't be bought but a lot of them were up for rent. Cabinet papers were spirited away to South Africa along with the mess silver from Rhodesia's regiments. I strolled into ComOps HQ. Guerrillas in dreadlocks were not exactly throwing darts at pictures of Ian Smith, but the mood was as if the Vatican had been taken over by the Mafia. Perhaps it has.

Some whites panicked and drove south, with just a few possessions. But after the first tidal waves of shock, many whites responded to Mugabe's calm calls for reconciliation. As one white right-winger observed: 'The war's over and we've got a strong leader.' The black Hitler had suddenly become the great white hope. And whites looked forward to the end of sanctions and to getting long-lost goodies like prawns from Mozambique. Ken Flower invited me to share some he had been given on a visit to Samora Machel, the Mozambican leader. He told me that relations between Mugabe and Soames were good. Maybe things were working out.

On 18 April 1980 Zimbabwe became independent. A right-wing British Conservative prime minister had caused, probably by accident, the first electoral triumph of a Marxist in Africa. White Rhodesians had hated Wilson in the 1960s; now their loathing was focused on Thatcher's foreign secretary, Peter Carrington. To many Rhodesians, Lancaster House had been a stab in the back, another Munich. They had been cheated, not defeated. My view was they had been saved from themselves and their own folly.

And what did I make of all this turmoil I had lived through? What had UDI brought but death? The Rhodesians had spat into the winds of change but had not been defeated militarily, although they would have been, despite their ingenuity. The history of the security forces was one of tactical brilliance but strategic ineptitude. The initial aim of the war was to prevent the passing of power to any black government, no matter how moderate. No clear political programme – beyond a vague preservation of the *status quo* – was ever articulated. There was little faith in far-reaching reform as a war-winner; it would have undermined the very reasons for fighting the war at all. White Rhodesians struggled long and hard against the only thing which could have avoided war – African participation in national politics.

Faced with the inner weaknesses of their strategies, the Rhodesians resorted to more and more desperate measures. The policy of winning hearts and minds was largely abandoned in the field just as the first moves towards a political strategy of a moderate black regime were coming to fruition. Political warfare gave way to slaughter safaris. As one senior ComOps officer admitted: 'We relied 90 per cent on force and ten per cent on psychology, and half of that went off half-cocked. The guerrillas relied 90 per cent on psychology and only ten per cent on force.'

The insurgents had a clear vision of their purpose: to break the back of white supremacy and establish a black majority government. This gave them remarkable stamina and their cause the strength to weather numerous political crises and almost consistent military defeat in the field. In the pattern of all colonial wars, the Rhodesian settlers simply gave too little, far too late.

Zimbabwe

I stayed in the new Zimbabwe for just over a year after the colonial war. Salisbury was renamed Harare and became more cosmopolitan. Cuba opened an embassy but the Russians couldn't – they had backed the wrong horse, Joshua Nkomo. The TV was Africanised. Everyone was comrade this or that. New TV heroes appeared: Yasser Arafat, Gaddafi and other great thinkers of our age. After an initial improvement with the end of sanctions, the shortages grew worse and more inconvenient. The disappearance of toilet rolls irked me.

Border posts were opened. Mozambique was too dangerous because of its civil war but I journeyed to Lusaka by road. I took lots of cigarettes to help remove gun barrels playfully stuck up my nostrils by Zambian soldiers. It was all part of my learning curve: never irritate, excite or plead with black soldiers – who in my experience were sometimes drunk – when they are carrying brand new guns which they are itching to use. Grovelling, my natural instinct, could be fatal. A polite, confident offer to share the odd few packets of cigarettes usually worked, but I always resisted the temptation to share my watch or camera.

Zambia depressed me. The long-term expatriates were like zombies, the white-owned farms were like forts, the seediness and corruption of the towns were glaringly evident, and I disliked the regular attempts to mug me in broad daylight in the main streets of the capital. I chatted to a black Zambian businessman who was surprisingly frank: 'We took ten years to bugger up the little the British left us ... The Zimbabweans are much brighter, they'll do it in 18 months.' Perhaps he was trying to appeal to what he thought were my racist tendencies, because he then spent an hour trying to prise some foreign currency out of me.

The Kaunda government screamed for sanctions against South Africa but the only decent consumer goods in Lusaka's shops were South African. Only the middle-class elite could afford to buy the rows of Cape wines. I used to think it was a racist legend that a white ex-pat businessman returns for a brief holiday to Kenya/Zambia/Zimbabwe and meets one of his ex-employees, half-starved, sitting dejected outside his former employer's shop/business/farm. The black is overjoyed to see his former 'exploiter'. 'Are you coming back, boss? When's this "independence" going to end?' Zambia convinced me that the stories were true. Starvation and unemployment are worse than capitalism. There is one thing worse than being exploited in Africa, and that's the departure of the white exploiters.

Leaving all the massive pot-holes behind, it was a joy to return to Zimbabwe; by comparison, a paradigm of good management. But civil war loomed once again. Mugabe's ruling party took its tribal revenge not on the whites but on the Ndebele, who made up about 20 per cent of the population. The integration of Nkomo's and Mugabe's soldiers had been only a superficial success, despite the Herculean efforts of the small British army training mission. By 1981 full-scale fighting had erupted around Bulawayo. Nkomo's angry guerrillas advanced in tanks and armoured vehicles to wipe out their Shona rivals. The white-officered Rhodesian African Rifles and aircraft flown by white pilots were once more in action against insurgents, as many whites cheered on 'their' side again.

The white exodus increased. Older whites were financial prisoners; they could take just a pittance with them, and had to stay despite the decline in standards of medical care, law and order, and education. Younger whites could afford to leave with nothing and start again in Australia or Britain. Many went 'down south', intending to use South Africa as a springboard to America or New Zealand, but got stuck in the cloying *déjà vu* of apartheid.

There were many improvements for the Shona people, especially the fat cats in the ruling party. Schools were reopened, new clinics were built, and some under-utilised white land was reapportioned to the peasantry.

Schools and clinics had been destroyed by the guerrillas and now white taxes were used to rebuild them, or so many 'ex-Rhodies' argued. For most whites the lifestyle and servants remained, despite niggling shortages, high taxes and the impossibly dull TV. A white architect put it this way: 'The whites are spiralling up on their social life but spiralling down on their business.' Comrade Mugabe's drive to a one-party Marxist state did little to encourage foreign investment. Nor did destabilisation by the South Africans, who stirred up the Ndebele dissidents and held up trade at border posts. One white businesswoman was more fatalistic: 'We had paradise here; now we're becoming part of the normal world.'

At the renamed University of Zimbabwe I gave a short course on guerrilla warfare, unaware that I would be teaching some of Mugabe's seasoned warriors. They quoted huge chunks of Mao to me. I don't know if I passed the course. I chatted in the comfortable senior common room bar to some of my old colleagues. White liberals who had espoused black rule were the first to leave Zimbabwe; the old colonial hard-liners seemed to be taking independence in their stride. Why? I asked one lecturer, who was Jewish, feminist, pro-Mugabe, forthright, and impeccably politically correct on everything. 'The liberals believed that "kaffirs" [marking two inverted commas with her fingers] were human beings, but they're disappointed, while the right-wingers thought they were baboons and are pleasantly surprised.'

The great losers of the Rhodesian war were the Ndebele. A North Korean-trained fifth brigade savagely pioneered a form of 'ethnic cleansing' in Matabeleland. Nkomo, forced out of the government and into temporary exile, said: 'We stand a cursed people. Independence has meant nothing to us.' More than 60 white farmers were also killed in postwar Matabeleland.

The Mugabe Cabinet had more degrees than any other in the world (except West Germany), but it presided over a series of disasters, mainly of its own making. Corruption was rampant. Given preferential treatment and lacking the capacity to use them, African businessmen sold their foreign currency allocations at a 50 per cent mark-up to white businessmen for whom imports were crucial to survival. The cold, austere, intellectual Mugabe seemed untouched personally by corruption, but his half-hearted manipulation of clan and ideological politics in his central committee suggested he still thought he was running a guerrilla army not a country. He maintained the tough emergency laws inherited from Smith.

Whites were allowed 20 separate seats in parliament until 1987, the majority of them filled by supporters of Smithy – perhaps out of habit, nostalgia or to raise two fingers to Mugabe, or because they thought that in the end he was right. Smith always said the economy, education, law and medical services would collapse under black rule, and that the Ndebeles and Shonas would fall on each other's throats without whites to stop them. Sadly, most of Smith's prophecies were self-fulfilling through white intransigence. At least Smith had the courage of his convictions and stayed in Zimbabwe. I didn't. I was taking the gap.

I regarded many black and white Zimbabweans as my friends. I had admired the courage and decency of white Rhodesians but detested their unthinking arrogance towards their voteless compatriots. I had come to love the country but none of its rulers. I had enjoyed an exhilarating five years as a writer and I wanted to keep some good memories. The transition from white to black rule had been spell-binding, but – this must sound racist (and sexist) – watching a country die is like observing a beautiful woman you once loved growing old before your eyes. I decided to take up an offer to teach politics at South Africa's most liberal and distinguished university, Wits. Down South was where the action was.

The transformation of Rhodesia to Zimbabwe was the replacement of an efficient, racist, white elite with an inefficient, tribal, black elite. It was inevitable and should have happened without bloodshed. If Harold Wilson had been more courageous or had had a few more seats, and if some of his military advisers hadn't been kithier and kinnier than was realised at the time, the bluff of UDI would have been called.

I handed in my police uniform; I had eventually served as a reservist in the dying days of the British South Africa Police, but only after Mugabe won and the police force fell apart. I also discovered a female police uniform in my house. Glenda had been sharing with me on and off for two years. I was helping her pack before she moved to Zambia to get married.

'What's this police uniform?'

'It's mine.'

'I didn't know you were in the police.'

'I was in SB; that's why I was on the Quill Club committee.'

'So you've been spying on me for years?'

'Yes. I sent a report on you every month,' she said, putting on one of her big smiles.

'But I'm your best friend. How could you do it?'

'Because I loved my country...'

'More than our friendship.' It was a stupid comment.

'You owe me a favour actually.'

'Sure, I confide in you and you're a spook.'

'I gave you a clean bill of health. You've been such a nosy bastard for the last five years, and they were convinced that your books on the country were a cover, and your Sandhurst background, and your friendship with the Flowers … Christ, SB were just as suspicious of Ken [Flower]. It was me who helped to get your clearance to go everywhere. They were thinking of deporting you. A lot of people were pissed off with your "Short Thousand War Stories" [my book entitled *A Short Thousand Years*].'

I had loved Glenda like the sister I never had. I should have been angry and hurt. I wasn't. Later I was godfather to her first child. I said goodbye to her and the country I loved.

2

South Africa – the government God made in anger

It is the dawn of creation and God and Jesus are parcelling out goodies. God says: 'I'll give Britain lots of fish and coal to make up for all the bad weather. And I'll give Saudi Arabia plenty of oil to compensate for the sand ...' God works his way through the countries, balancing bounty and deficiency, until he comes finally to South Africa. 'I'll give the southern part of Africa beautiful beaches and mountains, an exquisite climate, a vast range of minerals, superb fauna and flora, a wonderful cocktail of peoples ...' And so he continues until he is interrupted by his son.

'Why are you giving South Africa all these things?'

'Wait till you see the government I'm giving them.'

Every country has its quintessential joke, and this story summed up South Africa for me. I loved the country but hated the government. The conflict in this strange, fascinating, achingly beautiful land was far more complex than the comfortable stereotypes imposed from thousands of miles away. I never saw it as a straightforward case of good versus evil. I felt sympathy for *all* the inhabitants of that sociologist's paradise but statesman's hell. In olden days men turned to God for solutions, now they resort to politicians. Many white professionals left South Africa but the brain drain, alas, didn't include politicians.

South Africa, unlike Rhodesia, was not a case of thwarted decolonisation. The three million or so Afrikaners were a genuine white African tribe. They had nowhere else to go. Africa was home. South Africa was unique in having a large poor white population, and apartheid, initially, was the racism of the poor whites. But the ruling National Party enshrined racism in its constitution when it won power in 1948. That was a bad PR move just three years after the fall of Hitler. The Afrikaners were honest or stupid enough not to disguise their degraded political philosophy. Like Ian Smith in 1965 – from West European and American perspectives – the Afrikaners should have learned to lie like white men.

Much as I came to despise apartheid and its vicious implementation,

South Africa

I had few doubts about the genuine philosophical, even moral, impulse behind the Afrikaner desire for self-determination. The nineteenth-century history of southern Africa records the savage duplicity of English imperialism, especially during the Boer War. Lloyd George had shown sympathy for the Boer struggle and so did I. The Welsh were like the Afrikaners – too near the English and too far from God. I did my best to learn Afrikaans, that feisty derivative of Dutch which was the official language alongside English. Unpopular though it may be, when I started living in South Africa I was predisposed to understand the Afrikaner, not indulge in knee-jerk moralising. I was wary of the African National Congress not because of their aims, which I supported except for their socialism, but their methods. Yet I knew the ANC would win in the end. And I came to support sanctions and to accept, finally, the armed struggle, although not attacks on civilians.

Revolution and war were inevitable as long as the whites, 13 per cent of the population, controlled 87 per cent of the land. If the government had been serious about its homelands strategy then the only logical solution was a white homeland approximating the size of the white population. That would have furnished equity and equality, and removed the oppression of the majority. Whatever its (many) demerits, a white homeland was better than endemic civil war and the possible Lebanonisation of the country.

I arrived in South Africa in 1976 when the Soweto insurrection was at its peak. The government's political position seemed hopeless: all bullets and no ballot, repression without reform. But reform would have led inexorably to majority rule. There was no half-way house, so I could understand if not agree with the short-term thinking of the National Party. Throughout the 1970s and early 1980s I watched it potter around with half-baked 'new dispensations'. Yet at the same time I would compare white Rhodesians. When I read Denis Hills's *The Last Days of White Rhodesia,* a sentence stuck in my mind: 'Whatever the rights and wrongs of their cause, it is comforting to be among whites who decline to grovel before blacks. Does it ever pay to grovel?' But unlike Hills I hadn't been inside one of Idi Amin's prisons.

I disliked the ceremonial angst of the white liberals, who patronised selected members of the black middle class. It is just as insulting to fawn upon a man as it is to discriminate against him. At plush, polite, multiracial dinner parties I used to think that these Progs – members of the liberal Progressive Federal Party – should get shot at once or twice. And maybe live for a while in Zambia or Zaire. They might no longer think that goats are just sheep from broken homes.

Many Afrikaners were utterly sincere in their belief that the Bible ordained the policy of separate but equal. I thought they were sincerely wrong in believing that God wanted them to keep blacks from the ballot box. Among the wealthy English-speaking liberal community, however, politics was more etiquette than conviction. In South Africa 'liberal' had a special meaning. The terms 'left' and 'right' bore little resemblance to northern European models. Most South African liberals, for example, opposed universal franchise.

There was no doubt about the volcanic impatience of the young blacks in Soweto. But in the countryside and homelands, where blacks had been shoe-horned into gulags without fences, I found great passivity. A black Mao would have had a hard time mobilising these demoralised masses, although Lenin would have had a rousing reception among the urban lumpenproletariat. South African cities appeared more ripe for revolution than Russia in 1917. For a black radical I could see the attraction of the South African Communist Party. To him or her, apartheid was synonymous with capitalism.

In 1976 I didn't think that revolution was imminent because of the sheer efficiency of the security forces. As in most authoritarian systems, the thing that worked best was the secret police. South Africa, unlike Russia in 1917, had not been defeated in war. It was a regional superpower, a military and economic giant while remaining a moral pygmy. In this sense apartheid worked. It had created a cargo cult on a vast scale for the whites in the 1960s and 1970s. And it had worked psychologically. As intended, it kept the races emotionally apart. Ken Owen, a South African editor I came to respect enormously, observed: 'White South Africans tend to profess an undying love for a country they hardly know, whose people often frighten them, and whose stark beauty they constantly change in imitation of Europe.' To be in Africa, yet think like the most noble of Europeans of a century before, was the damning paradox for Afrikaners.

Cape Town

My introduction to Afrikanerdom was in the cradle of the culture, Cape Town. My stint at the University of Cape Town was a half-hearted political baptism enlivened by elegant vineyards and the finest Cape Dutch architecture.

Cape Town was the capital of Cape Province, which was bigger than France, and the republic's summer and legislative capital. About 25 miles from the Cape of Good Hope, it is one of most geographically isolated and yet also one of the most beautiful of the world's great cities. The

Cape peninsula seemed remarkably undeveloped, an impression exaggerated by the grey-green, untameable Table Mountain that forms part of its spine. The city itself was marred by motorways on stilts, but relics of the British and Dutch colonial era combined to give a special sense of history. The excellent restaurants and parks, plus the mountains, beaches and surrounding wine farms, made Cape Town an easy city to live in, provided you were white. Like all South African cities, Europe and Africa, first and third world, mixed uneasily. Parts of Cape Town, such as the cafés in Sea Point, could be found in any cosmopolitan city, but the shanty towns on the bleak sandy flats could only be in Africa.

I had a so-called 'Coloured' (mixed-race) girlfriend, whom I met at the university. We both loved eating out, dancing and the cinema. And we enjoyed making love. But the apartheid laws made it illegal for us to do any of these things together. I didn't intend indulging on my own, so we were forced to break the law. I had no problem in contravening this kind of law, but even though Cape Town was more racially tolerant than other South African cities, I knew my friend felt understandably awkward in public places. Because she could almost 'pass for white' – to use the local parlance – there were rarely any comments. Only once were we asked to leave a restaurant. We spent much of our time in my flat, where she felt more comfortable. Life in South Africa for 'non-whites' was not a street of joy.

My friend warned me that the security police, who were not above raiding the beds of mixed couples to examine the sheets, might try to plant drugs in the flat. Deporting a foreign journalist and university lecturer in politics on a drugs charge would be more expedient, she explained, than the bad publicity of arraigning me on offences against the Immorality Act. She explained some of the more arcane mysteries of apartheid: the various grades of 'Coloured' – Cape Coloured, Malay, Griqua, Indian, Chinese, 'other Asiatic' and 'other Coloured'; how the Race Classification Board worked; the 16 different grades of pigmentation based upon a person's public acceptance as being white, black, Malay, and so on; tests such as whether the hair was crinkly enough to hold a pencil, or the width of the nose ...

Not only was apartheid damned but it was doomed. When I argued with white reactionaries and white liberals about one person, one vote I would ask a simple question: why should Archbishop Desmond Tutu, a Nobel Laureate, be denied the vote when an illiterate, unemployed Afrikaner railway worker was enfranchised?

I found many of my all-white students at the University of Cape Town tediously dogmatic in their supposed progressiveness. I also lectured at the Afrikaans-language university of Maties at Stellenbosch, established in 1918 as the Afrikaner Oxbridge, where I considered the students much more open-minded. Simon van der Stel, a stiff Dutch bureaucrat, founded a frontier town on the banks of the Eerste River in 1679. Van der Stel loved oaks and the graceful boulevards he planted still adorn picturesque Stellenbosch. I was allowed to lecture in English, although sometimes I would be asked questions in Afrikaans. If totally stumped, I would occasionally say something in Welsh to make a point.

I spent as much time as possible in Stellenbosch because of the architecture. The Cape Dutch style contains elements from Dutch architecture, but it is also influenced by colonial Indonesian traditions and the local environment. The most characteristic feature is the graceful gabled section built around the front door, which is flanked by symmetrical wings, thatched and whitewashed, extending to either side.

I was supposed to be using my visiting lectureship to finish my doctoral research, so I became friendly with Retha, a librarian at Maties. She was a fund of knowledge on Afrikaans culture and offered herself as an intellectual guide. My scholarly investigations soon degenerated into a three-month tour of the local wine farms, for which I am eternally grateful. We drove through the old, beautiful vineyards of the valleys around Paarl, Franshoek and Tulbagh; then returned to eat in splendid eighteenth-century farmhouses converted to hotels, or join Maties friends in the Volkskombuis for *snoek* paté and *bobotie* with yellow rice.

Afrikaners, although traditionally hospitable to (white) foreigners, tended to be reserved in English-speaking company until they knew you really well. They were especially distant with journalists, whom they sometimes regarded as part of a communist conspiracy. Provided I wasn't working for the BBC, they would usually talk to me. Mixing with Afrikaners in Stellenbosch, or later in army and police camps in South-West Africa, and trying hard to follow a conversation in their own language, broke through many of the barriers. I was able to ask why they persecuted people – like my girlfriend in Cape Town – who shared their language, culture and religion.

'Agh, man. The National Party made a big mistake there. We need the Coloured people on our side. They must get the vote back soon. Good people, you know … I was brought up by …' Later in the evening: 'But they drink too much, man, and they're violent. They're OK when they're not on the *dop*.' *Dop* was a tradition of paying farm workers in kind – cheap wine.

I never got to grips with the peculiar variant of Afrikaans slapstick humour which was about as sophisticated as oompah *Boeremusiek*. Dances at Maties were as I imagined high school proms in the US in the early 1950s to be, although I didn't spot any chaperones. Beneath her frilly

Dutch Reformed Church facade Retha, my liberal librarian friend, was anything but a fuddy-duddy. On one wine tour, she suddenly stopped her Volkswagen on the side of a lake and pointed to a distant blob. 'Race you to that island.'

'But I don't have a swimsuit.' She just laughed and ran into bushes by the water's edge. The next thing I saw was a statuesque naked form diving into the lake. I had little option but to follow suit. Retha took about 15 minutes to swim to the island. I arrived there half-dead ten minutes later.

'Ag, shame,' she said in Afrikaans. 'There's bird shit everywhere. Race you back.'

When I eventually got back to the shore, I dived into the bush where my clothes were. Were. Retha had taken them and gone. Maybe I had asked one political question too many. I never really got to grips with the Afrikaners' sense of humour or their practical jokes. But it might explain why so many South African policemen thought it hugely funny to give flying lessons to black prisoners from the tenth floor of John Vorster Square, the police HQ in Johannesburg.

A shocking number of police detainees developed strange illusions that they could fly, and self-inflicted wounds took on epidemic proportions in cells. But Steve Biko was different. The police murder of the black consciousness leader attracted world-wide attention, as did the incredibly bungled reactions of the minister of police, Jimmy Kruger. He attempted to deflect outrage with his well-known sense of humour.

Kruger's tactlessness was aptly displayed in Sir Richard Attenborough's moving film on Biko, although the pathos was marred by two facts. Firstly, it was filmed perforce around Harare and too many of the settings were Zimbabwean not South African. Some of the local actors were friends and I was distracted by familiarity. Secondly, the film was more about the rapport between Dickie and Donald than the alleged close friendship of Biko and Donald Woods. Many of Biko's political associates agreed with the editorial in the right-wing *Citizen* newspaper: 'If the Donald Woods escape story becomes even more dramatised he will not only be the hero of the Liberals and the Left, but will also be the greatest fictional character of recent times.'

Kruger was displaying *kragdadigheit*, Afrikaner resolve, to please hardline whites before the forthcoming elections. Posters of the even tougher ex-police minister and subsequent premier, Johannes Vorster, were everywhere. One slogan, under a big photograph of Vorster, said: 'This time I vote NP.' It made me wonder what the National Party leader had voted for the last time.

Durban

I got a fresh perspective on South African politics in Durban, where I taught at the University of Natal. Both at Cape Town and Durban I had been an academic locum during the sabbaticals of the respective professors of politics.

In December 1497 the Portuguese explorer, Vasco da Gama, sailed along this coast while pioneering a route to India. As it was Christmas, the Portuguese called the area Natal. In 1824 the Union Jack was flown at Port Natal, which was later renamed Durban after the Cape Governor Sir Benjamin d'Urban. During the nineteenth century Durban witnessed great battles which spawned equally great leaders such as Shaka, king of the Zulus, and, later, Mahatma Gandhi. After the South African War (1899–1902) came peace and the union of the two British colonies, Natal and Cape Province, with the two defeated Boer republics in the Transvaal and the Orange Free State. A national convention to discuss the merger of the four territories was held in the city hall, now Durban's post office. Today's grand city hall and the facade of the railway station are reminders of Durban's imperial past. Many classical buildings have been bulldozed but central Pietermaritzburg, Natal's small inland capital, still retains a colonial mood.

Durban became a big sub-tropical holiday resort, with over a million visitors a year, mainly from the Transvaal. Most of the approximately one million South Africans of Indian descent live around the city. The old Indian market was burned down in early 1973, but many of the shops and restaurants have an exotic Asian atmosphere.

One man's shadow, for good and bad, hovered over Natal – Gatsha Buthelezi, the leader of the mainly Zulu Inkatha party. My impression was that Inkatha was essentially a huge protection racket, a ticket for blacks to secure houses, schools and jobs in the kwa-Zulu homeland run as a personal fiefdom by the chief. White businessmen cosied up to the mercurial warrior-politician as insurance against their mutual rivals, the ANC.

I travelled around kwa-Zulu, the successor to Zululand, to satisfy my historical curiosity. Sometimes I went on organised battlefield tours; at other times I strolled around on my own conjuring up ghosts from the imperial past. I had seen the brilliant South African TV series *Shaka Zulu* at least twice. Shaka was a black Napoleon in the early nineteenth century; later conflicts are better known. The Anglo-Zulu war of 1879, for example, composed a pattern which became almost compulsory for the later military campaigns of the British empire: the opening tragedy, the heroic redemption and the final crushing victory.

The tragedy was Isandhlwana, the worst British military defeat since the Afghan retreat of 1842. The heroic redemption came at Rorke's Drift, where 110 mainly Welsh troops conducted choirs and battles simultaneously (at least in the film), gallantly warding off waves of charges by 4,000 Zulus. Six months later the crushing victory came at the Zulu capital of Ulundi. The imperial forces formed up in the classic hollow square, four deep with fixed bayonets, with Gatlings and artillery at each corner. There was no digging in, no Boer laager. 'They'll only be satisfied,' said the British commander, Lord Chelmsford, of his critics in London, 'if we beat them fairly in the open.' The Zulus flung themselves in suicidal waves against walls of disciplined fire. Not a single warrior got within 30 yards of the redcoat square. When the impis faltered, Chelmsford unleashed his cavalry. Zulu power was broken; Zululand was divided up and later incorporated into Natal.

In the mid-1990s, if Buthelezi gets his way, Zululand will suck in white and Indian Natal. Zulu warriors now cut down his black ANC rivals. I gave a lecture at the University of Zululand, where the white lecturers were conservative Afrikaners who all seemed to be called van der Merwe. When I was introduced, I almost told them to call me van der Merwe too, so as to avoid confusion. Many of the Zulu students were pro-ANC and resented Buthelezi's autocratic and conservative dominance.

In Durban I gave a talk to a branch of the New Republic Party, a feeble descendant of the United Party which ruled South Africa until 1948. The UP was led by Jan Smuts, an Afrikaner who fought the British and then became an imperial pro-consul. Most of the senior citizens I addressed there seemed to think that Smuts was still premier. Some sat knitting in the front row; when I came to the punchline of a longish story, one of the knitters had a heart attack and died in front of me. After the old lady was taken away in an ambulance, I was just about to recommence my talk when a colleague whispered in my ear: 'That's the last time you'll use that joke.'

The NRP ruled in the provincial assembly and even hinted at UDI to escape Pretoria's heavy hand. Natal was the one province where English-speaking whites were in the majority, reversing the normal ratio of 60 per cent Afrikaners to 40 per cent English-speakers. Some English-speakers, especially in the prosperous farming communities, affected a cut-glass Oxford accent and the foppish mannerisms of upper-class England. These Natalers were patriots of a country that no longer existed. Many ex-Rhodesians, however, found the atmosphere quite congenial.

The university was very well-mannered in an English sort of way, although the student protests sometimes got out of hand. Most of the time the white students seemed rather apathetic. Witwatersrand ('Wits') and Cape Town universities were for the activists; many of Natal's tanned, skimpily-dressed females were said to be studying for a BA *Mansoek* – 'man-hunting'. Metaphorically, I tripped over surfboards to reach the lectern to gaze down on a sea of vacant Madonnas waiting impatiently for husbands.

City of Gold

Cape Town and Durban were forays from my base in Salisbury, but Johannesburg became my home in June 1981. At first sight, and even after regular visits, Johannesburg was an ugly, scary city. It is the biggest conurbation south of Cairo, with six or seven million inhabitants, and part of the Vaal triangle, which includes Pretoria and interlocking industrial towns. Census figures are very rough guesses. Just over one hundred years old, its existence has nothing to do with natural beauty, convenience, rivers or trading routes. It was founded on top of a gold reef. Brash, fast, crime-ridden, well-armed and architecturally a dump, Jo'burg had three redeeming features: wealth, energy and an excellent climate.

I started teaching international relations at the University of the Witwatersrand, the largest English-language college in South Africa, and arguably the most distinguished university in Africa. I had secured a year's contract because I needed the money, having been forced to leave Zimbabwe with almost nothing – except three manuscripts.

Wits was invigorating intellectually, but my department was very conservative and led by a cold-war warrior of Prussian extraction. He waged trench warfare against the politics department, which was of a liberal-Marxist tinge. Much to his disgust, and deliberately fatal to my career advancement, I used to drink with the Marxists. I could not help but recall Kissinger's quip – 'The politics of university are so bitter because the stakes are usually so low.' About the only thing that united Wits was a second-rate heating system.

My political fence-sitting plus my reluctance to attend the morning and afternoon tea-ceremonies sealed my fate. The final straw was the childish habit of some of my correspondents of sending me letters addressed to 'Professor Moorcraft, Department of Sexual Relations ...' I was accused of impersonating a professor. The normally irascible departmental secretary cracked her first joke: 'I don't know what you're teaching, Paul, but I'd like to see your visual aids.'

Wits was a springboard for my assault on the local media. I started a weekly political column in *The Star*, the biggest English-language daily in

Africa, and later wrote a similar column for the *Sunday Express*, edited by
the Cassandra of South Africa, Ken Owen. Later I worked with a
distinguished South African film-maker, Marie Bruyns. I had confidence
in her but not the *apparatchiki* in 'Dithering Heights', the South African
TV HQ in Auckland Park.

I ended up presenting as a freelance on a number of TV shows.
Although I was reluctant to class myself as an advocacy journalist, I
genuinely felt that it was possible to address some of the real issues in
South Africa even under conditions of censorship. Marie, an Afrikaner
intellectual whom I admired, agreed with me that there were indirect
means of skinning a cat. We were probably both wrong and naive but we
did have successes. Some of our best work, however, was canned because
of censorship, and our investigation of corruption in horse racing led to
my being the first person to be censured by the new Media Council. Some
films won awards; one, on black taxis, had a major political impact when
reaction to the documentary stopped the government banning so-called
'pirate', black-owned, Kombi taxis which were the safest and most
popular transport system for thousands of black commuters. I am sure
the minister of transport had never travelled on one.

Although we couldn't tackle apartheid head-on we investigated all
sorts of abuses – in transport, housing, education and crime – which had
far-reaching political implications. But I grew frustrated with SATV's pig-
headed bigotry, especially after Marie was unceremoniously sacked, so I
set up on my own as a producer. I tried to cover stories in neighbouring
states, with mixed results because stricter censorship, general mayhem
and warfare made investigative reporting more difficult than in South
Africa. Africa was and is a poor yardstick of press freedom but South
Africa, despite its panoply of media restrictions, was a lot freer than
nearly anywhere else on the continent. In some areas you could bitterly
attack the government but investigation, especially into anything to do
with prisons, the police and the army, was very risky.

The media gags were voluminous. You could be fined or imprisoned
for even 'embarrassing' the government, an idea which seemed as
preposterous as making Ghengis Khan blush or Margaret Thatcher
change her mind. I was occasionally harassed by security police, and
sometimes films were pulled only hours before transmission by SATV's
unofficial internal censors. On one notable occasion I was live on air and
the producer, via my ear piece, told me to tone down my questioning of
a senior official because the foreign minister, Pik Botha, had just
telephoned to complain. I carried on in the same fashion and my days of
live interviewing were over. But, by and large, most of the bad news was
reported, especially by the foreign media. In South Africa it was almost

impossible to hide a massacre, unlike in most of the countries to the north.

South African journalists were barking dogs who were chained. If you broke the chain you could be imprisoned. Foreign correspondents were deported. Pretoria made the mistake of kicking out the best foreign reporters – such as Peter Sharp, Michael Buerk and Allen Pizzey. The deportees, usually old Africa hands who had an understanding of South Africa's complex problems, were often replaced by young, inexperienced and crusading journalists determined to win their Pulitzer by sensationalised lop-sided reportage.

I became a resident, after a great deal of bureaucratic hassle from the immigration department. Bottom of the list of favoured people were lecturers in politics, journalists and musicians: I scored on two and was as interested in the stupendous local music as in political journalism, so I was lucky to get residence. It made it easier for me to travel in and out of South Africa, but it meant that infringing the censorship laws could lead to imprisonment, not deportation.

Melville

Johannesburg was a hard city with little soul but, as in all big cities, some of the suburbs can be like urban villages. I chose to live in Melville, the 'creative suburb' dubbed 'little Hollywood' by the locals. It was full of writers, artists and actors revelling in the little restaurants and quaint shops. People actually walked around rather than drove. Yuppies had Chelseafied the homes. For three years the reigning Miss South Africas lived next door to my mock Cape Dutch cottage, which made for pretty dinner parties and very light conversation. The chief drawback was the infestation of 'Parkhurst Prawns': big, Alien-look-alike mole crickets which liked to wrestle with you. Melville was spiced with history, laid-back kitsch architecture, parklands, and 'beautiful people'. A little Bohemia on the Reef. And, of course, all-white because of the Group Areas Act. Even the richest black capitalist had to live in a black area.

Beyond occasional forays into the battles in the townships, I lived a comfortable suburban life, along with the rest of white South Africa. The Soweto insurrection had been forgotten. Until the townships erupted again in 1984, the white suburbs were immersed in what Nadine Gordimer called a 'dreadful calm'. Most whites regarded politics just as Californians thought about earthquakes; the black townships were out of sight and usually out of mind. The torture chambers of the police HQ at John Vorster Square were just around the corner from the Market

Theatre, where white liberals could learn about black suffering from Athol Fugard or Pieter-Dirk Uys, South Africa's version of Dame Edna.

Until the war lapped around their cities in the mid-1970s Rhodesians didn't want to talk politics or war. In the early 1980s in affluent South Africa it was the same. Sport, the new pool or BMW, Waterford crystal, Gucci shoes, Dunhill belts, Georg Jensen silver and Balenciaga dresses came before ritual jokes about President P W Botha. The war was 'out there', on the border with Angola, a thousand miles to the north. That suited the government, which hadn't even told its own citizens that its army had invaded Angola in 1975.

My talks with government ministers suggested that they too wallowed in wishful thinking. If ignorance is bliss, then sometimes the South African government appeared as the pure embodiment of the politics of joy. They waltzed on the edge of schizophrenia. The Afrikaners were desperate to avoid foreign contamination – hence the absurd bans on films such as *Guess Who's Coming to Dinner?* and works by Daniel Defoe, William Faulkner and even *A Book of Common Prayer.* Some of South African Wilbur Smith's books were prohibited. *Black Beauty,* however, was on sale. Television – quaintly termed 'the little bioscope' – was not allowed until 1976. I used to keep awake in the cinema by counting the cuts, exchanging my brain for a pack of popcorn.

Pretoria said it was not only part of the West but was in the vanguard of Western Christendom's battle with Moscow's evil empire. The Afrikaner government had a Ptolemaic view of the world: Pretoria, not Berlin, was the centrepiece of the cold war. Pretoria therefore had to allow a free press, as integral to its defence of Western values, but it had to curb Moscow's total onslaught aided wittingly or unwittingly by the local and foreign media. The government wanted to be treated as part of the West and explained that there were similar problems with terrorists elsewhere. 'Look at the IRA.' On the other hand, it said, treat us differently. There are special problems with democracy in Africa. 'Look what's happening north of us.'

South Africa was third and first world, Australia dumped on Nigeria. You could change worlds by travelling a mile or so from rich white Sandton to the desperate poverty of the black township of Alexandra. But the third world analogy permitted a soothing psychic balm. For the comfortable whites the problems were not happening in the next township, which they very rarely visited, or in the dust bowls of the black homelands hundreds of miles away; no, the starvation and turmoil were another *world* away. It was much easier to ease the conscience by discovering black Africa in the Market Theatre. There was a bar and even a multiracial restaurant.

The complacency was shattered when Alexandra went up in flames in the 'unrest' which began in 1984. Ex-Rhodesians in Johannesburg were once again planning to become uhuru-hoppers. Most of them could claim British citizenship, but Afrikaners were stuck with their 'Green Mamba' passports. Dinner parties were full of 'kugel-speak': the whining tones of wealthy young white females, many of them Jewish.

'So, do you think we can get into Australia? Mannie's over there, you know.'

'Britain's too cold. I fancy California, doll.'

'I'm staying here. It'll come right.'

'What's the difference between an emigrant and a refugee? Timing.'

'Bloody sanctions. Business is so quiet, you can hear the turnover drop.'

'When we Jews leave you know there's a problem. When the Greeks go it's bad. When the Porks [Portuguese] start to leave, it's too late.'

'What are you taking with you? Sharon went over to New York with a R50,000 silk Persian rug in her suitcase.'

Rich Johannesburgers suddenly started taking a keen interest in portable art. Sydney Kumalo's statues were a bit heavy. John Meyer's hyper-realist paintings sold well in the US but he painted only 20 or 30 a year. Ndbele beadwork? Pretty but not much profit.

The increased pressure of conscription (the only aspect of apartheid which excluded blacks), sanctions and ungovernable townships shook the whites, but SATV news broadcasts served to reinforce the membership of the Mushroom Club, waging war on truth with a scorched air policy. Troubles abroad and trivial good news at home were emphasised. It was often so muddled that one was left thinking Lebanon had been invaded by Cabbage Patch dolls led by Brooke Shields wearing a very sexy number.

Second-rate celebrities visiting South Africa were given super-star treatment. Bella Harrison, an SATV hack, would meet them at the airport and gush: 'What do you think of South Africa?' Heavyweight politicians were interviewed by Cliff Saunders, who looked like a permanently untipped waiter when he was talking to Pik Botha, which took up half the news items.

I talked to the celebrities, too, including the stars of *Dallas,* which became a South African obsession. Some big stars, such as Rod Stewart, risked international opprobrium for big bucks, performing at Sun City in the so-called independent homeland of Bophuthatswana. It was part of the one-person, one-casino, one-vote-once system which allowed petty dictators to run sham countries funded by Pretoria and gambling. Most forms of gambling were forbidden in South Africa.

Because of the delayed advent of TV, white South Africans were traditionally big book buyers. Lots of authors did the circuit. Joanna Trollope was the most elegantly serious; Jeffrey Archer, surprisingly, the most friendly, at least to me. He was almost humble – but South Africa often affected people in strange ways.

The funniest interview was not with an Afrikaner politician but with a comic, Pieter-Dirk Uys. He was famous for imitating the 'Great Crocodile' – P W Botha. Uys, who described himself as 'a half-Jewish, half-Afrikaans actor-producer who makes his own dresses', claimed that he made more money pretending to be P W than P W did being himself. And without paying taxes. 'They're royalties, not taxes, because the government writes my scripts.'

'What if you were really P W?'

'I'd get Mike Hoare [who led the abortive South African coup in the Seychelles] to organise a coup on another island – Robben Island – to free Mandela.' Whites rarely mentioned the imprisoned ANC leader. He could not be quoted in any publication. He was an 'unperson'. But how often did I hear a variation on: 'If Mandela dies in prison, I'm off. I won't even bother to leave the key with the mortgage society.'

My favourite South African collocutor was Denis Beckett, who looked and sometimes acted like Gene Wilder. He edited *Frontline*, a beacon of irreverent, if eccentric, opposition to apartheid's lunacies. He formed a coterie of writers – whom he usually forgot to pay – which produced some minor masterpieces and in one case a major masterpiece, Rian Malan's *My Traitor's Heart*. Denis consumed much of his time, and my beers, in trying unsuccessfully to make me an optimist about South Africa and teaching me South African English. What Wordsworth's *Prelude* did for plain-spoken poetry Denis did for the peculiar and snappy mix of Afrikaans and English street-*taal* (language) which suffused his own and the magazine's prose. The famous little magazine was all Denis; he couldn't help but rewrite every contribution. He had a wonderful ear for slang, and a finely tuned built-in bullshit detector.

According to Denis, *uitlanders* (outsiders) had great difficulty with South African terms. Very few foreign journalists bothered to penetrate the Afrikaans core of South African politics, depending (initially) on English-language newspapers. English was the language of commerce but infiltrating politics, the army, the police and the bloated civil service usually required Afrikaans.

In the early 1980s the buzzwords were *verkramptes* (white conservatives) and *verligtes* (those who thought of themselves as enlightened). In English, traditional *verkramptes* would say things like:

– My Bantus [blacks] look on me as their father.
– We made this country what it is today.
– If you raise their pay they just get drunk.
– You have to show them who's boss, otherwise they'll think you're weak.

In Afrikaans they would say:

– Every white man could take ten kaffirs with him.
– The problem is that our forefathers didn't wipe them out like they did in Australia or America. We were too damn soft.
– It's been scientifically proved that their brains are smaller than ours.

Verligtes would say in English:

– Apartheid is dead, but the trouble is they've always been given everything.
– What we need to do is create a black middle class.

In Afrikaans they would say: 'Agh, man, they're also people ... but they're not ready to run a country yet.'

It is wrong to assume that all right-wingers were Afrikaners. The English invented apartheid, the Afrikaners codified it after 1948. Many old-time colonials, especially in Natal, hadn't forgiven Jan Smuts for losing in 1948, and the Nats (National Party) for declaring a republic and leaving the Commonwealth (before they were kicked out) in 1961. Many English-speaking reactionaries looked for a less Afrikaans variant of the neo-Nazi groups which sprang up in the mid-1980s, while English-speaking *verligtes* sniped at the 'hairyback' Afrikaners:

– What I don't like about the hairybacks is that they're so bloody rough on the Afs.
– I'll never forgive them for giving the blacks their own TV channel while we're still expected to share with the Afrikaners. [The original single 'white' channel was divided at 8pm between English and Afrikaans, without subtitles.]

English *verligtes* would tell you that their maid was 'part of the family', but neglected to mention that this 'part' didn't have access to a bath, hot water or a sitting room.

I went to dinner parties two or three times a week. They were so common because servants did the washing-up. If I became irritated by the pretentious display of 'progressive' attitudes I would ask two simple direct questions. What is the surname of the maid who has been 'part of your family' for so many years? And, have you been to the [black] location/township to which you have lived next door for X number of years? Nobody passed with a 100 per cent score. Surprisingly, I was always invited back, and even became a popular hair-shirt for the guilt which swamped white liberals. It sure beat cooking for myself.

These liberals, or pseudo-liberals, at least stopped introducing their maid to me as 'a very dear friend of the family' before dismissing her to the kitchen. But they continued to say:

- The only place we can go to understand things is the Market [theatre].
- The blacks have a right to be bloody angry. I would be too.
- It's a great pity that more blacks don't meet people like us.

There were also a few black liberals, who would be wheeled out on official tours of Soweto. They were elderly, old-fashioned, often ministers of religion, and polite and hospitable to the point of embarrassment. They said things like:

- Time is running out.
- [Jokingly] It's going to be a real mess when we're running the place.
- At least there's more freedom of speech here than in Zambia, Zimbabwe or Angola.
- I'd rather be in a prison here than in Zambia ...

The worst kind of white political hypocrisy came from the radicals who swarmed around Wits. As Denis put it: 'They are strong on the dictatorship of the proletariat, and dream about the grateful proletariat asking them to help do the dictating when the time comes.' Often rich kids from up-market suburbs, they flaunted phrases like 'the progressive forces of the people's will,' and 'students are workers'. Real black radicals would say privately that they couldn't stand pampered white kids pretending to be black. I suspect Biko might have written something like that about Donald Woods in his diary. The Wits radicals often drove big cars, claiming, 'It's only a very old Merc/BMW.' Denis, too, once had a big Merc – but it was very old.

Gangs

I spent the best part of a year chasing stories on various kinds of gangs in South Africa. Marie and I made a 40-minute film on the widespread gang culture. It was no good simply blaming it all on apartheid: that didn't explain the white middle-class gangs in Johannesburg. I started off with the Hell's Angels. The first thing I noticed was the strict hierarchy

– many of the gang leaders were mini-Führers. Although some Angels sported swastikas, Joe Pereira, el supremo, was a major fund-raiser for charity. We might all say no to a little old lady on flag days, but not to a hulking leather-clad warrior.

When I first contacted Joe for a drink to discuss filming he asked: 'Can I bring my wife?' Then he and his wife Joy had to leave early because of baby-sitting problems. But Joe, like all the gang leaders, was a male chauvinist. The female members of the 'crew' wore 'Property of Hell's Angels' on the back of their 'colours' or uniform. The lady Angels had to act with propriety: fidelity was in and orgies definitely out.

Marie and I were invited to a Hell's Angels rock 'n' roll night. Strict protocol applied. The camera crew had to pile their side-arms alongside the mini-arsenal belonging to the Angels. 'It's rude to dance with guns.' Protocol also applied on the dance floor. Only one couple danced at a time and the others formed a circle around them. The Angels story went uneventfully except for one Neanderthal who thumped a cameraman who put a light-meter near his face. But he apologised: 'Hell, I thought it was a breathalyser.'

Next was *West Side Story* revisited. We hung out with Jo'burg's Lebanese and Portuguese gangs, the cutting edge of new immigrant groups trying to prove themselves. They chatted amiably about protection rackets. Macho, territory, belonging – these were also the themes of the gangs in the coloured townships of the golden city.

Soweto was more difficult. Before the ANC comrades took over the South African townships in 1984–85 many of the same youngsters were in *tsotsi* (young criminal) gangs. I worked on the gangs in 1982–83. When I used the trains or black taxis, after initial surprise and suspicion at seeing a sole white man in their domain, I usually got a friendly response. Leaving the 'white' town centre to go underground to catch a train to Soweto, I entered a different, bustling world. I was reminded of the future in H G Wells's *The Time Machine* ... in daylight the polite, idyllic life, then at night the dark underworld. In order to film in the train the Railway Police insisted on a small armed escort. I don't know if we needed protection but we certainly required some help to make enough room to squeeze in a camera. It was a pickpocket's Nirvana: so jam-packed no one would know if a train-*tsotsi* slipped a sharpened bicycle spoke between your ribs. But I enjoyed the impromptu singing and train preachers making the most of their captive audience of sardines.

In the beginning it was easier with a film crew, later you had a 50/50 chance of being stoned, robbed or worse. Housebricks and stones were called 'Soweto confetti'. Mark Peters, a tough ex-Rhodesian, worked as a photographer for *Newsweek*. After working in a Durban township during the 'unrest', he said: 'I have spent a lot of time in Africa but I have never before witnessed so much hate in one day. Blacks were killing Indians. Indians were after the blacks and whites. And everyone was trying to kill the press.' That was not usually my experience in Soweto, but I didn't stick my neck out like Mark. I was nervous of Soweto at first, although I usually had a black companion or knew where to find one if I went in alone.

I began the first of many booze tours of the shebeens. In those days liquor outlets were largely controlled by whites. It was very difficult for blacks to sell alcohol legally; hence the 4,000 illegal drinking dens – the shebeens. Lucky Michaels, a liquor king, gave me my first lessons in shebeen lore. He said shebeens were the victims not the cause of the gangs. In his pseudo-American accent Lucky told me about the notorious 'wire gangs': a black Albino would dress up as a policeman and get people to open their homes at night. The gang would swoop in, tie up their victims with wire and steal their valuables. This was pretty tame by later standards, when houses were raided by feral youngsters toting AKs.

South Africa's 'supergangs' were to be found in the Cape. The Cape Town Scorpions and Born Free Kids had branches as far away as Jo'burg and Port Elizabeth. Experts guesstimated that on the Cape Flats about 600 gangs operated with approximately 80,000 members. Although the Cape's coloured gangs portrayed themselves as Robin Hoods, they often fed like parasites on their own people as much as on the rich 'whities'. Their gang philosophy was straightforward. Them versus us, 'Boer en bandiet' (Boers versus bandits). Yet, ironically, this rejection of Afrikaner-dom was always couched in the most robust Afrikaans. Indeed, the street *taal*, as much as smoking a white pipe (mandrax mixed with dagga [marijuana]) and their tattoos, was a cultural bond for the gangsters.

For youngsters in the Cape and Soweto, gangs were a brotherhood for survival in a tough environment where families had been divided by apartheid's 'relocations' (in total three million people) under the harsh dictates of the Group Areas Act. Some gangs included men in their forties. Some grew out of gangs, especially when they had regular girlfriends. Most gang leaders lamented women as the main cause of gang disruption – not the police. Others stayed in and became pro-fessional criminals.

As well as drugs, the professional gangs organised big bank heists, protection rackets, prostitution, and contract killing. For white gangsters the price ranged from R3,000 to R5,000 (today, around £1,000). One gang leader took a great liking to Marie and offered to bump off someone for her for free. I could see Marie's brain whirring around the hatchet men in the SATV, but she declined the gallant offer.

I spent a long time talking to Dennis Holmes, an infamous Jo'burg gangster, crippled after a mob shoot-out. He explained that his career started in school: 'It went from marbles to murder.'

'Why?'

'Instinct.'

In the Cape there were special junior gang branches, and some joined as young as ten. When the youths had proved themselves – usually in fights with rival mobs – they joined the adult gangs. After further education at the reformatories, gangsters climbed the gang hierarchy. The universities of crime were the prisons.

South Africa had the highest prisoner-to-population ratio in the Western world according to the University of Cape Town's Institute of Criminology. Seventy-five per cent of South Africa's convicted prisoners were members of prison gangs, which dated back as far as the nineteenth century. Their nation-wide and highly organised structures mirrored the titles and styles of the British colonial administration. In the 1880s a man nicknamed Nongoloza established the *Umkosi wa Ntaba*, the Regiment of the Hills, which operated inside and outside the prisons.

The Regiment formed the basis for the so-called 'Men of the Number', the main prison gangs called the 26s, 27s and 28s. Membership was supposedly voluntary. Each gang had distinctive (but mostly imaginary) uniforms, tattoos, salutes and other military paraphernalia. The gangs distinguished themselves by their roles. The 28s pampered and protected their catamites or 'wyfies'. The 26s were the thieves; the 27s were the knife-wielding enforcers of the various codes or 'The Book' of the gangs. Other gangs, such as the Air Force, organised escapes.

The Men of the Number had a school–university relationship with the street gangs, training new recruits and helping them organise outside prison. Once you joined the Men of the Number you were a 28 or 27 for life. And it was difficult to hide the numbered tattoos. The gangs held near-absolute sway over the inmates; prisoners feared the gang kangaroo courts, which frequently imposed immediate death sentences, much more than conventional ones.

Marxists liked to portray these gangs as regiments in a 'lumpenproletariat army at war with privilege'. When the townships were engulfed in insurrection some of the gangs joined the ANC and others sided with the authorities. Most of the gang leaders were in it for profit, although they might mouth revolutionary slogans. Politics initially played a minor role. Poverty, boredom, family break-ups, search for status – all the usual sociological explanations – were part of the cause. Bruce Lee and Mad Max were heroes who transcended race barriers. Many gangsters seemed really to believe that the movies were true-life stories.

Soweto had a homicide rate proportionately six or seven times worse than New York's. Black rule will do little to change this horrific fact. It will probably get worse. South Africa was often termed a police state, but in comparison with Western countries it was very *underpoliced*. While the white liberals in the relatively well-policed northern suburbs of Jo'burg were demanding that police powers be curtailed, the underpoliced inhabitants of the Cape Flats and Soweto said that the police were too *soft* on crime. Vigilante groups sprang up: the *Makgotla* vigilantes in Soweto insisted that *tsotsis* were not intimidated by the police. They claimed that their traditional methods, usually a good beating with a *sjambok* (whip), worked better. The *sjambok* was also used in traditional courts to discourage infidelity, hardly a vote-winner in the white suburbs.

As the producer, Marie won a number of awards for the gangs documentary. She deserved it. She had shown true grit. Only once did the male camera crew and I force her to remain in the crew mini-bus. We were running around back alleys in Soweto with the vigilantes, with stones flying, whips flailing and filming at a fast jog. It was no place for a beautiful woman in designer clothes, and I didn't want her to be thumped, raped or lost. She stood an equal chance of being taken into a tiny immaculate house and given tea – Soweto was always unpredictable during riots.

One of the most controversial films I made in South Africa was on religious gangs. Fundamentalists flourish in all societies in turmoil, and born-again brigades were sweeping South Africa. I could see the point of a Second Coming: Jesus might be the only one capable of resolving this conundrum, alhough I suspect Pretoria would have locked him up if He had heeded the call.

South Africa's new Christians insisted that the wave of faith-healing, visions and glossolalia were proof that Christ was due. I concentrated on Ray McCauley, a hot gospeller and one of the most unlikely converts since Saul. This once notorious body-builder hung up his dumb-bells and reached for the Bible to thump it in real style. I spent much time at his Randburg Lourdes, a store-turned-church run by an ex-bouncer turned priest. His happy-clappy audience obviously found him exciting but I cringed in embarrassment, although the services were certainly lively and full compared with the dull and empty pews of conventional Christendom. With all the American razzmatazz the revivalists were obviously filling a gap in the market, giving what the people wanted: an easily-digestible showbiz gospel.

Like ex-smokers the urge to proselytise is overwhelming. Ray told me: 'Don't go to heaven alone. Take someone with you.' The doctrine was simple: everything good is from God and all sickness is from the devil. As a well-known local actress, Marloe Scott-Wilson, said with fervour: 'There's no grey. There's a wrong or a right. There is no ambiguity. Doubt is sin.' Because her hair was died shocking pink, and she was dressed all in pink and driving a pink jeep at the time, I couldn't quite concentrate on clever theological refutations of the McCauley line. When I had recovered I thought, 'Yes, sometimes faith does require a denial of reason, but the mature believer must also face the possibility that he or she could be wrong.' I debated hiring a pink jeep and driving around to tell her just that.

One of the most worrying aspects of McCauley's Rhema church was its concept that material prosperity was a mark of God's favour. The churches were run like big business corporations, dependent upon tithes, plus the large impromptu donations of their ever-growing congregations. They were erecting massive new buildings. Why, if Christ was about to come? I dug into their finances and worried even more about the credit-card theology of the new supermarket churches. What happened to it being as difficult for a rich man to get into the kingdom of God as for a camel to get through the eye of a needle? Sometimes the sermons seemed to be bargaining with God.

If many churches were perhaps preachy cargo cults, what of their political ties? Some did have National Party affiliations. When it came to key social matters, such as conscription or the ANC's concept of a just war, the pastors were dumb. They rendered unto Caesar what was Caesar's, fortunately for Pretoria. On the other hand there seemed little debate about multiracialism, which so exercised the conservative white churches. Whites ran the Rhema show, but lots of black believers mingled happily.

I witnessed thousands of miracles. Cripples walked and spoke in tongues. The deaf heard; the dumb spoke. I questioned some of them closely. They couldn't all have been Oscar-winning actors; they were often very convincing, especially when they threw away their wheelchairs. Marie's bad foot, she said, had been healed. I had been wounded in my right eye and blinded so I tried it, but nothing happened. I'm a cynic, however. Doctors I interviewed told me that often new converts dropped their much-needed medicines. Sometimes patients were cured; at other times they regressed and blamed their lack of faith. They lost their faith and sometimes their lives. Were these fast-talking new breed of pastors con-men on the make, or maligned miracle workers? Were they suffering the condemnation that the early disciples of Jesus endured? The ones I met looked genuine, but so did Jim Jones and David Koresh, apparently, when they started up. Ray McCauley was adamant: 'Everything we do in this church has a scriptural foundation.' That's how they explained the Spanish Inquisition.

I witnessed fervent youngsters burning thousands of rands' worth of pop records 'because they were Satanic'. If they had incinerated heavy metal stuff or, please, Cliff Richard, I would have clapped with them, but I was tormented when someone threw a Chuck Berry LP on the fire. McCauley caught my anguish: 'If you think we're fanatical, we're gonna get more fanatical because Jesus was a fanatic.' I thought South Africa had enough fanatics, but I knew better than to argue when someone has that manic gleam in his eyes. Those glazed looks, the emotionalism, the unquestioning, if honest, fervour. Better Rhema, I supposed, than joining the neo-Nazi *Afrikaner Weerstandsbeweging* (AWB) or going to church just to show off your new hat.

What happens to their faith or mental balance if and when the new converts burn out and leave the hot-house atmosphere? The organised authoritarianism of the hot-houses bothered me; total rejection of doubt, whether in politics or religion, often leads to extremism. The movements may have been hugely successful, and even God-directed, but they were not my cup of tea. If Christ did die for our sins, dare we make his martyrdom meaningless by not committing them?

Pretoria

The screening of the born-again film led to literally hundreds of rude or pious messages per day to SATV and my home. The irate pastors had organised a mass phone-in: my answering machine was red-hot. It had gained a minor notoriety because of my unusual outgoing messages, which I changed almost daily. So, besides angry viewers, deservedly I received lots of idiot calls. I was stupid enough to be listed in the phone book, so I logged the cleverest audio graffiti. For originality I liked: 'This is the National Sperm Bank. You're overdrawn.'

The handy thing about apartheid was that I could separate my investigations and smug derring-do in the townships from my sheltered life in the white suburb of Melville. Except for the crime – Johannesburgers became the world's greatest wall-builders and razor-wire enthusiasts – you could pretend to forget about the big, bad, black world out there.

There were dangers, of course. Most Johannesburgers never worked out whether to drive on the right or the left. Proportionately more South Africans are killed by cars than in any other country. The 1993 death toll, for example, was about 10,000, three times the number killed in political violence. With so much general aggression, people used cars as weapons. Driving within the speed limit was often considered to be an act of provocation. Forty per cent of drivers didn't take tests; they bought licences in the homelands. Good cars, good roads and bad drivers were a lethal combination. Too much drink and the fatigue of driving in a big country caused lots of minor accidents, which could turn into shoot-outs because so many (white) drivers were armed.

Bus-drivers, especially the numerous PUTCO buses, operated their own total onslaught. I liked the story about the PUTCO driver who went to heaven and was given precedence over Billy Graham. The US evangelist objected and asked: 'Haven't I converted thousands?' St Peter replied: 'Ah, but this driver has put the fear of God into half of Johannesburg.'

My favourite (true) story happened when I passed two black window-cleaners who had stopped work to watch TV in a shop window they were cleaning. It was the royal wedding of Charles and Di. It was a sunny day in Melville, and I was bored enough to devote five minutes of my time to my miniscule interest in royalty.

'Is this taking place in Pretoria, *Bass*?' one asked me.

As I patiently explained the location of London, I realised how far away Pretoria seemed. It was all of 50 minutes' drive. Pretoria was the Afrikaner capital, an uncompromising Boer rejection of both blacks and Brits. Some of the ugly, massive buildings were a manifestation of the worst nightmares of Stalinist and Nazi architects. The size of the monuments implied a neurotic fear of impermanence. There were attractive structures around Church Square; in the middle was a statue of Paul Kruger covered in pigeon droppings. Compared with hectic Jo'burg it was like a country town, and pretty in October and November when the jacarandas flowered. This is where the embassies were, or at least the remaining ones from enlightened regimes in Chile, Paraguay and Britain.

Night life in the Calvinist city was out, unless you liked flood-lit putt-putt (mini-golf). But if you were interested in Afrikaner psychology and history it was well worth a visit, if only to enter the holy of holies, the Voortrekker monument. To the untrained eye the inside might seem like *Wagon Train* carved in stone, but the 64 ox-wagons celebrated the Great Trek and in particular the Battle of Blood River on 16 December 1838. Under the brilliant command of the eponymous Andries Pretorius, 470 Boers defeated 12,000 Zulus. The final score was 3,000 Zulus killed for three Boers. The Boers swore a sacred convenant to God and 16 December became a highly significant date; the calendar opposite of 16 June, Soweto Day, a symbolic day for blacks.

If you were a fan of uniforms, Pretoria was paradise. If you hated bureaucrats, it was hell. This was where you had to come to sort out your papers, queuing for hours to reach the counter on the stroke of 3pm, when the shutters came down as you tried to thrust your documents under the descending iron curtain. You suppressed a scream as your fingers were half-guillotined. You did not want to upset the lace-frilled, immaculately-coiffured dragon on the other side. 'Closed. Move your blerry fingers, *asseblief* (please).'

Pretoria was where I begged lifts from the military, usually to the Angolan border. You could see lots of interesting places in a Casspir armoured vehicle or a Puma helicopter. The inmates of these vehicles hated journalists, but I was tolerated partly because I had written a book on the SADF (South African Defence Force). Despite the catcalls from some of the UN, many of whose regimes were led by half-crazed officers, in military terms the SADF ran a highly professional show. My book said just that, while bashing the Afrikaner politicians who used the military to buy time that was wasted.

When the book was launched in Pretoria, the generals duly pitched up. Incautiously, I chose to give half of my short speech in what I thought was well-rehearsed Afrikaans. When I switched from my hello in English to Afrikaans, I unintentionally dropped my voice two octaves, clicked my heels and jerked my back ramrod straight. I thought I had done a good job until some English journalist friends reported on the reactions. An editor of an Afrikaans newspaper was sitting next to Chris Munnion of the *Telegraph*. 'Tell me, Chris, is this man a friend of yours?' he said in a thick clipped Afrikaans accent.

'Yes,' said Chris defensively.

'Is he a violent man?'

'Not that I know of.'

'Then why,' asked the editor, 'has he just murdered my language?'

Gail Adams, a friend from Zimbabwe who was undoubtedly South Africa's best radio journalist, said simply: 'You sounded like Adolf Hitler reading a nursery rhyme in Dutch.' A total stranger told me in an impeccable Oxford tone: 'You have the most marvellous accent without a hint of Afrikaans.'

I gave up my pretensions as a linguist but not as a socialite. My little cottage in Melville became a doss-house for visiting hacks. For all the agonies, journalists – despite their printed indignation – found Johannesburg a comfortable base for a good running story. For a while the 'frontline' states – Zimbabwe, Zambia, Angola, Mozambique *et al* – warned that foreign correspondents based in Jo'burg would have to move north to Harare. But it didn't work partly because of the better communications and, frankly, better life-styles, especially if the kids' schooling or the spouse's medical condition had to be considered. One top correspondent bought a wine farm, another a string of racehorses.

Melville was a nosy place. When I disappeared for a month to make a film in Morocco, I asked my very correct Afrikaans girlfriend to house-sit my cottage. When I returned my neighbours rushed to tell me that a man had parked his Porsche regularly overnight outside my house. After all the Dutch Deformed piety, an affair in my bed while I was away was a little over the top. Before I could get angry, Hettie told me an African parable: 'An ant was stuck in the quicksand when Jumbo the elephant walked by. The ant screamed for help and Jumbo tried to assist him. He extended his leg and then his trunk but they were too short. Eventually Jumbo extended his phallus which just reached the ant, who managed to crawl out. The ant thanked the elephant profusely. Such is the way of the jungle that a year later Jumbo fell into the same quicksand. The same ant passed by and Jumbo asked him to return the favour. The ant tried and tried, but was obviously too puny. Then he disappeared. Five minutes later he reappeared driving a Porsche. The ant jumped out, threw a tow rope around the elephant's head and attached the other end to the tow bar. Then Mr Ant revved up the engine and pulled out Jumbo.'

'Nice story, Hettie, but what's this got to do with the price of eggs?' I had never lost my temper in my life but I was getting close to it.

'Let me finish. Jumbo thanked the ant. Then the ant said: "There's a moral to this story, you know. When you have a Porsche, you don't need a tool like an elephant's."'

The relationship didn't last long after this, but it was a bravura display of effrontery and, for once, Afrikaans humour was well-placed.

SATV HQ continued to distil a farrago of idiocy, sheer exasperation and unintended humour. Because I was deemed a security risk my pass was taken away, but as I was still presenting on some of the main programmes, although rarely live, I had to go there regularly. I did interviews never knowing whether they would be broadcast, even if they were highly successful. There was a black-list of prohibited people, but it was never written down in case someone smuggled it out for publication. The list would change from day to day. One minute a union leader and Tutu were in, then they were out. It was Kafkaesque. I did a programme at the beginning of 1984 on Orwell's *1984*. I knew I was asking for trouble but I interviewed worthies such as Helen Suzman, Alan Paton and Pieter-Dirk Uys. Tutu refused, understandably, to take part: he was in and out of the black-list like a cuckoo clock. Our *1984* was heavily advertised, then Big Brother pulled the plug just before transmission. A desperate Marie asked whether I could put out an unfinished programme (the racing film I mentioned earlier which caused so much controversy). Then SATV banned Stevie Wonder's records. I recalled a similar ban, 20 years before, on the coloured South African cricketer, Basil D'Oliviera, which had begun the sporting boycotts. The ruling Afrikaners were like the Bourbons; they never learned anything and never forgot anything.

The new SATV chairman, a former ambassador, went on a tour of inspection. By chance he popped his head around the door as I was editing a film on the 1985 Zimbabwe elections. Bishop Muzorewa, admittedly wearing a moustache, was up on the screen.

'Is that Bishop Tutu?' the great man asked me.

'No, that's Bishop Muzorewa. It's a film on the Zimbabwe elections.'

'Has Muzorewa won?'

The chairman's aides shuffled in embarrassment. When the boss left, one whispered in my ear: 'He has a great sense of irony, nê?' Bullshit, I thought. This man headed the national television service and was a top ambassador, yet he knew nothing about politics in the region. That was the end of my patience with my Afrikaner rulers.

A topical joke summed up popular feeling about SATV. Bishop Tutu and P W Botha met for a pow-wow on a boat in the middle of a river. P W's hat blew off and floated downstream. Tutu jumped out of the boat and walked across the water to retrieve it. That night SATV news ran the headline: TUTU CAN'T SWIM.

As a final act of Afrikaans humour, Hettie gave me an Alsatian puppy, which I called Gelert. 'You need some responsibility in your life,' she said. She was right and I loved German shepherds, but such a gift was impractical for someone who was always travelling. Besides, I had a tiny garden, so I said I would keep Gelert for a week; then I moved to a house with a bigger garden and Jenny, a 25-year-old Australian lawyer, moved in to look after me and Gelert. He became the world's most travelled and pampered dog over the next ten years. Jenny, who stayed for nearly two years because she loved my dog, made our house into the unofficial Australian embassy.

In the first week I got an abrupt introduction to Oz culture. I had laryngitis and couldn't make a rehearsal for a programme at SATV. 'Please ring in for me and make my apologies,' I croaked.

Jenny, sweet, innocent and fiercely intelligent, lifted up the phone: 'Sorry, Paul can't make it today. He's crook and in bed with a wog.' (Wog, I learned, is Australian for flu). If the presumably racist Afrikaner on the other end of the phone had penetrated her Oz accent, I was apparently a criminal homosexual fornicating across the colour bar. That one sentence breached a whole range of Afrikaner taboos. 'Thanks, Jenny, for ruining my TV career and teaching me Strine in one sentence.'

It was the start of a beautiful friendship. She diverted my growing anger with political life in South Africa by making me share her love for the bush. 'You always want to go where people throw things at you or want to shoot you, can't we go somewhere nice?' I had been waiting for somebody to say that.

Oz odyssey

Australians are great travellers, perhaps because anywhere compared with their vast, empty country looks cosy and accessible. Jenny wanted to see animals so we went to the Eastern Transvaal, whose lyrical landscapes were evocatively captured in one of South Africa's few 'international' films – *Jock of the Bushveld*. If you have read Percy Fitzpatrick's charming novel or seen the film you'll understand how hard it was to drag an ox-wagon over those towering heights.

Motorists would probably start from Nelspruit, the commercial capital of the Lowveld. From here oranges, grapefruits, lemons, paw-paws, mangoes and bananas were shipped all over the world. At White River we forked left to pretty little Sabie village, the centre of South African forestry. Patches of indigenous forest survive in some valleys. There were numerous waterfalls in the area – the Bridal Veil Falls, the Lone Creek Waterfall and the Horseshoe Falls along the scenic track which follows the north bank of the Sabie River. Route 536 took us to the Kruger National Park, probably the best run state-owned game park in Africa, and provides an entry to the privately-owned parks of the Sabie Sands game reserve. Names such as Mala-Mala and Londolozi have become justifiably synonymous with luxurious game viewing. Expensive by local standards, but cheap in US dollars.

I always preferred Sabi-Sabi, not just for the richness of game and creature comforts but for the quality of the rangers. They were prepared to spend hours explaining the finer points of conservation. Londolozi ran it a close second because of the sympathetic symbiosis built up with the wildlife, especially the leopards. It was primitively awe-inspiring to watch a leopard hunt down a small buck at night and drag the carcass up a tree away from other predators. With a ranger, downwind and carefully, we followed the leopard back to its lair to watch it play with its three cubs. I had trailed all the big cats many times (always with a ranger or experienced hunter) but that night's contact for over an hour with the leopard, the most elusive of the big cats, was very special.

I also asked the rangers about other aspects of the natural habitat. On the other side of the game fences were the poverty-stricken and eroded homelands of Lebowa and Gazankulu. The earth was almost bare and the villagers had to walk miles for wood, in stark contrast with the luxuriant game park, teeming with animals and US dollars. The rangers explained how they tried to involve the locals, not least with employment. Without the (increasingly scarce) tourists there might be no game, no lush bush and no work.

In the opposite direction, Route 535 led to Graskop and, after some dramatic twists and turns, Pilgrim's Rest, a resurrected ghost town preserved almost exactly as it was in the heady days of the 1870s gold-rush. Pilgrims in the 1980s could stay in the cute tin hotel, the Royal, or one of its annexes. The period feel was enthralling in the state-run hotel – indeed, the whole village was a national monument. Unfortunately, the service and cuisine could have benefitted from privatisation. Adequate compensation was found in the hotel's period bar, reputedly made from a small Catholic Church in Delagoa Bay (Mozambique) but transformed to worship more earthly gods.

Little homes and shops, clean, white-painted tin with red roofs, perched on either side of the creek; a creek once full of gold, as Alec 'Wheelbarrow' Patterson discovered in 1873. (He was so named because he trundled all his possessions around in a wheelbarrow.) Another prospector, Bill Trafford, called the area Pilgrim's Rest, because he believed he had finally reached the end of his travels by discovering his pot of gold. On average, prospectors fossicked out about £3.50 worth of gold a week during the boom years. They could live quite well off that, even with the inflated prices demanded for whisky and gin imported from the Portuguese coast.

The miners came from all over the world, with names culled from the *Police Gazette* or the boxing ring. They were hard men, although – unlike the American West – little gunplay and few stabbings were recorded. Every profession was represented on the diggings. One entrepreneur advertised his services on a pole outside his tent: 'Surgeon, Barber and Tentmaker.' There was a golden rule amid this rough-tough camaraderie: all things could be dug up but not a man's past. Sadly, the colourful individual prospector gave way to the machinery, organisation and capital of big companies. Gold continued to be mined commercially until 1972.

From Graskop the scenic route meandered along the edge of the Drakensberg escarpment to Blydepoort. We made detours to see the Lisbon and Berlin waterfalls and the view from God's Window. The road traversed forests of wattle, conifers and eucalyptus. At Bourke's Luck Potholes, a series of extraordinary natural holes formed in the rock, the road crossed the Blyde River, rich in connotations of the Afrikaner *trekkers*. Just as today, one of the main Afrikaner hobbies was squabbling among themselves if there was no one else to argue with. A major dispute in the early nineteenth century was over the correct route to the

Portguese coast. One party, led by Hendrik Potgieter, was away a long time, feared lost. Their womenfolk left behind called the nearby river Treur (sorrow) and another river when they reunited the Blyde (joy).

In those days travellers had to risk malaria and the tsetse fly – the same fly that killed off Percy Fitzpatrick's oxen and bankrupted him. Most twentieth century visitors came to this rugged area to explore the Blyde River Canyon by air-conditioned car and with few problems, except perhaps a bit of banditry – AKs were sold for a few rands on the nearby Mozambique border. The canyon's trails provided some of the most isolated and breathtaking scenery in southern Africa. A few days' hike along the trails was exhausting: not the exercise but meeting twitchers. There was only one other human in 100 miles and it had to be a back-packing bird-watcher, who told you in great ornithological detail exactly what tripled-billed, five-legged turd-warbler he'd just seen. And being the only victim in the area, I had to listen. I liked birds but came to hate bird-watchers.

I sometimes felt stir-crazy in the landlocked Transvaal. Jo'burg, they said, was a place to live in to make enough money to live somewhere else. That somewhere else was usually in and around Cape Town. Visiting the Cape and Morocco in the same month made me realise that Africa ends as it begins; the same Mediterranean climate of dry summers and winter rains. Even the Cape's folded, sometimes snow-tipped mountains are reminiscent of the Atlas range.

If I had time I would go by train, especially the Blue Train, which ran from Pretoria to Cape Town. Unless you paid through the nose, you got a seedy broom cupboard called a compartment. A 'suite' with its own loo cost R2,500 return. (The average servant's monthly salary at that time was about R200, although he or she would also receive some kind of accommodation and rations.) Into the late 1980s foreign tourists could pass a stream of apartheid signs on platforms, subways and toilets, even though the South African ambassador to the US and amateur comic, Piet Koornhoof, said repeatedly that apartheid was dead. I asked an American on the Blue Train, 'Have you seen any apartheid signs?'

'Can't say as I have, sir,' drawled the Texan politely. I was too polite to say that I had counted 67 of the signs from central Jo'burg station to the outskirts of town.

I met wealthy Germans and Americans who took first-class holidays at wonderful, efficient hotels and had the time of their lives on safaris, shopping expeditions and wine tours at quarter the price of Europe. They didn't see a surly face or a hint of trouble. 'Apartheid? Trouble? I ain't seen no problems.'

I never worked out whether Afrikaner tourist officials were stupid, or smart enough to know that most foreigners were even stupider. For example, in the luxury cosmopolitan Blue Train where 98 per cent of my fellow passengers were foreign (I checked), the South African Transport Service had thoughtfully placed a magazine called *Momentum* on the tiny table in my broom cupboard. It was monumentally dull, full of self-congratulatory articles about obscure public servants, and included an article in Afrikaans on how to move abnormal loads. The piece concluded with the advice that monolingual readers could write for an English translation. What a thoughtful gesture for all the French, German, Japanese and American passengers on board. The radio provided little light relief; three of the four channels were in Afrikaans. Very handy for the hairybacks in the goods van.

The food was inoffensive, the hectoring and inefficient manner of the dining club manager very offensive. But the seriously androgynous waiter was excellent. I took refuge in the bar. 'Ah,' lamented the barman, 'we've gone downhill ever since 1984 when the tourist slump meant that less, well, classy people started coming on package tours. Lowers the tone, doesn't it?' he said, giving me a sniffy, sideways look.

The scenery, especially through the dry Karoo, was breathtaking. The Blue Train could have been better than the Orient Express, but for too long too many inbred Afrikaners had run the state transport systems with few other objectives than to stop black employment and start their pensions.

As always I was overwhelmed by the grandeur of the Cape vineyards: great estates, languid mountains, rolling fields of grapes, the little white-washed cottages of the farm labourers. It was a passionately beautiful feudalism, provided you were a passing foreigner, not a serf. On this occasion I was writing about marinas. In the Port Owen yacht club, international sailors had inscribed fond farewell messages on the bar-room walls: 'Veni, vidi and loved the place ... still chasing vicki though.' Port Owen was to the north-west of Cape Town on the Atlantic Ocean, to the south-east lay the Indian Ocean. I lived on the Melville ridge, which was the exact watershed. Piss to the left and I swelled the Atlantic, move to the right and I added to the rivers which ran into the Indian Ocean.

In trendy Indian Ocean resorts such as Knysna or Plettenberg Bay, you didn't see many Indians swimming in their ocean. The waters were not polluted, they were pure. Purely for whites. Beaches were desegregated in the mid-1980s; until then the neo-Nazis who wanted to drive blacks into the sea were frustrated, because most of the beaches were reserved strictly for whites.

Plettenberg Bay – 'Plett' – was a well-worn 'kugel' paradise. I preferred the simpler if more exclusive St Francis Bay, 63 miles from Port Elizabeth

(South Africa's scaled-down version of Detroit crossed with Bournemouth). St Francis Bay had an hotel which was superbly indifferent to the pressures of modern tourism and the passage of time – my time. I preferred to rent one of the small cottages which dotted the Kromme River. The river, I found, was relaxing; it afforded the serenity to philosophise, or fish, which may be the same thing. The river offered grunter, white steenbras, cob, leervis and elft. Nearby, at Jeffreys Bay, the supertubes had made the area famous among surfies. The *Endless Summer* surfing documentary, which I have proudly never seen, claimed they had discovered the 'perfect wave' there. I felt so happy for them when I heard this – I spent days looking for one.

Involved in such minutiae sometimes I could forget the atrocities of South African politics and succumb to the seduction of the country's scenery and its people. That was Africa: great people, shit-awful governments. The world could forget, too. Until the revolutionary turmoil of 1984–86, Western governments tended to cast a Nelson eye at apartheid. They were confirming one of the prime directives of journalism: the further away and darker-skinned the victim, the less the interest.

3

Morocco – endless souks

There was a brief and intriguing message on my answering machine in Johannesburg: 'Please proceed to Timbuktu as soon as possible,' accompanied by an instruction to ring a phone number in Pretoria.

The message came from the assistant of an Afrikaner film-maker called Albertus Johannes Venter. A cryptic message relayed by a third person seemed odd, but I soon learned that such eccentricities were Al's stock-in-trade. I had met Al, or Big Al as he was sometimes called, once before. I admired his *chutzpah*, but was wary of his reputation for sending people off on crazy and usually dangerous missions. They came back with little help from Al, and on occasion after a stay in the calaboose.

A day later Big Al rang from the Big Apple. I was to go to North Africa to make a film as a possible prelude to a venture in the Hindu Kush. Al was a Cold War warrior, addicted to conspiracy theories. His had a peculiar South African bent: he was targeted by both the CIA *and* the KGB, as well as other journalists who were trying to steal his film projects. He rambled on about 'mission security'.

Within 48 hours of the first call, I had dropped everything and was on my way to Timbuktu via Casablanca. I felt Al was testing me: I had to show form, even though I had lots of TV and writing commitments in South Africa. In Casablanca, I waited for Al. I had seen the film for the umpteenth time just a few days before: more people have heard about the town than the country, maybe because the film is better than the country. Casablanca seemed like the Jo'burg of Morocco, a brash, bigoted, rich and trendy commercial capital; bulging with elegant cafés and wealthy sports clubs, with dirt-poor shanty towns sprawling in the outskirts.

Nevertheless, Morocco was the most welcoming of the North African states. Compared with its neighbours, it was a model of hospitality and stability, and quite permissive by Islamic standards. Hashish was forbidden to tourists but openly smoked by the locals. On the other hand, tourists could drink alcohol but the Moroccans weren't *supposed* to; they had to make do with the ubiquitous mint tea, always choked to death with sugar.

Morocco

Casablanca's core was the huge Place des Nations, where an impressive fountain spurted multicoloured jets of water to the somewhat incongruous sounds of Strauss waltzes. Fine buildings stood to attention on the perimeter of the square. The greater part of the central city was designed by colonial French architects, but the tree-lined boulevards had been renamed after Moroccan heroes. Most of the Europeans had left after the advent of Moroccanisation but Casablanca was still very French – in cuisine, architecture, administration and education. In contrast with the consequences of the bitter struggle in Algeria, the French tradition was respected.

Despite the legends, Bogie never even visited Casablanca. Nor did Al. After sitting around for a day, I was summoned to the nearby capital, Rabat. As I travelled there by bus, I reflected on my quick cram of Moroccan history. It read like a who's who of soccer hooliganism: constant invasions, bold exploits and Moorish pirates. Well into the twentieth century Moroccan warlords had dangled the heads of their opponents from their fortress walls. The desert kingdom was never totally pacified by the colonial armies of France and Spain, although it was perhaps the most pro-western of the Arab League states. European, African and Oriental cultures blended: modern hotels and Old Testament casbahs, chic bikini-clad beaches and the stern dictates of the Koran. It was this cosmopolitan style which made Morocco the most easygoing of Islamic nations

In Rabat, Al was on form. He insisted that he had a booking for the best (and fullest) hotel in Rabat, although he'd never even heard of the place until he walked in. He berated the receptionist, a tiny man, for losing the non-existent booking. Towering over six foot, Al leaned across and, in his inimitably affectionate way, pulled the man across the counter by the scruff of his collar. 'You are a little shit,' Al growled, his voice subsiding to a confidential yell. The little man had guts. With his feet dangling in the air and his nose three inches from Al's beard, the Moroccan replied with calm dignity, 'And you, sir, are a big shit.' We got rooms.

Al introduced me to Nick della Casa and Henry Bautista. Nick was a stranger, despite his claims to know me from the Rhodesian war. Henry, one of the best film cameramen around, I knew a little by reputation. Al was excessively vague, rattling on about Henry, Nick and me travelling for 90 days by camel across the desert to Timbuktu. He implied we would make a film on the Polisario guerrillas in the Spanish Sahara. Eventually, however, we were instructed to make a normal documentary on Morocco, one of a 12-part TV series called *Africa in Focus* which won a number of awards and was shown in over 30 countries. Henry was on camera and Nick, ex-British army and ex-Rhodesian Grey's Scouts, was the sound man. Al said: 'Do a good job here and you're on for the big job I'm planning.' Although he made it sound like the Great Train Robbery, Henry, Nick and I set out innocently to explore and film Morocco.

Before he left, Al commented on the similarities between his native South Africa and Morocco: 'They're about the same size. They're both sports mad, puritanical, authoritarian with a small elite and a weak political opposition in parliament. They are both misunderstood, surrounded by hostile neighbours and very pro-western. And they're both crazy about royalty.'

Rabat was snobbish, conservative, and riddled with political intrigue. The king, Hassan II, usually lived there, although he had palaces all over the country. His picture was everywhere, and his eerily-familiar gaze transfixed me. Eventually the centime dropped: his features were an amazing amalgam of Frank Sinatra and Herbert Lom. Our official guide, Zakaria, insisted that the king was very popular because of his religious influence. I tactlessly reminded him of the country's least successful garden party: in 1971, over 1,400 military cadets burst into the summer palace and wiped out 90 guests. The king, who had shown a great deal of personal bravery in a number of earlier attempts on his life, escaped unharmed.

For once I decided to forget about politics and just enjoy the sensuous images of architecture and landscape. Rabat's old town exuded a sense of well-earned calm. The modern town, well laid out, merged easily into the medieval walls of the old city. Even the shanty towns tumbling down the steep hillsides to the water's edge appeared less appalling than the *bidonvilles* of Casablanca.

The market, or *souk*, of the old town seemed more sedate, less exotic, than other Moroccan market-places. Fewer little perishers begged or offered their services as guides. Fewer shopkeepers importuned us with how laughably low their prices were. You had to be prepared to haggle – that was half the fun. Traders thought you were a fool if you didn't bargain. If we asked in English, the trader demanded double the price in dirhams, the official currency. Nick, who spoke fluent French, thus implying a foreigner who knew something of the country, managed to persuade the shopkeepers to drop the price considerably; and the new price came in old francs. If we had been brave or foolish enough to ask in Arabic, which obviously commanded the lowest price, the shopkeeper might have come back at us in riyals. Good bargains demanded a linguistically adept mathematician.

On the other side of the river from Rabat slouched Salé. This old

Roman town became a nest of pirates called the Salé Rovers, the same privateers who captured Defoe's Robinson Crusoe, who roamed the Barbary Coast of North Africa and raided as far as Spain, England and even Canada.

Filming the coastal cities went reasonably smoothly, although Henry accidentally managed to blow our expensive borrowed lights, and I had a terrible time trying to do a piece to camera in a Casablanca park. Even though we had a hard-won (and expensive) permit to film, a park attendant kept jumping up and down like a demented Rumpelstiltskin and shouting near the mike for half an hour. Our permits were demanded, with menace and bribes, everywhere; the lower the uniformed one was in the pecking order, the more vociferous the officiousness.

After the bustle of the cities, Nick, Henry and I, plus our amiable driver, Abdul, set out for the southern coast. It was a scented drive: daffodils, tulips, violets and roses evoked northern Europe, while the hibiscus, bougainvillea and bright yellow puff-balls of mimosa recalled Mediterranean and tropical climates. The road passed walled coastal fortresses where the Portuguese had defended tiny trading centres for centuries. The Moroccans used these ancient ports to fish for sardines.

Agadir, the main tourist resort of the south, had been destroyed by an earthquake in 1960. We found the rebuilt town depressingly modern and charmless, except for the tanned Nordic beauties positioned nonchalantly around the beaches and cafés. Nick seemed to speak everything except German, Henry was fluent in Spanish, but for some reason they specialised in finding monoglot German-speaking females and then press-ganging me as translator. Being a gooseberry in German for hours on end was not my idea of fun: through either a sense of humour or insensitivity, Nick asked me to translate the lewdest remarks. I am not sure whether I helped or hindered this rake's progress by my on-the-hoof censorship. Probably hindered, because my regular throw-away line in German was: 'Ah, but Nick is inordinately fond of camels …'

Soon tiring of this bit of Europe in Africa, we set out over the Atlas mountains to film the desert and its peoples. In former times, warlords would exact a levy from travellers trying to cross the mountains, which form the spine of Morocco. Mountain shepherds in long *jellabas* assumed an air of timeless tranquillity – it was easy for the men to strike this pose, because most of the hard work was done by women.

We tried to film some of the colourfully-dressed Berber girls, but they kept covering their faces. Henry – or 'Moustache', as the Moroccans insisted on calling him – tried the old trick, pulling out a Polaroid and giving the girls one of the instant snaps. They immediately started posing like starlets. Bar this fascination with Polaroids, the women in the countryside were very reserved; in the cities they were much friendlier and, apparently, sometimes available. But innocents abroad did well to concentrate on the topless French tourists at the hotel pools and leave the local women alone, not least because Morocco had the highest proportion of female criminals in the world.

The Berber women of the mountains were notoriously independent and divorced quite readily. The rules of the veil were not iron-clad: when their husbands were away working in Europe, the women deployed a polite fiction of 'a child sleeping in the womb'. This allowed a two-year pregnancy, and a child born within that period was usually accepted by the husband on his return.

Once past the mountains and the Berber women, the scenery changed. Long strips of oases reached out from the watered foothills of the mountains like tentacles to the Sahara. The fertile strips luxuriated with almond and olive trees, bordered by towering date palms which, as the saying goes, 'like to have their feet in the water and their heads in the fire'. We headed due east to Zagora and the shabby, once distinguished Grand Hotel, where the large film crew who made *Lawrence of Arabia* had stayed because it was right on the edge of the desert. The Regency-style bedrooms added a surreal touch.

Zagora's market was real: for the locals, not marauding packs of tourists. Traditionally, a Moroccan market was the one place where enemies could conduct their business in peace, for it was a strict rule that all had to go unarmed. As we tried to film, however, we found ourselves surrounded by armed soldiers. Eventually, after much gun-display, haggling and permit-waving, we carried on filming the traders: a barber, a tooth-drawer, and even a judge helping to arrange a marriage. Locals bought coffee beans mixed with cinnamon, ginger, sesame, aniseed and peppercorns, which they claimed improved the flavour. The butchers' stalls were set a little apart to avoid the host of *jinns*, evil spirits supposedly attracted by blood.

Zagora was the trading centre for the desert nomads, who asked for very little beyond sugar and salt. In exchange they sold baby camels, animal skins and wool. The so-called 'blue men' sold carpets. These nomads wore deep-blue floating robes over their *jellabas* and indigo turbans; even their skin was blue-tinted where the dye had rubbed off. An enterprising English merchant called Thomas Windham visited Agadir several times in the sixteenth century and introduced calico dyed indigo blue. The customers have been coming back ever since.

I visited the local military governor to seek a special permit to travel onwards. A screaming lunatic, a pathetic bedraggled young man, was chained up at the sentry post. I wondered how long he had been kept waiting for his permit. Eventually, after clearance from Rabat, we pushed on into the desert. An occasional mud-walled fortified village shimmered through the heat haze. The last outpost before the deep desert was M'hamid, a Beau Geste fortress-village, although the Foreign Legion had long gone. It had not rained for literally a decade.

Soldiers immediately rounded us up and took us to the military commander. We sat and listened politely to a long speech in French. Then the phone rang and an animated conversation ensued in Arabic. One word cropped up regularly, at which the commander chuckled ominously.

'What does that word mean?' Henry asked me.

Despite my smattering of Arabic I had no idea, but I said 'beheading'. Nick could hardly stifle his laughter. After chatting on the phone for nearly an hour, the commander had shown us who was boss and let us go.

M'hamid was the beginning of the war zone. In 1975 Madrid gave up its colony of Spanish Sahara and Morocco took over. Polisario guerrillas, backed by the Algerians and sometimes by Colonel Gaddafi, immediately started fighting King Hassan's American-trained forces for control of the arid territory. The war dragged on for years until, to cut his losses, the Moroccan king adopted the old Berber saying: 'Kiss the hand you cannot cut off.' He tried to make friends with the deranged Libyan leader to stop supplies to the Polisario rebels.

Except for phosphates, the empty Western Sahara must be the most useless place on earth to fight over. Around M'hamid the desert seemed bent on exacting its revenge for futile human strife. Piled up against doors and windows, almost covering some of the mud hovels, sand was taking over man's ephemeral habitations. The essence of the whole country was passivity, but M'hamid more exemplified the Moroccan saying: 'Never run when you can walk, never walk when you can stand, never stand when you can sit.' The most exciting movements we filmed in the town were endless games of the local version of draughts, played with sheep droppings. Such passivity saves energy, which must be replaced by water.

We also filmed a sign saying 'Timbuktu – 55 days by camel', the closest we got to the legendary town. Nomadic Berber tribesmen used to bring back black slaves from across the burning Sahara; now blacks, whites, Arabs and Berbers formed a Moroccan fusion of colours which – to a visitor's eye – excited very little racial prejudice. Islam had been a great unifier. It also allowed men to have four wives, but only if they could afford them and the women agreed.

We left the desert and crossed back over the mountains to Marrakesh, the town of hippy fable. Crosby, Stills and Nash's 'Marrakesh Express' was actually a damn slow milk train. In the 1980s even the drop-outs dropped in by plane. Marrakesh looked south to the Sahara and black Africa; it had the liveliness of Africa rather than the Muslim quiet of Arabia.

After the waterless desert, we were flooded out in our hotel. We were cramped into one small suite with all our equipment; Nick had made it more difficult by smuggling in a woman. Ours were the only rooms to be flooded, but the burly manager declined to offer us alternative accommodation. He fulminated at our Western decadence, lack of permit for the woman, and insensitivity towards Moroccan culture and plumbing, although the dignity of his tirade was undermined by the fact that he was standing in a foot of water with his trousers rolled up.

After a few hours of great merriment for Nick and Henry as they filmed me falling off camels, we explored the crowded *souks*: over 20,000 little lock-ups and sentry boxes policed by Arthur Daley look-alikes. If a traveller didn't suffer from claustrophobia, the narrow lanes offered the chance of a lifetime to get lost. Some of the minuscule stalls sold the highly unusual: dried chameleons, dead owls and jackals' feet for spells and traditional medicine. We were offered aphrodisiacs which looked marginally more nauseating than Madonna – bits of dried dead animals that were enough to put you off sex for life.

Much of the medieval charm of Marrakesh was hidden from the casual tourist: the harems, palaces and inner courtyards were private, but everybody could enjoy the heavy scent of orange blossom, the jacarandas in May and the ancient mellowness of the terracotta colour that the natural mud gave the old town. Jemaa el Fna square was the heart of tourist town, dominated by the twelfth-century Koutoubia minaret. Musicians, sword-swallowers, snake-charmers and beggars competed to grab as much cash as possible from gullible visitors and film-makers with expense accounts. Colourful watersellers, with bells tinkling and copper cups shining, made money posing for photographers – the water looked undrinkable. Crowds assembled around the charcoal embers of kebab men, or heated dust-bin lids simmering with *harira*, a soup which contained just about anything plus beans. The square seethed with vitality and charm. The town council planned to make it a parking lot.

Next on the itinerary was Meknes, a more dignified place. Along with Fez, Marrakesh and Rabat, it made up the four imperial cities of Morocco. Meknes was developed as a military centre by the tyrannical Sultan Moulay Ismail in the seventeenth century. His security was assured by a vast army of black troops; his palaces and great walls were built by hordes of slaves, many of them Christians. Thomas Pellow, an English slave who became an officer in the sultan's guard, recorded that some 30,000 men and 10,000 mules erected the walls of Meknes. The sultan would personally flog his slaves and, in the days before unions, frequently sawed them in two from head to toe. He would put on yellow clothes (he called it his killing colour) if he felt in a sadistic mood. Christians were his favourite victims.

Nearby Fez had a long intellectual tradition and boasted the world's oldest university. Founded early in the ninth century, it became known as the Athens of Africa and the Mecca of the West. In the eleventh century it had a population of half a million, including Moors, Berbers, Jews, Negroes, Turks, Christians and 'renegades' – Christians who had converted to Islam. By the fifteenth century it had become famous for its inns; there were also 100 public baths. By the stench of the place, none had survived into the 1980s.

Yet Fez was immensely interesting; one of the few cities where an extensive area had remained unchanged since the Middle Ages. A film of the Arabian Nights had recently been shot in the medina. Walter Harris, a correspondent for *The Times*, visited Fez at the turn of the century and summed up the city precisely: 'There is scarcely a glimpse of Fez that is not beautiful, scarcely a glimpse that is not sad.' A stoic air of permanence pervaded these historic towns: despite the vicissitudes of history, I sensed that one kind of civilisation or other would inevitably survive. In other parts of Africa a pall of inexorable decay pervaded; jungles or sands were irresistible conquerors.

Heading north from Fez the road reached Tetouan, capital of the former Spanish protectorate of Morocco. General Franco assembled his fascist army here for the conquest of Spain in the civil war of the 1930s. The market was full of Spanish goods smuggled in from Ceuta, one of the two small strips of Spanish territory in Morocco and the last European colonial possession in Africa. The area was the centre of fierce resistance to European rule, and bellicose traditions surfaced again when a large and aggressive crowd tried to stop us filming. Covering Henry's back, I took a few well-aimed stones. After a few scuffles, our government escort arranged for a police guide.

The final stop was Tangier, which until independence was an internationally-controlled port famous for its spies and corruption. This was the place for night life and the team made the most of it, especially filming belly-dancers.

Our Moroccan trip was over: we had made a 40-minute glossy film in just over three weeks, filming impulsively on the trot. I edited in my head and did the to-cameras pieces spontaneously. I had made a hash of one in Tangier, using a radio mike in a crowded bazaar when the camera was out of sight on a balcony. The mike's radio signal kept breaking up when I was jostled; crowds of street urchins stared at me in amazement as I appeared to be talking loudly to myself. The effect was unintentionally hilarious, as were my presentations on a camel. I had also made an idiot of myself in a mock-up of Rick's Bar in Casablanca, playing the film's famous theme song on a piano. I couldn't play the tune; it was an automatic modern pianola. A child stood alongside in utter delight as I appeared to play 'As Time Goes By', then asked me to play 'Happy Birthday'. Nick fell about laughing. Later we discovered he had erased the sound from this section. Old film lore re-learned: never work alongside animals or kids, especially in a crowded bazaar.

The team had got on well and had made the film relatively quickly and cheaply, but we had all spent enough time in other Arab countries to know Morocco was not typical. Lebanon was, well, dynamite; Saudi women were much more reclusive and dangerous to talk to; and Moroccan hotels were a lot better than most. We had enjoyed the richness of Morocco's history, although the ghosts of yesterday were being shooed away by package tours and ham-fisted local bureaucracy. I found it a land of extremes: ancient and brashly modern, simultaneously both dazzling and seedy.

4

Pakistan – carry on up the Khyber

During our enjoyable month in Morocco, Henry, Nick and I had heard no more about Al's projected film in war-torn Afghanistan. Not a gunshot to be heard. And nothing from Al. After the Rabat meeting he disappeared, his favourite pastime. Henry and I became good friends; we both became fond, and protective, of Nick, an inexperienced and eccentric young journalist. We speculated whether Al was really going to send us to Afghanistan, or perhaps to Cambodia to do a story on the Khmer Rouge's elusive and genocidal Pol Pot. Al tended to clarify his 'missions' at the last minute.

Then, after I had finished producing the Moroccan film, Al rang me in Rabat and asked me to fly to London to make contact with Afghan exiles. After some initial explorations I flew back to Johannesburg to put my affairs in order. Al said I would be away for three months.

I flew to Cape Town for a final word with Al. He asked me to bring 'a few things' of his with me: Al-speak for a ton of film equipment plus a briefcase. While I was staggering with this load across the mezzanine floor of Jan Smuts airport, a high security area, the unlocked briefcase fell open. A rifle with a sniper's scope and around 200 rounds of ammunition rolled out. It was like the *Day of the Jackal*. A kind African helped me pick up the ammo and I put it all back in the case. Nobody said anything. I could have been hell-bent on shooting the president.

I had to check in the weapon at security before the flight. 'Do you have a licence for this?'

'No, it belongs to a friend.'

The security man looked suspiciously at the sniper-scope. 'What's all this fancy stuff for?'

'Duck shooting.'

The man didn't believe me, nor did I. But it was South Africa, and I was a respectable-looking white man. 'OK.'

Al met me at Cape Town and immediately resumed his security paranoia. 'You haven't discussed this mission with anyone?'

76

'No. But you could have told me what was in the damn briefcase.'

Al laughed and said: 'Duck shooting.'

'Like hell. But that's what I told the security check-in.'

He laughed louder. Things like mentioning carrying a gun and 200 rounds were not important to Al. He was not a man for details, except when they impinged on his definition of 'security'. At his luxurious mansion he gave me a drink and finally told me what he wanted me to do.

'You will lead three separate expeditions to penetrate Russian lines in Afghanistan. On the first one I want you to march to Kabul from Pakistan, and make contact with the *Mujahedin* guerrillas on the outskirts of the city. You might have to dress up in East German army uniform to get in.'

The rest of his briefing consisted of my sitting alone through three hours of videos on the Afghan war. I had never been to that area of the world, and was horrified by the filth, the rugged terrain, the death and suffering. After this televised horror, only partly softened by the best Cape wine, Al rejoined me.

'This is all soft background stuff,' he said casually. 'We need real front-line action. Our film, commemorating the fifth anniversary of the Russian invasion, is going to be the best film ever made on the war. Can you do it?'

'Sure.'

I spent a few days preparing things in Johannesburg. Henry and I had talked about getting fit for the arduous trip: I was grossly unfit, despite regular squash, and certainly unprepared for the tasks ahead. Although I had taken the occasional chance when covering unrest in the South African townships, in truth I had hardly heard a shot fired in anger. I was more worried about my fitness than getting shot at. To make things worse, Henry decided not to come because of family pressures. I was 36 and had no ties. I made out a will – I didn't own much, but I was a trifle disconcerted to overhear two close friends discuss which pieces of furniture they might get. It didn't boost my self-confidence.

I left for London on 18 June 1984. On the long flight I thought of the old adage about fools rushing in, but could I get out? Hopefully the experienced Afghan hands in London would provide the answer.

I gave myself two weeks in London to develop my initial contacts. The city seemed full of odd-ball exiles from this or that 'liberation front'. In the past I'd had infrequent contact with the occasional self-professed IRA man, bombastic Zimbabwean guerrilla and bitter Palestinian; now I discovered that Afghans in exile were more fractious and secretive than my other back-street-and-trenchcoat acquaintances.

The first Afghan I stumbled on was a Dr Helmandi, an exile who spoke fluent Russian. He said he would help but wanted one or two things in exchange, like surface-to-air missiles and a return ticket to Pakistan. My main job had to be done in Peshawar, capital of Pakistan's North West Frontier province, where most of the forty or so squabbling guerrilla groups had their headquarters, and I didn't think I needed the shady Dr Helmandi holding my hand. I took emotional refuge by ringing up a few adventurer friends from my Sandhurst days. Dick Snailham, who had led umpteen expeditions up the Nile and Amazon, went into minute detail about catching scorpions. 'They plague Afghanistan,' he said reassuringly.

A few mates who had been in the British SAS told me about lice, zinc oxide for tender feet, and plastic bags for film should the horses drown in the Afghan rivers. They hinted at nastier bits, such as the tactics of the 150,000-strong Soviet army of occupation and the bizarre habits of Afghan tribesmen. Since I was quite open about my ignorance of tribal warfare, I risked some teasing of my freshman status. Inevitably, I was treated to a lengthy discourse on the uncomfortable rearrangement of certain tender parts of the anatomy which the Afghans indulged in with estranged friends and relatives. I also heard stories about Russian prisoners being flayed alive, tribesmen buggering film crews' horses, and whipping unfit journalists for not keeping up on marches or for showing fear under fire. I had the vague feeling that people were trying to discourage me.

Tim Cooper, a man from the London Afghan Support Committee, was helpful. He looked and talked like a dapper, if slightly mad, Hussar, straight out of a Flashman adventure. I explained my elaborate logistical plans in detail. He laughed. 'All you need is a blanket, a couple of pills, and a shell dressing wrapped around your chest in case you get shot somewhere.'

I began to think the British experts were as crazy as the Afghans sounded. Then Al telephoned to suggest I visit my family in Wales before I left for Pakistan. Another confidence-booster.

Dr Helmandi was still tugging at my heels, nagging about his plane ticket and missiles. As I delved deeper into exile politics, it was hinted that he was KGB. Didn't he get his degrees in Moscow? Even if he wasn't a Russian agent, he was aligned to the wrong party, one of the conservatives. I was told: 'Try the fundamentalists, the ones who support the Ayatollah in Iran.'

I was given the address of an Afghan fundamentalist greengrocer on the Clapham Road. Then came an anonymous tip-off: 'He's definitely KGB. He'll warn the Pakis and you'll be turned around at Islamabad airport.' I decided I didn't have time to visit the Clapham Road.

Journalism is about bashing away even when every contact turns out a lemon. If you try ten times, you'll get there; but if you stop depressed on the ninth, you won't. My breakthrough was meeting the Gailani family in a plush Hyde Park apartment, paid for by supportive Saudis. After explaining that I was organising two, maybe three, film crews to enter the war zone to make a big anniversary-of-the-invasion film, the Gailanis offered to help. They promised a whole array of what proved to be useful contacts in Pakistan and Afghanistan.

It was time to leave. Although I now had contacts and knew something of the political problems, I was still worried about the logistics of getting a film team into Pakistan. The military dictatorship covertly helped their co-religionists in Afghanistan, but didn't like foreign journalists. Handled properly, however, and after greasing a few palms, it was possible to send a crew in. The Pakistan government was not averse to lots of money pouring in for the millions of Afghan refugees in Pakistan, some of which could be siphoned off for its own use, so journalists were allowed in to report on the plight of the refugees. Then they could slip illegally across the Afghan border. But to do all this I needed help on the ground in Pakistan.

It came out of the blue. I tracked down Peter Jouvenal, an ex-British Army paratrooper turned news cameraman, who had been in Afghanistan more than any other journalist. He was flying out of London the next day; so, unable to meet up with him, I contrived to book a seat next to him.

On the final night a strange apparition appeared at my hotel: Tim Lambon. Short punk haircut, worn-out leather jacket, jeans, big and menacing. I was drinking in the bar with a pretty, friendly blonde (it would be a long, no-women, no-booze trip). Tim was direct, a man of few words: 'Al sent me. He said I should come with you. I've just flown from Cape Town.'

I offered him a beer.

'I don't drink alcohol, but I'll have a Coke.' He knocked it back, and I thought he was going to eat the glass as well. When he went out to get his kit from the lobby, the blonde said urgently: 'He's got that killer look in his eyes.'

Tim came back, looking more relaxed, but I could sense he was thinking: 'Do I have to go into this strange number with that fat little Welshman? Will I have to carry the bugger?' As it happened, he did. His military background (ex-Special Branch of the Rhodesian police, active in an infantry role in the war), his skills as a medic, and his robust humour, wit and shoulders were to prove invaluable on our expedition.

Peter Jouvenal had said he would meet me the next morning at the exclusive Diner's Club bar at Heathrow airport. The Gailani family had also insisted that one of their brigadiers talk to me before we left. I was due to meet both parties at midday, and rushed by taxi to the rendezvous feeling the after-effects of one night's intense preparation for months of no wine, no women and no kissing on the movies.

At the Diner's Club reception an irate lady asked how I could invite so many strange-looking people to the exclusive facility when I wasn't even a member. Just as I was about to explain, the phone rang on her desk. It was for me: the blonde from the previous night wanted to say goodbye. Bad timing. The receptionist was furious. I offered to join Diner's Club on the spot, but she said I would need references and so on, implying that my sort wouldn't be wanted anyway. The only member there, Peter Jouvenal, had still not arrived.

Inside the club, Tim had been keeping the bald Gailani brigadier happy. Various surly Afghans, not invited by me, mumbled in barely muted hostility across the other side of the lounge. Tim was fondling a long, sheathed knife. It was like a waiting room in a Moscow railway station full of Bolsheviks circa 1917; the air was heavy with conspiracy.

The brigadier explained that he knew the Afghans opposite; they had once been friends but were now supporters of rival groups. We discussed our project. Ever security-conscious, Tim became agitated by our loud voices and use of maps. I put the maps away and lowered my tone, trying to be very secretive, then picked up my briefcase. It was not closed properly. All the maps and project plans fell out. Tim glowered at me – another black mark.

Finally, Peter Jouvenal appeared. I introduced myself and apologised for the uninvited Afghan horde. Within a few minutes we scurried off to catch a flight to Islamabad. No one was more pleased than the Diner's Club receptionist, still glaring at me with undiluted loathing.

Tim had to part with his beloved dagger at the check-in, which made him grumpy. I also suggested we sit apart and enter Islamabad airport separately. On the plane I tucked into European food and wine as though I was on my way to a Siberian gulag. Between mouthfuls I swamped Peter and his partner, Julian Geary, with questions about Afghanistan. Both were amazingly tolerant of my ignorance.

I was particularly concerned about how we should describe ourselves at Islamabad airport, suggesting that Tim should pose as a student and, if asked, say he was planning a walking tour of the mountains. Peter thought Tim should take off his tough-looking biker's jacket. I was wearing a suit and had 'businessman' written on my second, clean, British passport.

Peter and Julian felt I was worrying too much. 'Getting into Pakistan will be no problem,' Julian said, smiling. Perhaps my two weeks of talking to paranoid Afghans in London had got the better of me. One 'businessman' entering Pakistan was not a real worry, but the rest of the film team's equipment would probably need some smart thinking, or heavy paperwork and bureaucrat-soothing, on my part. I'd bribed my way around Africa and the Middle East, and now speculated on my first encounter with Asia.

The long war

As a historian I had read Flashman's memoirs of the fighting on the North West Frontier. British policy towards Afghanistan had been shaped by fear of a Russian drive south and the need to contain the turbulent tribesmen. Afghanistan had never been colonised, although the country's survival as an independent state had more to do with the competitive imperialisms of Moscow and London than the diplomatic skills of Kabul. Afghan leaders have always blamed foreigners for their ills – but internal blunders invited foreign meddling. In the early twentieth century Afghanistan tried to play off the predatory empires. Later it squabbled with its neighbours, especially Pakistan, because Kabul claimed large swathes of Pakistani territory.

Various regimes in Kabul tried to modernise the backward kingdom. In the 1960s the king experimented with liberal reform. A parliament, made up of MPs satisfying very minimal standards of sanity and hygiene, was established with limited powers. As all would-be conquerors and local civil servants soon learned, however, Afghans are the most ungovernable of peoples. Fiercely independent, they resented any central authority interfering in their traditional ways, even if it was for their own good, like sewerage, running water and schools.

Nowhere else in the world did the past live so closely alongside the present. Physical inaccessibility meant that, outside Kabul, the twentieth century had bypassed the country. It had the world's shortest railway – less than half a mile long. Much of the country was only passable on horseback or by camel. It was, above all, a tribal society, far worse than even Celtic versus Rangers. Each tribe passionately defended its local customs. In the south the people were mainly Pathans; in the north, Tajiks, Turkomans, Kirghiz and Uzbeks; in the central mountains, unruly Hazaras. The wildlife was pretty wild: wolves, hyenas, jackals, wild dogs, wild cats, leopards, bears and, fittingly, vultures. The tribesmen were like their land: harsh, unpredictable and brutal. The main unifying factor was Islam: belief in God and country amounted to the same thing.

Then hatred of the Russians was grafted on to raw nationalism, local tribalism and religious fervour. Soviet intrusion began with Lenin and reached a political climax in the so-called revolution of 1978. Before President Babrak Karmal was installed by Moscow in 1979, three of his predecessors had left office the hard way: variously shot, strangled or poisoned. Russian tanks rolled over the border at Christmas, 1979. While the citizens of the West were digesting their turkeys, Russia gobbled up independent Afghanistan.

The *jihad*, holy war, was declared *before* the Russian tanks rolled in. Anti-communist guerrillas in the countryside vowed to return Afghanistan to Islamic rule. The tribesmen disliked *any* government, let alone a communist one backed by foreign infidels. Attempts at land reform and improvements in the medieval condition of women had incensed rural conservatives, both landlords and peasants. The population numbered 19 million (five million subsequently fled during the war), of whom 90 per cent were illiterate. Local religious leaders believed that communist centralism – even if it brought schools – would deprive them of their authority, so the mullahs whipped up religious passions. And the arrogant behaviour of the Soviet conquerors made matters worse. The Russians soon discovered that defeating and controlling the Afghans were two different feats. The ungovernable tribesmen had simply never learned the habit of submission.

On the other hand, Afghanistan was not exactly Russia's Vietnam. The Soviets were fighting on their own doorstep. Despite the mounting body bags, press and public opinion were stifled. No Jane Fonda squawked defiance in Moscow. And, although Afghanistan was ideal guerrilla terrain, the tribesmen – despite Hollywood movies and star-struck American reportage – were not natural soldiers. They seemed to believe fervently in the sentimental claptrap written about them. Convinced of their innate martial qualities, they were very reluctant to be trained, and spent as much time praying as working out tactics or maintaining their weapons. They hated orders. Their incompetence in technical matters was surpassed only by their faith in technology (and God) to solve all their problems for them.

By sheer doggedness they had managed, however, to keep a super-power at bay for five years. The Red Army controlled the cities, towns and, crucially, the air. The *Mujahedin* (holy warriors) loosely controlled perhaps 80 per cent of the country. But their guerrilla war was undermined by tribal and political feuds; the *Mujahedin* spent as much time ambushing each other as venting their indignation on the invaders. Their rigid individualism was the guerrillas' main strength and weakness. No Tito or de Gaulle had emerged to seize overall leadership. The divisions were partly a legacy of traditional social structures in which decisions were taken by village elders, and fighting groups were often hesitant to venture outside their own neighbourhoods. The holy warriors had to work out a fundamental dilemma: to fight a modern war they had to give up their instinctive individualism and tribal ways – the very things they were fighting communism to defend.

Peshawar played host to a wide variety of guerrilla groups in exile, ranging from eccentric royalists to fanatical Maoists. The six most effective groups had formed two rival coalitions: one, the Alliance, composed of Islamic fundamentalists; the other, Islamic Unity, a more moderate, middle-of-the-road lot, like Saudi Arabia. They spent most of their time intriguing against one another, but they did provide some linkage with the outside world, and a channel for funds and arms from friendly countries such as Egypt, Pakistan, China and America.

By 1984 local commanders fighting inside Afghanistan – not talking outside – had grown heartily sick of Peshawar's fat-cat exiles. Able leaders such as the renowned 'Lion of the Panshir', Ahmed Shah Massud, were co-operating with commanders of rival parties, who had organised training inside the country and set up full-time combat units. Many of the part-time *Mujahedin* – numbering perhaps 150,000 men – regarded military operations as a highly individualistic ritual, performed on a whim or to save face according to their eccentric, if sometimes ferocious, code of honour.

The intensity and tide of the war varied immensely. The conflict in the Tajik-inhabited highlands of northern Afghanistan often bore little resemblance to the fighting in the Pushtun regions of the south east. A heavy Soviet offensive, tribal feud or the death of a popular commander could quickly and dramatically alter local conditions, although the news could take weeks or months to trickle back to guerrilla headquarters.

Initially the Soviets concentrated on the proverbial hearts and minds and left the guerrillas to the deserts and mountains, chased by gunships. But the Marxist-Leninist-trained Red Army seemed incapable of fighting a political war, and resorted to crude military power. In 1984 the Russians stepped up the pace of the war, deploying their occupation force more effectively and reducing their over-reliance on armour, which was more applicable to fighting a war on the flat plains of Europe. Crack airborne troops, more attuned to mountain warfare, were deployed. In June and July of 1984 they operated a scorched earth policy along Afghanistan's border with Pakistan, to wipe out the guerrilla supply columns and force the remaining villagers to flee. Nearly five million refugees were living in squalid camps dotting the border areas of Pakistan and Iran. The guerrillas' backers in the West and the Islamic world realised that without better weapons – such as surface-to-air missiles and the training to use them properly – the *Mujahedin* might face defeat.

That's when we arrived on the scene. The information gleaned in London, reading press clippings, and Peter's careful briefing on the plane had given me this much background. Above all, I knew that Afghanistan was not a media war, like Vietnam and Lebanon. Few American TV teams had reached the heart of the fighting. Covering the war was risky, film crews had to be prepared for days and days of long, hard marches, and walking seemed to be almost an un-American activity. No press helicopters commuted to the battlefields from the plush hotels and massage parlours of Saigon. Inside Afghanistan available women and booze were very rare commodities. It was hardly a popular war for journalists, and I knew it was going to be tough.

Making the right connections

Islamabad loomed below the low cloud. The whole green, low-tiered landscape looked permanently tilted, with rivulets streaming across the red earth. We circled and touched down at 6am. Customs officials were polite and we had no problems, although the baggage people had lost Tim's dagger. He seemed to have a very sentimental attachment to it, a sort of macho security blanket, so I refrained from commenting that a student on a walking tour probably wouldn't carry a military dagger.

We passed out of the building into the mad, teeming, shouting, smelly welcome of the third world. My first taste of Asia. Everyone dressed identically: long, scruffy shirts, baggy pants and leather sandals. Many of the men had dyed ginger hair (I learned later that they thought this made them look younger). I was determined not to be ripped off, so I asked an experienced-looking American how much a taxi should cost. Fifty rupees. Besieged by at least ten Pakistanis clamouring for my custom, I saw a large, new car parked at the edge of the passenger terminal in front of me. An insistent taxi-man kept tugging at my sleeve and pointing to the car. He agreed to the 50 rupees. I turned around to check Tim and our luggage. Julian was coming with us, with some light camera equipment; Peter would take the heavier stuff to our destination, the Islamabad Holiday Inn, in the hotel's courtesy bus.

'I've got the taxi fixed up,' I said assertively to Julian and Tim.

'You expect us to travel in *that*,' Tim said, laughing.

A dilapidated 1958 Morris stood where the gleaming new vehicle had been. The ginger-haired Pakistani taxi-driver gave me a toothless grin. He'd already loaded our kit on, and in, the car. I had been well and truly had. Despite my anger, the three of us squeezed in with our equipment. I didn't want to make a fuss and perhaps get entangled with the airport police. Julian and Tim thought it was hugely funny.

In sanctions-bound Rhodesia I had developed a genuine affection for the reliable old Morrie, but this wasn't of the same ilk. The engine chugged vaguely into life and we jerked through a series of red lights, while the one reluctant windscreen-wiper failed to cope with a heavy downpour of rain. Hooting and weaving from side to side, just missing cyclists, gaily-painted lorries and buses that looked like mobile shrines, we coughed along, firing on two or three cylinders. Great puddles swamped the pot-holed roads, criss-crossed by streams and tinged everywhere with red mud. My window was stuck open; every passing lorry sent a backwash onto the suit I had worn to play the 'businessman'. Tim, his eyes just visible above a mountain of kit in the back seat, kept chuckling away, as did Julian. They could afford to laugh: I was sitting in the front shielding them from the spray.

We navigated through a series of bigger pools – just. Instead of stopping on an unswamped section, the toothless wonder jerked the car to a sudden halt in the middle of a muddy river deluging the road. He braved the torrent and fiddled under the bonnet, obviously with little hope of resurrecting the drowned engine. Tim was still convulsed with laughter. Julian said: 'Well, I must be in Pakistan.' I just cursed. The ginger-haired non-mechanic flagged down another taxi, a slightly more modern Datsun, painted in the standard taxi livery of black and yellow. We took off our shoes and socks, rolled up our trousers and waded to the relieving vehicle. The equipment was transferred in sodden haste. My SAS advisers in London had talked about keeping equipment dry in the raging torrents in Afghanistan, but everything was soaked and we were only a few miles from Islamabad airport. I was not doing too well.

For six miles we drove through warm rain along the badly-mauled dual carriageway. 'Stop!' I shouted imperiously, suddenly convinced we had left my case on the other vehicle. Nobody remembered loading it. The taxi-driver carried on. He couldn't speak a word of English. By sign language and Julian's few words of Urdu we turned him around; very reluctantly, he drove back to the marooned Morris. No driver and no case. In the pouring rain we looked up: my case was on top of the second taxi. Julian and Tim laughed like demented stooges.

We started again, but our driver indicated that he had no petrol. We crawled, eventually, to a petrol station. It had no petrol; same story at the next two garages. Finally, the driver managed to procure a few pints of fuel. Then he got lost; he didn't know his way to the biggest hotel in Islamabad. Meanwhile, the courtesy bus with Peter in it had long since passed us; Peter had given us a regal wave.

We dragged ourselves barefoot into the sanity of the hotel lobby like shipwrecked mariners, an hour and a half after leaving the airport. It should have taken 20 minutes at the most. After the derelict symbols of the third world we had just endured, the hotel was a marvel of plastic Western efficiency. The very beginning of our journey to Asia had been a catalogue of blunders. Mostly my blunders.

We stayed for two days in the hotel. I went to see the political officer at the British Embassy – in other words, the intelligence man. He was politely helpful as we drank a colonial-style gin and tonic. We also had help from other journalists. Normally, international hacks are very cliquey and most reluctant to assist newcomers. Particularly in a war zone such as Rhodesia, Lebanon or Vietnam, old hands jealously guard information and contacts from the Johnny-come-latelies. It can take months for even the most professional journalist to break into the charmed circle. Afghanistan seemed to be different. There were only a few 'old hands', and they appeared ready to help. I asked Peter, who was on assignment for CBS, why.

'I'm helping you because you're serious,' he said. 'You're not just nipping over the border, like some American reporters, and standing there saying, "Here I am in Soviet-occupied Afghanistan", and then hopping back a few hours later.' Hopping sounded fine to me.

Peter was 100 per cent serious about his involvement, and the Afghans responded to him with the warmth of a brother. He always treated them with the greatest respect, and I determined to do the same. Everybody was quite happy to talk about Afghanistan, but none of the hacks would discuss Pakistani politics inside the hotel. Tim couched matters in his usual Rhodesian war patois: 'It's spooksville, man. I checked this number out. Foreign journalists are always given the same rooms on the same floor.'

Tim and I were very careful about the food we ate, and had been told to clean our teeth with Coke or whisky. But next morning Tim said casually over breakfast, 'The foxtrot has begun.' So had mine. After breakfast we met two leaders of rival Afghan guerrilla groups. The first was late: Ahmed Gailani, son of the patriarch of the National Front for the Liberation of Afghanistan. His father was an hereditary saint and the son also acted the holy man. Tim commented afterwards: 'Too sweet-smelling.' The Gailanis had rung Ahmed from London and told him to help us. Ahmed was vague about details, but gave us contacts in Peshawar.

Because the Gailani group was late, the meeting ran over into the time allocated to their main rivals, the *Jamiat-i-Islami*. I was worried, knowing of the depths of traditional feuds. Would they pull out knives if they met? But when Massud Khalini of the *Jamiat* arrived he greeted Ahmed with a hug – just like rival communist leaders in public. The Gailanis left and Massud, in excellent American-English, sized us up. He suggested we do a three-to-four-month trip to Afghanistan's northern border with the Soviet Union; the war needed coverage there as no film crew had gone that far. 'I can arrange that for you,' he said straightforwardly. Was this a serious offer, or a test of our commitment?

I explained that we had two penetrations in mind, one for a few weeks, and a longer one, perhaps two months. The duration of our trips was to prove a major bone of contention: I worried about my stamina on a long trip; Tim was superfit but had to get back to Cape Town to finish his degree thesis. Al had talked about two or three penetrations as though they were trips to the beach. As we were to discover, getting in and out was about the hardest part of the journey.

Massud seemed much more organised than the Gailanis and I grew to respect him. The *Jamiat* people took us to the airport, from where Tim and I flew north to Peshawar in an old Fokker which stank of stale vomit. Stickily hot, Peshawar was the capital of the infamous North West Frontier, whence soldiers of the Raj had sallied forth to fight the tribesmen. Winston Churchill, soldiering there in 1897, described the locals as 'among the most miserable, brutal creatures of the earth. Their intelligence only enables them to be more cruel, more dangerous, more destructive than wild beasts.' The troops referred to service on the frontier as being 'on the grim'. But Peshawar was colourful as well as grim; full of passionate political intrigue as well as drug trafficking, arms smuggling and currency black marketeering. Half-crumbling relics of the Raj lingered everywhere; old steam trains were still working.

Dean's Hotel was named after a former British governor-general, and had sounded a romantic sort of place in my historical reading. In fact it was filthy, and the dirt bothered Tim a lot. He was always scribbling in his journal (he later gave me a complete copy, even though it was very critical of my leadership of our expedition) and described Dean's thus: 'The colonial charm has definitely been tropically rotting for 40 years ... my room smells like there was a dung fire lit not too long ago here.' We had been advised to stay there because the bungalow-style accommodation allowed easy access for visiting Muj, and the ubiquitous if invisible Special Branch – like most totalitarian systems, one of the few efficient things in Pakistan – could not monitor our movements so readily.

The first night we met the foreign hacks. Ken Guest had just come out of Afghanistan after a long trip with the 'Muj', as journalists called the guerrillas. Three times he had tried to get into the Panshir Valley, but

Russian attacks and Muj ambushes had prevented him. Ken went into some detail about the air attacks and Tim was fascinated. We also noticed how spare Ken's kit was. Peter's was the same. They must have thought our elaborate logistical preparation ridiculous, especially for such relatively short trips, but were too polite to comment. As Tim diarised, 'We're like kids asking big brother what it's really like in the army'.

We had dinner in the Nanking – Peter insisted that Chinese restaurants were the safest place to eat, and Tim and I were still nursing our 'foxtrots'. Other expatriate characters joined us. Ed Girardet, a correspondent for the *Christian Science Monitor*, and one of the most charming people I have met, had just finished a book based upon eight trips into Afghanistan. And there was Vladimir Dremlynga, a Russian who had spent six years in jail for protesting in Red Square against the Soviet invasion of Czechoslovakia.

'That was the first political demonstration in Moscow since the Revolution,' he said proudly. He was trying to get hold of Russian prisoners in Muj jails to take to America as part of his anti-communist crusade. I liked him, even though I was suspicious of him. Al's paranoia was infectious.

I went to bed brooding on the USSR and our forthcoming trip behind Russian lines. It was a night of fever in that ugly, dank room. I didn't know whether it was the beginning of dysentery or malaria. It felt like both. I had terrible dehydration, but the hotel said there was no room service at night. Tim came in next morning and saw what an awful state I was in. Thank God he was a trained medic. He gave me some suitable pills for my shits and fever. Tim was succumbing to the same thing, so we decided to move to a better hotel, the Khyber Intercontinental, which at least had fridges with cool drinks and in-house videos on the TV. No wonder Julian and Peter had booked in there. We were put in the usual rooms reserved for hacks. We supposed they were bugged. I lay in a daze for two days. Tim was not much better, but at least I was not vomiting as he was. In my waking hours I watched videos, including *The Russians Are Coming*, which I hoped wasn't a portent. The films were infuriatingly censored – even a gentle kiss between married couples was cut. Sometimes one had to endure five or ten minutes of snow on the screen; they were not even censored properly.

After two days we both felt better, so Ed and Julian took us on a tour of Peshawar. We ventured into the famous Qissa Khawani, the storytellers' bazaar, with its rows of matchbox-sized shops. Herbert Edwardes, an early British administrator of the area, called it 'the Piccadilly of Central Asia'. Brassware, kids, donkeys looking dead on their feet, heat, smells, and everywhere the multicoloured three-wheeled taxi motorscooters.

In contrast to the bustle of the bazaar we saw quiet relics of the old Raj: run-down St John's Cathedral and the overgrown military graveyard. We took refuge in the famous Peshawar Club, once the centre of the Vale of Peshawar Hunt. During the bloodshed and chaos of independence in 1947 a hunt official went around the stables and kennels putting down every horse and hound, unwilling to leave them to whatever fate might spread from the tormented Punjab next door. The club was still and empty, with an almost tangible feeling of ghosts.

The history lesson over, Ed and Peter took us around some of the guerrilla HQs. Tim observed the slackness of the guards and the filthy condition of their new AK-47s. I eventually firmed on two parties, the left-wing *Jamiat* and the Gailanis on the right. Both began to arrange for our two expeditions.

Tim and I concentrated on getting well and acclimatising to the poor food and heat. Tim gave me an anti-hepatitis injection in the backside, then said I must do the same to him. I certainly trusted him with the big needle, but I was very surprised that he trusted me.

We also found an excellent taxi-driver who spoke English well. He said he was a former member of the Indian army during British rule. 'I miss the days of the Raj,' he confessed. 'At least we had food to eat then.' But the friendly Mr Azar, according to Peter, was probably on the police payroll. Peter explained how we should play the game. Everyone knew that we were heading for Afghanistan, but we had to be a little subtle about it. When we started wearing local dress, we said we were dressing to climb in the local hills.

I also had to kowtow to the bureaucrats in Peshawar and Islamabad – an endless and thankless task. I visited a Mr Afridi in Peshawar's dark, scruffy press office to get permission to film the refugee camps inside Pakistan. That was allowed: it showed how humanitarian Pakistan was, despite the bad image of its military dictatorship; and, more importantly, brought in lots of money. Afridi said I had to go to Islamabad, where I saw a pompous little man called Ismael Patel.

'You are a British team.'

'Yes.' It wouldn't have helped to say that Al had chosen a crew of tough South Africans.

'Then you must get permission from our embassy in London. That will take two months.'

'No. The crew is arriving in a few days.'

'Then tell them not to come.'

'I can't. They're on contract. They've come from all over the world. You see, we're not used to all these permits [a big lie, because South Africa was a very permit-ridden place then]. We just follow the news. It's

very important that we get this film done before the fifth anniversary of
the Russian invasion.'

I had already bribed my way around officials with envelopes full of
rupees or, for staunchly religious fundamentalists, a *Playboy* inside a *Time*
magazine – more effective than a 1,000 rupee backhander. I felt Patel
didn't want to be bribed. He said he would try to help; but with the crew's
arrival imminent, we would have to smuggle in the equipment somehow.
Getting it out, plus 50 rolls of exposed film, would be much harder.

Back in Peshawar I made final arrangements with the Muj. The main
trip would be with the Gailanis. They would take us through the tribal
areas, forbidden to all outsiders, then we would walk for five days to meet
Commander Wali Khan, who would arrange for some daylight action,
preferably an ambush on a Russian convoy. The cameraman and I,
dressed in communist troops' uniforms, would be smuggled into Kabul
to film there secretly. Hardly any footage taken in the capital by a western
cameraman had emerged since the invasion. Then we would all walk
back. Simple, if we were all lucky and fit. The second trip would be
arranged by *Jamiat*, either in the cold north or in the hostile desert region
around Kandahar.

Tim and I flew to Islamabad to make final arrangements for the film
crew's arrival. We could not get a film permit for them, as I explained on
the phone to Al in London. I asked him to approach the Pakistani
embassy in London. 'Get a night-scope, too,' I said. 'That's vital. Most of
the fighting is done at night.'

Al mumbled a vague OK, then dropped his customary bombshell:
'Paul, I've had a crew problem. The sound man has dropped out in
London. Lost his nerve. And I can't find a second cameraman. There'll
only be *one* crew and I want you to organise three trips with that one
crew.'

'Al, that's not so easy. It's damn hard getting in and out of there. I
haven't even sorted out getting you guys into Pakistan, let alone
Afghanistan.'

'That's your job,' he said testily. 'And I'm keen on a trip to the south.'

'Al, it's too dangerous by my reckoning.'

'My contacts here in London say that there's no problem with the
south.'

'Look, I'm on the ground with these people here in Peshawar, and the
general consensus is that with the Soviet build-up and the lack of cover
around Kandahar ...'

'We'll sort it out when I get there. Bye'

Then Mr Patel phoned to say there was no chance of receiving a film
permit.

'But the crew is arriving in two days.'

'If they try,' said Patel, very curtly, 'their equipment will be impounded.'

Tim and I had done everything we could. We filled in the two days by visiting the famous ruins at Taxila and then Rawalpindi to find gear such as water bottles. Some of the tiny shops in the bazaar were full of British Army surplus, sold or stolen in 1947 or 1948, or so it seemed. A man followed us through the bazaar, finally approaching us to sell some precious stones. Then he asked if we wanted to buy any heroin. We politely declined. 'Probably a cop testing us,' said Tim, the ex-cop.

We were not being unduly suspicious. That day a letter arrived from the blonde I had met on my last night in London, making all sorts of raunchy comments about my sex life, or absence of it, in Muslim countries. The letter had been clumsily opened and resealed. Dirty fingerprints marred the words, especially on the page making exotic references to camels. At least the police had some idea of what we were up to.

The BA flight to Islamabad arrived on time. I had hired a small bus for the crew and equipment. Four men – Al, Chris Everson, Joe Wilkens and Ian Robbie – arrived in the customs hall with a mountain of equipment. Six bulky green bags held the camera gear. Besides personal kit, Al had brought in ten boxes of what we later called 'moon food' – special pre-dried, packaged edibles used in NASA space flights.

A large customs official stopped Al. 'What are those big boxes for?'

'It's for the expedition,' Al said arrogantly.

'What expedition?'

'Haven't you been told about our famous expedition?'

'Oh,' said the embarrassed customs man. 'All right, but you haven't got any alcohol, have you?'

'No,' said Al assertively, in the full knowledge of whisky and *Playboys* stashed away.

Another customs man approached Chris and his trolley-loads of film equipment. 'What's inside there?'

'Personal items ... the odd film magazine and lenses, things like that,' he said with studied vagueness.

'Any drink?'

The official had just started poking around in one of the green bags when Al arrived: 'Hurry, the bus is waiting. Hurry.'

'I'm really sorry, but I've got to go,' Chris blurted out. 'The bus is outside. I'm in a terrible hurry.'

He said afterwards, 'The customs man was like a stunned mullet. We just walked out. That was it.' Al, big and resplendent in an official-looking blue blazer and tie, had out-bullied the practised bullies in the customs hall. The bluff had worked. No bribes and very little hassle. We piled into my bus for the three-hour journey to Peshawar. All four newcomers were transfixed by the bad driving and chaotic roads.

Gradually we began to size each other up. I vaguely knew Chris from Rhodesia, where he'd had a gung-ho war in the army and been badly wounded in action. After he recovered he was transferred to the mounted Grey's Scouts. Chris was big, strong and difficult, but a first-rate cameraman. Ian had also served in the Rhodesian Army. This gentle giant was very close to Chris, for whom he was acting as sound man. Joe Wilkens was the odd man out, an Afrikaner with vague credentials as a freelance journalist. Al, who wasn't going into Afghanistan, had been persuaded to bring him along. Joe could accompany Tim as a 'runner' to bring out after a few weeks any 'bang-bang' news footage, before Chris, Ian and I made our 'long-range penetration', to use Al's phrase.

Our team had been haphazardly shaped by events – the first big mistake. On such trips a definite leader must be selected or elected, and he must choose his own team. Tim was obviously worried about my physical capabilities on the coming operation, but was even more sceptical about Joe. In his diary he confided his thoughts about Joe's intelligence connections, adding: 'He is a granny and will be uphill on the trip.'

Arriving at Dean's, we immediately began to organise the finer details of the trip. First we went shopping, kitting ourselves out in local gear: *salwar kamizs* - long shirts and baggy pants – Chitral hats and *patous* – light blankets to sleep on and act as camouflage during air strikes.

Then I introduced the new boys to the Muj. *Jamiat* would arrange our second trip, but the first would be hosted by the Gailanis. The Gailani people insisted on entertaining their guests (the Afghans must rival the Welsh and the Irish as the world's greatest self-deceiving story-tellers), and briefed us on routes and customs. We were entrusting our lives to what, at least to the newcomers, seemed beturbanned weirdos, all putting on a striking display of nose, beard and whiskers. We must be raving mad to have volunteered. Given that, the long march and difficult filming seemed logical enough.

Julian, Peter and Ed were sceptical of the Gailanis; they preferred working with the more hardline *Jamiat*. I opted for the Gailanis because they had a good, safe record for working with 'English' journalists and tended to steer away from the heavy fighting zones; *Jamiat* would be a rougher ride. A safer, shorter expedition seemed preferable for apprentice Afghan hands. Al agreed with my decision, anticipating a series of incursions behind Russian lines, but Chris sniped at the plan.

Peter and Julian gave us a technical briefing, mainly on medical and photographic issues. Tim briefed us on some of our more esoteric medical kit, like the drips we would carry in big, adapted South African Defence Force rucksacks. We also gave some of our moon food and medical kit to Ed, Julian and Peter, who were about to leave on the arduous northern route into the Panshir through Nuristan, where little food awaited them. Chris busied himself with meticulous preparations of his camera equipment. He and Tim persuaded tailors in the bazaar to make, almost instantly, straps and bags for our kit, especially the camera and heavy tripod. Joe kept himself to himself, drinking the awful soapy beer and chain-smoking in his room. Al left for Djibouti to supervise another film shoot.

As we sorted out the mass of kit and tried to reduce it to five rucksacks and some long, green canvas bags, we all indulged in the usual, slightly nervous, pre-op camaraderie. We tried the moon food – it was delicious – played with the gas stoves, and checked out our commando knives. Chris said: 'What are we supposed to do with these? Creep up behind a Russian and stab him to death?'

I had sized them all up pretty well by then. Chris was professional to the core: tough, but touchy. Ian would be entirely reliable. Tim was a bit moody but hardy, energetic and very resourceful. Joe and I would be physical liabilities, I felt sure. I would find out soon enough, for we were leaving early the next morning. The Muj would collect our gear that night to pack and disguise it.

As we rushed to complete everything, we started to joke about what we would miss. None of us mentioned women. Tim was scribbling away as usual in his log, and we asked him to read out bits. He had written something about 'convoy cock' – erections as a result of vehicle motion. 'Don't let your missus get hold of that diary,' Chris warned. 'Especially if the camels turn you on as well.'

I went to bed at midnight and lay sleepless. I was apprehensive, but also had a feeling of elation, almost euphoria, that I'd never experienced before. My confident expectations surprised me.

The Wild West

We assembled at 4am dressed like a cross between Dad's Army and Lawrence of Arabia – Afghan gear and Second World War webbing and pouches. Vladimir, the ebullient Russian who was looking after our remaining equipment, waved us goodbye as we left Dean's in an open truck. Just outside Peshawar we transferred to a Toyota Hiace ambulance

with our kit already stuffed under the seats and stretcher. Five of us, plus
two Muj, squeezed into the back. Dr Khalid, our guide, sat up front with
the driver. We entered the forbidden tribal areas of the North West
Frontier a few miles out of Peshawar.

The tribal areas snaked for nearly 3,000 kilometres from the deserts of
Baluchistan to the mountainous borders with China and Kashmir. No
foreigner was allowed to enter, as there was no formal law. Technically,
Pakistan kept order on the few roads. Beyond a perfunctory police
presence, each tribe was ruled and fought according to ancient customs.
The tribes were united only by a common aversion to their neighbouring
states.

The British never fully controlled the tribal areas. From the annexation of the Punjab in 1849 to independence in 1947, they tried to
maintain a semblance of law and order through an elaborate system of
political agents backed by frequent army forays. It was all part of what
Kipling called the 'Great Game' to prevent any Russian threat to India.
Occasional acts of chivalry and mutual respect for the other's martial
prowess encouraged both the British and the tribesmen to treat clashes
as a blood sport rather than warfare. But treachery and savagery
sometimes turned sport into massacre. During the British retreat from
Kabul in 1842 the tribesmen wiped out all the women and children after
agreeing to allow them safe conduct.

Despite the complicated alliances forged by British political agents,
treaties were often dishonoured. A former governor of the Frontier
province addressed a tribal *jirga*, or meeting, by saying, 'You are married
to us, you can't now go and flirt with the Afghans.' Hardly had he finished
his sentence when a grey-bearded elder interrupted: 'We are Muslims
and can have four wives, so why should we worry about sticking to one?'

Much of the mythology of British India grew from tales of exploits on
the Frontier. John Masters wrote of the 'sense-sharpening chance of a
sudden storm of bullets, a rush of knifemen and bloody hand-to-hand
fighting'. *Our* senses were sharpened by road-blocks and trucks full of
tribesmen letting off volleys from their AKs. Some were just exuberant,
others were celebrating wedding parties with firepower. We passed
through five road-blocks, covering our faces with our scarves and moaned
like plague victims – not exactly Oscar-winning performances, but luckily
the police hardly bothered to peer inside. At two road-blocks the police
looked serious. Heavily armed, they tried to seal the road by standing
across it. On both occasions the driver started up the ambulance siren
and sped through the line of police, who fortunately had the sense to
jump out of the way in time; nor did they open fire on an ambulance.

Tim had a cold. Joe kept smoking in the confined space, which annoyed Chris. Ian started to panic as the driver sped along roads that helter-skeltered around mountains on the edges of precipices. I slept.

We reached Darrah, an infamous centre for smuggling heroin and gun-running. It was also famous for the Darrahwal Topak – the local rifle, unreliable replicas of the AK family. We peered nervously around the edge of the ambulance's curtained windows. Every tribesman carried a rifle of sorts; some sported old .303s, others nursed real rather than homemade AKs.

We wound tortuously along the banks of the Kurram River past broken-down British cantonments and a Mogul fort, the dramatic backdrop to M M Kaye's *The Far Pavilions*. Turning off the so-called road, we bounced and banged across an old glacial scree valley towards the border. Driving cross-country at least meant there would be no police road-blocks. We passed eerie mud forts; literally, each tribesman's house was his castle. Dr Khalid told us to keep our heads down as we bumped along the stony valley floor beneath the mountains of the Afghan-Pakistan border.

After seven hours of extremely uncomfortable travelling we reached our destination, Terrimangel, a real bandits' nest. No Cecil B de Mille film could have captured the drama, filth and romance of the place: camels, tents, guns, squalor, rickety wooden houses, and Pakistani and Russian spies. Everything was over-decorated, especially the trucks, which looked like gaudy mobile temples, and the rifles, beaded and dangling with charms. Tim said simply, 'Kitsch is king here.'

The ambulance slithered into a narrow, filthy alleyway and stopped outside a jerry-built, two-storey wooden construction – a Gailani safe house. We were greeted by a band of ruffians, armed to the teeth with RPG-7 rocket-launchers and AKs nonchalantly hanging on their shoulders. Khalid told us to climb a ladder into a top room, where we ate kebabs and rice washed down with Cokes. Full marks to the Coca-Cola company for their marketing and distribution. American capitalist products – admittedly at inflated prices – were available even in the inaccessible foothills of the Afghan border, while overhead Russian communist jets bombed and strafed the enterprising merchants and bandits below.

We relaxed while I pulled out some of the thick wads of Afghanis, the Afghan currency, I had obtained on the black market in Peshawar bazaar. Khalid helped me work out how many horses to hire and for how much. We hired three with their handlers, old men with faces rich in character and beards whom we dubbed the Three Wise Men.

I doled out some Afghan currency to each team member should we be forced to split up. Chris distributed film cans and batteries in case any supplies were lost or stolen. The rucksacks were loaded on the horses, along with the precious moon food and our medical supplies. The horses also carried the tube containing the heavy wooden tripod, which looked for all the world like a big rocket-launcher and from the air might have enticed a Russian chopper crew to think just that. Ian wore a flak-jacket-style contraption he'd had made for the sound gear in Peshawar. Chris had his Arriflex 16 camera on a sling over his shoulder. Tim lugged a big black bag with spare film magazines and lenses. Joe and I carried our light personal gear, a still camera each, and medical supplies.

At 8pm we left, joining a procession of Muj who looked like characters from Chaucer, and started to climb the mountains that towered above Terrimangel. At the top was the Afghan border.

Afghanistan/Pakistan

5

Afghanistan – Hollywood heroes

Kabul or bust

We climbed, seemingly almost vertically, in mist, darkness and rain. Almost immediately Joe started to pay for his chain-smoking; he was in a dreadful state. The others had gone off into the night. I tried to encourage Joe, although I needed every bit of encouragement myself. In desperation he hung onto the tail of one of the horses, which upset its handler and the Muj, who took it as a sign that Joe intended to bugger the horse; not an unusual custom in the area, but hardly a gesture designed to gain respect for us infidels. Already our battle-hardened team was degenerating into extras for *Carry On Up The Khyber*.

A camel suddenly loomed out of the darkness, charging unaccompanied down the mountain, and knocked me over. I picked myself up and continued the nightmare scramble, sometimes on all fours. Somehow Joe and I reached the top, where our colleagues waited impatiently. Khalid – we called him 'Doc' – told us to huddle in the middle of a large group of Muj to pass the Pakistani border post. In the night, mist and confusion we sneaked past without detection, as there were no individual security searches. We had made it into Afghanistan.

A few hundred yards over the border we passed a knocked-out Russian armoured personnel carrier lying on its side. Then came another, not quite so terrible, climb. Our group began to take shape out of the amorphous mass of Muj at the crossing point. Besides ourselves, our guide Doc and the 'Captain', an officer who had defected from the regular army, there were eight Muj.

We crossed a valley floor, well-watered with fields and streams, but hard going in the dark. Just before midnight the Muj stopped, reluctantly, at a small village. Already their Christian companions were disappointing them. Our tardiness was laughed at or, worse, treated as an insult to the Muj, *jihad* and even Allah himself.

Compressed into a small room in one of the square mud houses, we drank the first of many cups of *chai*, green or black tea, heavily sugared and rarely offered with milk. Like the British, the Afghans' sovereign remedy was to stop for a cup of tea. The householder's grandchildren, timid little waifs, brought us *nan*, unleavened bread. I grew to like it, but at first it tasted like cardboard. After ten or 15 minutes the children left with the cups and 12 of us prepared to sleep on the rough quilts. Joe coughed endlessly; the others snored loudly.

Next morning we left at 6am. It was Friday 13 July, and the day lived up to its omens. After a few miles we stopped to film a bombed village, where locals proudly showed us a Russian anti-tank gun captured when the Muj overran a government fort the previous year. It was stuck in a cow-shed, as the Muj had no ammunition and no idea how to use it.

We carried on down the valley until what Tim called a 'glacial re-entrant' opened on our right. On the floor of this vale of stones, the Jagi Valley, we stopped at a *chai-khana*, two rough huts dispensing tea. Two DSHK 12.7mm guns stood at the entrance; the Muj called them 'Dashekas'. We filmed them clowning around and posing with the guns. Just as they started serving tea in dirty little cups, four MiGs appeared over the crest of the mountain.

'Hello war,' said Tim.

A number of thoughts flashed across my mind. Firstly, I wanted to grab a cup of tea before everything was spilled in the melée. Secondly, I spotted a small ridge behind me, a good place to take shots with my still camera of the expected attack and the Muj firing back (hopefully). But this wasn't a film set: I would have been totally exposed on the ridge, just a few yards from the gunners. Then I guiltily told myself that I was there to make a movie, not hide or take photos. I tried to help prepare our equipment.

We were not the targets that day, however. We listened tensely to the roar of the jets bombing in the next valley: heavy thumps indicating that someone was catching it. Two planes flipped out of their bombing runs and rolled away out of sight over the mountains. Chris was using a new type of long-life lithium battery, as no electricity was available to charge up conventional camera batteries. Unfortunately, the battery hadn't been connected properly to the camera, so we missed this dramatic aerial diversion.

Leaving the huts behind we marched up a desolate valley. It grew hot. After two and a half hours the wide valley became a narrow cleft and we began to climb out over a never-ending series of false summits. The dry, sparse vegetation provided no shade. Tim was striding out in front with the lead guerrillas. Part of his self-image was founded on his ability to outperform everyone else physically. Joe and I reached the top half-dead, and downhill wasn't much better. After scrambling and tripping for two hours we reached Azara, a hamlet nestling in a pretty valley of apricot trees, flecked with small patches of maize, and watered by an elaborate irrigation system. Asian magpies, mynahs and small hoopoe birds darted here and there. A pine forest bordered on the Gailani house in which we overnighted.

We found a small pool and, assuming it was out of sight, took the chance of stripping off to wash. Out of nowhere a woman, heavily veiled, approached. We had been told to be very careful not to expose any part of our bodies, but now a village woman had seen us. She passed by and nothing was said.

After 11 hours of marching all we wanted to do was sleep, but we had to sit in a large room with the village elders and our small group of Muj. We were not hungry, but felt obliged to eat some of the sheep just slaughtered in our honour before excusing ourselves from the tea ceremony and climbing onto the roof to sleep under the brilliant stars.

At 4.30am we awoke and hurried to load up and leave. Doc had hired a fourth horse to accommodate Joe and me, the slowcoaches. I decided to walk first, but after two hours my feet, already badly blistered, began to hurt horribly. Laughing at our heavy going, the Muj kept up a fast pace; to them it was a Sunday afternoon stroll. Strings of young Muj passed us on their way out of the country, pointing and saying something like '*Ax, ax*'. Had they learned the word 'hacks'? I found out that it meant 'camera' or 'photograph'. Every Afghan I met loved posing and having his picture taken.

A Muj commander who had joined our group earlier in the day insisted on mounting a horse with some of the camera equipment. I asked Doc to explain that this could damage our kit and so perhaps abort the trip. Pretending to misunderstand, Doc loped off, obviously not wanting to confront the senior man. Furious, Chris berated the com-mander in front of the Muj, despite my attempts at diplomacy. The commander stayed on the horse, but we had made an enemy and a grudge which would later make our trip more difficult.

As the march grew hotter and dustier, we came to a narrow, steep defile. Joe had been riding the spare horse for hours. Although Chris did not seem to be tired, he asked Joe for a spell on the horse – out of boredom perhaps, or because he loved horses. Passionate expletives followed, and the powerfully-built Chris leant over Joe from the side of the defile, either to pull him off the horse or his head off his shoulders. The Muj looked on in amazement: so these infidels fuck horses and fight over them! Chris subdued his anger, but the incident established a permanent and bitter rift in our team. Although I was probably the weakest physically, I was nominally in charge: a testing paradox. What I lacked in strength I would have to make up for in diplomacy to keep the peace, both within our crew and with the mercurial, heavily-armed guerrillas.

A second Muj doctor, a burly and inevitably bearded fellow, joined our merry band, on his way to set up a small mobile clinic. He was accompanied by a former medical student, a wiry, friendly little Muj who could speak fractured English. We dubbed him 'Little Doc'. We passed horses and, occasionally, camels loaded with medical supplies in small wooden crates inscribed 'People's Republic of China' in English and Chinese. A camel in one such supply column took a peculiar dislike to me; for some reason – presumably malicious humour – the beast's handler asked me to lead it for a few hours. First it spat at me, then sneezed over me, then spent a good part of an hour trying to bite me. I encountered this animal on several occasions at tea-houses and pit-stops; even when tethered, it would try to make my miserable life even more miserable.

I took some consolation in the fact that the horse, which Joe shared with me after a while, seemed to like me. It had no saddle, proper reins or stirrups: I just sat on the wicker stringing which contained fodder and light equipment, with a bedroll on top. Usually I felt guilty riding, as Tim and Ian steadfastly refused when I offered them my mount. Occasionally Chris took up the offer for a brief change of pace. He walked nearly all the way with the heavy Arriflex camera cradled in his arms or hanging from his shoulder.

We were determined not to be separated from our equipment. An ITN crew under Sandy Gall had been forced to watch in exasperation the dramatic fighting in the Panshir for a whole month without being able to film, having had the bad luck – or lack of caution – to be moved away from their baggage. Sometimes I would wear Ian's bulky flak-jacket-cum-sound-kit if I was riding. Thus burdened, on an extremely uncomfortable seat, riding was only marginally easier than walking. But at least it gave my heavily-plastered feet a break. Some of my toenails had already fallen off.

We walked and walked, although my progression on foot was more correcting stumbles than a steady gait. The Afghans who passed on the track gave us infidels very strange looks, but nearly always issued a hearty greeting. '*Salaam Aleikum.*' (God be with you.) I learned the reply: '*Aleikum Salaam*' (And you), but never quite mastered the string of pleasantries which followed.

I started studying the architecture. A typical house consisted of bricks and dry earth, covered with a kind of stucco made of straw mixed with mud. Many adjoined laboriously-constructed irrigation channels and sometimes a village defence system which formed a network of little forts, often with a watchtower.

We marched through exquisite valleys, rich in apricot and mulberry trees; occasionally the Muj would climb and shake the trees while their companions collected the falling fruit in their *patous*. At these stops we would ask Doc the inevitable question: 'How much further?' He grew as tired of our enquiries as we did of his vague replies: 'It's a short walk', or 'Only an hour from here'. We called this 'Afghan time'. 'English time' meant what was said: an hour equalled an hour. In 'Pakistani time' an hour could equal two or three. Afghan time meant that an hour could be a day or even a week. No wonder American teams, addicted to rigid schedules, found Afghanistan so tough. J B Priestley wrote: 'A good holiday is one spent among people whose notions of time are vaguer than yours.' I doubted whether Afghanistan had ever featured in his travels.

From a quasi-Alpine valley we moved into a semi-desert plain with no cover apart from thorn bushes. I contemplated the risks of throwing myself into one if we were caught in the open by gunships. The standard, and only safe, tactic was to stay absolutely still, preferably with a brown *patou* over your head. In the Rhodesian bush war the guerrillas nearly always broke this golden rule: although they usually had good cover, especially in the rainy season, if the choppers persisted they broke and ran, hitting the army stop groups or getting shot up by the helicopters. I was engaged in a purely theoretical discourse on this subject with Chris, a veteran of the Rhodesian war, when two Hind-24 gunships emerged a long way off.

They were moving fast and we were completely in the open. I was on horseback, wearing the sound equipment. A few hundred yards away lay good cover of trees and mud buildings, so I urged my horse into a canter and accidentally knocked Joe over. It was mainly fear or instinct, but I shouted an apology, saying I had to protect the sound gear. I made the cover and the choppers flew over, ignoring us. The village among the trees was derelict: carcasses of dead animals and bomb holes scarred the tranquillity. My horse sensed death and reared. I controlled it, but it had a mind of its own. '*Shur! Shur!*' was Afghan for 'Move! Move!' but nobody had bothered to tell my horse.

The arid landscape grew hypnotic. Outlandish mud forts occasionally tipped the edge of the horizon. Suddenly we came into a fertile valley with a large stream running through it: Alamkach. About twenty mud houses nestled in the trees and donkeys brayed unbelievably loudly. A stream babbled. Children's voices filled the air. Young boys were working in small fields. Golden patches of wheat contrasted with the green, and a man was winnowing corn. It was like a summer morning in England a long, long time ago.

Gailani's men greeted us in the shade of a big walnut tree, making us feel very welcome. Under the tree, with the sound of the stream lulling us, we relaxed for 24 hours, cleaned our equipment, and changed for the first time in three days. We were waiting for a message from Commander Wali Khan.

On Sunday morning, Joe, a staunch member of the Dutch Reformed Church, suggested a prayer meeting. 'We must show these Muslim people that we are devout too.' In theory it wasn't a bad idea, but to Chris, as he put it, 'It went down like a turd in a punch bowl.' Tim, despite his rough ways, was a devout Christian too, but his faith was more personal. Chris thought it would be hypocritical, and said so.

Joe gave his commando dagger to the Captain, so all the Muj started crawling through our kit looking for our knives. We had a hard time being persuasive with our heavily-armed hosts, explaining why we didn't want to part with our daggers. It infuriated Chris, who began imitating Joe's heavy Afrikaans accent. Tim, Ian and I were also annoyed, but we didn't want to fight the Boer war all over again; we had enough on our plates. Joe was well-meaning, but he seemed to try too hard with the Afghans. Like many Afrikaners, he tended to patronise the natives even while appearing genuinely fond of them.

We were becoming preoccupied with our health, especially our bowel movements. Chris had the runs, but Joe asked if I had any laxatives – which summed up their differences. I was the worst: my loose bowels gradually degenerated into dysentery, although I was swallowing eight to ten strong anti-diarrhoea pills a day, and I suffered continual cramps. We had brought water-purifying tablets but discarded them: we were either too eager to sip from a mountain stream when totally dehydrated, or too reluctant to quibble with our hosts if offered water or tea. We just took our chances, and I had the most vulnerable guts.

I liked the urbane, if occasionally slippery, Doc Khalid. He spoke excellent English and good French. We sat munching apricots as he explained why he had left Kabul to join the Muj.

'I was living in Kabul when the *Shuravi* [Russians] came. On the day of the invasion I was studying for my final medical exam. I couldn't work properly because of all the aeroplanes waiting to land with the invasion troops. I eventually got to sleep, but I woke up to find Russians and tanks on the corner of every street in Kabul.'

He had waited for his parents to obtain permission to fly out, then he walked out by the same route we were on and joined the guerrillas in Peshawar. But Doc was more interested in the West, especially its social conventions, than talking about Afghan history. He said he understood our Western weaknesses. 'I tell the *Mujahedin* that they must not laugh when you cannot walk as fast as them. I tell them you have escalators so that you don't have to move, but they don't really believe me.'

Doc often extolled the virtues of an American ABC team he had worked with previously. Apparently they had been mountaineers and doctors as well as cameramen. 'They kept on walking and carried big rucksacks,' he told us. I grew tired of hearing about these supermen.

'Ah, but they did make one big mistake,' said Doc. 'We were crossing a river and some Russian tanks came around the bend of the road. The man with the sound equipment just dropped down under the water to hide. That ruined their sound gear.' Some consolation at least, but we hadn't been in action yet. We might not fare any better.

Doc and I talked about women, a subject in which he was very interested. Filming Afghan women was a big problem. They rarely appeared, even if they had cooked our food. If a woman approached in the distance, her menfolk would start to bristle and treat us as though we were the vanguard of an advancing army of sex maniacs determined to violate every female under 90. The women were covered totally in *burqas*: head-to-toe shrouds with a small vent for the eyes. The nomads had a reputation for branding their women with the same irons they used on their animals. We were much too exhausted even to think about sex; and the savage stories told of the Muj suggested that a bit on the side (in the highly unlikely event it was offered) was a trifle risky.

Although Doc was a fairly conservative supporter of Afghan customs, he confessed to a secret desire: he desperately wanted to screw a black woman. He knew roughly of Joe's origins, but could draw no comment on black women from our resident Afrikaner. Doc's quiet but persistent interest in this subject became a standing joke.

'Our men do not see their wives until they are married,' he said sternly. 'Of course, she has seen him in the village and so on. But he has never looked at his wife until they sit back to back on their wedding night. Both hold mirrors and gaze on each other's face in the mirrors.'

'What if she's ugly?' I said, rather obviously.

'No, the parents have made sure that there are no physical problems.'

'And will your parents choose your wife, Doc?'

'That has not been decided yet,' he said vaguely.

I told Doc about when Lord Curzon, destined to be Viceroy of India, visited Kabul to meet the Amir of Afghanistan. According to Curzon, the Amir called monogamy 'a most pernicious system' because there were more women than men, and it was unnatural for some women to remain unmarried. But the Amir excused the system in Britain, saying it was due to the damp climate. The British, he conjectured, were raised in water and mud like rice; whereas Eastern people, who lived in dry soil, were like wheat and could manage four wives.

Doc liked the story, but had no answer to my question: 'Who would want four mothers-in-law?' The conversation drifted on to censorship and Muslim double standards: despite the cuts in videos (even the kissing), and the strict control of booze and girlie magazines, nearly every Afghan we met (when not with any other Muslims) would devour *Playboy* or take a drink. Chris didn't say much, but he had a pithy sense of humour: 'That's why they like cowboy movies in Pakistan. Cowboys don't kiss, they only fart.'

The talk had descended to the normal lavatorial tempo. It was time to go. The day's rest had restored spirits and eased the pain, as well as the blisters we were all developing. Besides resting, we had some beautiful scenic shots in the can plus an interview with the two doctors and the story of the Captain, who had defected after nine years in the regular army. We started walking with zest.

The going was rough at first. We walked through a stony river bed, slipping and cursing all the way. Joe tripped and sprained his ankle. Then we climbed over a steep pass. At the top was an amazing desert panorama: an arid landscape of sandstone, rocks and occasional tufts of grass. After a mercifully short march – just three hours of hard slogging – we climbed up another river valley until we reached a clump of trees in a cleft between three low, steep hills. This was Serracheena – 'the place of the red spring'. We were destined to spend ten days there.

The cesspit

The camp at Serracheena was filthy. Chris summed it up in his usual blunt fashion: 'Meningitis is crawling over this place like that thing in *Alien*.' The camp consisted of three bombed buildings, one roughly repaired, set among a clump of trees in a small cleft halfway up a bare hill. Some 30 or 40 Muj used it as a base. 'Moustache', the commander whom Chris had tried to eject from our horse, was in charge, and it was clear he didn't like foreign intruders in his eyrie.

Almost immediately two Mi-24 helicopters glided across the sky like big sharks. A Dasheka just above the camp let rip, exposing our position even though the gunships were out of range. Then a machine-gunner in the camp fired a burst accidentally and almost blew off the head of a fellow guerrilla. I said to Tim: 'They look fierce and can probably do a lot of damage, but more by accident than intent. There's more chance of us getting hit by a Muj's AD [accidental discharge] than by the Russians.'

There was no order, no discipline, no training, not even enough organisation to build a latrine: the Muj just shat in ever-increasing circles round the camp perimeter. The smell might keep away the Russians, but not the flies. We camped in the open in a small mud clearing in front of the one useable hut. Beside it was a tiny cave which served as an ammo store.

As we sat drinking tea Chris switched on the BBC World Service. Emlyn Williams, the Welsh playwright, was talking about his boyhood. I started to suffer from what the Welsh call *hiraeth*, but the bleak Kabul mountains mocked my homesickness for the Rhondda valleys. My nostalgia was contagious. The rest of the crew started talking about Rhodesia and comparing it with Afghanistan: 'Now we are the hunted guerrillas – no radio comms [communications], no choppers for a casevac [casualty evacuation], no bath in the officers' mess to return to each night …'

The plan was for the chief commander, Wali Khan, to organise an ambush for us. The possibility of a clandestine trip into Kabul would come later. Most attacks were at night but, as we had no night-scopes for our camera, we would have to attempt a risky daylight sortie. We talked about our chances of getting away with it and, as we stayed longer in the cesspit, the chances of being ambushed. Normally it was considered unwise to stay for more than two days in the same place. The KGB and its local equivalent, the *Khad*, had a country-wide network of informers, and foreign journalists were prize trophies. The Soviets were interested in all Westerners travelling with the guerrillas. Any they managed to capture or kill provided their version of proof for their (accurate) claim that the CIA was backing the war.

If grabbed, we knew we would be in for a rough time. A Frenchman caught previously had had a sympathetic socialist president to exert diplomatic pressure on Moscow. We all had military backgrounds and had been seen with weapons, usually during shooting competitions with the Muj to humour them. We would surely be branded as mercenaries.

Joe admitted: 'The only thing that worries me is an air strike. The Muj can say what they like, but an air strike can come in here.'

'I'm more worried about them putting choppers and troops on the hills around here,' interrupted Tim. 'We are very vulnerable.'

'Yeah, but what a position to film from,' Ian said positively.

'But we've got no film if we're caught,' I pitched in more soberly. 'Or if someone gets killed and we're forced to dump our equipment.'

'But we're here to get bombed,' said Chris.

I corrected him. 'We're here to get nearly bombed.'

More immediate dangers were to hand in the form of 'Donkey', Doc's nickname for the half-cunning, half-idiotic camp fool. He was the grinning Dasheka gunner and putative mine expert. Right in front of us he primed a Chinese land-mine, then jumped on it to test it. Joe, sitting nearest, did a passable impression of a Superman take-off while the rest of us threw ourselves on our stomachs. It didn't go off. We didn't find out whether Donkey was playing the real fool, or had deliberately misprimed the mine.

We spent a couple of days filming intermittently, but the bored Muj kept horseplaying. It made any filming, even with Doc's assistance, very tedious. We wondered whether the whole valley had interbred to generate a new subspecies of mutton-headed hillbillies. We grew as bored as the guerrillas, playing cards endlessly and trying to read amid the flies. Chris was reading *Schimitar,* Peter Niesewand's novel about a neutron bomb in Afghanistan; I was perusing Le Carré's *The Honourable Schoolboy,* about the KGB. In the circumstances it was hardly escapist literature.

In between we cooked our moon food, such a delightful contrast to the perpetual *nan* and stringy goat. Tim and Joe tried to teach the locals the art of the southern African *braai* (barbecue). The Muj boiled everything and didn't use any salt, even though they had ample stocks. Eventually the two Africans served up a very acceptable braaied goat.

Joe was still the odd man out. We tried hard to get him into a team mood, but it was difficult because he had little or no interest in the film. His original purpose – running parts of the film out – had been negated by the problems of getting in and out of Afghanistan. His aims were simpler: he had obtained some good still pictures and enough material for a few articles; now he wanted to leave. We all despised the filthy conditions and wanted to escape, but we had a film to complete. Besides being reluctant to split up the team, I could not ask Doc to provide an escort back to Peshawar, so Joe would have to wait. But Joe was determined to find his own escort out, further annoying Chris and me. Doc could not really comprehend the differences within the team, nor the absence of a clear leader and our habit of democratically discussing options. But later he developed an astute insight into our differing cultural and psychological make-ups.

We infidels had noticed a world of difference between the small, educated, Afghan elite and the illiterate, apparently witless, peasants who made up 90 per cent of the country. It was probably we who were witless; like many journalists in third world countries, we did not know the language.

It was our third night at the cesspit. As usual, we bedded down in our sleeping bags at about 9pm. But sleep did not come easily. We squirmed around like a row of huge, disgruntled chrysalises, listening very reluctantly to a Donkey Serenade. Donkey and his Muppet band were screaming out monotone songs while banging on oil drums for hours on end. Worse, they began pounding old rockets apart and gleefully throwing bits of explosives into the fire. Tim, our Samuel Pepys, confided in his diary, 'Donkey tried to entertain the troops, but the troops were not amused and contemplated going out there with an AK to fire a few rounds over the natives' heads.' All of us, including Doc and the Captain, shared his sentiments.

Finally, under the stars, we fell asleep. Then it rained. 'Just our luck,' moaned Chris. 'We're in a bloody desert and it's got to pour with rain.'

We moved into the small mud hut store-house. Just as we settled in, and had made sure our film kit was dry, the roof started to leak under the torrential downpour. Sleep was out. We busied ourselves keeping the film stock and camera equipment away from the wet. Then a Muj started raving at us. We had our shoes on and were told that the hut was also their mosque, all eight square feet of it. Although they could be grossly obnoxious by our standards, spitting and crapping everywhere, Afghans were ultra-sensitive about their religion and women – especially if there was a Muslim audience.

In the morning we witnessed a flash flood: a wave of water a few yards high swept down the dry river bed in the valley below. That was the highpoint of a day spent eating mulberries, apricots and grapes. Donkey challenged us to a stone-throwing competition, then duelled against Chris with catapults. The hill man had obviously spent most of his spare hours in such country pursuits, and we were hopelessly outclassed. We were gradually going native. Nervousness and frustration scratched at our boredom. Artillery boomed regularly in the distance; choppers and Antonov reconnaissance planes droned overhead.

We walked down the valley towards Jigdalek, the exact spot where a British army retreating from Kabul had been treacherously destroyed in the snows of January 1842. Major General William Elphinstone left the Afghan capital under a truce with 4,500 soldiers and 12,000 camp followers, as well as soldiers' and officers' wives. In one of the most savage defeats in British military history, only one British officer and a few Indian sepoys managed to reach the British garrison at Jalalabad. A famous Victorian oil painting by Lady Elizabeth Butler, popularly known as 'The Last Survivor from Kabul', depicts their arrival. The vivid detail of this painting did much to fix in British folk-memory the magnitude of the catastrophe that befell Elphinstone's army, and the image of Afghans as two-faced, merciless thugs.

Ours was a more leisurely trip. Without blood and snow, the valley was idyllic, full of plums, apricots and mulberries. It was well watered but the cultivators had fled from the bombing, leaving only a handful of shepherds and a few groups of *Jamiat* guerrillas. We looked inside bombed-out houses and examined walls where shrapnel and rockets had left their marks. In one house we discovered a host of shed snake-skins hanging down from the roof like spaghetti. Adding to the sense of death amid such natural beauty, huge 1,000lb bomb craters were testimony to why the former residents had abandoned their houses to the snakes. Outside, blackened trees bent over to weep, their backs broken by shrapnel.

Returning to Serracheena we found Donkey had brought a message from the Scarlet Pimpernel of the mountains, Wali Khan. We were to wait another two days, as the commander was preparing an attack for us. Having already waited for five days – a major security risk being in one place for so long – we no longer trusted Khan, and speculated whether he was capable of organising an attack. 'I don't think he's capable of even organising an appearance,' said Chris.

We restlessly debated our options, wondering whether we should hide the still photographs showing us with weapons in case we got caught on this promised attack. Out of boredom we climbed a hill to compete in target shooting with an AK-47. The rest of the crew were spot on. I rated pretty much the same as the Muj, but excused myself because of my blind right (shooting) eye. We went to bed early, listless, dirty and with the trots besieging our stomachs. Joe had given up smoking for a while, but he still snored.

The terrible Hind-24 gunships, the scourge of the Muj, operated from early morning to about 3pm, when the pilots returned to scrub up for an early mess dinner at Jalalabad air base, less than 40 miles away. Later on, after the heat of the day, thermal updraughts and swirling winds made contour flying in the mountains hazardous.

At 7am the next morning, ugly as sin, two of the squat killers hovered above us, accompanying six MiG fighter-bombers. The Hinds were big battlefield helicopters with five rotor blades and a total loaded weight of ten tons. Chris and I bolted for the small latrine gully; crouched there, with Chris resting his camera on my back, we looked up at the titanium armour-plating guarding the gunners' and pilots' cockpits, engines, fuel tanks, gear box, hydraulics and electrical systems. Difficult to knock out of the sky, the Hinds had a maximum speed of 229mph and maximum altitude of 18,000 feet. They were armed with 32 rockets and guided missiles, and a traversing four-barrelled 12.7mm machine gun with drums of 1,000 armour-piercing or HE incendiary rounds. All we had was Donkey blasting away on his pitiful Dasheka.

Anyone firing at a Hind had better be sure of knocking it right out of the heavens – anything less than a fatal shot would normally invite a lethal counter-blow. They dropped lower and lower, ignoring the Dasheka. One hovered right above us, and we expected napalm. But we were lucky: the gunships were busy co-ordinating the fighter-bombers blasting away in the valley below us. Fortunately the Russian or Afghan pilots were trained to stick rigidly to their assault plans; any Western gunship crew would have taken out the near-defenceless clump of 60 Muj stuck on an exposed hill below them, but the Hinds left us alone.

The attack lasted about 20 minutes. Then, a little shaken, we crawled out of the latrine gully. Tim and Joe had been snapping away with their still cameras, but Chris was furious that he had been caught out of position to film the staggeringly dramatic air attack. We were fortunate not to have been hit but unlucky not to have captured on film the bombing runs down the valley. But we felt sure they would come again soon – and next time we would be ready.

All we could do was sit and wait for the Soviets, and the elusive Wali Khan. We constantly harangued Doc for news of Khan, explaining that we had wasted almost a week's filming. Soon we would move on, with or without Wali. Doc tried to divert us with Afghan-style humour, which was Rabelaisian at the best of times. He told us about Brezhnev's barber – the dead Brezhnev, never Andropov or Chernenko, was always the butt of the jokes. Every time Leonid went to the hairdresser's the barber would ask about Afghanistan. Eventually the Soviet leader grew angry. 'You stick to cutting hair and leave politics to me. Anyway, why do you keep asking about that country?' The barber replied: 'Because every time I mention Afghanistan, your hair stands on end, and it's much easier to cut.' It seemed a good joke in the hills around Kabul. Doc had a boyish, lavatorial sense of humour, like most Afghans. I couldn't help but like him.

That night we listened again to the BBC World Service, a vital link to civilisation and sanity. A report from Islamabad said the Russians had landed troops to block supply routes. Russian, not Afghan, soldiers were now fighting behind us in the Jagi Valley. Our exit route might be cut off, but at least we hoped to film some action. Although it would be retracing our steps, we resolved to proceed soon to Jagi. We were sure the BBC reports were correct: we had seen large movements of troop-carrying planes and helicopters, as well as hearing increasing artillery barrages emanating from our rear.

We got up at 4am. Nobody wanted to be caught by gunships with their pants down or sleeping bags zipped up. The five of us trekked to a hill on the other side of the valley, a perfect spot to film the expected attack on our own camp. We had taken the precaution of stowing our kit in the cave, despite the ammo. The Muj didn't seem to care a jot that we were bloodthirstily awaiting gunships which would rain down HE rockets on their flyblown little home.

Our hill had practically no cover. Chris bravely opted to sit on the completely exposed northern slope. Since the camera would look exactly like a weapon from the air, we covered Chris in mosquito nets and pieces of bush and grass to disguise the glinting tripod. Tim and Ian hid nearby. Joe and I prepared rough cover 20 or 30 yards behind Chris just over the ridge, near a gully which could provide a Flashman-style exit if the Soviets turned on us.

The reconnaissance planes droned overhead at 6am, then it grew cloudy. We waited until 10am. Nothing. Chris was as chirpy as ever: 'Why don't we ring up Kabul and complain?' Out of sheer boredom, the crew asked me to sing some of my extensive repertoire of rock 'n' roll numbers. The fact that they actually asked for my musical impressions was a sure indication that we were slowly going mad. Donkey had become our mentor.

We gave up at noon. Chris stood up and shook his fist at the sky. 'Come back, you Russian bastards, and fight!'. What he lacked in tact and diplomacy he made up for in strength and courage. Although he had been badly wounded in the Rhodesian war, with five bullets in the lower leg and thigh, he could walk tirelessly carrying the heavy camera. Under fire he appeared fearless.

We repeated our dawn patrol the next day. The weather was fine and the recce plane went over again. Surely, this time, they would come back. We camouflaged Chris and took up our positions. I slept or read Le Carré. By late morning, with no show, we grew frustrated and angry; the film needed a good attack sequence.

We returned to the perpetual theme of Muj inadequacies, all worried about the same thing: the guerrillas couldn't handle their weapons sitting around a camp-fire, so how could they fight in battle? To be fair, Doc and the Captain were aware of their fellows' faults: the Captain was obviously embarrassed by the Muj's lack of soldierly qualities. Doc even asked Tim, who had impressed everyone with his knowledge and handling of weapons, to stay in Afghanistan as an instructor. Tim politely declined, even when Doc offered to put Tim's wife up as well. Katie, a vivacious ex-dancer, would not be at her best covered in a *chador.*

Tim's complex personality intrigued me. Although he spoke the patois of a Rhodesian troopie and had worked as a bouncer, his intellectual versatility constantly surprised me. One minute it would be a comment on Conrad's *The Heart of Darkness*, the next an astute aside on team psychology, after identifying a plant or obscure bird. From time to time he sported a small white object behind his ear. I assumed it was a hearing aid, although he seemed to hear quite well without it. Because the thing appeared only sometimes, and he never mentioned it, I thought the macho Tim was sensitive about his one physical weakness and never peered too closely to avoid embarrassing him. Eventually, I saw him pop it in his mouth. He laughed almost uncontrollably when I told him about my confusion as to where he stored his chewing gum!

For all his sterling qualities Tim was not perfect. He became paranoid when he lost his diary, blaming the Muj for taking it and remaining absolutely distracted until he found it in a spot where he had tripped over. He was also very fastidious, particularly about security. Mostly he was fully justified. I noticed he had made himself a small survival and get-away-quick kit: a passport, medical pack, exposed film, glucose tablets and lightweight sleeping bag, which he carried in his adapted ammo pouches at all times in case we were ambushed and he had to make his way back alone. I had done the same, though not so thoroughly.

Enough was enough. We had spent nine largely unproductive days in the disease-ridden camp and still no Wali and no film of an air strike. I told Doc that we would leave at 3pm to film the fighting at Jagi if no definite word had come from Commander Wali.

Suddenly, there was a commotion on the path at the back of the camp. A man led a young boy on horseback into the clearing, his hand swathed in a bloody, makeshift bandage. Nine-year-old Sadat Khan had lost three fingers picking up a Russian anti-personnel device which looked like a plastic butterfly, said Doc. 'The Russians drop them by the thousands to hurt children. This demoralises the parents.'

We were a little sceptical: we had seen some anti-personnel devices, but not one of the so-called butterfly bombs. Had the little boy been playing around with spare ammunition, I asked gently. Doc insisted it was the work of the demonic Russians. The brave young boy sat upright on the floor as Doc looked at his grisly wound. Doc could do little to help or avoid gangrene – all he had were some pain-killers. It was immediately decided that we would all march back to Alamkach, where the doctor we had met earlier on the trip had set up his small mobile clinic. Chris filmed my talking with Doc and the child, and we would film his arrival at the clinic. It was very moving material. And we were leaving Serracheena at last.

We set off back to Alamkach at a fast pace. It was hard going over desert and mountainous terrain but – for once – I felt really fit, almost euphoric, as I pushed my legs forward. Also, it was only a three-hour march, and *away* from our cesspit. En route I chatted to Doc about the difficulties of treating wounds in the field. Doc spoke with a mixture of quiet anger and resignation: 'We are educated in twentieth-century medicine but inside Afghanistan, because of the lack of drugs and equipment, we are doing the medicine of the Middle Ages.'

He launched into a long lecture on 'foreign occupiers' and 'ruthless Russians', but many of the problems could be blamed upon Afghan tradition, not Soviet atrocities. Some women, for example, died simply because a male doctor was not allowed to examine the patient. Doc confirmed how it was customary for the husband to describe the symptoms. The doctor had to prescribe at second hand, without ever seeing or speaking to his patient.

Nevertheless, Afghanistan's most recent invaders did not make war by the gentlemanly rules favoured by their imperial predecessors. A doddery 70-year-old villager told me, via Doc, 'My family fought the British. I had relatives killed by them. But the British did not kill old people, nor hurt women and children intentionally. They never aimed their artillery at innocent people, never.'

Up and down the hill again

Alamkach was jumpy. The Russians were supplying a fort at the end of the valley, less than two miles away, so the Muj were preparing to evacuate the village if the Russians pushed any further up the valley. We could hear artillery and tank fire. The immediate problem, though, was to attend to Sadat Khan. He was given one of our drips and the two doctors cleaned and dressed his wound. Dusk approached as we filmed this procedure, using some precious battery time on our 'sungun' for illumination. The doctor said surgery was required; the boy would have to travel to Peshawar. Many wounded Afghans had died on the route by which we had come in. But the lad seemed tough; Doc felt sure he would make it safely to a hospital in Pakistan.

We repacked our film gear ready for a rapid exit from the camp the next morning, and crowded into a small tent, pitched on top of a mud hut for some reason, to avoid an imminent downpour. I slept blissfully unaware of the artillery, but Tim stayed alert to distinguish the various types of ordnance being flung around in the storm.

We got up in wet darkness at 4am. During the night about sixty men had been seen marching along the ridge above us. The slack Muj hadn't posted any guards, so we didn't know whether they were Russian commandos or nocturnal Muj. We were jittery: it wasn't like the Muj to walk around at night in the rain.

We set off immediately to a camp higher up. The river had flooded the previous night but had already subsided, leaving a coating of red mud everywhere which made it even more difficult to walk over the slippery pebbles. After a few hours we reached Manay, a more organised camp run by allies of the Gailani faction, who welcomed us with sweet milk tea and killed a calf. We felt honoured, even though they slit the poor animal's throat right in front of us.

Unfortunately, the sweetness of the tea was soured by a letter from the mysterious Wali Khan: the ambush had been set up and we were to return to Serracheena immediately. We'd all suffered enough of both the cesspit and Wali's non-appearing acts; but Doc was under orders and there was the problem of maintaining face. Khan, a man with a reputation in the area, couldn't be seen to chicken out on fixing a hit for some Western hacks. Very reluctantly, and mainly out of respect for Doc, we decided to go back to the eyrie of flies rather than push on to the fighting in Jagi. In the midday sun, with heavy hearts and heavier boots, we set out to climb back into the desert hills.

I was exhausted and disheartened. The two things I hate most in life, marching and communal living, were beginning to overwhelm me. Tim wrote in his log that I was walking like a dead man. Even had I been fitter, no outsider could walk like an Afghan. They had a distinctive long, flowing step, gliding their sandalled feet over rough stones and scree. The Muj could walk all day, seven days a week. It was like a sick passion: they would never walk 100 yards if they could walk a mile, usually over the most rugged terrain, preferably the pebbly hell of river beds. Where I stumbled, they walked straight-backed, dancing along trails and desert tracks like scruffy ballet stars. Nor was there a pattern to their marches. At least in a Western army one could expect to rest for a few minutes every hour, even if the route march went on all day. The Muj walked on a whim as well as on air, stopping twice in an hour, or trekking without a break for six hours across mountains. I kept going with the mirage of a pint of Guinness shimmering in front of me.

Eventually we shuffled back into Serracheena. Donkey greeted us like brothers risen from the dead. Moustache pouted at us with his waxed nostril-piece, like a demon barber in a Victorian melodrama. There was a gleam of triumphant mischief in his eyes: the message which had dragged us back was from him, not Wali. He had made us pay for telling him to get off our horse.

We were told we had to march for another day and a half, then it might be possible to set up an attack. Doc was embarrassed; we were fuming. We paid Donkey, perhaps the only man we could trust in the camp, to ride one of our horses to Wali's camp for a direct response as to why we had waited for ten days for nothing. If no message came back we would leave at 3pm the following day.

It was another miserable night. Even Tim admitted to feeling unwell. 'My guts are like Niagara,' he put it, poetically. At 4am we tried our dawn patrol again: the hike back would have been worthwhile if we could film a rocket attack on the commander's moustache. Poor Chris was smothered with mosquito nets and grass again, but all to no avail.

Then something interesting turned up: we were invited to a weapon-training session at a *Jamiat* camp a few miles away. Moustache tried to stop us going but we ignored him, trudging off down the valley with one horse. Joe and the rest of the kit would meet up with us later. We passed craters of the 1,000lb bombs we had seen dropped a few days before. Some of the holes, now full of water, were six to ten yards across and about 15 feet deep.

The *Jamiat* camp was extremely well-fortified with DSHK gun emplacements. It was commanded by Mohamed Anwar, a well-known Afghan wrestler who had defected just before he was due to represent his country in the 1980 Moscow Olympics. Built like an ox, shrewd and intelligent, with a patient face, he was about 38 but exuded the authority and charisma of a much older man. He was a born leader.

Another surprise awaited us here: a big man in blue jeans under his long Afghan shirt, with a double, unshaven chin and Chitral hat sported at a jaunty angle. He shook hands with the insincere firmness of a politician – which he was. Michel de Guillenschmidt, a French Gaullist and the most senior Western elected official to enter guerrilla country, was accompanied by another Frenchman, the unfortunately named George Pons. I interviewed Michel, who advocated more Western support for the Muj. They were fighting, he said, for the same noble cause as the French *maquis*. I didn't completely understand his analogy, as many in the French resistance after 1941 were communists.

Then we filmed the training session, particularly the setting up and firing of a large DSHK Chinese recoilless rifle fired from a tripod and, unusually, from the shoulder. 'Our' Muj were clearly outclassed by the discipline and training of the *Jamiat* men. We were all impressed by Mohamed, who also had a good feel for PR. (Strangely, a Christmas card arrived for me in Johannesburg the following January from the wrestler-warrior.)

This diversion made us some hours late for our rendezvous with Joe, the Captain and the rest of our kit. The Captain was in a foul mood. It was very dark, so I suggested camping on the trail, dreading the thought of another rapid night march in my weakened condition. But a trek in the dark it was – across the mountain back to Manay.

In the moonless night we passed ghostly deserted villages, stepping around the carcasses of camels rotting next to bomb craters. After a hard day the treacherous mountain passes took a heavy toll on our tempers. Horses began to slip and stumble, particularly in dangerous passes. The Doc and Little Doc, who was still loyally with us, shone small pen-torches to help our poor night vision. Joe and I had the most difficult time.

The mood grew grim. Doc and the Captain exchanged bitter words, then blows. The Captain marched off into the night towards the border: we never saw him again, so Joe lost a friend and a possible escort out. Then one of the Muj thumped Sofi, the gentlest of our three horse-handlers. Joe swore at me as I attempted to guide his steps with the tiny torch. I tried to give him the torch and tell him where to stick it, but dropped it. It went out. While I stumbled to find it, a scorpion brushed across my hand. Little Doc quickly kicked it away.

After four hours' unhappy marching we reached Manay. More bad news awaited us: the Manay men had hit a Russian convoy the night before, nailing a tank and an armoured personnel carrier. They had suffered only two wounded, who had been ferried off to the border. The commander showed us his trousers with a neat bullet-hole punched just two inches from his calf. We had missed the whole show, and Chris was hopping mad.

Exhausted, we had a lie-in till 6am. Then another messenger arrived from the literary but never personally ubiquitous Mr Khan. Why had we steadfastly refused to move from Serracheena to his forward base? The letter contained a series of half-truths, misunderstandings and bullshit, and told us to advance to his forward base. We all said a resolute no; although, curiously, Joe – who had been so keen to leave the country altogether – voted for finding Wali. Our new plan was to return to Alamkach, lower down the valley, where the Muj had promised to hit the local garrison for us, then go back to Jagi and finally the border.

En route we filmed some lyrical shots: sheep herded by children, the jingling of goat bells, and, with permission, some workers in a field. Then we were rudely shooed away – apparently some of the distant figures being filmed were women. Dog-tired, we relaxed at Alamkach with the river tinkling away in the background. We munched wild figs and ate omelette and *nan*, trying to preserve our moon food in case we had to stay in the country longer than planned.

We indulged in a rarity – a proper wash. Chris tried to wash with the utmost modesty near the camp, but was pelted with stones by village children. Tim, Ian and I walked a long way along the muddy brown river and stripped completely for our first all-over wash in two weeks. I dropped the soap. They roared at my antics as I ran naked downstream trying to retrieve it, expecting to get shot by a tribesman outraged because a female relative was within a ten-mile radius.

That evening we bumped into the two Frenchmen again. They were accompanying a *Jamiat* group, so protocol indicated that after a brief hello we should be kept apart. We managed to chat later over a communal supper. Doc discussed various interpretations of the old Afghan story about why Alexander the Great skirted the country in his drive towards India. The Greek conqueror supposedly met six squabbling Afghans; suddenly one put a piece of Afghan soil on the ground, and instinctively they formed a circle to protect it. It was a pleasant little story, although we infidels privately thought the Afghans would strangle each other to grab a piece of the earth.

The next day a *jirga* assembly of village elders in the valley met to discuss the big attack which their foreign guests would witness. It took a long time to arrange because of the issue of who would sit where – indicating deference for this leader or that party. Chris was quick to add his usual acid comment: 'If they can't even organise seating arrangements, how the hell are they going to organise fighting the Russians?'

While we waited, Doc asked me to write a letter to Wali explaining our point of view, saying he would translate it. I did so, although I suspected the letter was kept for Doc's own defence later. Doc said Wali was an influential man; we should understand why he kept us waiting ten days. We knew we were exhibiting our own, perhaps narrow, cultural viewpoint, but we tried to explain that Western film crews might grow impatient of waiting for even the American president after a day or two.

Meanwhile, we tried to film equestrian scenes. Certain Afghan tribes had a reputation as horsemen and played a game called *buzkashi*, a very violent cousin to polo, although during the war it was played very little. As actors and horsemen the Muj in this valley fell far short of expectations. Again we had a great deal of trouble stopping them peering like grinning idiots into the camera at every opportunity. '*Camera tai magora,*' we kept saying. 'Don't look at the camera.'

We were supposed to film the *jirga* when it eventually began but were told it was inconvenient, so we sat and waited for the verdict. Bored, Chris asked Tim to read from his diary. Tim's prose had a deceptive simplicity and directness that recalled Bunyan's *Pilgrim's Progress*. His religious comments, peppered with psychological and military observations, further enhanced that impression. Chris also asked me to play some recordings from my daily mini-tape recorder log. My extract ran: 'The Muj are so disorganised they deserve to lose this war, because they refuse to think in twentieth century terms. Maybe the Soviets have a point; maybe they do need to be "socialised". They certainly need something.'

Chris was surprised. 'You're always defending the Muj when I criticise them. I didn't think you felt like that, or is it for the benefit of the Russians if they catch you.'

I just glared at him.

Into battle

We sat in our tent discussing the action planned for the next day, analysing Muj strategy, possible Russian responses and filming technical-ities. I wondered about my own grit and, more importantly, my stamina if we had to run far under fire. We had all shown courage, perhaps tinged with stupidity, in volunteering for the trip. Courage may be the grandest of virtues, but for combat journalism experience is every bit as important, both to control fear and to help in anticipating an enemy's behaviour. We all had African experience, but Afghanistan was a far cry from bundu-bashing.

The Alamkach commander outlined the rough plan of battle. We would march for an hour and a half to a garrison defended by 400 government troops. The fort also had two outposts of 150 men each. Muj forces would comprise about 80 men from the *Jamiat* and Gailani camps. The return fire was expected to be artillery, 105mm tank guns from dug-in tanks on the perimeter, 120mm mortars and 12.7mm guns. Our force would attack one of the garrison outposts. Attacking an entrenched position ideally requires a three-to-one ratio; we had 80 men rather than 2,100. They planned to make the assault in the late afternoon, giving enough light for our filming but also allowing a counter-blow from the air. We questioned the commander in detail on this crucial factor.

There were pro-Muj Afghan conscripts in the fort and the intelligence was good, he said. In the main garrison two Afghan officers were in charge of liaison with the Russian air base at nearby Jalalabad. Each supported a rival wing of the Afghan communist party, the *Khalq* and *Parcham* factions, effectively two separate parties. (Afghanistan was the only communist country ruled by two different and hostile parties. As author John Fullerton put it so succinctly: 'This is not the People's Democratic Republic of Afghanistan but Some People's Divided Repub-lic of Kabul.') Neither officer would want to be the first to lose face by calling up Russian choppers, thus signifying a lack of confidence in their own capabilities, so an air strike was unlikely.

In theory, our attack was clearly suicidal. Our Muj were half-wits who didn't clean their weapons and couldn't shoot straight. *Jamiat* were better trained, but 80 against an entrenched 700 backed by Russian Hinds looked like a one-way street to the Muslim heaven. If a Muslim kills an enemy in battle he is a *ghazi*, an Islamic warrior. If he is killed he is *shaheed*, a martyr for Islam and well rewarded in paradise, although we doubted if there was any room for Christian companions. On the other hand, the Muslims fighting with the Red Army were extremely reluctant to sacrifice themselves, as dying for communism was considered a particularly 'dirty' death with no entrance ticket through the pearly gates.

Our instincts and brief experience of the Muj suggested that no one was in a rush for martyrdom. They were not inclined to perform a Custer's Last Stand for the cameras. We had to play along, cautiously, for it was their war, their battlefield, their rules.

The thought that goes through everyone's mind at such times, especially in faraway places, is not so much the fear of death but of being maimed: on crutches for life, all for a battle between tribesmen in an arid valley in a country whose name many people can't spell. But I was too tired to dwell on such black thoughts, and fell straight into a sound sleep.

In the morning the clans gathered at a leisurely pace. Doc refused to come with us, leaving the major problems of liaison and translation to Little Doc, who spoke very poor English. We filmed the loading of the recoilless rifles, a Dasheka and ammo onto the horses. By 10am the sun in the clear sky was already suffusing our bodies as we set off in a long single file, eventually reaching the outskirts of Hesarak village. In front of us lay a huge ridge; on the other side, about a mile away, was the targeted outpost. The crew went up another valley to film the destroyed tank and APC supposedly bagged by the Manay men. I joined a small group of Muj in a little shady settlement, where we loafed for the rest of the day.

The enchanting rustic idyll contrasted blasphemously with the RPGs stacked against a tree. Children brought grapes and *nan*, while a bullock threshed corn around and around in time-honoured fashion, sweeping me back into the Middle Ages. I dozed. Erotic memories impinged on my dreams, then I awoke with a start to find a field mouse climbing up my baggy pants. I jumped up and laughed, as did all the Muj. The scampering children brought water and more grapes, which tasted like almonds. Obviously the guerrillas had the total support of the country-side. If the government forces had developed a similar rapport with the locals, they could easily have swarmed over the ridge to wipe out our small band, which had posted no guards and taken no security measures. So far it was like a picnic, not a killing field.

At 4pm we joined the rest of the force. Chris was fuming: they had been on a wild-goose chase. After a two-and-a-half-hour rapid march in searing heat they were led to two old lorries, not a tank or an APC. Was it language problems and cultural difficulties, or were the Manay men who claimed such a big victory deceiving themselves and us? Or was it like Africa, where tribesmen told you what they *thought* you wanted to hear out of sheer politeness?

The Muj milled around like boy scouts deciding where to pitch their bell tents. Each group had its own area with prepared positions: holes and emplacements for the Dasheka, and even little stone walls for the AKs. This was hardly a surprise attack, more like Saturday night on the town. We wanted to choose a good spot to film the kick-off; but no, we had to accompany our Gailani troops, who were to initiate the battle by firing a recoilless.

I peered over the top of the ridge from our firing position but could see very little – trees, a flag, and a crenellated wall. We moved along the ridge; carrying the tripod and equipment bag, I had trouble keeping up on the slippery, sloping shale. Tim suggested that I pull back down the ridge and take the kit back to the horses, as I would slow everyone down. He wrote in his log that I resembled 'a bag of the proverbial, tied in the middle with a tea cosy on its head and a bog brush instead of a chin'. Staggering all over the place with a cumbersome tripod and bag, he feared I would make an easy target. It occurred to me, too. I went down the ridge to find the horses but our handler had hidden them.

The recoilless boomed off at 7.50pm, and the Gailani commander prepared to shoot more shells, which his men had laid out in their carrier tins and primed. As the commander reached out for a new shell, he knocked half of them down the slope. It was Donkey-jumping-on-a-landmine time again. Then the incoming started: 82mm mortars, which went right over the ridge and landed at the bottom of the valley where I sat with the film kit.

Tim, Ian and Chris ducked along the ridge, now under heavy fire, and took cover in a ruined mud house, pulling out a few seconds before it was demolished by an RPG from the outpost. The large tank cannons started, but their fire was inaccurate as they could not depress enough, or elevate sufficiently, to get a short or flat trajectory. The Muj responded by letting rip with everything, although much of the AK fire went into the air or out of range. Weapons jammed frequently. There was more sound than fury. The Afghans matched T E Lawrence's description of his Arab levies: 'They thought weapons destructive in proportion to the noise.' The Muj despised the Soviets for hiding in their tanks, calling them 'beardless cowards living in iron tents', but were themselves keeping their heads well down behind their prepared defences.

The Muj had no co-ordinated plan. This was the real dictatorship of the proletariat; not the tyranny of the few but the total licence of the many. If Afghanistan was a nation of fractious villages, then their combat was an ill-assorted cacophony of squabbling individuals. They were supposed, like medieval crusaders, to be ready, even willing, to die for their God, but it was Tim who stuck his neck out for bravado.

The crew came across a Muj with a stoppage in his .303. Tim cleared it and fired three shots over the ridge, then cleared another dud in the chamber. Then, head up like an idiot, he told Ian to take a still photo. As he cocked the rifle an incoming round struck the dust a few inches from his face as he lay in a prone firing position. The Muj laughed gleefully. Wiping the gravel from his face, Tim kept his head up and let off another three rounds, which impressed the Muj no end. Tim later wrote in his log: 'A bit gung-ho, I suppose, but the whole thing was for the cameras anyway.'

A no-weapons neutrality is the golden principle of professional journalism. If we were caught by the Russians, participation in a battle, plus our regular shooting competitions and military backgrounds, would undermine our claims to fair treatment as disinterested film-makers. Tim broke the rules. But this was his first journalistic assignment, and he was still at heart a soldier.

I wasn't thinking much about ethics at the time. In my attempts to get out of harm's way, I was picking up more concentrated incoming fire than my battle-hardened colleagues. Behind me a mortar shell landed bang in the middle of an inhabited house about 500 yards away. I was half-bemused, half-fascinated, but it seemed surreal: I was witnessing the event as a journalist, not participating, not feeling. Another shell fell right next to me. I threw myself down, feeling dirt from the blast land on my back and neck. More mortars exploded around me. I crawled into a gully, hoping the valuable extender lens in my equipment bag was undamaged. The Afghan government forces displayed strange mortar discipline, initially sending in only one bomb at random instead of a pattern, so it was impossible to predict which way they were 'walking' onto their targets. Besides the mortars, an occasional tank round screamed overhead.

The Muj were disengaging, but the government mortars kept on landing beyond them, exploding in their rear around me. I hugged the gully and moved out. Just before dark I bumped into Little Doc and the camp commander, who began the skirmish by knocking over his shells. We trudged up the valley, meeting the rest of the crew half an hour later. Chris and Tim, believing I had been zapped by mortar fire, were just about to search the gullies for my remains. A Muj fired three tracers into the air to indicate our group was OK; three tracers were returned from the rest, straggling in the dark further down the valley. In the pitch black we took nearly three hours to stumble back to camp. Just as we reached the outskirts of our base, a tank shell whistled a foot or so in front of Chris and me – the camp was still within the two to three mile tank range.

Our battle foray had been something of a damp squib, more set-piece ritual than the real thing. The Muj didn't seem to have the heart, nor planning, for hard, close-quarter night assaults inflicting real damage on the enemy, apparently preferring long-distance sniping to close-range combat. That suited me personally, but it wasn't good for the film.

Doc had already eaten and lay dozing in the open on a rough wooden bed. We cooked some moon food, laughing and complaining about the battle. Nobody on our side had been injured, and we reckoned the other side would have been pretty damn unlucky to have suffered any harm either. It was Saturday night in Afghanistan with a bit of bang-bang. Done in, we fell asleep in our sweat-soaked clothes.

The march home

We awoke to the strangled cry of the camp cockerel at 4am, scheduled for an early start because of the possibility of retaliation from the air. We would have the luxury of a horse each for the return journey, although much of it would be too mountainous actually to ride. I gave a pair of binoculars to the Alamkach commander, and made a pompous little speech thanking him for sharing his battle with us and wishing him luck with the Russians.

We started off at 7am for a 12-hour day in the saddle, leading our horses over mountain passes. On a particularly narrow and dangerous pass Joe's gelding mounted Ian's big black stallion. Joe's face was a picture; Ian rapidly debussed; and in the pandemonium Chris's horse was almost forced over the edge of the cliff. Chris hugged the camera and quietened his horse. Everything was fine. We had a good laugh about the incident: the only bit of sex we'd witnessed in nearly three long weeks.

At a village market we stopped to buy yellow-green plums and bunches of grapes, and film the scene: a peaceful, verdant valley, with narrow paths meandering down between well-watered fields of maize and potatoes opening onto wider avenues enhanced by mulberry and walnut trees. Within an hour's travel the landscape had changed to arid semi-desert of loose shale and deep red-brown to blue-black dust.

We passed another tea-house, swarming with horses weighed down with ammo. Doc became very agitated when we stopped to film: this was a *Jamiat* convoy at a *Jamiat chai*-house. *Jamiat* had suffered numerous raids on their ammo supply columns, mainly from the rival *Hezbi* group. Doc emphasised our friendly status, but fussed over us to rush our filming. We soon left, riding on our uncomfortable, stirrupless, wicker-saddled horses for another three hours. Chris and I grew irritated by the accompanying Muj whacking the horses on narrow high ridges or, occasionally, putting a stick up the horse's rear just to test Chris's – luckily excellent – equestrian skills.

Horses weren't our only animal problem: snarling, vicious dogs often ran out of the mud compounds to threaten us. The Muj threw stones or, if the dog became very aggressive, raised their rifles just in case. It would be a lousy place to catch rabies.

Despite this, things were now better. We were riding, and were anyway walking much more easily when we had to, even Joe and me. At Azoar, the night stop on our second day in the country, our hosts had yet again killed a sheep for us. We usually paid them via Doc, in an attempt not to offend their strict code of hospitality. The *Pushtunwali* honour code granted total sanctuary to any guest; even if he uttered an unspeakable insult he was safe from retribution, although the host could hunt him down to kill him *outside* the house. On this occasion we knew we would have trouble eating the stringy meat, and allowed our hosts to feast off the sheep themselves. For politeness' sake we usually made a show of participation, but often resorted surreptitiously to moon food cooked on small gas heaters.

The next day we set off before the stars had even paled. It was very cold and mountains loomed ahead of us, each summit presenting another in a desperately frustrating string of false crests. We climbed, leading our horses up the steep paths, for an hour and a half. At the final summit stood a small mud hut with a pot of the ever-welcome *chai*. Anti-communist posters festooned the walls. Tim gorged himself with cookies and experimented – foolishly – with some sheep biltong. Joe complained of a hot-and-cold fever. I felt exhausted. Chris and Ian were fine physically, but Chris was in a foul temper.

Back on the road Tim's stomach had him bent over double in pain until a MiG strike in front of us, at the head of the Jagi Valley, made adrenalin pump out his sickness. Someone shouted what sounded like 'Choppers' in Pushtu. Joe and I couldn't hear much above the sound of the bombing and dashed into some tree cover. We must have misheard or misunderstood the Pushtu words, as we didn't see any Hinds.

Reaching the tea house where we had witnessed the air strike on that first morning, we were told the house we were making for had been bombed a few hours earlier. Our host and seven of his family, including small children, had been killed. Tim recorded the sad news somewhat phlegmatically in his journal: 'That's one for the record ... a day earlier and we'd probably have lost our kit or something more serious.'

We struck out towards the awaiting carnage. A welcome respite came at a pretty Afghan farmhouse, full of children, laughter and aromatic country smells. An oxen sled was going around in small circles threshing grain. Chris climbed onto the sled, with the farmer's permission, but it moved just a yard before the rope broke, much to the Afghan family's amusement. They repaired it and around Chris went again, filming an idyllic sequence as the farmer, ever watchful, held a dish behind the oxen to catch droppings before they contaminated the corn. The little girls were exceptionally pretty, so we filmed them as well. They sat happily posing, very shyly, smiling and covering and uncovering their faces.

Suddenly, they stared hard behind us and ran away. The bombs landed one second before the sound of the jets reached our ears. Chris swung the camera around to catch the second stick of bombs throwing thick black clouds of dust in the air. The unseen MiGs launched another three bombing runs right in front of us. Previously when we had heard the jets we had a few seconds to take cover; with supersonic MiGs there was no warning.

We sat in the field next to the house to wait for more Russian visitors, but they didn't oblige. It was a Mad Hatter's Tea Party in Bomb Alley: the farmer kindly brought out a pleasant picnic of milk tea, fresh *nan* and a tray of tasty apricots. A young man appeared carrying a 1944 PPSH Russian tommy-gun and sporting a Red Army belt. He chatted and posed for pics, but refused to sell us the belt.

Walking again, one of the Muj kept asking for my boots. I had given a pair of tennis shoes to a Muj a few days earlier because his boots had fallen apart. The going was rough; even Tim's new Rhodesian army boots were on the point of disintegration. As we had seen with Joe's commando knife, once one present was given, everybody wanted one. I asked the Muj what he expected me to wear – or did he expect me to go barefoot? This expedition was turning into a mobile cargo cult.

We reached the village of death. The house we had stayed in on our first night in Afghanistan had been totally destroyed: a big crater replaced the room we had slept in. Dead cattle, sheep, donkeys and chickens lay rotting and ballooning with decomposition after less than a day in the summer heat. Women wailed from nearby houses. The eight killed had just been laid to rest, as Muslims traditionally bury their dead almost immediately. Outside the village new scarves were fluttering on sticks marking the fresh graves. Everywhere in Afghanistan we had seen graves, often on mountain-tops, bedecked with scarves as tokens of respect for the martyrs.

We paid off our horsemen from Alamkach and moved to a house on the edge of the village, half-way up a hill. In the background soared a high mountain range. We camped in a large room covered with dirty, but comfortable, red quilts. A large window provided a panoramic view of the Jagi Valley, although the smell of the decaying animals wafted in waves through the open window.

We started filming. First, I did a to-camera piece standing in the ruins. 'There is no frontline in this civil war, it passes through the hearts and hearths of all Afghans,' I intoned; a poor epitaph for the dead family. All that was left of the father was, ironically, his membership card of the Gailani party in his scorched wallet. The rest was vaporised.

Then we trekked for an hour or so to the valley floor, to a government garrison overrun by guerrillas the previous year. We trod carefully along a path fringed with live anti-personnel mines, and filmed the stripped hulks of a Russian APC and four tanks. Spent rounds lay everywhere: from 12.7s, AK-47s, AK-74s and Tokarev 9mm pistols. Russian and Afghan ration-packs, peppered with holes, littered the battlefield.

We returned to a vegetarian supper: in the mourning period no meat – except chicken – was eaten. We were relieved; we'd had enough of stringy dead goat. Early next morning we climbed up the hill behind the house, having slept badly because of all the bugs crawling over the red quilts. The local Muj commander assured us no jets would arrive before 8.30am, but we knew that Russian pilots were not inclined to sleep in and reckoned on a 6.30am visitation. Spot on time, the MiGs, subsonic on this occasion, rolled into the Jagi Valley. A wall of fire came from the far side of the valley: the fundamentalist Alliance had installed nests of Dashekas, apparently supervised by Arab instructors, although we were not allowed to go across to see. For the next hour squadrons of MiG-21s and MiG-27s bombed four different sites.

After the excitement we settled down to scrambled eggs and coffee, but our breakfast was interrupted by a MiG-27 dropping two bombs on a village just half a mile away. They didn't explode. The next MiG swept in. We saw the bombs fall, open their corrective parachutes, and explode with a thunderous roar right in front of us. We couldn't ask for a better show. Chris got the explosions on film, but the MiGs' speed eluded the camera. Better still, we found out later that no one had been killed in the village, just for the benefit of a one-minute-or-less film sequence for bored couch potatoes in the West.

We were called down from the hill for lunch in the house. With so many MiGs wasting the area we all felt a bit fidgety sitting around relaxing, and the stench of dead animals put us off even a vegetarian meal. We asked Doc why, as a medical man, he hadn't suggested that the villagers remove the carcasses for hygienic reasons, let alone the smell. He gave a very vague answer.

We wanted to go to the adjacent village to film the results of the morning's bombings, but this started a long palaver. Visiting that village was a very delicate matter, said Doc, translating for the local commander. He could not take us there, as courtesy demanded: both villages were involved in a long feud in which 13 villagers had been killed, five of them recently.

Doc led a convoluted debate on the *Pushtunwali*, the Pathan code of honour, which operated alongside the stern dictates of the Koran. The code included a number of observances, of which *melmastia* (hospitality), *badal* (revenge), *teega* (truce), and *nang* (honour) were important components. The *jirga* decided on all important issues, peace, war and matters of honour. Most important of all, quarrels had to be settled honourably. Disputes arose frequently over *zar, zan* and *zamin* (gold, women and land), and each tribe or clan maintained an account of profit and loss, as it were, in matters of *ghairat* (self-respect). Traditionally blood had to be paid for in blood: killings would go on for generations of enmity which made even the Irish look forgiving and forgetful of slights. The harshest penalties were frequently reserved for fellow clansmen or relatives. More recently blood feuds were often settled by cash payments.

'Not all the roubles in Russian could compensate for the Afghan national *badal* against Moscow,' said the commander.

We discussed the fact that the blood feud was alien to Christian beliefs of turning the other cheek and forgiving neighbours, citing the parable of the Good Samaritan. Doc said that in tribal society the victim would evoke no sympathy, but rather tribesmen would ask whether the robber had made a successful getaway. He felt the Bible was full of tales of vengeance, not least by God; Allah was much more merciful.

Doc thoroughly enjoyed relating a series of old Pathan stories about asylum and truces, and modern ramifications, *Nanawatey*. 'In the past a man seeking a truce would go before his enemy with a rope around his neck as a mark of humility. In very serious cases, women wearing the Koran on their heads would go to the enemy's house to plead their family member's case.' The tribesmen did not accept *Nanawatey* when it involved female modesty, for a woman's good name was regarded as a sacred trust. Even tribal elders refrained from pleading the case of a woman who had infringed the strict sexual code.

If an unmarried woman became pregnant, usually through the advances of a cousin or brother, since females were kept away from everyone else, she could expect no mercy. Her own brother or father would kill her, and the man too – if they could find him. The previous year a woman who had killed her illegitimate baby was sentenced to death by a court in the tribal areas. Before death she was to suffer 20 lashes, serve seven years in prison, and pay a $200 fine. On appeal to the High Court, she was acquitted of the infanticide but found guilty of giving birth to an illegitimate child: her punishment was reduced to two years' hard labour and a fine of $100. Apparently she had been made pregnant by her cousin, who refused to marry her. In past cases of marital infidelity, if a husband didn't shoot his wife outright she could expect to have her nose cut off and sometimes her upper lip too, to mar her beauty and be a lasting mark of Cain whether or not she was guilty of the accusation.

The female role was not always passive: grandmothers frequently acted as guardians of the standards of the *Pushtunwali*. If *badal* was exacted, it was often the matriarch who knew the precise history of the dispute. For honour's sake she would expect her sons to avenge a killing, even if she knew that they in turn would be killed.

The commander was genuinely intrigued by our Western ways, asking about our codes of honour. 'What would happen if your woman was unfaithful? Would you kill the man?' he persisted.

'Well, some European countries recognise what are termed "crimes of passion", which allow more lenient treatment for a man who kills an unfaithful wife or her lover. But murder is certainly the exception. Often there are blows, but usually divorce follows or it is accepted and forgiven,' I said defensively. The commander could not hide his disgust at our wishy-washy ethics.

Doc was well-versed in the lore and traditions of his land, often referring to the warrior-poet Khushal Khan Khattack. I did not tell him that I knew his favourite poet had addressed most of his love poetry to a young man. But it was the wrong time for a cultural discussion. Chris was understandably itching to start filming. I was always the amateur anthropologist, and knew from long experience that in traditional societies these matters took time. The commander was stalling us, repeating his strong reluctance to visit the next-door village. If he went there he might have to kill someone, so Doc would accompany us. Even the war against the Russians could not take precedence over this little war.

The 'enemy' village was less than a mile away, and we found the locals slaughtering a bull in thanks to Allah for saving his followers from harm. Our welcome was warm. They showed us the bomb craters, and we filmed the unexploded block-busters. One had embedded a few feet from the entrance to an underground bunker – if it had gone off it would have killed 40 women and children sheltering there. We debated why the bombs hadn't detonated: faulty Russian workmanship or, far less likely, sabotage by loyal Afghan ground crews?

The welcome changed dramatically to hostility when a villager arrived to tell our hosts that we were from the rival settlement. Before a third front opened up, we departed gingerly along a path lined with sullen faces. Doc said we had come within a whisker of getting our camera equipment destroyed. As we crossed the two big fields separating the warring villages, an elderly man with a rifle blocked our way. Two women were working in the distance and our path went through their field, so he led us on a half-mile detour around the fields along a muddy brook. In the stream lay the cow and donkey carcasses which had been rotting under our window: either a total disregard for health measures or a shocking piece of deliberate bad neighbourliness, since the polluted stream flowed into the rival village and was its main water supply.

No wonder we all had gut rot. Mine was becoming exhaustingly acute, with attacks every five minutes or so. Joe also felt rough, so we returned to the bedbugs to rest while the others went to film another village. Chris tried to shoot some of the interesting stone houses, but our local commander stopped him because women were in the far background, even though Chris assured him they were not in frame. Admittedly, as Doc explained, the men were obsessive about their women's modesty in these border tribal areas, but Chris was irate and frustrated by his inability to film.

Tim wrote in his diary: 'Chris, rather unnecessarily I thought, lost his rag completely, adopting the attitude that he was making a film that would help them so why the hell didn't they want to help him to do it. Not correct. These people don't see the benefits from a film and couldn't give a fig whether it is made or how good it is. If it crosses their social structures then they won't make allowances but will get hosed off.'

Things were going sour. The fact that the border and our ambulance lay a few hours' walk away over the mountains tempted us all. Joe was more than keen to get out; I was sick; Tim and Chris had fallen out. Chris was generally very touchy, not least with my suggestion that we should leave because we had overstayed our welcome. The commander was already upset by the death of eight kinsfolk. To the peasant mind the suspicion that the Russians had bombed the exact positions where we foreigners had slept might have turned into more than a coincidence. Then Chris and the commander had argued about filming near the women. Ian agreed that our hosts had had enough of our less than delightful company.

We still needed some shots of MiGs, having filmed the bombing and explosions but not the delivery vehicles. Early the next day we positioned ourselves on the hill hoping for more aerial antics. Up in the sky aircraft, with the latest computer-guided technology, roared in the far distance as we stared blankly down on a medieval landscape. For three weeks we had not seen even a chair. No road, no electricity, no machines, only weapons. The single exception was a bright red tractor working just a mile from the border.

Waiting for the bombers, we discussed the film. We had captured some lyrical evocations of the countryside, and dramatic and moving footage of the injured boy, but precious little action. We had intended to stay in for at least six weeks, but events and Joe and Tim's limited timetables cut short our adventure. Chris, Ian and I dreaded the thought of coming back soon, and I doubted whether I was in good enough shape to go anywhere. Nor was I keen to split the team, as Chris suggested, to let him and Ian camp on the hill for a week after we left. Besides my determination on principle that we should all leave together as a team, I was worried that Chris might antagonise the locals into violence, without Doc to smooth things over and my occasional diplomacy. Chris thought he could stay there without Muj protection for a week or so, but I pointed out that this was a complex tribal society into which we were allowed to intrude – just – on great sufferance. Already, we were more than pushing our luck. Chris refused to accept this, saying I wanted to leave only because I was ill.

If the MiGs had provided some more action for us, and Chris had managed to get their attack on film, we might have left the country without a row. But the Russians simply wouldn't fight exactly when we wanted them to. So, unforgivably in front of our hosts, we had a rip-roaring verbal punch-up which left Chris ranting, the commander embarrassed, and Doc grievously offended. Ian, always the gentleman, remained aloof. We should have sorted out our problems privately instead of swapping insults in the commander's house. It was difficult for me to keep a lid on things because I was nipping outside every five minutes with diarrhoea. Thank goodness for the *Pushtunwali*.

We left at 3pm and trudged gloomily through the Alpine forest, reaching the unpoliced summit border crossing after an hour or so. We looked back to Afghanistan. Our last sight was a martyr's grave, freshly adorned with scarves and pieces of coloured cloth hanging from sticks. We clattered down the foothills into Pakistan.

Entering the bandit town of Terrimangel in daylight, we were told to disguise our kit, wear Muj headdress and speak no English, to avoid detection by Pakistani police. Tim wrote: 'The cover-up made Paul look like Rumpelstiltskin, Ian like one of Snow White's dwarfs after a dose of steroids, and Chris a foreigner with a *patou* wrapped around himself. Joe just looked cranked and I hate to think what I looked like.' With his very short hair and faintly Mongol appearance, Doc thought Tim could have passed as an Uzbek. But if Tim looked the part and walked almost as well as an Afghan, the rest of us had no choice but to brazen it out and hurry through, eyed suspiciously by local ruffians as we wove around tents, camels, chickens, donkeys and mess on the ground.

Doc said to me quietly, 'If you put your bag down there, a man could say, "It's mine," if he had a gun. What matters is force. There is no law here. You might film a man and he could shoot you because he thought you were taking a picture of his wife. They fight tribal battles here still – it used to be with old rifles, but since the war they use RPGs and mortars.'

We passed through unhindered. I hadn't washed properly for weeks, wore filthy clothes, and was tanned and bearded. I smelt rotten, so maybe I could pass for a local, provided I spat now and again. At the Gailani safe house we climbed up the rickety wooden stairs almost exactly three weeks after leaving. Outside about fifty Muj were loading up a big ammunition convoy, but we were told it was too risky to film.

Peter Jouvenal had said that returning from the Afghan countryside would make Peshawar look like New York: certainly, the mud hut's filthy loo seemed like the Hilton. Kebabs which three weeks before we had treated with grave misgivings we now munched like caviar, accompanied by seven or eight Cokes each.

When the British army soldiered on the Frontier a column reckoned to march about ten miles a day in rough terrain. We had walked or ridden for hundreds of miles behind Russian lines over rugged ground and sometimes under fire. Although the film was not complete, I treated myself to a cigar that had miraculously survived all the pounding. I lay back, puffed on the rich tobacco, and said a silent prayer of thanks.

Red tape

Although we had got out safely, our mood deteriorated. Peter had warned that even the fittest adventurers often fell apart once they got out, as though one relaxed one's guard after the sheer effort of will to keep the body going on gruelling Afghan journeys.

It was time to say goodbye to the remaining horsemen. We paid the loyal Sofi well, plus a tip (he, like the others, went afterwards to Doc for more *baksheesh*), and the persistent Muj eventually got my boots. The others bedded down while Tim and I joined some Gailani leaders for tea. The conversation turned to chemical warfare, a pet theme of Afghan guerrillas in conversation with Westerners. Doc told a story of when he worked in the main hospital in Kabul: 'Some Afghan villagers came in with minor wounds. Thirteen out of 25 died and we couldn't work it out. Eventually, we decided it was poison bullets.' Yellow rain, maybe, but Tim and I were very sceptical of 'poison bullets'. Tim thought it was probably poor hygiene.

Next morning, before boarding the Toyota ambulance, we tried to film the incredible squalor of the little street outside. Next to the rickety steps of our wood and mud house, at the side of a kitchen, stood a long-drop loo. Beneath this 'thunderbox' were other thunderboxes – crates of ammo. In the street chickens and children tripped over open drains. On the corner stood a junk-yard with an amazing pot-pourri of militaria: rocket fins, artillery and tank shells, bits of armoured vehicles and helicopters; a schoolboy's paradise and bomb squad's nightmare. A butcher walked casually by, carrying a large shoulder of meat swarming with flies. The village blacksmith hammered away, shoeing a horse. Donkeys brayed.

Chris tried one last time to film some Muj standing around or loading our vehicle. For the millionth time, '*Camera tai magora!*', 'Don't look at the camera' – but, as usual, they stared inanely into the lens. Chris cursed and climbed into the ambulance. Doc had forbidden us to film beyond our little street, which was a great pity because Terrimangel was an Ali Baba wonderland for the photographer, and Chris was reluctant to film through the curtains of the ambulance after we left the bandit hide-out.

Inside the van we made two piles of film, with the unexposed stock on top for any policemen who tried to seize the fruits of our labour. Exposed film was hidden, coyly marked 'Refugees'. We toyed with the idea of sending some of the stock separately with trusted Muj, but it seemed safer to keep everything in our sight.

The bumpy cross-country marathon began. At a little town called Sadda rival Muj had let off several bombs in the market, so the place was crawling with Pakistani police. Going through the road-block we covered our faces with scarves and pretended to sleep. If the police had looked inside, we wouldn't have fooled a soul.

We dropped from dry hills into valleys with strips of lush vegetation – heavy rains made the return journey much greener. Travelling on something approximating real roads, the Toyota picked up speed until we hit a massive traffic jam. Klaxoning our way to the front, the cause of the hold-up was immediately apparent: a bridge had been washed away by the rain. Twenty yards of the span had disappeared into the foaming muddy swell, and the bridge would obviously be down for days. Our excellent Muj driver vaguely remembered an old British Raj military road; after three hours of cross-country travel which would have worried a four-wheel drive, and fording two wide rivers, he found the old track. An hour later we were back on the road on the right side of the broken bridge.

Chris and Ian looked understandably forlorn: they would probably have to repeat this awful roller-coaster ride. Joe was very quiet. Tim nodded away through the back-breaking bumps. I was intrigued by the remnants of the Raj: old forts, classic Victorian railway bridges, 'dragon's teeth' cement tank-traps, probably from the Second World War, and occasional decaying cantonments, relics of grandeur. Joe grew interested too.

'Sad how this place has fallen apart ever since the Brits left,' he commented sombrely.

'Yeah, just like South Africa,' I said, to tease the Afrikaner. It was the only time Chris smiled that day.

A road-block loomed ahead. The police came forward to stop us, so the driver put the klaxon on, increased speed and the policemen jumped out of the way. A few miles on lay another block and more policemen: this time they were alert, with rifles at the ready. We slowed down as the officer put his hand out to stop us. Pretending it was a salute, Doc gave a smart salute back, and we slipped over the chain across the road before the surprised police officer could do anything. Our cheek worked. After 12 hours in the ambulance we reached Peshawar and switched to a truck to take us to Dean's Hotel.

Vlad the Russian gave Tim a mighty hug, and welcomed us as if we had escaped a Soviet gulag. All our kit was safe. The hotel manager, looking at our filthy condition, said knowingly, 'You've been to Afghanistan, haven't you?'

'No, we've been walking in the hills,' I replied unconvincingly.

The run-down hotel was full, so we happily switched to the more luxurious Khyber Intercontinental. I dreamed of a beer and a bath, but in usual Pakistani style the hotel could not serve any beer for some obscure reason. I kicked up a fuss. It isn't the badness of bad hotels which is so annoying, but the badness of so-called good hotels. Even without a beer, a bath was a primeval joy after stripping off my lice-ridden clothes. I was clean and lean; the trip had cost me 40lbs in weight.

At dinner with Vlad we caught up on the local gossip. Peter, Ed and Julian hadn't even entered Afghanistan: partly because of a Pakistani clampdown due to Russian pressure, and the trio's tardiness in offering bribes, they had been arrested near Chitral while trying to make the perilous entry through Nuristan. After three weeks of bureaucratic trauma they had set out again the day before we returned. In comparison, our trek seemed a bonanza of opportunity.

Vlad was very frustrated with the Afghan guerrillas, telling us dark tales of Russian prisoners-of-war kept for years in pits in Muj camps. One frightened 18-year-old Russian had apparently been repeatedly sodomised by his captors. After our meal we relaxed over a video, *FIST,* about a truckers' union. Half-way through it Vlad walked out, mumbling that he couldn't take any 'workers of the world unite stuff'. Vlad was an enigma: he showed obvious sympathy with the Soviet prisoners, as fellow Russians, but clearly detested the system imposed on a motherland he manifestly loved.

Tim and Joe flew off, and Doc helped us organise a second trip into the north. Nick della Casa was asked to fly out to join us; he would be a useful replacement, despite his occasional vagueness and habit of disappearing on his own private walkabouts. If Nick couldn't come, I would have to go back again.

It wasn't a thought I embraced willingly: I was still sick, and Al had agreed to my suggestion that I should fly to New Delhi to try to arrange for us to fly to Kabul and secure permission from the communists to film the other side. It was a long shot, especially as the Russians would almost certainly have inveigled a very comprehensive list of visiting journalists from the heavily-infiltrated Pakistani Special Branch, but worth a try. I was also busy trying to get permits to film in Peshawar and set up a third penetration of southern Afghanistan. Fortunately, however, Nick was able to join us.

I tried to read and think myself into Pakistani politics as part of my total onslaught on the local and national authorities. We couldn't even begin to film street scenes, let alone the sensitive refugee camps, without permits, which in turn would allow the export of the 'refugee' films. The Pakistani media reflected paranoia inspired by the fragility of the unpopular military regime. Externally, the crucial Washington axis was under fire because of Pakistan's lack of democracy, poor human rights record, heroin smuggling and nuclear weapons aspirations. Internally, the suppression of political parties and regional nationalism prevented stability. The answer usually was to blame India. I formed the impression that Pakistanis were so wrapped up in anti-Indian paranoia and Byzantine bureaucracy, and so busy shuffling permits and papers, that they wouldn't notice if they were invaded by the Russians.

Dislike of Indians, who were mainly Hindus, was rampant throughout the predominantly Muslim population. A taxi-driver lambasted them: 'You Christians and we Muslims are good people. We both have a book, the Bible and the Koran. The Hindus don't have a book. They have a stone. I hate them.'

Chris said simply: 'Instead of thumping them, why not lend them your book?'

The Flying Dutchman, as Chris called Al, arrived back in town in a bad mood: his case had been lost by Pakistan International Airways (PIA). It took three days of tilting against bureaucracy to get it back, half an hour before Al flew out. We nicknamed PIA *Inshallah Airways*, because before every touchdown an announcement would say the plane would land at a certain time '*Inshallah*' – 'God willing'. PIA certainly needed every bit of Allah's support.

Doc's family invited us all for a real Afghan dinner, a delicious *Narenge Pulau* cooked by Doc's mother. His father spoke excellent, if quaint, English, having been a student for six years in England. He explained why he had left his war-stricken homeland: 'Living in Afghanistan is like walking along with a bucket of boiling water on your head. You never know when it's going to fall.' Life in occupied Kabul was 'like a shift system,' he said, slowly enunciating and enjoying every English word. 'The Russians run Kabul by day and the *Mujahedin* control it at night.'

Once the parents had left the room, in his usual forthright manner, Al asked about Doc's personal life. Doc explained that he had a lady but marriage was not an immediate prospect. 'A person who doesn't have a country doesn't have anything. So now we have lost our homeland I have nowhere to put a wife or a house.' Al bluntly persisted in his enquiries about Doc's interim achievements with the lady. Doc smiled and said tactfully: 'She's a nice woman, but permission to land and take off has not yet been granted.'

The discussion turned to the very elegant women presenters on Pakistani TV, upon whose availability we speculated. By now we had a good grasp of the fanatical constraints imposed on Islamic women, although the rules were laxer in Pakistan than in the tribal areas of the Frontier. That day's newspaper carried a report of a married woman receiving 40 lashes and three years' hard labour for fornication. It didn't mention the punishment, if any, for the fornicating male. Gun-running, dope-smuggling, bank-robbery and murder were OK, but extra-marital love (for surely love it must have been with such penalties) was out.

It was decided that Chris would go into Afghanistan again. John Rubython was coming from Cape Town to attempt the hazardous trip to Kandahar. Although a well-known and highly competent stills photographer, John did not have Chris's experience with movie cameras. Chris was worried – rightly – about the overall quality of such a patchwork assignment. Al flew off again, having confirmed that my main job was to look after the new team – the Kabul angle was impossible, so my eagerly-anticipated trip to India was off. 'And get those permits,' he said, just before departing.

'They're worse than you Afrikaners,' I said. 'Anyway, you could have smoothed things over by going to the embassy in London like I asked.'

'I didn't have time – you must sort it out here. I'll ring you from Djibouti,' he shouted out of the taxi window. 'Bye. And get those damn permits.'

After further visits to Islamabad and the Peshawar press office, and much waiting, bribery and bullshit, I got them. We could now make a 'tourist' film about Peshawar, and film in one designated refugee camp. An authoritarian regime suits the film-maker better than the anarchy which often precedes and follows it, so long as your documents are in order.

While we waited for our stage-managed visit to a government show camp, we set out to explore Peshawar on film. We walked and walked the ancient city until we stopped getting lost; our forays before the first Afghan trip had been quite superficial. Peshawar derived its name from a Sanskrit word meaning 'city of flowers'. The old part of this Pathan city was dark with tall houses, narrow lanes and overhanging balconies, redolent with the smell of meat, fruit, tobacco and drains. The air was full of the raucous sounds of chickens, putt-putt motors of three-wheeled taxis, the tapping of hammers and the occasional shot in the air, usually to celebrate a wedding rather than a feud. Kebab and *tikka* meat sizzled on hot coals outside dirty tea-shops. In and around the Qissa Khawani bazaar, tiny shops sold *chappals* (sandals), and striking bandoliers and holsters. Gun shops proliferated. Here a shop sold lapis lazuli and there, sadly, the skin of a snow leopard.

A journey's end or long halt for caravans of antiquity from all over the Middle East and Central Asia, the seedy capital lay in the lush Peshawar Valley, well-watered by the Kabul River winding its way down to the mighty Indus. Vital, bustling and intriguing, every turn was a film-maker's delight. The locals were not so camera-conscious or vain as their Afghan kinsmen, and even policemen were helpful, rushing to beat anyone who obstructed us or blocked our way. After all, we had permits.

The British had built their own cantonment when Peshawar was their Frontier headquarters, full of gracious avenues and flaming bougainvillea. The sandwiches at the Peshawar Club were still good, but came with soft drinks rather than punch (the Marathi word for five, named after its ingredients: sugar, lime juice, spice, water and arak). An old retainer, who had worked at the club since 1945, mused about the changes. 'In 1945 many people were happy. Many gentlemen and officers and their ladies ... much dancing, many beers, much whisky, now nothing. Ah,' he sighed, 'the local politicians came and now no dancing, no beer, no people ... very sad.'

Indeed it was. The billiard tables were ripped. The ballroom had burnt down and had been roughly rebuilt; the chandeliers were missing. Yellowing photographs of colonels, huntsmen and drama societies were stacked in a mouldering, stuffy office. Decay suppurated in every corner of the club, despite its genteel, colonial facade. The library was still full of old, unborrowed, imperial tomes. The tennis courts were choked with weeds and there were no lights in the squash courts. The swimming pool was working, although females and males had to use it at different times. We heard the squealing antics of young girls in the water, but a big green canvas shield around the pool protected their youthful modesty.

Over our sandwiches we mused about the end of empire, discussing the fate of a similar club in Umtali, Zimbabwe. For once, Chris became philosophical. He talked about the respect the whites had lost in Africa, although he reckoned the French were an exception.

'But they seem to respect us here,' I said. 'Look how they make way for us in the bazaar. There's very little of the surliness and sense of lurking danger you experience in much of ex-colonial Africa. Sure, they all want bribes, but at least they don't stick gun barrels up your nostrils to remind you. Passivity rather than menace seems to be the essence of the locals.'

I walked around alone in the club grounds pondering this conversation. I understood the lust for gold, but what was the psychological motivation behind Britain's scramble for empire? What drove middle-class Victorians to leave a country they loved so jingoistically, and the company of the race they regarded as God's own, to travel in dirt, blood, sweat and fears among Asiatics and Africans whose morals and habits they usually despised? Some historians have suggested that many imperial adventurers were misfits. The squaring of the pegs perhaps began in public schools, with tales of bold Westerners challenging the sinister inhabitants of the enchanting East and darkest Africa. Mercantile Britain offered few opportunities to satisfy this romance and wanderlust; so they put on knight's armour and went to the colonies, if only to play croquet, cricket and polo.

In Peshawar cricket was still played – perhaps the most lasting legacy of empire – but the polo ground was closed. The most poignant relic of the Raj was the military cemetery near St John's Cathedral, filled with graves of young soldiers, mainly aged 19 to 25, from once-proud regiments now merged, restyled, rationalised and disbanded. We filmed some of the arresting epitaphs on the headstones: 'killed by assassins', 'murdered by Afridi tribesmen', 'died bravely during the siege of ...' We wanted to contrast the quiet relics of the Raj with the bustle of modern Peshawar; and compare the sound and fury of the Afghanistan war with the Muj political leadership safely ensconced in a city far removed from the battles. We also wanted to examine the fall-out of the war in the refugee camps and hospitals.

The Red Cross had set up hospitals and rehabilitation centres around Peshawar, where we filmed some amputation operations on war-wounded. Worse were the limbless children learning to walk with their stumps. A little girl, aged five, had lost one leg to a bomb. As she hobbled around with crutches, I noticed that the toes on her remaining foot were painted with nail varnish. A boy of about seven, with both legs taken above the knees by an anti-personnel mine, smiled bravely as he talked to the Swiss doctor in charge. This was the real tragedy of the war: not Soviet imperialism or injured Afghan pride, but the carnage thrust on the innocent.

A West German newspaper, *Bild am Sonntag*, had sent two journalists, Wolfgang Kempf and Dirk Hourticolon, to arrange for war-wounded children to be sent to Germany for hospitalisation. A local doctor assisted them in choosing ten children who could benefit from advanced Western treatment. It was like a scene from a biblical epic: hundreds of children on crutches, adults on stretchers, old men dragging themselves along on all fours – all seeking cures. The Germans had to play God and take just ten, not just from this camp, but from the whole Frontier province.

Even when the Germans had found suitable cases among the thousands of supplicants, local bureaucracy made the projected transfer to Germany difficult. On top of this Dirk and Wolfgang met with huge suspicion from the parents of the wounded kids, who feared their children would be converted into Christians in their few months abroad. One father flatly refused to allow his daughter to go for surgery; she died a few weeks later when she could have been saved. Preservation of faith transcended preservation of life.

We were taken to Nasir Bagh, a settled refugee camp with mud houses, which seemed reasonably well run. But it was a Potemkin village shown to all visiting journalists: illegally, we filmed other tented cities soaked in appalling squalor. In one camp over 200 children had died from polluted water in a month. A Pakistani official tried to stop us talking to the Afghan doctor in charge of the camp but the Afghan, showing obvious contempt for his titular host, insisted on telling us how it really was. Dysentery was obviously rife. As we stood on a hill filming the sea of tents, Chris, Ian and I were surrounded by a human wave of living excrement: hundreds of absolutely filthy children surrounded us, fascinated by our camera and stinking to high heaven. The stench was so appalling that we all retched; we could hardly stand up, so we walked away after snatching a few shots. It was far worse than even the smell of putrefying human flesh.

As in Palestinian camps, a new generation was being reared in bitterness. These Afghans comprised the largest single refugee mass in the world of any one national group. Day after day the mountains of Afghanistan disgorged their human misery. Some went back to fight every summer; others stayed in the sprawling camps. Built on unwanted land, the encampments resembled well-populated ghost towns. They had no water, no trees, only dead earth. The men were farmers without fields, traders without businesses, shepherds without flocks.

Pakistan officially welcomed its co-religionists, but the tidal wave of newcomers strained meagre local resources and tempers. The Pakistani public were less welcoming than their government. Afghans, who were free to travel throughout the country, were commonly blamed for Pakistan's spreading drug problem, unemployment and crime rate.

We had seen enough of the agony of the refugees: it was time to talk to their political leaders. We interviewed Professor Burhanuddin Rabbani, the head of *Jamiat*, who bore a passing resemblance in looks, and a close resemblance in ideology, to Ayatollah Khomeini. A soft-spoken, unworldly academic, he seemed too mild-mannered to lead one of the toughest guerrilla groups. He thought the Muj had already won, because they had survived over five years of fighting against a superpower.

Massud Khalini, the likeable but austere *Jamiat* official I had met earlier, translated for Rabbani. Afterwards, I asked him about the fundamentalist image the professor had in the West. It was difficult for Americans, still smarting from the Iran embassy hostage crisis, to sympathise entirely with what they saw as an Afghan version of the mad mullah in Teheran.

'People in the West,' Massud said in excellent English, 'don't have time to understand what fundamentalism means. They might just read about it in *Time*. He's no good because he looks like Khomeini; he's no good because he looks like Gaddafi. Ah, but he's okay ... he wears a tie.'

I wasn't so sure that Westerners distinguished much between good and bad Afghan guerrillas, who was fundamentalist and who was 'moderate'. The general impression was of plucky freedom fighters resisting the Russian bear with old rifles. They were on 'our side'. Ironically, the same type of people in Iran, holding the same Islamic viewpoint, were depicted as crazies, whirling dervishes, medievalists, and a threat to the West. I didn't say this to Massud, but asked how long the war would go on. 'It's not even started yet.' How right he was.

We interviewed the rather corpulent, sleepy-eyed Pir Syed Ahmed Gailani, leader of the Gailani faction, who talked about a possible political solution, with the exiled king returning as a figurehead.

Gailani's translator, the charming and chubby Wakil (*Jamiat* men were all lean, the pro-Western Gailani people seemed more prone to fatness) expanded on his master's voice: 'The Americans want the fight to continue, but cheaply, at the cost of Afghan blood. The West wants the war to go on to embarrass the Soviets.'

Next stop was Faisal Akbar, a PRO for all the Muj groups. He admitted that the main problem was lack of unity and the need for a single leader. 'Why not the Panshir's Massud?' I asked.

'Ah, he is a good fighter but he is young.' Faisal gave a convoluted explanation of why Massud had been criticised for his various tactical truces with the Russians. What he didn't say was that the brilliant guerrilla commander came from the wrong minority tribe. As in Africa, it was never polite to discuss with Westerners the crucial issue of tribe. In turn, most journalists and academics refrained from mentioning the indelicate subject.

I did ask him how long he thought the war would go on. 'Thirty or 40 years. We are indifferent to time. We will fight on.'

Maybe he was right. The Afghans were stubborn, enjoyed firing guns, and had no sense of time. But I would have liked to march all the major Muj politicians around the hospitals and camps I had just visited. Many of the politicos seemed to be sitting in fat-cat isolation. They issued blood-curdling war-cries, but the only pain they had experienced recently was indigestion.

Faisal showed us documents and photographs taken from the bodies of Soviet troops. I had a strange sensation sifting through the pictures of children, wives and mothers, family snapshots of weddings and birthdays, that somehow I had more in common with the everyday loves and lives of these dead men than the austere Muslim traditions of our hosts, even though I detested Kremlin politics.

Faisal also displayed his collection of military hardware, including two butterfly bombs. We filmed one that had exploded, then I held up the unexploded one for the camera. I discovered afterwards that it operated on a random ratchet principle which made it explode after a number of turns. It could have gone off in my hands. We all should have known better than to mess with unexploded devices; but Tim, our weapons specialist, wasn't there.

Our next film sequence was full of exploding devices at a Gailani training camp: Muj firing machine guns, and experimenting with homemade anti-personnel devices, grenades and booby-trapped radios and light bulbs. Both sides practised dirty tricks. As usual, our team was unimpressed with the Muj performance, particularly their misuse of weapons. Nick commented that it wasn't just an Afghan problem. 'I remember how many guns were buggered up in Rhodesia by using them as bottle and tin-can openers.'

Chris shot back: 'Soon they'll make a Swiss army knife that can shoot.'

At the camp we filmed two Russian POWs. One looked like a timid ballet star; the other was complaisant and bored. Caught selling guns to maintain their drug habit, their officers had punished them with electric shock treatment. Later they tried to sell more guns to the resistance and were captured by the Muj. This was the official translation, but it seemed somewhat rehearsed. The Russians explained that they had been told they would be fighting American and Chinese invaders; instead they had been forced to kill Afghan peasants. 'This is a dirty war,' said one. 'I don't like it.'

Nor would they have liked the possibility of long years of captivity in an Afghan prison. Some Red Army soldiers, from the Muslim Soviet Asian republics, had defected. A few had been allowed to fight alongside the Muj, but the process of gaining trust after switching sides was lengthy. Some prisoners even converted to Islam – perhaps out of conviction, but more likely to improve the conditions of their harsh confinement.

The camp commandant, Brigadier Rahmatullah Safi, who had briefed me in the Diner's Club at Heathrow, was helping Doc put together the second trip. The team would take two cameras to film a battle to avenge the killings of the family of eight at our last stop-over in the Jagi Valley. The Gailani group promised a dramatic and rare demonstration of captured artillery pieces, which would be towed over the border. We were suspicious of their promises but hoped the firepower would materialise.

That they were setting up the attack partly for the film led to a debate about 'creating facts'. Where do you draw the line between passively filming activity and actually encouraging it? Do you carry on filming a self-immolating Buddhist monk or do you try to douse the flames? In a sense, all journalists – by their very presence – are instigators. We discussed our recent experiences during the rioting in Soweto. Cameras definitely trigger off mob activity; it's theatre in the street. But we did not over-moralise; the ever-energetic Chris was keen to get a good battle scene in the can.

We had to wait a day or two before departure, so Doc took us around the carpet shops. Chris and Ian bought two exquisite silk Afghan carpets, $800 cash each. I purchased a cheaper woollen Baluch from Herat. Doc wangled a good price after explaining our contribution to the *jihad*. Nick's boyish amiability and old Etonian-style charm had recharged our spirits. It was once again a real team. Peshawar also was in festive mood, with pennants fluttering everywhere to celebrate Independence Day. Even the taxi-scooters, with their coloured dangling tapes and crudelypainted visuals, often of movie heroes or kung-fu action, looked even more garish. 'Set up a tinsel factory here and you'd make a fortune,' said Ian.

The last day was spent sorting out kit in the hotel. As usual, hotel staff kept barging into the room. It happened 15 times in one day, including an alleged cleaning man at 10.30pm when I was asleep. Special Branch activities plus incompetent rudeness, we assumed. In the evening we had a drink in the so-called bar. No Afghan friend could join us, we were told severely, as the bar was reserved for drinkers – that is Christians, implying that 'criminal' was an equal description. Ian, Nick and Chris left at 7am next day for their long journey in the ambulance, all in fine fettle as I wished them good luck.

I had a day to kill before returning to Islamabad to meet the second team, so the genial Wakil took me to see Niem, an 11-year-old captured Soviet spy. I was rather sceptical: the slightly-built, diminutive lad looked like any other ragged Afghan child. True, he displayed an arrogance tinged with fear, but I had seen that before in prisoners, although not in one so young.

Wakil related Niem's strange history. The boy was the son of a Kandahar schoolmaster, a Communist Party member. In 1982, because of his Party background and intelligence, Niem was chosen with ten other children to go to the USSR on a special study programme. The youngsters went first to Tashkent and later to Samarkand in Soviet Uzbekistan, a Russian Asian republic. There they were lodged with families of Party members. Their schooling included military training, weapons instruction, camouflage techniques, the use of marker panels to assist air strikes, and indoctrination in Marxist ideology.

As Wakil was telling me all this in English, the boy indicated that I should give him a cigarette. Wakil said I didn't smoke.

'Does he really smoke?' I asked.

'That and a few other things. He drinks, smokes hash, and has relations with women.'

My kind of fellow, I thought; but the journalist in me suspected Wakil was taking the anti-Russian propaganda too far. Wakil insisted that Niem was encouraged to have sex with the Afghan girls in his group, to break down Muslim taboos. They were persuaded to drink for the same reason. After six months' training Niem was sent to Herat, where the Russians told him to go into a bazaar pretending to be a homeless refugee and latch himself onto the local Muj by offering to help with errands. He was then to liaise with an older Afghan boy, who worked directly with the KGB. All this Niem did, passing on titbits of information about the Muj. Eventually one of the bazaar boys became suspicious, tailed Niem, and discovered the Russian connection. Niem and the older boy were taken by the Muj, who tried to trade both spies for some Muj prisoners in Russian hands. During negotiations the older boy was killed, so Niem was taken to Pakistan.

In translation Niem told me that he was surprised he was not killed by the 'bandits', as he described the Muj. The Russians had told him he would be tortured and killed. He was, however, treated reasonably well, but complained that he was not given enough cigarettes. Wakil looked at me and sighed with resignation. 'He's never going to change. He's a real little shit.'

Wakil gave me a lift to the airport, where I said goodbye to him and Peshawar.

The southern front

John Rubython and Mark Stucke were in good spirits, despite their 6am arrival at Islamabad airport. After an hour's row with PIA about tickets, we caught a plane for Quetta. I'd met John a few times in Cape Town; now he seemed tense, even though he had managed to slip his well-hidden camera through customs without any problems. Mark, a New Zealander working in London, was 22 and dead keen.

Eventually we circled over Quetta, the arid capital of Baluchistan. This old British garrison was still a military centre: fighters, mainly of Chinese origin, stood in concrete pens around the landing field. Hamid Nasser Zia, of the Gailani family, was waiting for us with a jeep. I had met him before; then, as now, he was cool, aloof, elegant and dressed all in white. We loaded up and set off for the best of the bad hotels, the Blue Star. I asked Hamid whether the jet fighters were facing north against the Russians or west to the Iranians.

'Neither. They're just for show.' Despite using Pakistan as a sanctuary, the Afghans here and in Peshawar had little respect for their hosts.

We arranged to meet the Muj later and decided to explore Quetta, the main town in the sparsely populated semi-desert region of Baluchistan. It was cruel and merciless country, worthy of its sons. The Baluchi tribesmen were divided – on maps only – by the borders of Afghanistan, Iran and Pakistan. In the 1970s, backed by the Russians, they had fought a long war against the Pakistani army for Baluchistan's autonomy. Situated in northern Baluchistan, Quetta marked the southernmost point of Britain's North West Frontier defence line. In the nineteenth century Kabul's potentates regarded all the province up to the sea as Afghan territory. If the Russians could control it, the coastline would give them a choke point to threaten the West's umbilical oil supplies. That, at least, was the Cold War warriors' angle.

Like Peshawar, four roads led to Quetta. To the south west lay old Persia and the lost kingdom of the Shah. To the east and south east were two routes to and from India. North west the road led directly to Kandahar, the base for the Afghan guerrillas' southern front and the target of our operation, whence Russian convoys ran through hostile territory to the ancient city of Herat. The name Kandahar is probably the only genuine relic of a Greek place-name to survive in Afghanistan, originating from the Arabic form of Alexander's name, Iskander.

I took John and Mark around the bazaar to kit them out in local gear. I liked Quetta. It was cleaner, prettier and more orderly than Peshawar. Much of the town was destroyed in an earthquake in 1935 which killed over 20,000 of its inhabitants. The British military rebuilt it, which perhaps explained the more disciplined pattern of the streets.

Back in the Blue Star, I briefed the new team. Al, I felt, had been too sanguine in his instructions. They would have no cover from Hinds in the open desert, and the route had been ambushed frequently by crack Russian airborne commandos. On the other hand, in the hotel we met a number of journalists who were about to go in, and two English women who had just visited Kandahar with the Muj. This obviously made the cameramen feel more at ease. We made friends with Hugo Delatude, who was with a French TV team from Antenne 2 scheduled to go in on the same day as John and Mark. What worried me about the pack of journalists was the ease with which we could be targeted by the local Special Branch and, worse, the KGB, who had infiltrated Quetta as thoroughly as Peshawar. My suspicions were later justified.

That night we met some of the Muj leaders, all Gailani men, including the red-bearded Suleiman Gailani. The team leader would be Engineer Ayubi who, besides speaking good English, had the crucial prerequisites for dealing with Western journalists – a sense of humour and plenty of patience. The military commander was a fierce-looking old warrior, aged about 50, who had been the Gailani representative in France. He spoke French, so I attempted in fractured franglais to discover some of the military parameters of the forthcoming operation.

John and Mark would be driven to Chaman on the Afghan–Baluchistan border and then join a camel supply train, which would take two or three days to reach Kandahar. 'Could you be more specific about the duration of the inward journey, bearing in mind the dangers of air attack?' I asked.

'Journalists are not used to riding camels, so I can't be exact,' he said with a Parisian accent. 'We will spend five days with the Muj in the city.

The whole trip should take about two weeks.'

When the Muj left we sorted out the equipment. I had brought medical supplies and spare film stock. John and Mark had transported a full-size Nagra sound system and a large wooden tripod, which might be all right on the back of camel but a real cross to bear if they were running down alleyways or trudging on foot across desert sands.

I was worried. Al had the habit of throwing teams together and, although his swashbuckling instincts were to be admired, his logistical techniques were deficient, to say the least. John, I guessed, was over 40, although wiry and fit. But he was not an experienced movie cameraman. This would be a dicey journey: open flat desert, not the mountainous cover we had travelled through in the north. The two-man team had never worked together before, let alone with unfamiliar equipment. It could be a recipe for disaster. I was so worried I almost gathered up enough courage to join them. I'm not sure whether I would have been a liability or an asset, as I was still almost chained to the bathroom.

Next morning we drove up a fertile valley north of the city. Painstakingly-irrigated apple orchards luxuriated in the middle of the desert. Stopping to buy some fruit from a roadside vendor, I determined to show off my carefully-acquired haggling skills to impress John and Mark. My lengthy session, including bits of Urdu (which they didn't speak in that region) would have done a Cairo street-merchant proud. Instead of getting a bargain, I embarrassed the taxi-driver into intervening to pay the small amount himself.

On the way back into town Mark discovered he had lost his bag, which contained some local clothing we had purchased as well as John's still camera. Mark thought he had left it in a carpet shop where I'd spent an equally fruitless bargaining session. He went back to try to retrieve it, but to no avail. I gave it a try, marching into the bazaar and confronting the Afghan merchants. I didn't know whether to buy the expensive carpet we had haggled over as a sweetener, threaten them with the police or our well-armed Muj allies, or appeal in the name of the *jihad* to give back the camera – vital, I said, for a forthcoming expedition which I implied was sanctioned by Allah himself. I probably made an ass of myself, threatening fire and brimstone as an angry Welsh Muj, for I got absolutely nowhere, although I was sure they had the camera. Afterwards, I realised that my aggressive behaviour in an obscure back street in a bazaar full of armed tribesmen might have earned me a sharp knife in the back.

When I got back to the hotel, John and Mark were gone. The Muj had arrived early to take them to the border, and I had not even been able to shake my colleagues' hands and wish them good luck.

I flew out of Quetta two hours later without even photographing the steam engines which had teased my ears for three days. At a stop-over in Lahore I confirmed my flight the next day to London. In Peshawar I had used my last *Playboys* trying to get a seat on the BA flight to Heathrow: PIA flights, besides being non-alcoholic, were booked up with pilgrims making the traditional *Haj* to Mecca. But all I got was a place on the waiting list, and I was desperate for some English beer and European cuisine. In the Lahore British Airways office a charming Pakistani woman secured my seat, without even a hint of wanting a *Playgirl*.

In my last few hours in Pakistan I finally lost my temper with their bureaucracy. After three security checks at Lahore airport – justifiable in view of recent hijackings by Sikh extremists – flight delays and incorrect loudspeaker announcements, I reached the boarding gate. PIA had already done everything to our teams except crash them; now a security man told me to go back to the long queue to obtain another security label on a plastic bag I was carrying. The flimsy thing must have fallen off. This was the last straw: I emptied the contents of the bag, containing newspapers, dirty laundry, underwear *et al*, on the floor in the narrow entrance in front of stunned security officials.

'I will not go through all that security again. You can have the damn stuff. I don't want it!' I said imperiously, drawing myself up to my full diminutive height. Everyone just stood and stared. I refused to pick up my scattered belongings. A polite customs man rescued the dumb-founded security guards, unused to defiance or Western petulance, and negotiated a fresh label for me. On the flight to Islamabad, I wondered whether anyone ever went to Pakistan for a holiday, or whether the rigours of the system always deterred would-be travellers from a voluntary trip to the natural beauties of the northern valleys like Swat or the rugged splendour of the Khyber.

In Islamabad I received a surprise phone call from Ian in Peshawar. I knew he had returned with the ambulance after making the journey into the tribal areas, knocked out by diarrhoea, but had gamely made a second attempt to rejoin the team.

'I was left in the tribal areas on my own. Rough-looking locals kept asking me how much my camera was worth and how much money I had on me. I was stuck in a den of thieves. Eventually, some of the Gailani people extricated me.'

'Why? Didn't Brigadier Safi meet you?'

'He didn't show up. At least I hope he pitches up for the artillery battle he's promised Chris.'

Full of anxiety about the two teams, and feeling guilty about luxuriat-ing in a hotel while they were slogging away in deserts and mountains, I was glad to leave for London the next morning. The customs officials had got to know me, after my raucous attempts to stop them opening cans of film in broad daylight, or retrieve lost daggers and cases. One had obviously decided that, for the sake of peace and quiet, discretion was the better part of bureaucracy. Uniquely, he refused a bribe proudly and politely, although he did ask me to write to the head of PIA on his behalf to formalise my unmoneyed gratitude. Which I did.

The film cans were not opened, as I had my permit to export film of the 'refugees', and loaded safely on board the BA jet. I relaxed with an English beer, even though it was early morning. Well, half-relaxed, because the film was only half-completed, and my colleagues were still *in situ* around Kandahar and Kabul.

I had suffered nothing worse than a massive dose of culture (and stomach) shock, but had probably failed a number of tests. Despite ten years of travelling, mostly in the third world, I had viewed my brief experience of the Afghan war through the narrow prism of my Western European prejudices. In three weeks I had endured a little of what the Afghan people had stoically withstood for over five years, and had made some friends among the Muj. By Peter Jouvenal's criterion, however, I had failed the ultimate test. He told me that there were two types of journalists who covered Afghanistan: those who came once, and those who came again.

New maps

The long-awaited Guinness tasted good, although the traffic chopper hovering over my hotel in the Strand gave me the heebie-jeebies for a few minutes as I sat discussing my adventures with a friend. Afghanistan had performed the amazing trick of not only reducing my bulk but also my ego. It's said that the superego is that part of the personality which is soluble in alcohol, and the Irish truth drug made me confess I'd learned more about myself in one week of campaigning with the Muj than in two years at Sandhurst. I didn't know whether they were brave, stupid or stubborn. 'They don't seem so keen on rushing off to Islamic heaven, either,' I added.

Nick della Casa arrived back in London. A former soldier, he had not been impressed by the fighting during Chris's second penetration, which lasted ten days. He was very scathing about the Muj: the promised artillery had not materialised; they had merely filmed a half-hearted attack on a fort, which had been met with Katyusha rockets, the Stalin Organs, and mortar fire. Perhaps Nick was being a bit blasé: when I looked at the film later, Chris's shots of incoming mortars suggested some bravado in staying to film when the enemy had obviously found the exact range. The second northern trip had not produced a great deal of exciting footage, but at least everyone was safe. But a big question mark still hung over Mark and John in Kandahar.

I phoned Pakistan during a weekend visit to my family in Wales. Getting Quetta from Cardiff was a time-consuming business but eventually I got through to the Gailani people, who told me there had been one or two hiccups... I made out the word 'ambush' on a very weak line, and 'held up by a tank offensive' and 'someone injured'.

Such bellicose echoes caused consternation in the Welsh household. Already some confusion reigned... 'Have you been with *African* or *Afghan* guerrillas this time, dear?' My mother always showed a heart-warming, if sometimes misdirected, concern during my occasional visits. After one or two more disturbing phone calls to Pakistan, it did indeed look like the worst had happened to the Kandahar duo. I readied myself psychologically to return to Asia when, indirectly from Cape Town, I heard that after a few close shaves the two men had got out safely.

I met them both in London. It had been a tough trip. 'There weren't enough camels to go around,' said Mark, 'Anyway, we couldn't handle the motion. So we walked, dodging all the camel shit.'

With no food and very little water they eventually reached Kandahar, where they hid for four days on the outskirts of the city. Then the Russians launched a major artillery and tank offensive. They spent five days in a small bunker, often under fire from Katyushas. They saw lots of action, aircraft and tanks, but it was almost impossible to film from the bunker. Eventually, fearing their capture, the Muj sneaked John and Mark out on the back of Honda scramblers, through a minefield.

But who had been ambushed and who was injured? The Muj, as usual, had got their wires crossed – it was not our team but the French TV crew who went in at the same time. Jacques Abouchar, a well-known correspondent for Antenne 2, travelling with the rest of his team and guided by our Quetta acquaintance, Hugo, had been ambushed 14 miles from the Pakistani border. They were surprised by tanks firing heavy machine guns. The 52-year-old Abouchar was shot and captured after being wounded, then led off like a trophy on top of a tank. (He was eventually released after a show trial.) The French crew and the rest of us at the Blue Star had been under close scrutiny by Afghan and KGB agents. They were ambushed by a combined Russian-Afghan unit with specific orders to capture Abouchar alive. This operation was directed at one audience: Western journalists trying to report on occupied Afghanistan.

Ten years later I still find it hard to forget the suffering I saw in Afghanistan: the deliberate Soviet policy of what has been called 'rubblisation' and 'migratory genocide' – destroying everything to make peasants become internal or external refugees. The tragedy is the Russians have long gone, but the Afghans are still killing each other with much better weapons than they had before the invasion. Afghanistan, never a nation, is a cluster of fortress towns surrounded by tribes warring among themselves. When they are not fighting they are busy growing opium (after Burma, Afghanistan is the world's biggest producer). Anarchy and plunder have returned as natural pastimes. Nick Danziger, an experienced traveller, put his finger on it: 'The civil war was more about tribal and sexual apartheid than about the defeat of a foreign invader.'

Despite the briefness of my visit, Afghanistan taught me a lot about combat and filming. Like Evelyn Waugh's famous greenhorn in *Scoop*, we blundered into a war like ignorant fools and came out, surprisingly, intact and with a film. Although most of the team found the physical conditions less arduous than I did, the trip had a profound effect on us all. The disabled children, exquisite valleys, Hind gunships, Chris's humour, Donkey grinning inanely, Tim's *braai* … These instants in the Afghan wind sweep back when people ask why I went. I did it for the money, but it was more than that.

When friends ask me the obvious question – would I do it again? – I prevaricate and recall Chris's constant quip: 'If you can't take a joke, you shouldn't be in Afghanistan.' Tim went back, but without me. It was not my first combat assignment, but my first team effort. I learned the hard way that such an expedition requires a clearly-defined leader who is fit to lead and who has carefully chosen his own team. The next time, if I were the leader, I certainly wouldn't choose me.

The most important personal insight came from reading Tim's log. It was largely unflattering and entirely truthful. To have an acute observer write in detail about you when you're under fire, sick with dysentery and trying to lead a team of fractious individuals in a primitive environment where people have a habit of poking a stick up the backside of the horse you're riding was bound to draw a new psychological map. And all for half an hour on TV or, in some countries, just a few minutes of bang-bang.

6

Angola and Mozambique – guerrilla chieftains

Angola's Patton

He looked about 13 but he was a soldier. His bush hat was much too big for him, as was the AK he cradled. His tattered uniform hung on his small, spindly frame. He sat on a captured Russian truck, which stood in the shimmering heat of the Angolan–Namibian border. A fresh-faced South African soldier, only a few years older than the boy, offered him a cigarette.

'He's too young to smoke,' said a fellow South African gruffly.

'If he's old enough to carry a gun, he's old enough to smoke,' replied the fresh-faced youth.

I was sitting on the back of an adjacent Russian truck waiting to be driven to the rebel capital of Jamba to interview 'Dr' Jonas Savimbi. It was August 1986 and the scene was being set for the biggest African tank battles since Rommel. The passing exchange between the two teenage smokers made me reflect on the tragedy of war in southern Africa – not only its almost total embrace of the young, but also how the fate of all the countries in the region had become enmeshed.

Until the outbreak of the war against the Portuguese in 1961, Angola was one of the least reported territories on earth. After independence in 1975 the conflict became a sadistic civil war, mainly between a pro-Marxist government in Luanda, the capital, and Savimbi, the bush warrior. Russia and Cuba backed the MPLA (Movement for the Popular Liberation of Angola) government in Luanda; Savimbi's Unita (National Union for the Total Independence of Angola) was helped a little by the Chinese and a lot by the Americans and South Africans. Angola, twice the size of France or Texas, was churned into one huge devastated battleground, when its oil and fertility could have made it a second Brazil.

Savimbi was one of the most interesting African leaders, a charismatic political chameleon. The former Maoist, trained in China, had been dubbed the 'Mrs Thatcher of Africa' – presumably a compliment. He was

Angola/Namibia

certainly tough, touchy, vain, intelligent and determined. And he liked yes-men around him. Whether his military qualities matched his PR genius is debatable, although he certainly led one of the best-trained and best-disciplined guerrilla armies Africa has ever seen. After 30 years of fighting the 60-year-old Unita chief is still campaigning, despite losing an election and his Western allies.

In 1986, Savimbi was Pretoria's key player in the wars of destabilisation raging throughout the region. South Africa was fuelling big wars in Angola and Mozambique and smaller ones in Zimbabwe and Zambia. These proxy wars disrupted the frontline states' support for the ANC and the transport systems required to make anti-apartheid sanctions work.

A pilgrimage to Savimbi's HQ was expected of foreign reporters on any serious fact-finding trip to southern Africa. There were two routes. One, courtesy of the CIA and Zaire, took longer and could be uncomfortable partly because Zaire's army was dangerously and drunkenly unpredictable. I took the easier route via Wonderboom airport near Pretoria. Old Daks, lovingly termed 'vomit comets' by troopies, flew over South African-occupied Namibia (then South West Africa), dropping to tree-top level in the final stages of the journey to avoid stray SAM-7 missiles. I had a romantic attachment to Daks; in Rhodesia I had flown on some which had taken part in the 1944 Arnhem campaign. Durable and reliable. Mine landed at Jamba at night. It was a full moon and the rough strip was lit by hurricane lamps. Guests were met by extremely well-turned-out Unita officers, searched, and offered the unique opportunity to have their passports stamped with 'Free Angola'. Most declined, as it would have invalidated their passports to travel elsewhere in Africa.

Sometimes journalists spent five or six 16-hour days bumping along flat forest tracks or stuck in endless quagmires if Savimbi wanted to demonstrate his latest advance on the capital. Access to Jamba, however, was much easier because it hugged the south-eastern border with Namibia. The Portuguese called this area 'the end of the world', with good reason. Savimbi's well-camouflaged, 50-mile-wide capital was very isolated. Pretoria poured in massive amounts of military hardware from bases in the Caprivi Strip, while South African and Portuguese businessmen traded in contraband: smuggled diamonds, poached ivory and rare wood.

Savimbi had summoned a small group of hacks because he wanted to announce his latest victories. It would be hype, but we were always afraid of missing out in case he really did have something important to say. We drove in trucks along empty dirt roads, signalled forward at deserted intersections by immaculate military policemen wearing spotless white gloves. We were taken to an officers' mess and regaled with South African wines and beers. I chatted to an amiable group called 'Black Americans for Free Angola'. 'If the US gives aid, there's less need for reliance on South Africa.' Quite.

This was a comfortable war to cover for the majority of newshounds who avoided, or were kept away from, the front. Savimbi, a self-publicist in the Robert Maxwell mould, garnered acres of favourable news coverage despite being an African nationalist who supped with the devil in Pretoria. The message, though, eventually palled. It was always 'next year in Luanda', but he never reached the Luanda station.

On the other hand, people had written off Savimbi so many times. He was a great survivor, an African Houdini. In 1975 his forces took part in the South African invasion which stopped just short of Luanda. When his allies retreated, Savimbi led 300 of his surviving troops on his own version of Mao's Long March. By the mid-1980s Unita was rampaging all over the country, running rings around crack regiments of Cuban troops. (But South African tanks and jets were always in the background when Unita stopped running.)

At this press conference on 21 August 1986 Savimbi was ebullient about repelling the latest offensive which experts had predicted would overwhelm his forces. There was an extra Patton-like swagger to the bearded warlord, who also sported a pearl-handled Colt revolver slung low over one hip. Savimbi did not openly admit that the latest American Stinger missiles had turned the tide of battle for him, but said: 'We have got all we asked President Reagan to give us and it has arrived in a very quick manner.' Artistic appreciation of that generosity was displayed in a massive mural of Savimbi and Reagan which dominated the central parade ground. Savimbi, with characteristic rhetoric, dismissed the threat of an attack from his old friend, the ever-lachrymose Kenneth Kaunda: 'There is a difference in having soldiers for parade and having soldiers for fighting. Mine are seasoned soldiers for fighting, those in Zambia are for parade.' Actually, Savimbi was being kind. Zambian troops couldn't even manage a proper parade.

Savimbi droned on about the enemy's use of chemical weapons which had blinded some of his troops. A Unita colonel gave an eye-witness account: 'The leaves of some trees became totally dark, the sand became very, very dark as well ... The smoke was yellow and green.' Observers of other wars, such as Afghanistan, will have noted how often guerrilla spokesmen harp on the theme of chemical and biological weapons. They know it is the type of story Western journalists want to hear.

My favourite Unita story concerns a small, pilotless Seeker drone which the South Africans used for spying. Unita soldiers observed the plane being shot down. A South African colonel with a sense of humour told a search party to hunt for it, as the matter was sensitive politically: 'The pilot is a very small Japanese.'

Unita liaison officers with the South African Defence Force were more tactful. The South Africans spent a small fortune dropping tons of propaganda leaflets on the rival MPLA forces before Unita officers gently informed their allies that very few of the MPLA troops could read. Other South African propaganda ploys were equally disastrous. They used 'skyshouts' – loudspeakers in aircraft and on the ground – to amplify sounds of hyenas. But this gimmick also unnerved the superstitious black troops in the South African forces.

The South Africans fought with great skill and bravery in Angola, although they were always outnumbered and often outclassed by modern Soviet equipment, but they never mastered psychological warfare or press relations. During and after Pretoria's first big lunge into Angola, Afrikaner troops were instructed to tell journalists they were American or English mercenaries to disguise the extent of South African involvement. Blacks might all look the same to some foreign correspondents but Afrikaners – with very thick and often broken English – couldn't really pass for Texans or Geordies. From then on South African troops talked about 'going to the States' when they crossed into Angola.

Before I left Jamba I asked Savimbi about his relations with the anti-Marxist Renamo guerrillas in the other big Portuguese-speaking ex-colony, Mozambique. He was quite dismissive, implying they were in an altogether different junior league. I was interested because I was about to interview Savimbi's approximate counterpart in Mozambique, General Afonso Dhlakama. Jamba was the Las Vegas of guerrilla HQs; next I would visit the seediest of bandit hideaways. Mozambique made even the Afghan camps look plush.

Mozambique's Scarlet Pimpernel

The challenge was: 'No one has ever done it before' – made a professional film about Renamo. Few were crazy enough to try. Their reputation made the Khmer Rouge look almost polite. One or two journalists had managed to wriggle into Renamo-controlled areas, but no one had been deranged enough to attempt a long-range penetration with modern, heavy, professional video equipment. It was all Tim Lambon's idea. After our trip to Kabul, I knew he was the Rambo type. But he had a fatal flaw: he was prepared to work with me again.

The civil war in Mozambique was definitely not a media event. The (then) Marxist Frelimo (Front for the Liberation of Mozambique) government in the capital, Maputo, did not allow Western press much access to the fighting in the interior. (Much of the time the government didn't even know what was happening in the bush, except that it wasn't nice.) So the international media largely fed on government disinformation. Like all communist dictatorships, Frelimo was efficient in two areas – propaganda and the secret police. In contrast with both Savimbi and Frelimo, Renamo – the Mozambique National Resistance – had the worst PR of any guerrilla organisation. Even Pol Pot could have given them lessons in how to win friends and influence people. Part of the reason was the complexity of the story. Another was the almost total inaccessibility of the guerrillas. And also, to be frank, Renamo was in the massacre business.

Portugal's grip on its 400-year-old colony had always been tenuous outside the few coastal cities. The entire white population, concentrated largely in Beira and the colonial capital, Lourenço Marques, numbered only 27,000 in 1940, although subsidised waves of poor immigrants pushed the total to 200,000 by 1970. A handful settled in military-style *kibbutzim* in the rural areas, but most preferred the sheltered employment and racial privileges of the urban fleshpots. This sudden surge of white settlers made Mozambique the largest white 'tribe' in sub-Saharan Africa after South Africa, Angola and Rhodesia.

The neo-fascist thugs who ran Lisbon were not the type to dabble with democratic experiments, especially in the colonies. Forced black labour continued until 1973. The secret police, animals officered by intellectuals, ran a tight ship. But Mozambique was one of the poorest colonies of the poorest state in Europe (after Albania), and survived largely by servicing its richer neighbours, Rhodesia and South Africa. Trade, transport fees, tourism and black miners working in South Africa made Mozambique tick ... albeit with typically Iberian *mañana*.

In 1964 Frelimo began a guerrilla war against the Portuguese. Mozambique had a black population of about seven million, made up of 19 tribes from nine major ethnic groups speaking about 17 different languages. It was a war won mainly by default, although by 1975 Frelimo claimed 10,000 men under arms. Frelimo squabbled endlessly and murderously, encouraged by the colonial police's manipulation of tribal rancour.

The first guerrilla supremo was Eduardo Mondlane, who was the country's first PhD and also the first Mozambican recipient of a CIA donation ($10,000 in 1963). Frelimo argued over the correct role of chiefs, churches and socialism; unresolved disputes which resurfaced as causes of the post-independence civil war. In 1969 Mondlane was assassinated in his Dar es Salaam office by a letter bomb, probably planted by internal rivals but with a little help from the secret police. It was briefly and bizarrely mooted that his American wife, Janet, take over as interim leader. A white American female guerrilla leader might have done wonders for Frelimo's image in the salons of the West but little to induce conservative black peasants to join the cause. Instead, a diminutive former hospital orderly, Samora Machel, succeeded Mondlane.

As with France in Algeria, Portugal was not making a profit by holding on to its African possessions, especially when the insurgencies expanded. The colonies were an anachronism of Europe's oldest empire led by its oldest dictatorship. Something had to give. After many years and with very little bloodshed, the dictatorship and empire collapsed in the 1974 military coup in Portugal. Flowers and optimism filled the streets of Lisbon, but chaos and a brief counter-coup erupted in Lourenço Marques. The feeble but bitter UDI lasted about as long as the generals' *putsch* in Algeria. The Portuguese army, helped by Frelimo, put down the white coup. A Portuguese exodus began. By June 1975 half the whites had fled; within a year only ten per cent remained. The towns were full of scavenging stray dogs, abandoned pampered pets. White farmers killed their cattle rather than leave them. Mechanics sabotaged their machinery. Some blacks looted and raped. The few skilled whites who remained – either financial prisoners or committed socialists – were desperately needed. Few blacks had been trained to take over the reins at any level. Of the 350 train drivers, only one was black.

While few South Africans visited Angola, Mozambique was a popular holiday resort: glorious beaches just an hour's drive from the Transvaal border. Gambling, cheap prawns, wine and sex, especially the multi-racial variety banned in South Africa, attracted many whites, including the conservatives who needed to taste sin before they could adequately condemn it at home. The colony's LM radio was a youth cult for young white South Africans. LM played the Beatles, banned by the half-wit censors in the South African Broadcasting Corporation. But suddenly the 'Yeah, Yeah, Yeahs' were replaced by martial music, then African voices attacking neo-colonialism. Overnight the lucrative tourist trade evaporated. Over 30,000 prostitutes were suddenly out of work in the renamed capital, Maputo.

Mozambique was free from Portugal but not from war. The new president was sucked into the rebellion in next-door Rhodesia. Frelimo had co-operated closely with the guerrillas fighting Ian Smith, so the Rhodesian Central Intelligence Organisation headed by the genial Ken Flower started recruiting dissident Mozambicans to form an anti-Marxist army: Renamo. It became a Frankenstein's monster. In March 1976 Machel closed the border with Rhodesia. Direct Rhodesian army raids and Renamo sabotage were bringing Mozambique to its knees. When Mugabe was victorious in Rhodesia, Renamo moved to Pretoria for its patronage and arms supplies. Mozambique entered the very heart of darkness.

Renamo was the bastard offspring of Flower and apartheid, but it was not simply a puppet of white racists. Patriotism intruded. Much of the original political rhetoric was cooked up by Rhodesian intelligence officers and, by the style of it, late at night after too many whiskies. But initially Renamo attracted much genuine support among the peasantry: those who objected to attacks on the Catholic church and the mosques, farmers hostile to Marxist land collectivisation, traditionalists who resented the down-grading of the chiefs, youngsters looking for adventure and food ... During the carnage of the 1980s most of the *povo* – the masses – came to detest both sides in a war that killed tens of thousands and created more than three million refugees.

The South African military backed Renamo for the same reasons it aided Savimbi. But the doves in Pretoria's foreign affairs department, led by Pik Botha, realised that destabilisation in the neighbouring states was destroying Pretoria's image abroad. It had become apartheid's second front. And the violence was contagious. Guns were flooding back into the Eastern Transvaal from Mozambique. In 1984 Botha doubted whether 'Renamo had the capacity to run anything more than a Mercedes and a few atrocities'. But to army hardliners the Renamo boss, Afonso Dhlakama, was an anti-Marxist who was beating the Russians at their own game. Renamo deployed classical guerrilla warfare to undermine Soviet satellites whose Eastern-bloc military advisers had been transformed into defenders of the *status quo*. The Red Army's revolutionary ardour had dimmed. And many in the CIA agreed. The Contras, the *Mujahedin*, Unita and, maybe, Renamo were the vanguard freedom-fighters in the war against Reagan's Evil Empire.

But Renamo's alleged passion for cutting off ears, noses and lips relegated Dhlakama to a horror chamber with a million dollar price-tag on his head. The Black Pimpernel was hunted by over 60,000 Frelimo troops backed by Cuban advisers, East German intelligence officers, 2,000 Tanzanian soldiers, and over 20,000 reasonably effective Zimbabwean troops, whose officers were trained by the British army. Ex-British SAS men were sniffing around as well. Dhlakama was a difficult man to pin down for an appointment.

When Pretoria made half-hearted peace with Frelimo in 1984, some South Africans were keen to get rid of Dhlakama, although Renamo still had friends in military intelligence. Amid the ballyhoo of the Nkomati agreement, Pretoria said it would stop helping Renamo if Frelimo kicked out ANC guerrillas. South Africa gave Frelimo £1 million in vehicles and radio equipment. Playing both sides against the centre was not the deal struck at Nkomati, however. Soon Machel realised that some Afrikaners were acting in bad faith. The resurgent Renamo was, to quote a senior Frelimo official, 'unpicking the social fabric'. Frelimo held the cities but – throughout the country – Renamo owned the night.

Some Mozambicans were Frelimo by day and Renamo at night. Renamo held – or ran riot in – vast swathes of territories, while Frelimo reinforced the towns. And even the few major cities were more scrap-heaps than modern conurbations. Renamo, adopting classic Maoist tenets, hoped that once the rural areas were fully consolidated, the Frelimo-held cities would fall like ripe plums. The economic collapse and Frelimo's military performance were so dire that by 1986 Mozambique could hardly be called a state any more.

This beautiful Eden became a fertile wasteland. Over 60 per cent of the people lived in absolute poverty. Over 70 per cent of the gross national product came from aid. As one cynical aid worker put it: 'The People's Republic of Mozambique has become the Donor's Republic.' The abiding images, for me, were lushness and fear. Two punch-drunk armies trampled the famished peasantry like bull-elephants locked in mortal combat. So when Tim Lambon suggested a little trip to find Dhlakama's HQ in central Mozambique, I didn't expect much of a holiday.

A colleague, formerly British SAS, had just spent six weeks at my Johannesburg house planning to use black camouflage cream to attempt night work with the highly elusive 'Super-Zapu' insurgents in Matabele-land. He wanted to do a story on Mugabe's genocide of the Ndebele. Wisely, in the end he didn't try it. When Tim came along with a more crack-brained scheme, I immediately agreed.

With much effort Tim made contact with a Renamo man in Malawi. We would try to cross the border illegally from southern Malawi. It was fairly easy to hide in the swamps along the Shire River, but the main difficulty was getting a professional camera through Malawi's main airport. Hastings Banda, the paranoid geriatric who ran Malawi, didn't like journalists and wouldn't even let them holiday there, let alone work. After six months' notice he would occasionally make exceptions for the SATV and BBC. Everything in Malawi revolved around *Ngwazi*, the conqueror. Like General Pinochet in Chile, *Ngwazi* claimed to know where every leaf fell in his domain.

Malawi was conservative because Banda was ultra-conservative. Malawi was Banda squared: small, disciplined and notably intolerant. He ruled as a modern African monarch, dressed in black homburg, three-piece suit and thick spectacles. Photographs of the highly eccentric autocrat were everywhere. Dr Hastings Kamuzu Banda, LRCP and LRCS (Edin), LRFPS (Glasgow), Life President (Paramount Chief) of Malawi, Minister of External Affairs, Defence, Justice, Agriculture, Works, Women and Children's Affairs and Community Services, was a busy man for his 90-odd years. He was also a puritanical bigot. The most respectable female visitors might have their mini-skirts or bell-bottomed trousers confiscated; males without a short back and sides could expect compulsory haircuts at the airport. When his people displeased him Banda would go into fits of terrible temper tantrums, shrieking that they should 'rot, rot, rot' in prison. And they did. Lucky ones were hunted down by the secret police and covertly murdered. Malawi's police killers specialised in staging car accidents; opponents would be 'accidentalised'.

Malawi is also a beautiful, green, mountainous land adorned by the thin blue Lake Malawi. Banda was good at PR and there were no riots or wars, so Malawi was sold to white tourists as the 'warm heart of Africa'. His refusal to indulge in racial politics meant good business with South Africa and the encouragement of ex-pat skills. Malawi initially prospered because it retained white expertise and, a rarity in Africa, an efficient and honest civil service, modelled on the British system. Provided you avoided politics, Malawi was a safe and pleasant little country: Banda kept out journalists in case they found out the really nasty political downside of his benevolent dictatorship.

Malawian customs officials were industrious and difficult to bribe. The only way to pass through the airport without physically going through customs was in a wheelchair, because the space between the customs desks was very narrow. So Tim would go to Malawi in a wheelchair, recovering from a bad accident (although not as bad as the one he might have if he were caught by the Malawians). The dismantled camera would be in a bag hanging on the back of the wheelchair. The trouble was, even in such an apparently disabled state, Tim's military bearing and haircut advertised that he was still capable of launching a successful one-man assault on the presidential palace. I suggested a wig and a cosmetic grey facial pallor. In the end we decided on a distraction: an attractive blonde with lots of silk underwear. It would have to work first time. Unlike other TV performances, boogieing through borders brooked no rehearsals.

At Jan Smuts airport, Johannesburg, South African Airways staff rolled Tim onto the plane. In Malawi another SAA air hostess wheeled him safely past the customs hall while his blonde companion's collection of exotic underwear caused maximum embarrassment to the most puritanical customs men in Africa. She was ushered through; the video tapes were under the knickers. Tim kept up his act and limped for a week, despite the discomfort of a thick plaster cast in the sweltering October heat and rains. After finally contacting the Renamo liaison man, he rang me in Johannesburg: I had to bring more tapes and a battery-charger.

I hollowed out some books and made them look terribly suspicious, especially the wires from the charger. There was an educational publishing conference on in Blantyre, Malawi's old capital. I flew there via Harare loaded with books and video equipment, plus some camping gear 'for a walking tour'. Heading into customs, I met a Zimbabwean publisher I knew. 'You *are* loaded down; going to the conference, are you?'

'Of course.' He knew I wasn't, but he didn't let on. Ex-Rhodie white solidarity and all that.

One has to tell lots of porkies in the line of duty, but I always hated this part of the job. Digging at truths attracted me to journalism; paradoxically, my stock-in-trade was dissimulation. I even became good at it. Putting piety aside, I managed to persuade customs that my funny mix of dismembered books, tapes, electronic equipment and camping gear all made sense on a walking tour. My small Pentax camera fitted the story, as did my luminous orange rucksack.

Tim met me in a bar in Blantyre and took me straight to a Renamo 'safe house'. He took off his cast and we set to work on the wheelchair, cannibalising parts to make frames for our rucksacks and using the foam to stop shoulder straps chafing. We spray-painted the orange rucksacks olive green. Tim converted one of the crutches into a mono-pod for the camera, which also had its own green carry-pack. Besides the video camera gear, two still cameras and a medical kit, we each carried one change of clothes, a sleeping bag made out of light parachute material and some emergency rations. We also adapted one rucksack to carry a solar panel to make electricity for charging camera batteries.

We worked through the night, finally leaving at 3am with two missionaries. Carrying Bibles for passports we were waved through three road-blocks of disciplined (and sober) Malawian troops. On the edge of the Shire River we contacted the local headman, who helped us negotiate a lift in a very crude dug-out canoe. We paddled and poled our way across the river and through swamps for an hour and a half. Halfway across we realised we had forgotten our mono-pod, but it was too late to go back. Wobbling against fast currents, with hippos grunting alongside, pushing through croc-infested swamps, we fretted over our four heavy packs and the sensitive, expensive and uninsured equipment.

The canoe dropped us on a small island. This was Mozambique. The fisherman pointed to a mountain for our bearings and left. We kitted up with rucksacks on our backs and fronts. Tim, much the stronger, also carried the camera. We trudged forward, sometimes waist-deep, through the swamps. I admired a kingfisher darting down to seize a fish. Lily-trotters hopped dementedly. We reached drier land, where soldier ants started biting like small piranhas.

We found a track and headed due south towards the mountain, about 20 miles away. I was never a great walker and after an hour or so my shoulders and back began to ache with the load. But it was not like climbing an Afghan mountain on all fours, and I felt at home in the familiar smells and sounds of the African bush. I felt good about the trip. The ever-resourceful Tim, who had spent nearly two years sneaking around Mozambique during the Rhodesian war, was unusually negative. He had domestic troubles at home in London. This trip taught me that mind over matter was not just a myth. My head was in the right place so I kept my spirits high, despite my physical weaknesses. Tim was physically a very hard man but his mind was elsewhere. For once in our many adventures I was psychologically the motivator. I carried the mental load, even while he was piled up like a pack donkey.

We passed small mud-hut villages. A woman, with one breast like a dried pea and the other dangling down to her waist, stopped and stared in utter disbelief. The villagers didn't wave, nor were they hostile. They were just stunned. Perhaps the younger ones hadn't seen whites before – certainly possible in this utterly remote area. I started thinking about David Livingstone, grateful that we had a modern first aid kit and, above all, anti-malaria tablets to protect us against the constantly aggressive mosquitoes. Soon we could not place a finger on an unbitten, unswollen piece of flesh. Tim, an experienced army medic, reminded me not to scratch, despite the itching. 'It can go septic in hours in this place,' he warned.

Three unarmed men stood waiting for us on the edge of some bush; our contact man in Malawi had got a message across the border before us. We greeted them with a traditional African handshake and Tim went into the accepted series of Shona formal exchanges. This wasn't exactly Shona-speaking country but we were understood to be friendly. We didn't say we were looking for the Renamo warlord; we did not mention Renamo at all. After the greeting we did not speak. They were there to guide us. They certainly weren't porters, dancing along unladen while I started to stagger. They didn't offer to help, unlike Unita soldiers who were wonderful about carrying equipment for journalists.

Tim knew me of old; he didn't have to read my thoughts. 'Don't ask them to help with the kit. They are testing us. And we are being watched from the bush. Ignore them and try to march properly, you old Welsh bastard. If you fall over now, I'll kick your arse.'

I pointed to the far distance. 'Race you to that tree?'

He smiled. That set a pattern. No matter what shit came down on our heads, it was my job to make Tim laugh. It's funny how on dangerous trips your subconscious pops up with psychological maps to guide you.

A strange apparition wheeled an old black Rudge bicycle from behind a tree, reminding me simultaneously of *Easy Rider* and *Macbeth*. I had expected a Khmer Rouge-style ruffian bandoliered up to the eyeballs, not a genial-looking, bespectacled figure in blue jeans (tucked into his socks) wearing a clean checked shirt and a purple, mohair tea-cosy as a hat. He was carrying a symbol of Renamo rank, a transistor radio in a gaudy bag made of curtain material. Unlike the smartly-dressed officers in Savimbi's 'Free Angola', he didn't want to stamp our passports. Our three silent guides drifted off.

We talked to the unarmed tea-cosy with great politeness in a mix of broken Shona and Portuguese to establish our bona fides, although we were circumspect. Blacks thought whites in Africa were always in a hurry; Tim knew from long experience that taking time with the greeting rituals was vital. Everything mattered, from the handshake to the eye contact to the sitting position. The Renamo man avoided eye contact initially as a form of deference. He was not being shifty. If I had offered him a gift (which I didn't), he would have accepted it with both hands upturned, as in supplication.

It was established that he would take us to a nearby Renamo forward base. He loaded two of the rucksacks on his bike and walked ahead of us. Suddenly two ragged, bare-foot teenage sentries materialised out of the bush alongside us. One carried a PPSH Tommy gun and the other a 5.56mm commercial hunting rifle. At the sight of each new weapon Tim, a walking encyclopaedia of armaments, would launch into a detailed history of its make and history. More usefully, he was just as adept at using them. Two more ragged soldiers joined us carrying folding-butt AKMs.

Tea-cosy indicated that we should stop. The seven of us sat in a circle and smiled at each other. The four soldiers dared not speak in front of tea-cosy, who seemed reluctant or incapable of answering our questions. Two cowboys in denim jackets arrived on 100cc trail bikes. The sentries carried our kit as we were whisked off on the back of the bikes to be shown off on a circuitous roar around the camp. The Renamo base was an exact replica of the type Mugabe's guerrillas had built in the hundreds in Mozambique during the Rhodesian war. We dismounted and went through the greeting ritual with a Commander Zimba.

Not much more than 12 hours after I disembarked from the plane, we were in a Renamo base: arrogantly, I thought I had done more in 12 hours than most London commuters would do in 12 years. Tim had organised well and everything was going to plan. We had been lucky. In Afghanistan we were hostages to the whims of the unpredictable *Mujahedin*. Both Tim and I felt at ease in Africa, the old Africa, where the white man was treated as boss. We knew something of the languages and cultures. We thought we knew how to treat Africans. I also had a niggling suspicion that this confidence might be misplaced: we were in the middle of one of the biggest wars in the world, with tens of thousands of casualties every year. And the polite and friendly African troops around us spent a lot of their time cutting people up.

Commander Zimba produced a large hunting knife and gave it to Never, one of his sidekicks. Zimba led us in prayer, then we were fed with chicken and *sadza* (ground corn). We ate this for three weeks, three times a day. I grew sick of the scrawny chickens but fortunately had already developed a taste for *sadza*, although Tim and I took vitamin supplements to keep our strength up. Sometimes we were given rice and occasionally captured Frelimo tinned food, usually Russian fish or Australian cheese.

Our first meal was accompanied by raucous Shona music from a transistor radio. Night was falling. The guerrillas were mainly in T-shirts but we put on all our clothes and waterproof ponchos with the hoods up, despite the overpowering and sticky heat, to guard against mosquitoes. It was an eerie gathering in the light of homemade candles. We popped purifying tablets into the water and gratefully drank two bottles of Fanta orange smuggled over the border.

Zimba described his heroic experiences while Never translated in adequate English. Never was patently pleased to be sitting on the officers' table. Tim entertained the troops with his Polaroid camera – I used my torch to show the pictures materialising from the black. Our hosts oohed and aahed at the magic. Everyone wanted a pic, laughing long and heartily at the poses, especially Never scratching himself under both armpits like a monkey. I pulled out my Portuguese phrase book, as most Renamo officers could understand something of the still official language of the country. Tim thought I had gone around the bend as I persisted in reading out lines like: 'Would anyone care to partner me in a waltz?' I fell about laughing and the guerrillas appeared mildly amused, albeit confused by my antics. I was already bush-crazy and thoroughly enjoying it.

We retired to our mud-walled thatched hut to sleep. We were in swampland and the air was clouded with malarial mosquitoes. Tim constructed an elaborate cage of bamboo and gauze to cover his upper torso. I took the lazy sauna route and pulled my plastic poncho over my head with a small air-hole. I was soaked in sweat. Music blared outside the hut and the locals kept popping their heads around the door to examine the new monkeys in the zoo. I fell instantly asleep.

We awoke with the dawn, eager to continue our journey. Zimba had promised to take us to the main camp on the back of the bikes. The guerrillas had been given a week's notice of our arrival, but only thought about petrol at the last minute. 'Why didn't they plan to get petrol before?' I asked Tim.

'Stop thinking like a white man,' he replied. 'This is army life – hurry up and wait.'

We tried to film their radio hut containing a hand-cranked generator for communications; probably an old Mortley-Sprague, according to Tim. But the guerrillas were understandably hostile to our snooping around the communications equipment.

We eventually left the base in mid-afternoon on two small Hondas and a Yamaha. With so much gear on our backs and chest it was an uncomfortable back-seat ride, but I would do anything to avoid walking. The *vleis* were full of yellow flowers, just like the Burmah valley in Zimbabwe. We passed deserted Portuguese trading posts, and I wondered why the locals didn't live in them and repair the roofs. Was this forbidden by the guerrillas for security reasons or was it some kind of superstition? There were no white survivors in the whole hinterland of Zambézia province.

The Renamo HQ in Zambézia was 35 miles from the Shire outpost. We went across country on rough tracks, sometimes crossing streams with crude bamboo bridges and ditches traversed on single railway sleepers. With so much weight on our backs the constant jolts made Tim and I wince with pain after a few hours. For a while we drove along roads, once intended for four-wheel drives but turned into narrow tunnels in the undergrowth by encroaching nature. We had to duck constantly to avoid low branches.

The HQ, well-hidden among mountains and forest, held about 500 rag-tag troops and perhaps two to three thousand camp followers (as well as a much bigger army of rats). The camp was made of wood, mud and thatch, with bits of looted furniture indecorously adorning the primitive style. After Jamba, this was very crude. Fortunately it had one generator providing occasional electricity: our solar panel experiment was not working properly and we needed to charge the batteries.

We were taken immediately to meet the camp boss, Commander General Calistu Matade Meque, whose mad bloodshot eyes made it clear that we were at the mercy of a dangerous eccentric. Our translator, Roberto, had worked in Rhodesia and, when sober, did a good job of interpreting the commander general's rapid staccato speech. We had decided to use translators where available or speak Portuguese, keeping

Tim's command of Shona in reserve.

Meque invited us into his mess, a tiny European wooden construction. It was like a surreal recreation of what the locals thought the Portuguese would have; a dark, dank, frilly doll's house. Curtains were draped all around the room, except for the odd triangular windows, which actually had glass in them. There was a table cloth with serviettes which no one except Meque and whites dared use.

The general offered us each a brown Malawian beer. Tim was a teetotal, non-smoking fitness fanatic, so it always fell to me to drink the booze. Imported beer was OK but rare; some of the camp moonshine was tough going. Meque knocked over the second bottle, but everybody pretended not to notice. I think he was too drunk to notice himself. After an hour's pleasantries we came to the point. Would Meque please provide us with a guide and, if possible, bikes, to take us to central Mozambique to visit the president at his Gorongosa 'capital'?

The general went into a long explanation about the president's absence in the Beira area. In a radio communication with the Shire base the president had agreed to meet us within the week at or near Gorongosa, about 150 miles south. But Meque was not keen on us carrying on to central Mozambique, wanting us to film his planned attacks in the north. We were happy to video some bang-bang, even with these crazies, but both Tim and I felt that finding the president and filming him for the first time was the essential core of our trip. If we managed any action en route, fine. Tim had pressing reasons to return to London within a month. Once we started wandering around the country we could be delayed for ages. Guerrilla promises of attacks were always to be treated with caution. The longer we stayed, the greater the risk of being wounded, falling sick or, worse, being captured by the opposing forces. We reckoned Frelimo must be monitoring Renamo's signals, and two Western journalists visiting Mozambique's most wanted man would be a very tempting target.

It was clear that the general was an egomaniac who wanted us to film his great victories. We had become his hostages as much as his guests, and would have to be very careful if we were to be able to proceed into the interior. Initially, his whimsically autocratic manners were reminiscent of Shaka Zulu's not-so-gentle court. When he was half-sober and in a good mood he would allow long discussions about Renamo's struggle. There were complaints about the harassment of religion and traditional chiefs and the forced communisation of land, and talk of free elections and the end of Marxist tyranny. This was partly Shona territory, so the old ways, spirit mediums, the need for polygamy and *lobola* (bride price) were also discussed.

Meque was first and foremost a soldier, not a politician. He might also have been a homicidal maniac. Our meal-times were always strained affairs, especially if he became drunk. After one difficult dinner, as we stood outside his mess hut, the general (shaking somewhat with intoxication) drew his revolver, looked me in the eyes, aimed at me, and fired at a range of about six feet. I didn't throw myself to the ground because I saw him move his hand slightly to the right. It was a bloody good shot. He took the head off a puff-adder. The general enjoyed his little joke, having made it clear that our lives were in his hands. It was the only time he smiled.

We lived in a small wooden hut furnished with two old beds. It was on much higher ground, making 'mozzies' less of a problem, but both the hut and camp were plagued with rats. It was difficult keeping them out of our survival rations and there was little we could do about them scampering over and around us as we tried to sleep. The generator flickered on occasionally, so we could sometimes read at night and charge the batteries. Meque, who always put a very polite veneer on his dictatorial ways, allowed us to use his toilet and crude shower facilities. Unfortunately they were close together, and I managed to drop the general's treasured bar of soap down the black hole. Wisely Tim suggested I replace it with my only bar.

We were woken by sirens in the middle of the night. Tim was always anxious about an air strike, partly because he had been in Maputo a few weeks before and had noticed numerous Soviet gunships lined up at the airport. We slept in our clothes with our kit handy for a quick exit. We shot out of the hut ready to scramble into the surrounding bush, but the guerrillas were calmly sitting around a camp fire. It was a 'training exercise'. We went back to our rats. We couldn't sleep so we listened to the sanest thing in Africa – the BBC World Service – on Tim's small radio.

The insurgents were clearly under formal discipline, and not the disorganised 'bandits' painted by Frelimo. The worst infringement of discipline was to intimidate the *povo*, the peasantry. The Renamo code was similar to that of Mugabe's Zimbabwean guerrillas, which was breached as much as it was observed. Male soldiers were not supposed to fraternise with the numerous female cadres in the camp. Both sexes volunteered, or were shanghaied, for the duration of the war. Morale appeared high, but the camp's inmates were all understandably terrified of Meque. Military standards were low. Ordinary soldiers wore rags; officers dressed in a bizarre array of Rhodesian, East German, Tanzanian, Zimbabwean, Portuguese and Frelimo camouflage. Weapons were in a terrible condition. They were never cleaned, except with soap and water!

There was sometimes Malawian or home-made beer for the officers but no oil for weapons. They could have used petrol or some of the lamp paraffin. A minority of the officers kept their AKs in good condition.

Renamo officers were second-generation guerrillas. Frelimo absorbed perhaps 30 per cent of the expertise of their Eastern bloc or Chinese instructors during the 1960s. In turn Renamo soldiers, many of whose officers were ex-Frelimo, adapted a percentage of that original training, beefed up by Rhodesian and South African advisers. During the whole journey of hundreds of miles we did not see any direct evidence of South African involvement, however, except the radio network, apparently donated before the 1984 Nkomati agreement.

Meque decided to put on a weapons and training exhibition for us. Like many African guerrillas they tended to shoot up in the air with their eyes closed. It was all automatic fire: nobody seemed to have heard of a target and firing on single rounds. Then the general rolled out a galaxy of ill-assorted hardware, ranging from old German Mausers to Russian AGS-17 grenade-launchers which, according to Tim, were very rare in Africa. They also had Russian SAM-7 surface-to-air missiles which Meque modestly said he didn't know how to operate. Tim did, and was itching to have a go. But we thought better of it and politely refused. Zimbabwean gunships and the Frelimo air force, when it managed to fly, were a major problem for the rebels, who had no effective defence against air attacks. Otherwise, Meque boasted, 'Zimbabwean troops run away just like Frelimo when we attack them. They always call for air support.' Renamo claimed that it captured all its weapons; Frelimo said the rebels' arsenal was largely comprised of Russian weapons seized in Angola and donated by South Africa.

We filmed a flag-raising ceremony, but whenever we started to film something interesting the camera would pack up, the tape ran out or the battery went flat. On the roller-coaster ride in, part of the lens had been damaged. Tim had great difficulty focusing properly. Then Meque announced a football match. Armchairs were pulled out for us on the edge of a dusty field. The general sat in the centre wearing Ray Bans and listening to a ghetto-blaster at full volume. The shooting on the football pitch was as bad as their weapons handling.

We had been in the camp three days and were heartily sick of this pirates' den. We kept nagging the general to let us proceed with our mission, but got nowhere until Meque mentioned his stomach ailment. Tim listened carefully and made a concoction from our medical kit. After a few hours the general was mightily pleased with his miracle cure, and proceeded to thank us with a two-day drinking spree. Looted beer had just arrived. The officers went through that in a day and then turned to palm wine. They had also found, traded or pillaged some batteries for what Tim called 'wog-boxes': ghetto-blasters which boomed around the camp. The party got into full swing, enlivened by the odd playful burst of rifle fire.

I felt it my duty to join in the fun, but the abstemious Tim was becoming more and more irritated and stayed in the hut while I danced and drank with the guerrillas. Meque kept asking where Tim was, so I felt obliged to drag him out. There were rumblings of bad vibes: some officers might have thought Tim a racist. I explained that 'Tim's religion won't let him drink' but he could hardly refuse to dance. He did so, but he was not a happy man. Tim had led African soldiers and lived with them at close hand, but his Rhodesian upbringing made him wary of partying with African women. I encouraged him by pointing out how attractive some of the women were, especially one who could have strutted on a Paris cat-walk.

Tim was always frank and, to me, he could be racist. 'You've been in the bush too long, Paul. You know what they say, "In the bush absence makes the blacks grow blonder".'

I looked again at the guerrilla-model. 'Don't even think about it, boyo. They'll cut your balls off,' said Tim.

Instead I did something crazier. There was always great anger and violence burning inside Tim that sometimes he only just managed to suppress. Despite my often exasperating habits it had never been turned on me; Tim seemed to have almost endless patience for my manifold inadequacies in the field. Now he was reaching the end of his limited racial tolerance. I had to get him out of what he called a 'chamber of horrors party' without insulting Meque, who was fired up on brandy.

I asked the general to stop the music because I wanted to say something. Clearly annoyed, Meque stood up – all the 70 or 80 followers jumped up like Muppets – and clicked his fingers for silence. With alarm on his face, Tim muttered: 'Whatever you've got in mind, this had better be good, or we're in real shit street. The general's totally out of his skull.'

I cleared my throat. The group of officers and ladies sat down in the dust. Meque's eyes were rolling around the back of his head; only the red-inflamed whites were visible. Roberto had long passed the stage where he could understand his native tongue, let alone translate anything. All the senior officers had their mouths and eyes gaping wide; no one had dared to stop one of the general's parties before.

I groped for phrases in Portuguese and sought words in Shona from Tim. This was clearly an emergency. 'We are very honoured by the general's great feast. I wish to thank him by showing our gratitude in my own language and culture. As we have no proper gifts worthy of the

Mozambique

general, I would like to sing a song praising him.'

Tim looked at the ground, hoping it would swallow him up. The guerrilla band sat mute and immobile, like a row of extremely well-armed tailor's dummies. This could be a tough audience. Perhaps some of my words were understood through the drunken haze. I started with a spirited version of *Sospan Fach,* then led into 'Swing Low, Sweet Chariot' with lots of rugby club actions, and finished with the Welsh national anthem sung at the top of my voice. I think I was in good form that day, and the canopy of trees and huts made my voice bounce around a little.

When I had completed my party piece I was met with utter silence. My audience was confused, bemused and perhaps amused, but it had defused the tension with Tim, who slunk away. No one would show any response until Meque reacted. Concerned, I saw him reach for his gun. This was not good. The general let off a few rounds in the air, which seemed to indicate approval, for the odd clap and cheer emanated from the dummies. The ghetto-blasters were turned back on and the cultural standards were once more elevated to the camp norm. I staggered off to the hut. That night my guts were ripped apart by the palm wine.

We had a day of quiet while the officers nursed their hangovers. The heavens opened and Tim and I played mindless games of battleships on bits of paper. When the rains stopped Tim went out to forage for bananas. I watched two giant chameleons mate. Utterly bored and feeling dreadful, I lolled in the damp heat gazing at massive snails sliming their way across the floor, too tired to chase away the chickens which regarded our hut as their roost.

Meque relented the next day and said we could leave that afternoon. We spent the morning filming the clinic, a mud hut which dispensed only aspirin. The chief motor-bike mechanic doubled as the doctor. In the nearby school the teenage teacher had one book, a Frelimo textbook, with the pages containing Marxist propaganda torn out. The children sang beautifully.

Tim thought we had a 50/50 chance of getting to Gorongosa and back to Johannesburg with our lives and film intact. I wasn't so pessimistic but knew we could be picked up by Frelimo and jailed as apartheid mercenaries for our military and South African connections. Jail in Maputo would be very bad news indeed. I recorded a short to-camera piece explaining my British background and our serious endeavour as disinterested journalists. I wrote a brief note to my father in Wales. I already had a will taking care of my German shepherd; my Australian girlfriend had just left for the UK. I had no responsibilities, which made it easier. I felt more lightheaded than alone. Tim, though, fretted and wrote a long letter to his wife. We packed these letters with our used tapes and still film, wrote a covering note to the British High Commissioner in Malawi, and asked Meque to send it to Blantyre if we didn't return within a set time. We were ready.

Of course the guerrillas were not. If they had only spent less time drinking ... Three men were to accompany us on two decrepit Honda 50ccs and another, better, 100cc bike. Hardly suitable for bundu-bashing across very rough country with five men and lots of kit, plus weapons. But that's all Renamo had scrounged from South Africa or stolen from Frelimo. They treated them roughly so they were always breaking down. Alberto, the doctor-mechanic, was a genius with all things technical. He also looked like a good soldier. Pedro was a pleasant duffer. Zacharias was certifiable and arrogant. After a series of mishaps, punctures, major repairs and false starts, with two farewell drunken bouts from the general, we left the next morning.

We were making for the great Zambezi River about 120 miles south, travelling through virgin and primitive forest. But it was hard to enjoy the scenery. Either the going was rough and we had to carry the bikes and kit, or on barely discernible tracks the three rebels drove with great speed and little skill. Alberto was OK; Zacharias kept forgetting he had no brakes; Pedro was obviously a frustrated speed-way driver. Tim was on the best bike with the safest driver because he carried the camera. I took the spills with the other two.

Often when we stopped, or crashed, villagers would come to greet us, sometimes bringing *sadza* and water. We passed a religious college; people waved Bibles at us. There seemed little starvation, although the peasants were dressed in rags or bits of sacks and occasionally bark. Long columns of porters passed heading north, carrying bags of ground corn on their heads for sale or barter in Malawi. I didn't feel there was any PR fix. We stopped where we (or the bikes) wanted. The peasants did not appear cowed. In that raw, primitive, regressive society there appeared – on the surface – to be few local problems with hearts and minds.

We hopped from base to base in what Renamo called liberated zones, passing abandoned Portuguese stores, farms and once-pretty little colonial towns painted in light pastel shades, faded now, but their gardens ran riot with the colour of flame trees and poinsettia. Everything was deserted. Locusts had picked one large area clean. A beautiful, isolated, desecrated cathedral arched towards the heavens, as if crying for help. Blasphemous graffiti despoiled its walls. On a tarmac road, a bright red tractor stood forlorn and gutted. A train was strewn across an embankment, its carriages overgrown by fast-devouring bush. Once this part of Mozambique had teemed with wildlife. We saw just four deer, a few monkeys and some tree snakes during the entire journey.

Tim fell sick after two days of non-stop travel. At one small camp where we stopped to scrounge petrol, I called a halt. Tim had lots of old war wounds, his back was in agony, and he had to lie down for at least eight hours. He even accepted some brandy from my hip flask. I foraged for food and managed to make some soup. It was a change for me to look after him. We camped in an abandoned Portuguese store, which had a little wooden structure outside, a real longdrop with a seat. What luxury, especially as I was still suffering from the palm wine. Just as I sat down a great big hairy thing lashed at my naked posterior. Fearing Africa's biggest spider, I flew out through the door. It was just a large bat.

Tim had bad news. 'I've been listening to their conversation and something's wrong. I'm not sure what – I get the impression that Alberto has been ordered not to take us to Dhlakama. Meque is up to something. We might have to disarm them and make our own way south.'

'What do you mean, "disarm them"?'

'Take their guns.'

'And what if they resist?'

'Then we'll have to shoot them.'

I went into some detail about the bad PR, lack of guides, and the simple fact that I had no experience in taking on some of the world's fiercest guerrillas.

'Alberto's the one to watch. He's one tough son of a bitch. The other two are berks. And, anyway, they might shoot *us*, if the general ordered them to.'

'It doesn't make sense, Tim. Renamo want us to make a film about them. Dhlakama knows he needs the publicity.'

'You keep saying they know bugger-all about PR.'

Tim thought for a while and added: 'I think the general is his own man. He may not be as mad as he makes out. He has his own agenda. Act in your normal amiable buffoon way and I'll try to get to the bottom of what's going on. They haven't cottoned on to the fact that I can handle their lingo.'

I had become fond of Alberto, admiring his expertise and stoic endurance. I didn't fancy shooting him. Besides, I had just watched him making a clutch plate out of tin cans. Without him, I might have to walk.

'What you could do, Paul, is flatter Alberto and ask to see his AK. Tell him what great condition he keeps it in. And I'll sort out the other two, if I have to. I'll give you the word if I think the crunch is coming. You remember how to use an AK?'

I mumbled a reluctant yes. Tim gave me one of his long looks. 'If you're in trouble, don't panic and don't leave the safety catch on.'

This gung-ho stuff just wasn't me at all. I had trusted Tim with my life on a number of occasions and would do so willingly again, but I wondered how sick he was. He definitely had a fever.

I did ask Alberto if I could see his gun and he gave it to me proudly and trustingly. I felt awful. But I had to see if I could do it. The crunch never came. We got the impression that Alberto later confided in the president, and some action was taken against the wayward general. Tim got better. And the gun thing seemed nonsense, because in the inevitable unloading, bike-carrying and crashes, the AKs were often piled on us anyway. It was against all journalism ethics to be armed and technically we deserved to be shot as combatants, but it was impossible to play by the rules when you had five people on three bikes in the middle of one massive madhouse.

The bike I usually rode had no mudguard. It was raining hard, and we churned through mud in a long, hellish descent to the Zambezi. Then the sun came out. I reached the river happy but covered in stiff, dried mud. A half-finished bridge stood guard on either side of the river. A large substation for the Cahora Bassa hydro-electric scheme – one of southern Africa's biggest disasters – mourned its own crippled and useless state. Bits of transformers decorated the roofs of the villagers' huts, although hardly any of Mozambique had regular electricity. Petrol was king – for the Renamo elite's motorbikes and for boats to cross the wide, surging river. Everything was cannibalised to keep the few machines and motors running. 'This is something out of Mad Max,' noted Tim. A Russian Antonov reconnaissance plane droned overhead as an unpleasant reminder that some things still worked properly. On the other side of the fast-running river, crossed in a captured Frelimo inflatable, bikes and all, were millions of pounds' worth of heavy plant. Massive cranes bent, as if in pain, marooned like Martian machines from Wells's *The War of the Worlds*.

Not far from the southern bank lay Caia, a largish small town in Sofala province recently captured from Frelimo. It had a big, empty airstrip. Caia was absolutely deserted, as though vultures had picked clean its carcass. A child's tin rocking horse and a 1930s' typewriter were the only artefacts left behind after the flight or pillage. It was as if a neutron bomb had been dropped. Indeed, all I had seen of Mozambique seemed to irradiate a dread, post-apocalypse feeling. Renamo troops were camped outside the town. Was this a Khmer Rouge addiction to the ideological purity of the countryside or prudent fear of Zimbabwean gunships?

There were also hundreds of Frelimo prisoners, whom Renamo said would be freed after a time. Those who wanted to enlist could. None would be kept against their wishes. That seemed dubious, as did the Renamo officers' explanation that Caia had been ravaged by retreating

Frelimo troops, not advancing Renamo. The prisoners were lined up and we filmed them: it seemed a mere propaganda opportunity, especially as Renamo were reluctant to let us talk to the prisoners. No one speaks English, we were told. We slipped away from the Renamo officers and managed to snatch brief conversations with the POWs. One had worked in Bulawayo for 20 years and spoke excellent English. He refuted the bullshit about not being kept against their wishes. They were not beaten but there was no food. Our conversation was disrupted by a sudden charge to a nearby river, where a hippo had been caught. They were all desperate for meat.

In broad daylight, for the first time the bikes raced along good tarmac roads. Pedro was in his element, going flat out with no brakes. He pretended to misunderstand my instructions to slow down. We reached the edge of the Gorongosa forest and camped at a satellite of the main HQ. The Gorongosa 'capital' was, I realised later, something of a movable feast if not sometimes a mirage. Zimbabwean paratroopers had destroyed big bases in the area on a number of occasions. But Renamo clung to the Gorongosa vicinity for political and strategic reasons. It was a convenient place to disrupt Zimbabwe's vital Beira Corridor, the road, rail and (Lonrho-owned) oil-pipeline link with Beira harbour.

A smartly-dressed aide told us that the president would see us that night. Was Afonso Dhlakama a nationalist committed to an African variant of, say, Dr David Owen's (egocentric) brand of social democracy, as Renamo propagandists implied, or the most vicious mass-murderer since Hitler, as Frelimo insisted? Was he a super-patriot or a crude puppet of Pretoria? We were led into a small clearing with one freshly-made thatched hut. Two young bodyguards patrolled nearby. Dhlakama sat quietly and alone in the hut, an unprepossessing, chubby young man dressed simply in a blue shirt and dark slacks. There was no Savimbi-like posturing with fancy six-guns. With his glasses on he looked for all the world like a timid bank clerk, but no doubt Genghis Khan had his good days.

He was 33, he told us, and looked like a younger version of his arch enemy, Mugabe. Dhlakama, too, was Catholic trained. He said he was a family man with two children. He was confident, quietly spoken and relaxed. Obviously intelligent, he spoke a very precise Portuguese, although he understood English. Unlike most politicians and generals he was prepared to listen. He discussed international affairs and asked why everybody rated his movement as the most cut-throat of the international mafia of insurgencies. He offered us a Coke, the most common capitalist symbol in Africa (although not in Mozambique), and a suitable counterpoint to the Russian AKs that surrounded us.

Dhlakama had not had much to do with journalists. That was obvious because he was (apparently) open and trusting. We were invited to dinner, where we politely devoured fresh bread rolls, Australian cheddar and, what luxury, some Nescafé. The fourth man was Vincent Ululu, the president's amanuensis, who was an excellent linguist and something of an expert on Charles Dickens. After the meal he showed due deference in the imperial court by asking permission to smoke. As Ululu lit up, a boomslang slithered across the tree above his head.

Dhlakama gave his first TV interview next morning, mainly speaking Portuguese. We needed some soundbites in English, and Ululu helped the president with his pronunciation. Dhlakama was a bit hesitant so we suggested cue cards – not telling him what to say, but advising on technical delivery. Tim then referred to an 'idiot board', a common term for a large cue behind the camera. The warlord showed some displeasure at this word. It was bit like mentioning a favourite Jewish grandmother to the Führer, I suppose. I over-explained hastily to Ululu, who luckily saw the funny side and translated the correct nuance in Portuguese.

After the interview, we talked for two whole days. Dhlakama was open but not stupid, and predictably denied that he relied on South Africa. He emphasised in almost Maoist terms his self-sufficiency. 'We have no complex theory. Our strategy is simple, and based upon the support of the people.' He claimed to control 85 per cent of the country, denying any part in the grand scheme to destabilise southern Africa. He had no contact with Savimbi, he said, and proceeded to attack Unita's overtures to Frelimo following Savimbi's condolences on the recent death in a plane crash of Samora Machel, the Frelimo president.

On the way to Malawi, on my stop-over in Harare, I had witnessed the riots and protests against South Africa, which was blamed for Machel's death. The presidential plane came down just inside the apartheid republic. I told Dhlakama that South Africa's deputy foreign minister, Louis Nel (who had met Dhlakama several times), also sent a letter of condolence to Machel's widow.

'That was kind of him,' said Dhlakama.

I couldn't stop now. 'Ah, but, Mr President, the letter arrived a week before the crash.' Dhlakama didn't laugh. Tim was always telling me off for trying to tell jokes and stories in languages I could hardly speak. They always went off half-cocked but I couldn't help myself.

Most of the conversation was serious. How could it not be in the midst of so much death? In between the long dialogues, Tim and I sought light relief by using a paraffin lamp to project shadow figures with our hands against the white walls of our tent.

I enjoyed talking to one of the world's most dangerous and secluded men. I'd like to think that he also enjoyed talking to me about world affairs, and I tried not to give a Welsh nationalist spin on everything. He was so eager to learn about the outside world. The West, particularly America, he said, had no idea of what was really happening in Mozambique.

'The people of Mozambique are now independent, but they are not free. Everything is done by force. People are taken by force to live in communal villages; children are sent to Cuba without their parents' consent. We believe independence has nothing to do with this sort of thing. The ideals which drove us to take up arms against Portuguese rule haven't yet been fulfilled.'

Dhlakama launched into a tirade against the US State Department, 'who have been doing a good job of promoting the cause of Marxist Frelimo'. He also accused Pretoria of betraying him. As he had spent ten years being hunted by thousands of troops, I couldn't really blame him for being a touch paranoid.

'Renamo is winning,' he insisted. 'We are not the *desperadoes*, it's Frelimo that's desperate … All the aid money is being used to buy weapons to keep them in power, not given to those who are dying of hunger… They spend their days watching the ports along the coast, hiding and waiting in Maputo for the arrival of a boat from the US bringing food and everything else that's necessary for the survival of Frelimo which is surrounded in the city of Maputo. In fact, Frelimo survives only in the big cities.'

I asked why, if he was doing so well on the ground, Dhlakama had such an atrocious external image. 'The Marxists have traditionally been brilliant at propaganda,' he conceded.

'You could do better at PR and propaganda,' I said, 'by releasing the Western hostages you are holding.' There were three: a Brit, a German and a Portuguese. Because Dhlakama had an obsessive interest in Britain and a much-inflated view of Britain's influence in Africa, I spent hours explaining how the release of the Briton, especially just before Christmas, would help his cause. It might even help procure a visa for his much-cherished plan to visit London. Dhlakama subsequently released all three but nobody thanked me, not even the British Foreign Office. Sir Robin Day later interviewed me for the BBC and asked how I did it, so it wasn't a secret. And the freed Brit could at least have sent me a Christmas card.

We parted on good terms. Dhlakama said: 'You were the first TV journalists to come all this way. You will be the first to be given a TV interview when I enter the presidential palace in Maputo.' I'll keep him to that, I thought.

Dhlakama's off-the-record remarks confirmed his naivety if not his integrity. Tim and I were utterly cynical about some of his claims, but the fact remained that we saw no evidence of current South African involvement. And we looked hard. Tim used all his expertise to examine radios and weapons. Some of the trade marks and registration numbers could have been interpreted, with just a bit of licence, as apartheid stock. Our film would have made a small fortune if we had done so. But we played it absolutely straight. After travelling for over 300 miles we did see a basic and nationwide indigenous organisation. We saw food being grown. We witnessed no cruelty to the peasantry, although Renamo was hardly likely to stage a quick atrocity for the benefit of our cameras.

On the harsh return journey we stayed at camps where no sentries were posted, lacking even basic defence perimeters. 'The Viet Cong would make mincemeat of this lot,' said Tim. We concluded that Renamo guerrillas were doing so well militarily not because they were any good, but because Frelimo was so bad. The journey to 'Free Mozambique' had been instructive but we left as sceptics, still wondering about the amazingly coincidental congruence of Renamo's and Pretoria's strategies.

We almost didn't make it out. Three miles before the final Shire River base, Pedro drove us straight into a low branch. The bike went on and stopped in one piece. To be fair, we had been driving cross-country for days, it was pitch black, and the lights didn't work. Pedro was at last too dazed to drive, so I piled all the kit and his weapons onto myself, let him flop on the back seat, and drove the last stretch into camp. Tim was some way behind. I saw a hut with a light on and walked in cursing: 'Where's the fucking Dettol?' I must have looked strange: a Rambo headband and bandage over my head, three weeks' growth of beard, covered in cuts, bites, bruises, an AK and ammo belts.

'You look like you need some whisky, not Dettol,' said a deep American voice. The hut was dimly lit by a candle and the tall American was covered with what looked like a bee-keeper's helmet. It was Holger Jensen, a massive Vietnam veteran working for *Newsweek*. I knew him from drunken binges in Salisbury. 'Whisky? Yes, please. I like your hat.'

'Yeah, it keeps the bugs out,' said another American, Tom, a chain-smoking acquaintance not too far removed from friendly relations with the CIA.

Holger was also on his way to Gorongosa: we had started a stampede of hacks. I wondered how he would survive on the back of a tiny bike and whether it would even move with his weight, although he didn't have any cameras. Seeing Holger was a bit like thinking you were climbing Everest for the first time and finding a can of Heinz baked beans at the summit. Renamo had asked us not to disclose the very tenuous route via Malawi.

We didn't, both to keep other hacks out and to ensure we could get back in later. And we had given a promise. Nick della Casa, who was a near neighbour in Johannesburg, decided to try our route a month later. Although I saw him nearly every day, he never asked my advice. He was caught up a tree stealing pawpaws near the border: Renamo locked him up for 18 months, thinking he was a spy. Others were arrested in Malawi and deported. One or two unfortunates were handed over to Frelimo.

Nick was treated well, according to his own account when he returned to London. I tried to use my Renamo and British contacts to speed his release, even though he had done very little to help a mutual friend imprisoned in Botswana despite being directly responsible for the man's arrest. Nick was a born trouble-maker, for all his immense personal charm. He led an amazing life, right out of Kipling. His early death at the hands of the Kurds was sad, but almost biblically inevitable.

Tim joined us for five minutes of war and mosquito stories, then we had to move on. Surprisingly I had kept a cool head the whole time, but on this very last stage I panicked in the dug-out canoe when Tim offered the boatman double the normal fee to go faster. He reckoned there was a chance of catching a bus on the other side of the river. We started to wobble almost uncontrollably in the fast current. I quietly offered our excited sailor four times the amount to disregard Tim's offer.

'We've gone through all this shit, and there's no way I want all this film to tip over into the river.' I knew how to balance in a single kayak, but this was like trying to juggle on a highly unstable hollow log in the middle of a massive stretch of fast-flowing deep water full of crocs.

'Relax, Paul. He knows what he's doing. Nobody would hire him if he tipped this thing over. He makes his living from it.' As if in rebuttal, the young fisherman gave Tim a toothless idiot smile. I closed my eyes, concentrated on balancing, and wished I could levitate.

There was no bus but a government Land-Rover eventually picked us up, unconvinced by our walking tour story. It was obvious we had been in a battle zone. I was keen to get away from the government man, who dropped us off at a ramshackle bar. It was a brothel, and we persuaded the madam to hire us a truck. We diluted our whiteness by picking up two black hitch-hikers: Anglophile teachers, both desperate for pen-friends in the UK. On that premise they befriended us immediately. Very fortunately, they had relatives on the first three road-blocks, where we were introduced as bosom buddies. That's one of the good things about Africa, the ability to bond quickly. And I replied to all the letters from my Malawian pen-pals.

We arrived at the Mount Soche hotel in Blantyre after picking up our European gear from the safe house. I wondered what the person cleaning our hotel room would think of the abandoned crutches, medicines and bits of wheelchair. 'Miracle cure. The Soche Lourdes,' said Tim. He restrapped his leg caste and limped all the way to Johannesburg plane. We had made it.

The film didn't sell too well, despite our pioneering efforts. TV networks which were interested in Africa – and there weren't many – wanted anti-apartheid stuff. The dogma of conventional wisdom reigned in most Western newsrooms. Some didn't believe our film; those that did, didn't care. I became irritated by London executives pontificating on guerrilla warfare with all the embattled *savoir-faire* of the Northern Line. In Johannesburg some of the better journalists, such as ITN's Peter Sharp and Mike Nicholson, took the trouble to ask me how we did it. They had tried and failed. Allen Pizzey, a good friend from CBS, thought we had been duped. Others said we had flown into Gorongosa in a South African helicopter, just as Louis Nel had done. As it happened, the South African security people tried to stop us, not help us.

I made enough money from the limited film sales and photo-stories to more than cover my expenses, but the trip did untold damage to my academic reputation (such as it was). At seminars at Oxford, for example, I listened to worthy experts talking in detail about Renamo bandits. Because Frelimo was on the side of the angels, *ipso facto* Renamo had to be bandits with no organisation or goals; mere starving wolf-packs scavenging for food. Just as happily I would have made a film about the other side (Frelimo in fact asked me make one later). And I would have made more money. In my opinion, both were just as bad as each other.

What irritated me most was the self-righteous omniscience of my Oxford-type friends. They knew everything about Renamo and wrote books based on their long-distance learning. But they refused to visit or at least try to visit the areas they described, relying almost entirely on Maputo's government news service. Seldom has such a big civil war been analysed so often from just one side. They refused to sully their prejudices with experience. This kind of intellectual Stalinism encouraged me to switch from ivory tower academia to the real world of journalism. A kind of Gresham's Law applied: the further you are away from experiencing first hand, the greater the sum of intellectual knowledge. Coward that I am, I came to believe that there is nothing like being shot at occasionally to sharpen your wits, and prose.

Perversely, I resolved to return. I had actually enjoyed myself in Mozambique, not least because despite being the continent's worst walker I liked the bush. And it was partly psychological. Other arduous trips had displayed my physical limitations very quickly; on the Renamo foray I had largely transcended them. I wasn't suicidal but I didn't care what happened to me. I had no job, no debts, no family to worry about and there was no particular woman in my life. All that mattered was what was happening that minute in that place. And there had been a goal, not just aimless adventure. I also had Tim. Once again, I played Danny de Vito to his Schwarzenegger.

The next time, Tim wouldn't come.

Hotel California

I planned to spend Christmas 1991 in Wales. It would be a chance to be with my family for the festivities for the first time in nearly 20 years. Then I received a call from David Hoile, a Renamo contact in London. The war was playing havoc with the Malawian economy; settlement talks between Frelimo and Renamo had been stumbling along for months. Publicity about a possible total end to the war was OK with the Malawians. Peace was breaking out all over southern Africa. Or so it seemed. 'President Dhlakama will give you an interview. He wants to discuss the ceasefire and a settlement. Can you fly in next week?'

'Fly in? You mean, no bikes?'

'No, a light plane, low under the radar, straight to Gorongosa.'

'Sounds good, but it's Christmas.'

'You can get in and out before Christmas Day ...'

Tim was busy, and also negative about the sales possibilities. I just wanted to get back there and hoped to cover my expenses; Tim was in the big league now. Most of the bang-bang stuff was done by freelancers, often at great risk and usually without insurance. Tim was still adventurous but the bottom line had become more important. He made a lot more money than me. But he was a highly skilled cameraman, and I was nothing special: I could organise, write, research, present and produce but network staffers could do all that, and often better. Combat cameramen were an elite breed, and rightly so.

J J Swart said he would come. We had worked together in South Africa but now he was based in London. He was fit, young, adventurous and used to the bush, having done national service in the South African army. Not that I expected much action on this trip. David was coming too, with a female journalist, Fiona, who had never covered a war or been to Africa. It was David's show: he had arranged with the Malawian Special Branch to get us through without hassles.

We were met at the airport by two top security men and escorted through customs. I had remembered the dress code and made J J wear a hat with his pony-tail rolled up inside. But Fiona had slacks on. J J was quick. He dragged out a long cloth he had in his bag, then asked an Indian woman to make it into a formal sarong for Fiona to satisfy the officials.

We resorted again to the Mount Soche. I sat by the pool and listened to the early evening crickets while a waiter in a fez brought me a drink on a tray. Fiona was immediately dubbed a female Indiana Jones when she came out in safari gear. She seemed good fun, and David was one of the wittiest people I have ever met. Back in shorts and in Africa after a three-year break, I felt alive again.

The next morning we flew out in a Piper Aztec with 'Pilots for Christ' emblazoned on the side. Sitting beside the missionary pilot was Domingos Adgira, a Mozambican living in Canada. We flew very low to slide under the radar, looking down at almost the same route I had endured on foot, canoes and on cannibalised bikes. It took a few minutes to pass over the Zambezi. In 1986 getting the inflatable pumped up, the engine working and the bikes loaded had taken hours, despite the chanting of a witch-doctor. I thought: bugger all the anthropological stuff, the bites and mad generals, this is the way to go.

I chatted to the pilot, who had been flying for only nine months. Then we circled where we were supposed to land. The strip had been made between very tall trees to disguise its role. It certainly fooled me. 'That's a footpath, not an airstrip.' The pilot didn't help much by saying a quiet prayer, but it was the niftiest bit of bush flying I had ever seen. Domingos was very emotional, perhaps from relief after a very tight landing or his return to Mozambican soil after 20 years of exile.

Renamo's bikes were now bigger and better. They had graduated to 200cc engines and proper trail bikes, not lawn-mowers with seats. They ferried us to a very well-organised camp. The rags had gone; the troops were wearing smart olive-green boiler suits. JJ and I were allocated a large hut with Domingos and three others. The beds even had sheets. Amazing. David said: 'Welcome to Hotel California.' There were still a few rats, one of which persistently raided our little food store, so I dubbed our mansion 'Casa del Raton Mickey'.

About 20 foreign Renamo representatives, mainly from North America, Germany, Portugal and Kenya, were scheduled to meet with local Mozambican bigwigs for the second national congress to discuss the internationally-brokered settlement talks and planned election. Meanwhile the war went on but there had been ceasefires in some areas. Frelimo had ditched Marxism. Since the independence of Namibia, the winding down of the war in Angola and the release of Mandela, hopes were high for the end of 27 years of war in Mozambique. Pretoria had actively aided Maputo, so Renamo had called Frelimo 'a South African-backed Soviet surrogate state'. With the collapse of the Soviet Union, Frelimo had nowhere else to go but talks with Dhlakama. The rebel president would discuss these changes with his main henchmen before the congress of 1,500 people at Gorongosa.

Dhlakama was due in a day or two, so we took it easy. The food in the camp was good and orderlies brought hot water for the showers. Either Renamo had got its act together or this was a very convincing Potemkin village. J J was obsessively interested in filming fauna and flora, which was a problem because I was producing a political film. He got bored easily. As we weren't short of tapes and the camp had electricity for the batteries, I didn't stop him filming ants mating and flowers growing. He also liked climbing trees at any opportunity. After drinking a half of bottle of duty-free whisky he swung around the camp like a chimpanzee on speed. Fiona, who had consumed the other half, did the same with almost as much athleticism. Both redheads, they looked and acted like twins. Suddenly a boomslang slithered in front of Fiona and both dropped out of the tree at the same time. She didn't go near a tree again. She was given the greenhorn treatment, suffering patiently our long lectures on forest animals, many of them invented; but, except for one large spider in the loo, she behaved like a pukker memsahib. She had even brought an elaborate, mobile, folding, all-dancing contraption that transformed itself into a sort of four-poster bed with mosquito netting on all sides. I had never seen such a thing in Africa before.

I had seen the old British army training films screened by Renamo, of the Biggles meets *Carry on up the Khyber* type, full of majors with clipped accents and obliging Scouse sergeants, made for national servicemen in the late 1950s. If such films had contributed to the Renamo resurgence then Frelimo must have been in a lot worse shape than I imagined. They also showed videos of black South African pop stars. Even in central Mozambique, Africa was getting too modern for this Colonel Blimp.

J J and I filmed the local clinic with just aspirin, village scenes of women grinding millet, and amputees, alleged victims of Frelimo. In one village I was delegated to maintain the visitors' honour by drinking the *skokian*, which tasted like boot polish, turps and semolina, but the old chief seemed pleased. He gave me two live chickens to take home. We also filmed an excellent sequence of tribal dancing which the soldiers were practising for the congress. It was the best and most authentic I had ever seen: horns, drums and animals skins, dust, colours … Later the dancers enacted various rituals and mini-morality plays which owed a little to Mao but much to ancient paganism. There was not a tourist in a thousand miles and it felt good.

I interviewed some of the delegates while we waited for Dhlakama.

Adelino, one of the last great white hunters, had lost everything to Frelimo's nationalisation and been tortured by Frelimo. He now lived in Madrid. The delegates from Kenya were shifty; the man from the US was brash and wore a baseball hat; the man from Frankfurt acted Germanic. It was interesting to see how exiled Mozambicans had exaggerated the customs of their adopted lands, as many forced migrants do. That was better than huddling in ethnic ghettoes and celebrating old rituals as the British tend to do. I interviewed Domingos, the Mozambican on the plane and the most humane man I met in Africa. I would have liked to round up all the Frelimo and Renamo politicians, put them on one of the beautiful islands off Mozambique, and keep them there, in comfort, to argue for the rest of their natural lives. I would make Domingos president, and let the people have a yearly referendum to see whether he should stay or go. If you share a mud hut with a man, you get to know him quickly.

I had a long chat with Almeida, the Renamo minister of information. He had spent a lot of time with Nick della Casa when Nick was imprisoned by Renamo. Almeida told me that they were desperate to get rid of Nick but the British – who had repatriated Nick on a number of previous occasions – had had enough of him. I asked about my old friend, the mad general. 'Ah, yes, he is a character but a fine soldier,' Almeida said warily. A number of journalists had lately suffered his hospitality. 'He has been reported killed many times, but he is still there.' I could see why so many people would want him out of the way, including – from the look in their eyes – some of his own officers.

Almeida did a lot of running round for us, so I gave him a small present of a new Swiss army knife – he had frequently asked to borrow my well-worn one. After I finished grilling him about Renamo's continued reputation for mutilations, JJ whispered in my ear: 'Great present. Now he can cut off ears, noses and lips with Swiss precision.'

Dhlakama arrived in a smart blue suit on a red bike. His female bodyguards were riding shotgun. Much podgier, the general had become a fatcat politician. He greeted me by name like a long-lost brother and asked after Tim. I suspect that the faithful Ululu had refreshed his memory. (I gave Ululu a copy of *Great Expectations*; he had asked me to bring him a book by Dickens when I last met him. He had also put on a lot of weight during the peace talks abroad.) Dhlakama did seem genuinely pleased to see me. Despite being busy with the delegates, he gave generously of his time. He had now travelled widely and his English had expanded as dramatically as his girth. The Portuguese were grooming his family for big things. His wife was taking an extended etiquette course in Lisbon.

We chatted alone about world politics. He still had a touching faith in British power. 'London has the key to peace. He asked why a Conservative government was spending so much training a still-Marxist Frelimo army in Zimbabwe while it couldn't afford to maintain some of its own famous regiments. A good question. He queried my reply that British support for the frontline states had been the Thatcherite alternative to full sanctions. But Thatcher – 'Machel's pal' – had gone, he said. Britain no longer needed to shop on both sides of the street – Mandela was free. Dhlakama also thought the British were prolonging the war. He wanted Britain to use its leverage on Mugabe to pull out Zimbabwean troops from Mozambique, and all British military aid to Frelimo to end. 'Because of Lonrho's investment in my country, Britain should want peace. Along with the Americans, Britain could bring peace tomorrow.' Dhlakama's political education had been good, but I didn't have the heart to dissect his misplaced confidence in British flexibility when it came to foreign policy.

He then took me shooting. That was still vintage Renamo. His female sharpshooters did only marginally better than Fiona, who almost wiped out the Renamo Cabinet with an accidental burst of automatic fire. On the way back he stopped for some electioneering with the masses, doing a number with a little kid which was an exact replay of Saddam Hussein's PR debacle on CNN. But the light was poor for the camera. We rode back through the forested camp. Lights twinkled around campfires. It was like Disney's version of Sherwood Forest.

We filmed the pre-congress cabal of Renamo delegates. Dhlakama in a dress uniform looked like the chief scout. Around him were old chiefs in 1930s' demob suits, the white hunter in safari gear, tense academics, some hoods, some *mestiços* ... an apparent attempt to balance the classes and tribes of the old Mozambique. Fiona, J J and I were the only journalists there. I didn't know if we were witnessing an historic milestone in southern African history or a remake of *Al Capone*.

I did a long interview with Dhlakama on the atrocities, all but accusing him of being a mass murderer. Asking what 99 per cent of the international media thought was a paranoid genocidal maniac in the middle of his army whether he killed people seems a little bold, in retrospect. I didn't think so at the time, because he struck me as open-minded. I had warmed to him. I still had doubts, however, even though our missionary pilot was totally disdainful of all politicians except Dhlakama. 'I trust him completely; he cares about the faith and fears of his people.' Dhlakama said of the planned elections, 'I will win with 85 per cent of the vote.'

Everything was in the can and we could go. Renamo arranged for the missionary plane to return for us. Dhlakama insisted on personally giving me a lift on his own bike back to the landing strip, reminding me that he would give me the first interview in the presidential palace. The whole trip had taken a week, and there had been no mishaps. J J and I edited the film in record time and it was screened internationally. It even made some money for the Christmas I managed to spend at home.

But a pat ending is not a suitable close for the continuing Mozambican tragedy. The war has wound down very considerably, but the land is ravaged. National reconciliation is a long way off. A year after our trip, Domingos wrote to me:

The film you made in Gorongosa, in December 1991, in which I appeared has had a devastating effect on Frelimo. I have heard from friends who have seen me in various countries, including Mozambique... In Rome, after the ceremony [signing a peace agreement], [Frelimo President] Joaquim Chissano came swinging to embrace me and shouted my name three times for the benefit of his bodyguards and the entire group of his security men. The act reminded me of Judas's embrace in the passion of Jesus in the Mountain of Olives. I have known Chissano since March 1968; he is still his old self – cynical, liar, etc. The embrace was simply 'this is the man'. Many eyes from the Frelimo delegation were on me wherever I moved in the packed hall. I knew I had been marked.

Paul, I am not afraid and thank you for making me so famous. President Dhlakama was impressed by the interview ... I thought I should tell you about all this because I expect some nasty things to happen. I am one of the few who know Frelimo really well; many have surrendered to Chissano over the past two years, through bribes and other false promises ... so if anything happens to me ... you will have an idea ...

Domingos is a good man and he is, so far, still alive. This poignant letter reminded me of the tragedy of civil war and that the media can so casually be an arbiter of life and death.

7

Zimbabwe – the lost legion

Zimbabwe

Zimbabwe revisited

It was February 1987 and I had just returned from Mozambique. Mugabe was at war with Renamo and the two film-makers, namely Tim Lambon and myself. I had got up Smithy's nose with my books and now I was in trouble with Mugabe. I was thinking of quitting Africa and wanted to see old friends in Zimbabwe before leaving. The British High Commission in Harare and the embassy in Pretoria left me in no doubt that the Zimbabweans would throw away the key and the Brits wouldn't help me at all if I chose to ignore their advice.

That made me more determined to go and I thought someone might help me. Ken Flower had remained as Mugabe's security chief for a year or so after independence and was still a consultant to the Marxist government. I couldn't contact him directly but I got a message to him. His reply said, in essence, that I was stupid but he dared me: if you can get a bottle of Chivas Regal to my house, I will cover your arse for two weeks, provided you don't cross any borders illegally and keep your word that you are just visiting friends. No politics, journalism or monkey business.

Just before I left I met Susan, a very attractive, blonde ex-Rhodesian, at a party. She insisted on coming with me, despite the risks. She wanted to see her sister and she liked adventure. 'Besides,' she said, 'a couple looks less suspicious.'

I knew my name was on the computerised wanted list at Beitbridge. I headed through Botswana to the Plumtree border, which had a reputation for being slack. With luck, there might be no electricity, let alone computers. I ran out of petrol en route, forgetting the prime axiom on long-distance travel in black Africa: if you see a gas station, fill up.

I boasted to Susan that I was a world authority on crossing African borders. I had traversed a few recently without passports, by paying small bribes to locals to take me on foot around any posts. This time I was in a car. I explained my affable berk routine: pretend to be stupid; it removes the racial tension and hostility to arrogant white men. I had added the refinement of posing as deaf, which stopped the long harangues and requests for bribes and sometimes evoked compassion. Underneath my glibness I was really nervous. I knew what happened sometimes to white politicals in Zimbabwe's prisons, having talked to a few sore-arsed survivors.

Despite her South African papers, Susan skipped through immigration at Plumtree. I didn't, although I had an elaborate British identity – I had a fairly wide selection of completely genuine passports and documents by this stage. Grilled for an hour, I tried to explain and was told: 'Shut up.

I can kick you out of here. I'm trying to help you.' Like hell. The tough-looking official, clearly an ex-soldier and a party man, was the political type. No chance of bribing him. When I was allowed to speak, I said I was a British tourist travelling through South Africa, Botswana and Zimbabwe, which was essentially true. It was just a very long tour.

'Where's your return air ticket to London?'

'I don't have one. I am not sure from where or when I shall travel back. I have more than adequate funds.' I showed him my traveller's cheques and credit cards. He wasn't interested.

I changed tack and showed my South African papers. He seemed most happy with my gun licence. So, I was a kaffir-shooting Boer. No longer confused, he had proved some kind of point and let me through.

Then came customs. After my humiliation, I decided to let Sue handle that. We queued at a counter which fronted an Ali Baba's cave. The huge safe door was open. It had to be: files, teapots, rugs, baskets and car parts poured out of it. Just as we got to the counter five officials disappeared, presumably for lunch. The one man left was clearly not quite educated enough for the Zimbabwean Cabinet.

We spent 40 minutes on the arcane details of South African motor insurance. He was obviously thinking of making up for his lack of schooling by doing a private thesis on the subject. Unfortunately his knowledge was rather out of date: quite a few of the companies might have been around in the Boer War, but were definitely not alive and well in 1987. We had insurance from one of the biggest insurers in South Africa and the documents to prove it, failing which we would have to buy large basic insurance plus the extra which allowed you to travel in Mugabe's People's Republic. Our company just wasn't on his list, so he spent a happy half hour reading the small print of our documents, our passports over and over again, our driving licences and any other official-looking bits of paper we shoved his way. He seemed passionately eager to devour anything in print. I almost went out to get him a *Reader's Digest* from the boot of the car. I don't wish to be rude and I am all for self-improvement, but he not only moved his lips when he read but also audibly sounded the words.

I was warming to the fellow but the 60-odd people behind us were not. An old man wordlessly handed our scholar a large engine part, which he had been cradling with some effort. The woman behind started breast-feeding her baby to stop it crying. A tour guide leader arrived with a busload of people. None of this influenced the customs official. Once we had paid some money, not half as much as he had originally asked for, he seemed happy. He raised the rubber stamp...then the phone rang. He conducted a 20-minute conversation in Shona with what was obviously the object of his desire: lots of giggles, 'Aieeeeees' and naughty 'Aiwas' ('Be off with you'). I waited for her to take his advice.

When he had finished his telephonic dalliance, he came back smiling and lifted the stamp once more. Sue said: 'It's so nice to be back in Rho ...' I gave her a sharp tap on the ankles. She recovered quickly. 'It's so nice to be in *Zimbabwe*.' He hesitated, then stamped the forms. We passed a queue that snaked around the building. Next the vehicle and luggage were searched. Then I was asked to drive the car over an inspection pit. It was Sue's car but I didn't think she had stacked explosives under the vehicle. We drove off.

It wasn't until we had a puncture that I realised Sue's car had its spare wheel under, not in, the boot. Of course, it had been whipped at the inspection pit. Happy to have passed through border patrols, I wasn't on my guard. Having overcome that tricky problem, we negotiated a series of police road-blocks en route to Bulawayo. The first one made a fuss about my British driving licence, which had no photograph on it. The soldiers passed it around with great suspicion. I had given them a licence issued in Wales: in Welsh (with English translation, admittedly). This caused great consternation. I shared some cigarettes and we were on our way.

At the next road-block I stopped and got out of the car. 'Stay inside,' I was told threateningly. 'Where are you from in South Africa?' South African plates, of course. I should have hired a car in Botswana.

'Johannesburg.'

'Why aren't you wearing your safety belt?'

'I was until I stopped.'

'But you are not wearing it now.'

'I was getting out of the car ...'

'I didn't tell you to get out.'

'Would you like a cigarette?'

'No. Have you got any beers?'

I hesitated. Would he get me for drunken driving? I had beer in the boot and in a cool box in the back seat. 'May I get out to get some beers from the boot?' He grunted, and let us pass after a few alcoholic presents. I wondered how closely these fellows liaised with Zimbabwe's tourist board.

We stopped at Bulawayo to visit Sue's aunt, who was delighted with our gift of a rare item – toothpaste. Eventually reaching Harare, I knocked on Ken Flower's door. He seemed pleased to see me, even before I gave him the Chivas Regal. We chatted about old times, although Ken lowered his voice, like all white Zimbabweans, when we broached politics. Some place, I thought, where the intelligence boss has to speak in whispers. He stopped talking when his cook walked into the room.

'Don't go into the Quill Club,' he said. 'See your friends unobtrusively and then get away somewhere quiet. Why not try Kariba?'

I rushed around my old friends and even risked one or two restaurants. The latest 'in' place was Aphrodite's Tavern in Strathhaven, which served first-class Greek food but no olives. The owner smiled as I left: 'If you want olives, bring some next time from South Africa. But big tins, big tins, not small jars, eh?'

Glenda drove down from Lusaka to meet us in Kariba and show me her latest baby. She always got straight to the point: 'Hell, you've put on weight. Why are you wearing that *moffie* [homosexual] pink shirt? When are you getting married?' She winked at Sue. 'Give up, Glenda. You know I'm a professional bachelor. Besides, I've only known Sue a few weeks.'

I loafed around Kariba, which was still full of very old-fashioned colonial characters. Some seemed lively, while a few appeared to have had all their vital juices squeezed out of them. Slightly open-mouthed I sat in a pub listening to a very loud racist conversation that could have escaped from Karen Blixen's time: two farmers discussing the driving habits of *munts*, the traditional derogatory Rhodesian term for blacks.

'I wouldn't let one of my *munts* drive my Merc. Are you mad?'

'How come you trust a *munt* with your $150,000 tractor or your $300,000 Scania truck but not your $30,000 bashed-up old Merc?'

The next day Sue and I crossed the lake to Spurwing Island. We were put in a small bungalow where a few years before her close friends had been trampled to death by buffaloes. Not a good omen. I walked around to find Rob, the game ranger. 'Herpes is a good omen,' he said cheerily.

'I beg your pardon?'

'Herpes, there,' he said pointing. 'That giant hermon means good luck.' The handsome bird stood nonchalantly on the jetty.

I fished, canoed and drank. Mostly drank. The island was isolated and romantic. I felt lucky to be alive after the rigours of my recent adventures in Mozambique. I was in my favourite place in my favourite country. Over dinner I got drunk and proposed. I had done this one or twice before but luckily no one had ever taken me seriously. Sue said yes.

There were only eight people on the island and they were all in the little dining room. Rob thought an immediate wedding was a wonderful idea: it would be useful publicity for his safari camp. The rest was a haze. The next day I tried to suggest to Sue that perhaps a pause for thought might be a good idea. Didn't she want to have her friends at her wedding? But by this time Rob had organised a special licence with a magistrate.

We crossed the lake, drove for hours to Karoi and back with Mr Chigagora, a chubby, genial man. He had been a political commissar in

Mugabe's army and was now the local magistrate. He was most affable even when I mentioned the war.

By the time we reached the lake it was dark, and a storm was whipping up three-foot waves on the water. It was quite dangerous. I suggested we stay at a hotel on the water's edge. I was stalling. But Rob was keen to get back; his wife would be worried. On calm waters in daylight the trip took about 15 minutes. An hour later we were still on the lake. The engine packed in; somehow Rob restarted it. I sat on the prow trying with a torch to find our way around sand banks and the forest of petrified trees which rose from the water like shimmering ghostly scarecrows. The storm and rain grew worse, and the waves grew more robust. It was pitch black. Then we hit a sand bank and I jumped out to push the boat off.

'Get back. *Now,*' shouted Rob. I did, and a croc slithered across the bank from which I had just leaped. The magistrate seemed quite unperturbed, beyond sea-sickness, assuming that the two white men were experienced sailors who knew what they were doing. Rob and I knew that what we were doing was stupid.

In the maze of half-submerged forest we eventually spotted Rob's wife waving a lantern to guide us home. Aching all over from sitting on the buffeting prow, I dragged myself into the bar. I was in double shock from my recent and forthcoming traumas, and sank three beers straight off.

An hour later I was married, in the open air, surrounded by buffaloes and elephants. I had scrounged a pair of socks to go with my khaki shorts and borrowed a ring. The magistrate gave a wonderful little speech about this being 'God's own place'. I could hardly disagree with him.

When I got back to Johannesburg I rang my mother in Wales and described events. 'Where did you get all the animals from?'

'They're not from the zoo,' I said. 'They live there.'

I took my honeymoon on my own. I had booked a seat on the famous Blue Train six months before. It had been given to me as part of a journalism award and the next vacancy was six months hence. The wedding had been most dramatic and so, incidentally, was the divorce.

The lost legion

I visited Rhodesia just once more – in an English garden setting. It was July 1990 and I was covering the 100th anniversary of the foundation of Rhodesia for *The Guardian*. Some of the lost legion were celebrating with beer, troopie songs and a few words from Ian Smith.

West Lavington, a peaceful, pretty, Wiltshire village, was an unlikely place to celebrate a conflict in far-off Africa. But hundreds of ex-Rhodesians – they would never call themselves Zimbabweans – converged there to commemorate the pioneer column's erection of a flag in what became Salisbury. They also came to worship their old hero, Smithy.

The event was sponsored by Rhodesians Worldwide, an organisation which supports the white diaspora in 50 countries. Peter Hagelthorn, an administrator at a private school in West Lavington and editor of *Rhodesians Worldwide* magazine, supervised the gathering. Hagelthorn, a patently decent man, insisted that the organisation was for charity not politics, aiming to help Rhodesians settle in their new countries. Strict government controls meant many refugees left Zimbabwe with very little money; some were civilians, others soldiers wounded in the bush war. But this weekend was not a wake, it was to celebrate the good old days.

It was hot, as though the Zambezi sun was broiling the Wiltshire hay-fields. Initially the strangers looked like ordinary Englishmen. Soon, though, the colonial garb emerged – shorts, *veldskoens* without socks, T-shirts and (apparently) wartime crimplene for the old women. As they greeted old friends in their peculiar clipped accents, memories tumbled out of wild, wide spaces of Africa, Kariba and Inyanga. It was long gone, but one colonial-type commented to a man struggling to unload his car, 'Better get the boy to help you'. Life was easier with servants.

The school was bedecked with the green and white flags of the rebel republic. In essence, perhaps, the ex-Rhodies were celebrating their UDI against Britain, not the foundation of the colonial state. They had come from at least 11 countries but here, for one weekend, they could all be Rhodesians again. As one observer noted cynically: 'It's like being at a gay club outing with everyone rushing to leave the closet.' That was unfair: a macho, heterosexual culture so typical of war veterans and also the normality of colonial family life, with kids galore, were more obvious. The men drank Castles and Lions, South African beers brought in specially, while the women gossiped about life without maids and gardeners.

Although the men embroidered on their war stories or, more often, understated them, some of the memorabilia on sale provided a less heroic view of the fighting. The slogans on the T-shirts read 'Rhodesians – an endangered species?' and 'We didn't make it'. The most plaintive said 'Rhodesian war 1965/1980 – we came second'. A few die-hards still sported T-shirts about 'slotting gooks'. Only one black attended this *hooley* (party).

The Saturday night dinner dance was attended by about 500 people. John Edmonds flew from South Africa to sing troopie songs in Rhodesian English, *Chilapalapa* and Shona. They were given a rapturous reception by the exiles as they recalled the flat dogs, chasing *gandangas* (terrorists) while drinking *shumbas* (beers) and taking *muti* (medicine) for hang-overs.

Smithy's short speech got an even better reception, bordering on adulation. The irreconcilable old prophet was once more among his own people. He hadn't changed a jot; the same phrases as in 1965 but his audience hung on every word. Instead of deceased Rhodesia, South Africa was now the 'last bastion of Western civilisation on the African continent ... You may not agree with everything they do, but at least you know where you stand with them.'

The 71-year-old ex-premier, now grey and stooping, spoke about Zimbabwe with some caution. He had often been rapped over the knuckles by Mugabe's men for speaking out of turn while travelling abroad. Smith had always said what he thought. Few doubted his courage, even while damning his bigotry. 'Things are not so good back home now, I must tell you ... when you scratch beneath the surface.' He cited the Willowgate government corruption scandal. 'Many black people have had enough,' he claimed. 'They say it was better in the old days and that "This is not what we fought the war for".' This was an interesting variation on Smithy's evergreen of 'We have the happiest Africans in the world'.

Smith told his adoring audience that the anniversary celebrations in South Africa were being organised around a Rhodesian flag-raising ceremony north of Messina, overlooking the border with Zimbabwe. This taunt brought a volcano of applause. 'You can't keep Rhodesians down wherever they are,' their leader concluded.

Amid the triumphalism no mention was made of the tens of thousands who were killed in the war. Yet I could see but not understand why 75 per cent of the whites kept backing Smith. Like Margaret Thatcher, he was a conviction politician. Charismatic without a discernible trace of personal charisma, yet people believed what he said because he was so patently sincere.

The evening ended with the most painful rendition of 'God Save the Queen' in the history of the empire. 'What do you expect from the rebels against the Crown?' muttered my cynical companion.

On Sunday there was the inevitable *braai*. The sun shone again as in the 'old country'. The pinched, sundried, prune faces of the old women contrasted with the healthy, tattooed, tanned bodies of the young ex-warriors, who performed various eccentric regimental rites. Edmonds sang again. Smith told his people that they should not mind being called 'When wes' (When we were in Rhodesia ... or Kenya). 'We should be proud of being this small group of people with the finest spirit this world has ever known.'

Rhodesians managed to defy the world partly because they were so well-organised. Ladies rushed around with black plastic bags clearing up the rubbish of more than 1,000 people at the *braai*. 'Rhodesians are a tidy people,' one said. A people? The last white tribe? A nation? Or a racist suburb masquerading as a country? The (fortunately) inimitable Rhodesian foreign minister, P K van der Byl, once said that the Battle of Britain spirit had not evaporated; it had migrated to Rhodesia.

All that remains of Rhodesia now are memories, a large supply of cripples and a breed of dog, the Rhodesian Ridgeback, many of which were in evidence in West Lavington that weekend.

8

South Africa – the endgame

Crossing the Rubicon

In 1984 the Orwellian nightmare began to assume a tangible form in South Africa: from the blasphemy of the 'necklace' (a burning, petrol-filled tyre around the neck of an alleged collaborator) to the frenzied doublespeak of government propaganda. At the beginning of that ominous year the armed struggle was just over 22 years old. ANC guerrillas had proved remarkably inept, even by African standards. White power looked more entrenched than ever. From the Sharpeville massacre to the June Soweto uprising 16 years had elapsed. On the cusp of each crisis capital and whites had fled. They had panicked but the security forces had not. Each wave of resistance was absorbed, diluted, pushed back, pumped underground. From Soweto the cycle of revolt had been reduced to eight years. But there was no ANC master plan: the exiled leadership in Lusaka was always slow in keeping up with, let alone controlling, events forged in the crucible of black anger in the townships. From 1984-86 blacks in both urban areas and countryside would rise up once more, hyped by foreign media as the beginning of another 1917. It was not to be.

For the first half of 1984 P W Botha's imperial presidency was riding high. He had humbled Marxist Mozambique into signing a peace agreement, and won a referendum at home to proceed with his new 'dispensation', the tricameral parliament for whites, Indians and coloureds. There was precious little wrong with the old Westminster system: perhaps all it needed was the extension of the franchise, equally, to blacks. As with Hitler in 1933, Botha gathered up the business community in his drive against the Bolshevik menace. After all, this was 'a step in the right direction'. It was not – it was a declaration of war on 75 per cent of the population, who were arrogantly excluded from the new system.

The 'unrest', in Pretoria's parlance, began to snowball. The cycle of insurrection fed on itself as one area emulated the tactics of another. It

Southern Africa

was all recorded, faithfully and otherwise, on TV – thus stimulating further pressure, especially from the USA. There Bishop Tutu whipped up the sometimes prefabricated moral fervour of the chattering classes. American pressures on South Africa duly encouraged the 'young lions' in the townships. The South African government believed that TV cameras, ravenous for blood and guts, sometimes created rather than merely recorded the grim events. Pretoria's almost total ban on non-SATV coverage of the unrest was thus unsurprising; more remarkable was the year or so it took to implement. It was a cynical gesture which seemed to work. Perhaps Pretoria had adequately sized up the attention span of Joe Public in America. But in 1985 being an anti-apartheid groupie was the moral fad in the USA. Even Ronald Reagan noticed.

The vicious pantomime of death was endlessly recycled – boycotts, stay-aways, rent-strikes, demonstrations, riots, police retaliation or provocation, single shots, tear-gas, panic, confusion, concentrated automatic fire … funerals and more funerals. At the burial services – one of the few legal outlets for the outpouring of political and personal grief (before funerals were also restricted) – ANC and Russians flags were openly displayed, along with wooden replicas of AKs. The cutting edge of the insurrection was arson and murder of suspected informers, black councillors and policemen, perceived to be the main, and available, local representatives of apartheid. The 'necklace' became a trade mark of the young comrades in their war on collaborators. In the compressed, often breathless, reportage on TV screens in Europe and America, South Africa was going up in flames. In contrast, little of the violence, except the occasional necklacing to emphasise black barbarity, was shown on SATV.

I attended a meeting of 'concerned citizens' in Johannesburg city hall, sitting by chance next to Harry Oppenheimer, the richest man in South Africa. We exchanged a few pleasantries and I looked around for any heavies minding the ageing boss of Anglo-American. There were none that I could see. Crazy violence was everywhere in South Africa but he couldn't have gone solo like this in the US. Worthies such as Beyers Naudé and Helen Suzman sat alongside empty chairs for proscribed organisations. Suzman claimed that if only the locals could see just a little of the barbarous police behaviour shown on foreign networks, 'tens of thousands of decent white South Africans' would raise their voices in protest.

I wasn't so sure. Some whites wouldn't believe the pics if they saw them. One of Pretoria's prime weapons against its own electorate was ignorance. Blacks in the closely-knit townships relied upon a very effective news grapevine; whites had a less effective gossip machine which, in the twilight world of censorship, produced epidemics of alarmist rumour-mongering and the conditioning of Huxley's *Brave New World*. For blacks the regime's aim, if not the result, was intimidation along the lines, though not the extent, of Orwell's *1984*. It was ironic that, as in Rhodesia, government propaganda was internalised by the whites but usually scoffed at by blacks, presumably the most important target. The Angolan war, with real-live Cubans and Russians involved and captured, added flesh to the abstraction of a communist onslaught. But for years Pretoria had whipped up a less tangible, groundless paranoia.

South Africa's 'alternative' press, like the *Weekly Mail*, and sometimes the more establishment-oriented English-language papers such as the *Star*, the *Cape Times* and Ken Owen's blistering editorial and columns in the *Business Day*, played Russian roulette with the censorship laws. According to opinion polls most whites relied upon, and trusted, SATV for their news information; but only bits of truth escaped the mindless censorship of local television. Liberals beat their breasts or emigrated, while the silent majority of whites adopted hard-line stances on security. As one Afrikaner farmer's wife said: 'We will never give up. We will fight to the last Afrikaner. We did not accept English rule and we will never accept Bantu rule. We don't mind sanctions. We will go back to ox-wagons if they cut off our petrol.' Another woman, from a Jewish, liberal, business background, was ruthlessly candid: 'Let's be completely logical. We can hand over peacefully now, fight and lose, or we kill the lot of them.'

On 21 July 1985 Botha declared a state of emergency in some areas, the first in 25 years. The security forces already possessed extensive powers of arrest and detention, exempting them from potential prosecution for any act carried out in 'good faith'. To the comrades, this seemed a licence to kill. By the end of the year over 1,000 blacks had indeed been killed, many by police action. Over 7,000 people had been detained, usually without trial.

On 31 July 1985 William Butcher, the conservative chairman of Chase Manhattan, refused to roll over further loans to South African borrowers. The republic's most serious financial crisis ensued. Despite its fundamentally sound economy, Pretoria's credit rating was now lower than even chronically mismanaged Zaire. To restore confidence government officials hinted strongly that the president would deliver an epoch-making speech at the National Party congress in Durban on 15 August. As the crisis mounted, so did the expectation that P W Botha would finally break the political deadlock. The least that was expected was the freeing of Mandela. It was billed as the Rubicon speech.

Jenny, my Australian girlfriend, and I watched the televised version of the speech with growing amazement, then disappointment, and finally cold rage. P W dug in his Achilles' heel. During a bleak performance watched on TV around the globe, Botha wagged his finger and contemptuously dismissed his critics. He offered little beyond threats. Some of his backwoods Afrikaner faithful might have shivered with wicked delight when their man once more gave two fingers to the world, but the Rubicon fiasco finally switched off the English-speaking business magnates in South Africa. The influential *Business Day* called the president a 'hick politician'. Not only was the content diabolical but so was the exaggerated and bellicose presentation. The mannerisms were like Botha's renowned impersonator, Pieter-Dirk Uys: the president stuck out his jaw while uttering tired clichés, with an occasional flash of lunacy in his eyes as he shouted arrogantly. Botha was obviously totally oblivious to the PR disaster he was inflicting on his country.

'I am too embarrassed to live in a country which is ruled by such people,' Jenny said. I agreed, and we both made plans to leave. Botha's speech was the final straw after ten years of watching racist *folie de grandeur.* But what really did it for me was a conversation an hour after the speech with some top SATV officials, who told me how wonderful they thought P W's performance was. I searched in vain for a hint of irony. It was hopeless.

Money talks loudest: the rand fell to an all-time low against the dollar. Foreign investors deserted in droves. With a performance like Botha's Rubicon, market-led sanctions became much more important than official government-sponsored pressures. Once again, Pretoria had shot itself in both feet. Desperate top white businessmen started to talk officially to the ANC in Zambia.

Pretoria blamed nearly all the violence on the ANC, and more particularly the South African Communist Party. The ANC had not instigated the revolt that began in 1984, and was taken by surprise by its outbreak and enduring scale. And the SACP was an important restraint on the *Umkhonto*, the ANC's military wing, which wanted to hit soft white targets. In June 1985, however, the ANC adopted a strategy of 'people's war', intended to take the struggle into the comfortable and almost untouched white suburbs.

Botha would not talk to ANC 'terrorists' and looked for elusive 'moderates'. No one stepped forward, not even Buthelezi, who insisted that Mandela's freedom was a precondition for serious talks. The roller-coaster of often savage repression and occasional wilted carrots of reform had become mutually exclusive. As veteran journalist Stanley Uys noted: 'Botha's reformism in South Africa today is like a lift going up in a building that is coming down.'

The major reform of 1986 was the scrapping of the hated pass laws and influx controls. More than 18 million Africans had been arrested for infringing these laws. In March 1986 the partial state of emergency was lifted. The violence was endemic but appearances mattered: keep the violence off foreign TVs, tell them apartheid is dead often enough, play with doublespeak at home, rule by loud semantics and the quiet sword. The ending of pass laws was a real reform, but Chris Heunis, the minister in change of constitutional change, obfuscated the central issue of political power for blacks. He babbled in Pretoria-speak. The legislation in question had been passed as 'The *Abolition* of Passes and Coordination of Documents Act', but actually *tightened* up pass laws. The classic was 'The *Extension* of University Education Act', which forced established universities to kick out blacks. Heunis made incoherency into an art form.

The comrades struggled to make South Africa ungovernable. 'People's courts' were set up to establish their often arbitrary rule. Sometimes adults were terrorised by bands of feral youngsters, especially for breaking consumer boycotts. Often victims were forced to consume all their 'illegal' purchases on the spot, sometimes fatally in the case of cooking oil, washing powder, soap and paraffin. Parents grew frustrated with the long school boycotts and self-defeating demands for 'liberation before education'. During 1986 the liberation mania began to dissipate. After two years the severity of the repression, sheer physical exhaustion, and frustration with the excesses of both disciplined comrades and roving bands of *tsotsis* and psychopathic elements had taken their toll. Chaos in the townships was not the same as people's power.

But black–white polarisation escalated. In June 1986 George De'Ath, a freelance cameraman working for the BBC, died from head wounds received from axes and pangas deployed in the fighting between *witdoeke* vigilantes, the police and the comrades in Cape Town. He was the first foreign correspondent to be killed while covering the civil war. The Cape *Argus* newspaper described the mood in the black communities: 'You can reach out in front of you...clench your fist and squeeze fear out of the air.'

In June 1986 the state of emergency, lifted in March, was reimposed. By the end of 1986 more than 23,000 people, including 9,000 children, had been jailed under the June decrees. The South African Defence Force smashed the pretensions of the liberated zones in the townships. Pretoria was back in charge. The details of the crackdown could not be analysed adequately because of the total ban on all but official reports of black unrest. The ludicrous, but powerful, Bureau of Information handed out leaden lumps of newspeak. At daily briefings in Pretoria, Brigadier Leon Mellet (a former journalist) told pressmen what the government thought they should know about the insurrection. The police brigadier insisted on being called 'Mr' Mellet, in case anyone should think the police were running the country.

Jenny's cousin came over from Australia. He was a fire chief in Perth, not one of nature's radicals. In a Melville restaurant, over sensual local wines, he said: 'I love the countryside but socially the place is like a prison. And those bars,' pointing to bars on all the restaurant windows. 'I don't feel they're keeping the other fellow out but me in. I feel caged.'

South Africa's main trading partners were lining up against her. The logical, economic arguments against sanctions, and there were many, no longer mattered. Imposing sanctions was a question of standing on the side of the angels; you were either for or against apartheid. The tide of opinion swept up even stonewallers like Reagan and Thatcher. I asked the boss of a once highly profitable small business how things were. 'Oh, wrist-slashingly normal,' he sighed.

Despite the military defeat of the comrades, a psychological corner had been turned. It would take time, but belief in ultimate victory had been implanted in the popular psyche. The Great Crocodile led his followers into the May 1987 election with all his customary Teutonic charm. The emasculation of the liberal opposition and the increase in seats of the right-wing Conservative Party – the first time since 1948 that the official opposition had been on the right – indicated that the voters, especially English-speakers, had moved to the right, attracted by the security ticket. With this new reliance on English-speakers, the Nats probably no longer represented even the majority of the Afrikaners. Botha now led a minority of a minority tribe.

The wind-down of the unrest brought renewed confidence to the whites. Except for the liberal minority, South African whites seem naturally (or desperately) inclined to be optimistic. Their peculiar political environment demanded constant psychological reassurance. 'There's nothing wrong with us, the world just doesn't *understand* us.' Hence the importance of rebel sports tours and bimbo starlets. Few people bothered to pay to watch them perform but that didn't matter. The important thing was that foreigners 'come to see for themselves'. Township violence was off the world's TV. Tourists started to trickle back, as did a handful of the whites who had taken the 'chicken run' to Australia and Britain.

The ANC kept up its bombing campaign. In July 1987, 68 people were injured in a bomb attack in central Jo'burg. As long as the ANC waged war and the white right wing bayed for tougher action, Botha found it difficult to move ahead with his stalled, if not moribund, reform programme. The rise of the Afrikaner Resistance Movement, the AWB, mesmerised Pretoria. Pretoria hoped that given enough rope the AWB leader Eugene Terreblanche, a spell-binding orator, might hang himself.

In April 1987 I attended an AWB mass rally in Jo'burg city hall. I was chilled to my marrow ... and, sitting at the front-row press table, covered in Terreblanche's spittle. In an action replay of 1930s' Germany, long swastika banners adorned the hall, jackbooted storm-troopers raised a Hitler salute, little blond children waved flags and powerful rhetoric raged against liberals and communists, anyone who questioned the Afrikaners' divine right to rule. The gleam in the eyes of the wildly enthusiastic audience boded ill for the future. After a series of antics, including a well-publicised dalliance with an English liberal ex-beauty-queen-turned-journalist, and the habit of falling off his horse in public, Terreblanche became a music hall Hitler for some. For a while. The conspicuously armed right wing grew, so did underground cells. Terreblanche, the dark messiah, bided his time.

In 1989 President Botha, enfeebled by a stroke, had reached a political dead end: Rubicon, the curt dismissal of a Commonwealth peace mission, and the public humiliation of his coloured and Indian allies lit up his tricameral parliament as a ship of fools. His successor was F W de Klerk, a brighter and more sophisticated figure. But the political log-jam remained: no credible black leader could talk to Pretoria until the ANC was legitimised.

P W Botha had once warned that the whites had to 'adapt or die'. Pieter-Dirk Uys responded: 'People have adapted a little...and died a lot. And we have swapped a laager for a bunker.' On 2 February 1990 de Klerk finally dragged his party out of the bunker and across the Rubicon. The ANC and the Pan-Africanist Congress were unbanned. On 11 February Nelson Mandela was finally freed after 27 years in jail. De Klerk and Mandela haggled long and dangerously over the details of a transitional government and the elections scheduled for April 1994.

I didn't see the whole endgame. I had stopped presenting on local TV, although I sold occasional anonymous films. I had opposed sanctions in Rhodesia because of the massive pious hypocrisy oozing from the sanctioneers, and had a certain sympathy and occasional involvement with the swashbuckling sanctions-busters. But in South Africa I thought sanctions might save lives by bringing the Afrikaner government to its knees, or senses, that little bit earlier. My own small business ventures suffered – for example because of the extra costs of film. Non-comprehensive sanctions prolonged the war in Rhodesia but shortened it, I believe, in South Africa.

And I was angry in a way that I hadn't been in Rhodesia. I became aggressively argumentative at dinner parties, wanting to shake people by the throat and make them see sense. It was bad journalism. I had become a talker not a listener. In late 1986 Jenny went to study at Cambridge. It was time for my dog and me to leave, too. Little things in the last few months confirmed my decision. Partly it was the crime. A shot went off nearby and some of my friends drew guns in a Hillbrow restaurant as though it was the Wild West. Jane, a dashing extrovert, pitched up at my house and insisted on showing me her new derringer and garter holster.

A hundred yards from my house I saw two coloureds kicking a black holding two apples, who was lying semi-conscious on the pavement. It was outside a grocery shop but I had no idea whether the prone figure was a thief or not. Whatever the cause, I feel you shouldn't kick a man when he's down. Armed only with a squash racket – I was on my way to my squash club – I managed to persuade the attackers to desist and told the dazed black to run away if he could. Just as I was helping him up, two burly, scruffy whites started shouting at me in Afrikaans. One drew a gun and pointed it at the black while the other kicked him in the head. I told them to back off, advancing on two armed white men wielding a squash racket. If I had thought about it, I wouldn't have been so damn stupid. But I was indignant and white enough to persuade the assailants to desist. They drove off cursing me in Afrikaans. The black man disappeared, seemingly unfazed by it all; perhaps he was in a state of shock or drunk. Five minutes later a group of black and white children was playing soccer on the same spot. Nearby an elderly white woman asked me to sign a petition to get a police station in Melville. Yes, crime was bad, I agreed. 'Trouble is,' she said, 'the police have been told to treat the natives like porcelain.'

In my last week in South Africa, May 1987, I revisited my old campus at Wits and stumbled on a student protest and riot police charge. I knew enough to decide where to stand – behind the police lines and a little to the side, downwind. I followed the line as it charged, whipped and launched tear-gas grenades. When I stopped to help a student – who was not part of the protest but had accidentally walked into it – I, too, was gassed. In a confined space you have to vomit immediately; in the open you can get away with feeling nauseous and headachy, especially if you put a wet handkerchief over your face early enough.

As I was packing up the house, a coloured knocked on my door and said he was canvassing for the National Party. 'I support the ANC,' I said briskly (and illegally).

'Right on brother, so do I.'

'But why are you canvassing for the Nats?'

'Agh, man, I needed a job.' He pushed a leaflet into my hand and walked out of my gate. South Africa was a funny place. I left Melville with sadness, but Johannesburg with relief. I was going to write in Spain.

A year or so after Mandela was released I thought that sanctions should end. Apartheid had been totally and irreversibly scrapped. De Klerk had shown courage and gone the whole way, unlike that other reforming lawyer, Gorbachev. I did worry about the increasingly dangerous right wing and its alliance with Inkatha. South Africa needed help quickly. After 40 years of anti-apartheid campaigning, a host of vested interests had mushroomed. Sanctions were almost the *raison d'être* of the Commonwealth and thousands of anti-apartheid groups in Europe and America. For too long, belief in sanctions had been seen as a litmus test of morality. To borrow Desmond Tutu's phrase, ending sanctions – except on arms – had been enveloped in 'moral humbug'. It took nearly two centuries for the American constitution to reach the black underclass. South Africa looked like it had a few years before it exploded – unless economic and political conditions improved rapidly. Sanctions withered, de Klerk and Mandela maintained an uneasy rapport, and the killings went on.

The international media were less interested now, unless there was a big massacre, preferably involving whites. The Inkatha/PAC/ANC conflicts were 'black-on-black', too confusing to explain to America. But calling Inkatha versus ANC 'black-on-black' was about as helpful as describing the Second World War as white-on-white.

South Africa is a microcosm of every conflict known to man: black versus white, terrorism versus militarism, socialism versus capitalism, tribalism versus nationalism, federalism versus centralism, group identity versus individual rights... And the proffered solutions varied: state socialism for the Afrikaners, capitalism for the English and Indians, booze for the coloureds, and fascism for the blacks. If the constitutional issues are ever properly resolved, the real post-bellum problems will start: land and wealth redistribution, nationalisation, education, mass unemployment, AIDS, drought, soil erosion, overpopulation... The bitter anti-apartheid campaigns were rich in slogans but poor in offering solutions.

Much of the rest of Africa had slid off the political and economic maps. Once attractive capital cities looked like they had been carpet-bombed. Parts of former Portuguese Africa had reverted almost to the Stone Age. Now Mozambique was trying to woo back Portuguese businessmen. Zambia was desperately trying to persuade white farmers from Zimbabwe and South Africa to travel north to restore agriculture in that fertile land. Africa had already been recolonised partly by the World Bank and the International Monetary Fund.

Some liberal African experts were talking of formally recolonising areas such as Somalia or Mozambique, where government had effectively collapsed. Schemes would be set up to seduce back ex-colonial powers and settlers who knew Africa and could speak the local languages. Many would go back armed with external financial guarantees. Such schemes would of course have to adopt a politically correct name, say 'government restructuring'. They would operate under the UN, supported by the EC's former colonial states and, once some order had been restored, with the popular consent of the African people expressed in a referendum. After all, black Africa had been nagging the world for decades to enforce one person, one vote in South Africa. Now they could start introducing it into their own countries. While the vast majority of African politicians who have specialised in ripping off their own subjects and banking foreign aid money in Switzerland could be expected to howl, millions of African peasants would undoubtedly welcome the return of the colonial powers. 'When will independence end, boss?' has a core of truth.

Such a solution is unlikely. Africans could rightly point out that Austria or Turkey would be better advised to recolonise the Balkans. But Africa is dying, Europe (outside Bosnia) is not. The colonial era might come to be regarded as the zenith of African development. (It was also responsible for the crazy patchwork quilt of colonial boundaries which sliced through tribes and geographical logic. Many of Africa's territorial wars could be ended if the sacred cow of maintaining artificial imperial borders was sacrificed.) If the whites return they may be able to rebuild roads, hospitals, schools and clinics. And they could earn the plaudits of the Greens by perhaps saving what remains of the big game. So long as whites can survive in black-ruled South Africa (or 'Azania'), the new state could become the breadbasket of Africa, not another basketcase; the engine for continental renaissance, not its holocaust.

South Africa was a difficult conflict to cover. Some journalists felt it was a special case, apartheid a special evil. After witnessing a massacre or two it was easy to take sides. No wonder Pretoria accused foreign journalists of incitement. Afrikaners said that many overseas hacks had a Jericho complex: one more blow or one more trumpet and the whole edifice would implode. Most journalists did not crusade against Pretoria. Nevertheless the vast majority, even the crusty old Africa hands, were frequently appalled by Pretoria's ham-fisted manipulation of the media.

It was always difficult in Africa to balance moral convictions with professional standards. Just giving a rough balance, say 50 per cent blame to Mugabe and 50 per cent to Smith, sometimes created a legitimacy by default. Maybe Smith didn't deserve 50 per cent of the moral argument. Yet it was better to make this kind of mistake than give in to advocacy journalism and crusade against apartheid. I certainly felt like putting on shining armour at times. But – to mix metaphors – it was the thin edge of the wedge. Once you started accepting apartheid as a special case, where did you stop? Haiti? The Khmer Rouge? You could make the argument for a whole series of special cases. Professional detachment is blown out of the water. It is like a doctor refusing to treat, say, Saddam Hussein, or Richard Nixon, or the Yorkshire Ripper.

Those journalists who took up cudgels for the ANC should remember that revolutions tend to devour their own children. Are partisan journalists prepared to stay in South Africa and accept personal responsibility for what follows? The Shah gave way to the Ayatollah, Obote to Amin. Were conditions better after those revolutions? Mandela became a secular saint but what happens if he plays Kerensky to a despot? Should we judge Africa by Western standards? Or should we patronisingly make allowances? Who should decide what these universal standards are? I do not know the answers. In my experience, independence in most African countries seemed to mean a lot less press and personal freedoms and, more importantly, less food. But what do I know? I'm only a white man.

Spain and Gibraltar

9

Gibraltar – Europe's last colony

The paper war

Paper clips can be more injurious to your health than bullets. That was my experience of Spain's bureaucratic Leviathan. Give me Russian gunships any day over a semi-literate Spaniard on the make – but I don't want to appear too obvious in my Hispanophobia. Great for holidays or retirement – provided you weren't sick – but you had to be criminally insane to try to work there. I lived there for exactly three years, seven days and 11 hours, for most of which I subsisted without a phone. For a journalist that's like losing a limb. I also gained an appendage: a mother-in-law, who bought a house next door. My *madre politica*, to use the Spanish phrase, was kind to my dog, tough and omnipresent. So some of the arguments I had with Spain were problems with me. Temporarily, I was trapped between family pressures and an Everest of forms.

I lived near Altea, on the Costa Blanca. The colours and light in the old town could produce an instant orgasm for artists and photographers. But nearby loomed the breezeblock paradises of expatriate ghettoes where Scouses and Brummies pursued the English dream – a house with more bathrooms than people – or at least *a* bathroom. Altea was beautifully old and shockingly new. That was Spain all over; so many different styles, peoples and languages. To define Spain as one country is to call the Equator a town.

When I lived there all the talk was of 1992. The year of the Seville Expo, the 500th anniversary of the Italian Columbus's first voyage to the New World, the summer Olympics in Barcelona and, perhaps most important, full membership of the EC. Personally I think Spain should have joined not the EC but the Organisation of African Unity. Provided there were no organisational disasters, the year would be billed as a triumphal symbol of the end of centuries of Spain being cold-shouldered by the rest of Europe. But there was always potential for mayhem, induced by the volatile Iberian mix of incompetence and overconfidence. A million-dollar reproduction of the first Spanish ship to circumnavigate the globe was launched in 1991 amid massive publicity. It sank in 20 minutes. You could almost hear a collective groan from the thousands of Columbus statues dotted around the country.

Spain's dark history intruded upon the glitzy dash for modernity; 1992 was also the 500th anniversary of the expulsion of the Jews and Arabs from a country which launched the terrors of the Inquisition. Similar terrors were inflicted in the 1980s on foreigners, who queued for years for endless permits. There was a technical requirement, presumably never observed, for permits to wallpaper your own house. Beleaguered foreign residents hoped 1992 was the beginning of the end of a system which regulated everything except farts.

Altea was one of the last areas to fall to Franco in the civil war, so the local council had a strange complexion: 1930s' Popular Front socialists, anarcho-syndicalists, peasant Marxists with a soft spot for Stalin, and a sprinkling of Valenciano nationalists. The council decreed that the union leader who ran the main post office should refuse to sell stamps. He despised foreigners anyway, especially the 99 per cent who couldn't speak fluent Valenciano, and used an electronic random selector to calculate prices for those who couldn't count in his native tongue. Tobacconists were given the monopoly on selling stamps, although they had trouble prising any out of Madrid. I suppose the millions of tourists were expected to take their postcards home with them. That was a lot safer than risking the Spanish unroyal mail, even if stamps could somehow be purchased: some letters were fed to goats or used to fill potholes.

The communications 'system' was particularly irksome at a time when I was trying to send five copies of an academic thesis to South Africa. I completed it with great difficulty: floods (temporarily) wiped out the roads and the remnants of the postal system; electricity surges or no electricity at all played havoc with my computer. Without a phone I resorted to using the fax at the South African embassy in Madrid, 12 hours' drive away, to communicate with a university professor in Pretoria. The embassy appeared to think I was involved in some arcane sanctions-busting, because the professor was also a colonel. I didn't disabuse them. Eventually the thesis was finished and I looked for a bookbinder. I found Moscow Printers, a Marxist co-operative in Alicante. The chief binder spoke English and objected to working on something which would be sent to South Africa. I showed him sections which attacked apartheid, at which he reduced the price. He reduced it further when he printed the title upside down. (Spain seems to be the only country in Europe which prints the titles on book spines upside down as a matter of tradition.) Then I had to find the sole rapid photo-copying machine in town, operated by a *pied noir* Algerian who gave me a discount because I listened to his anti-communist ravings in a nearby bar. We toasted Generals Salan, Challe, Zeller and Jouhaud separately and collectively. I hadn't realised the French army's botched coup in Algiers had been so much fun.

Leaving the bar I ran into a *Guardia Civil* road-block. What is it about me and road-blocks? Uzi at my head, I was dragged out. Since I was unshaven, portly, swarthy, moustached and smelt of garlic and booze they spoke to me in Valenciano. Foolishly I replied in Castiliano, standard Spanish – but my Spanish was not up to anyone's standards. In the panic I muddled genders and said: 'My wife is next door. He speaks perfect Spanish.' A drunken poof trying to pass as a noble Valencian. They didn't like me. They told me to get back in my car and follow them to the police station. I turned left as they went right. I suppose foreigners usually went quietly to the *Guardia* shop because they had such a fearsome reputation. I wasn't being a tough war correspondent. In my confusion I simply took the wrong turn.

The next day, with my bound thesis, I sought a courier company. Their politics were not apparent but they invented every excuse under the Spanish sun not to send a parcel to the world's polecat. In the end I flew to London and used a courier at Heathrow. I exaggerate but slightly.

I do not exaggerate at all my surprise at how many unreconstructed Nazis I met in Spain. One or two were old SS men in retirement, but even younger Germans seemed reluctant to accept any responsibility for the Holocaust. Nearly every German I met said the genocide of the Jews had been grossly exaggerated or completely invented. As both Sue and I spoke German we were sometimes invited to German dinner parties. Sue always gave me the John Cleese line: 'Don't mention the war', but it inevitably came up when people asked about my war reporting. At one party two German army officers treated me to a highly intelligent if historically bogus version of the extermination of the Jews.

The one German I met who was politically correct on the genocide was a doctor. I asked him what his speciality was. 'I am a medical doctor but working in research.'

'What research?'

'On pain thresholds.'

With all the crooks, red tape and roaring Nazis, I wondered about the 'new' democracy, thinking Spain was not ready for Europe *sans frontières*. Cynics said Spain was not ready for the twentieth century, let alone 1992. Some parts of the country were on the move, however. *La movida* was true of Madrid, where everything except traffic moved quickly. It was an elegant, sophisticated city but its outskirts were afflicted by shanty-towns. Spain was full of such contradictions, always ready to confirm or confound every cliché.

It was third and first world at the same time, both a 'fragment nipped off hot Africa', as Auden called it, and the most European of all EC states. It was collectivist but attractively individualistic. Even anarchy was too organised for most Spaniards. You could see that in their homicidal driving, madcap parking, compulsive littering, and sheer delight in chain-smoking in very confined public spaces such as lifts. Tax evasion was a national passion, along with gambling. *Mañana* sleepiness held everything up but visitors always asked, paradoxically, 'When do Spaniards sleep?', because they caroused so late, so often and so noisily. It was a country dedicated to the worship of the Virgin Mary, but whores outnumbered nuns by six to one.

The contradictions, inherited from an often humiliating past, were reinforced by sudden, recent democratisation and the resulting swings of the moral pendulum. Spain revelled in, or raged against, the new-found freedoms. It became legal to smoke dope. Almost naked Spanish girls relaxed on the beaches where their mothers would have walked well-covered, accompanied perhaps by chaperones. Imperial isolationism was also to blame. Like Britain, the Spanish often referred to 'Europe' as though it were somewhere else. Both nations ran empires in which they expected everyone to learn *their* language.

To the fascist right, especially during the 39 years of Franco's dictatorship, 'Europe' was a dirty word representing heresy, immorality and liberalism. To the left, 'European' was interchangeable with 'open-minded'. After 1975 democracy brought political freedom and economic advance – but EC membership in 1986 also threatened the feudal business monopolies and xenophobic bureaucracy. Some economic reforms predated the constitutional monarchy of King Juan Carlos: Franco's reactionary government presided over the most far-reaching economic and social changes – partly induced by the tourist boom – since the Catholics drove out the Moors. The 1980s tourist bonanza also accompanied a big increase in drugs, crime, political corruption and pollution.

The most centralised state in Europe mushroomed into a quasi-federation of 17 autonomous regions, each with its own flag and capital, and in some cases its own language. The most bloody- and independent-minded were the unruly Basques, my favourite 'Spaniards'. I also liked Barcelona, capital of Catalonia. Ever since the wonderfully named William the Shaggy made the title Count of Barcelona hereditary in the ninth century, Catalans had exhibited a fierce sense of independence. Barcelona was the most fashionable and go-ahead city in Spain. Even the phones and lifts worked. The cuisine was excellent, and the local champagne, *Cava*, compared well with the original, despite what the petulant French said. Barcelona was an arty place, forever associated with such names as Picasso, Salvador Dalí and, above all, Antonio Gaudí, whose brooding genius was best exemplified by the Sagrada Familia cathedral.

Sun, sea and sand, not culture, attracted 53 million visitors per annum, more than the 38 million inhabitants. Roughly seven million of the invaders were British. Benidorm was the capital of the coastal culture-free zone. With justification, many Spaniards described these Brits as *animales*. Every year Benidorm, which had more hotel beds than the whole of North Africa, expected the worst, and was not usually disappointed. Not surprisingly, Spaniards applauded their king when he said that the tourist industry should move up-market. Cut back on Brits, whom the Spanish seemed to dislike far more than their old fascist allies from Germany and Italy. Recession in the UK, and in Spain the over-valued peseta, air traffic congestion and strikes, tawdry hotels, dirty beaches and inflation, reduced the number of low-spending bucket-and-spades brigades.

Many working-class Brits sold their semis in London and bought Spanish villas with pools. Despite the English bread, bars, video shops and newspapers, the Costas were not Brighton or Blackpool with more sun. It was a different country with a different language few ex-pats bothered to learn. Usually they were not allowed to work. Spain's unemployment rate was touching 20 per cent, the EC's highest, although many of the 'jobless' worked in the black economy. Welfare benefits were the lowest in Western Europe. And the country was haunted by its poor infra-structure: bad roads, medieval postal service, disorganised health, legal and educational systems, and my *bête noire* – the suffocating amounts of red tape.

For the tens of thousands of voteless, tax-abused foreign residents in Spain 1992 would not bring relief from permit-mania. As John de Zuleuta Greenbaum, one of Madrid's most successful businessmen, told me: 'Spain wanted to be isolated. It was self-imposed. 1992 will happen, but not in 1992.' I spoke to John Hooper, a British correspondent and author of the best-selling book, *The Spaniards*. He argued that the Spanish economy probably couldn't cope with the supposed free movement of goods, capital and jobs. 'The Spanish tend to regard 1992 as an *event*, like the 500th anniversary of Columbus, not a *process*, which involves hard work and sacrifice, such as giving up three-hour lunches.' Another Hispanophile author, Tom Burns, added: 'There is a touching idea that Europe will somehow have Spaniards form queues, put their litter in waste-paper bins and cease smoking in public places.'

Spaniards were proud that their country had returned to the main-stream of European life. The socialist government led by Felipe González had dragged his fellow countrymen into a new era. From a low base the economy had begun to catch up with its northern neighbours, but endemic paranoia about foreign competition produced an habitual hostility to competition at all levels. In their minds and hearts many Spaniards longed for the cloistered certainties of Franco. Such atavism meant that Spain, away from the coasts and big cities, displayed a primitive refinement. The castles, tiny villages and vast open spaces often recalled Europe of the Middle Ages. Spain was like a massive Hollywood set: behind the modern facade lurked a backward, traditional society.

Spain had flair and style, leading Europe in fashion and design. Spaniards wore or drove their new-found wealth. As José Ortega y Gasset, the country's greatest modern philosopher, noted: 'Spain has an absolute genius for art and absolutely no talent for economics.' From my perspective, Spain was committing economic suicide in keeping out foreign professionals who could help to rationalise the cumbersome systems in preparation for the big bang of 1992 and 1993. From one-man bands to big business it was made almost impossible to circumnavigate the permit system – legally.

Part of the problem was the *gestors*, legal middle-men unique to Spain and her corrupt ex-dominions in South America. They were a throwback to the days when illiterate peasants had to employ educated professionals to deal with the state. This applied even to driving licences late into the 1980s. The *gestors* had a vested interest in keeping the bureaucracy as complicated and corrupt as possible. And everyone from sanitary inspectors to estate agents formed guilds to use the permit system to keep out foreign competition. Spain had become one huge closed-shop union, even more bloody-minded than the most predatory of print unions in the old Fleet Street.

In the three years I lived in Spain I failed to get a permit to reside, work or even legally import furniture into the house I shared with Susan and her daughter Laura. Gelert, my dog, managed to avoid the paper blitzkrieg. Sue, a fluent Spanish-speaker and erstwhile Hispanophile, was threatened with deportation on several occasions. The family was genuinely European. We spoke the major European languages and had between us German, Dutch and British passports. But no rights in Spain.

My wife tried to run a business and pay tax. I helped to edit a small English-language magazine. But we were threatened, usually by fellow ex-pats, with a quaint form of social revenge – being 'denounced' to the authorities for having inadequate permits. (Technically, the denouncers would get ten per cent of fines imposed on the denounced. Spaniards, who also had to live with the permit-mania, usually disdained the *denuncia*.) We employed three Spaniards part-time and would have employed more if we could have secured permits to run a business. But no, we spent much of the first year in queues and going back and forth out of the country to get fresh visas. We spent a fortune on lawyers. In the end we gave up, and begged to be allowed to take our furniture out of Spain.

Standing in one of the endless queues, treated regularly like cattle, Susan said: 'Now I know what it's like to be a black in South Africa.'

'The difference is,' I replied, 'our maids have the vote but the madam doesn't.'

If you were retired or wanted to run a bar, you could secure permits. If you were a doctor, dentist or lawyer, you faced a paperchase lasting years. This was bonkers. Floods of aged ex-pat pensioners had already swamped the archaic hospitals and social services. Spain needed young, skilled foreigners, not more geriatrics. And the tidal wave of British bars was inexplicable. No one doubted the panache with which the Spaniards ran restaurants. The Alicante *comisario*, a cross between the Gestapo and a lunatic asylum, became my second home. Every day we were asked to provide extra documents. Then the original ones would be deemed to have expired. You would be asked to return in person to England or South Africa to have them attested. One bureaucrat was honest enough to admit: 'We do everything we can to keep foreigners out, especially those with skills or who want to run businesses.'

Inspectors would fan out from the *comisario* trying to catch people working, even professional, middle-aged ex-pats who might own a farm and a large villa. One Dutch woman in her sixties was almost deported for helping a colleague with some book-keeping on an informal basis. 'I went through the war,' she told me. 'It reminds me of the feeling of terror when the Nazis were rounding up Jews.' Van-loads of young EC foreigners doing casual jobs were herded together, taken to the border and dumped. I was incensed by articles in the Spanish press about how wonderfully European Spain was.

I nagged a friendly MEP to help me by taking my case to the European Commission on Human Rights. I also wrote a series of articles condemn-ing Spanish corruption, mainly under the pseudonym of D Shannon (others were B Holly and E Cochrane). One joke went down very badly: in a competition for the most corrupt country on earth, the Spaniards couldn't believe that Spain came second until they heard that Madrid had bribed the judges.

I was just finishing a book on southern Africa and the finale was to be the release of Mandela. Having eventually – oh, joy! – secured a phone without paying a huge bribe, I left my answering machine on to attend a cultural event in Benidorm with a group of *animales*, good friends from the UK. We arrived back at the villa, rather tired and emotional, after seeing 'Sticky Vicki', billed as the sexiest act in Europe. Vicki had removed light bulbs and sausages from parts of her anatomy. (This was the 'family version' of her show.) The message light flickered on my hard-won phone machine and my friends gathered around expectantly. There were eight messages. One was from South Africa confirming details of Mandela's release, the culmination of years of my research. The other seven, from all around the world, commiserated with me about the suicide of Del Shannon.

'Shows where your intellectual priorities lie,' said one friend.

'Del shot himself because of you,' said another hurtfully.

'Why? I was the founder of the Welsh Del Shannon Appreciation Society.'

'Aye, but you use his name as a pseudonym. He was on a big comeback tour of Europe and Spain was the main leg. But his tour permit was rejected because a certain D Shannon had been writing all these nasty articles about corruption. You killed him, mate.'

Passport to Pimlico

On such occasions I would take refuge from the modern-day inquisition in a little piece of England in Iberia – Gibraltar. It was a day's drive to Gib but there were some wonderful pit-stops. Old Granada, especially the Alhambra, has to be one of the glories of Islamic civilisation. I would dally for a day or two with unreformed criminals on the Costa del Sol. Occasionally I stayed with a retired conman in Fuengirola, which local ex-pats wittily called 'funny guerrilla'. My appetite for big dollops of sleaze and plastic opulence at places such as Marbella was limited, but inland were the Hemingwayesque bridges of Ronda, one of the oldest of Spanish towns.

I also liked Mijas, not for its over-visited prettiness, but for the magazine its massive palace of a town hall published. Its Spanglish and odd detail made it much funnier than *Private Eye*, partly because it took itself so seriously. It published, for example, how many contraceptive coils had been fitted in local clinics. Good taste prevents me from going into further detail. The glossy municipal mag played up two things, the town's unique square bull-ring and its even more unique and round mayor, who appeared on every page. The mayor's own publication described him as a 'fox-like man' who had very rarely been 'left with his behind uncovered'. He was also said to be an 'octopus that still hasn't even felt the need to use his ink'. I shared some of this unintentional humour with

John Gordon Davies, one of my favourite novelists. He lived in the hills above Coín and put me up provided we could swap African stories in his sauna over endless bottles of wine.

Then I would tumble down the steep Andalusian hills and slide into Gibraltar to revel in the red post-boxes, efficient phones that rang not burbled, Marks and Spencer's, post-offices that sold stamps, bank tellers who did not spend an hour reading your passport, Marmite...all the little English things to cheer up the jaded ex-pat...right down to the stale sandwiches in the (over 100) pubs.

Gib, or 'the Rock', as it's often called, is just that: a big rock which forms a tiny peninsula jutting out from southern Spain. The 30,000 inhabitants were packed into an area of 2.5 square miles. I liked Gib a lot, despite its claustrophobia. The streets were clogged with traffic, but the climate was sub-tropical and the crime rate very low. It was an historical and sociological curiosity, rather like a small English town frozen in the 1950s. And it was unusual – a colony that wanted to stay that way. It had an attachment to Britain and traditional hostility to Spain. Always essentially a garrison town, its Britishness and military past gave the statelet its special charm.

For anyone who liked militaria, the Rock was heaven. Its wars went back to Roman times, although Gibraltar is said to take its name from Tariq Ibn Zeyad, a Moor who conquered the area in 711 AD. Gibraltar is a corruption of Gibel Tarik (Tarik's Hill). Frequent sieges spawned the numerous fortifications and cannons. Nelson's body, apparently pickled in a barrel of rum, was taken there after the Battle of Trafalgar. The *Marie Celeste* was towed there in 1872.

With the run-down of British forces on the Rock, Ministry of Defence land was handed over to commercial and residential development. Some new buildings were strikingly modern, like the £140 million Europort financial centre. But, for me, the Rock's appeal was its traditional architecture. Gib was truly a jigsaw of history: an eighteenth-century British Regency town built on a fifteenth-century Spanish town, itself constructed over a twelfth-century Moorish settlement.

A tour of the churches clearly illustrated the different types of religious architecture. Under the Gibraltar museum, for example, was a well-preserved Moorish bathhouse dating from the fourteenth century. Gib's inhabitants have mainly been Catholics, with substantial minorities of Muslims and Jews, but during the wars with Spain the Rock was always portrayed by the British parliament as a bastion of Protestantism in Iberia.

The Rock itself could be climbed on foot, with a cable car for the less energetic. Near the top was the den of the famous Barbary apes. During the Second World War Winston Churchill ordered that the apes be secretly replenished. They had begun to die out and local superstition held that if the apes left so would the British. The apes are in fact tailless macaque monkeys; Gib is the only place they are found in Europe, supposedly having used an undiscovered tunnel that ran under the Mediterranean from their natural habitat in the Atlas mountains. The story goes that no one has ever seen an ape die or found an ape's skeleton.

Perhaps more interesting, though, was the Barbary partridge, also unique in Europe on Gibraltar. Their natural habitat was Africa. They couldn't fly across the straits; either they were better fliers centuries ago, or the Moors introduced them. That they have remained naturalised in such a small area is unusual. For such a crowded place, there was a lot to interest the naturalist, especially in spring and autumn when Gib became a staging post for migrating birds flying between their breeding grounds in Northern Europe and wintering areas in Africa.

The Rock also contained numerous caves and miles of tunnels. St Michael's Cave was the most interesting. Some tunnels were still MoD property and off-limits, but the 'galleries' – gun emplacements blasted out of solid rock in 1782 – could be explored.

Gib had dramatically improved its harbour facilities, especially for leisure craft. The new marina was one of the best in the Mediterranean, not least because of its good medical services, often deficient in other places. The Rock bristled with hotels, some of them rather seedy. On the other hand, many ex-military types had settled there and operated excellent restaurants with military precision. 'Main-streeting', walking down the narrow thoroughfares, was the major outdoor occupation for locals: the opportunity to show off new babies or beaus. Gibraltarian women, often astoundingly beautiful, wore their wealth, just like the Madrileños. The shops offered a wide variety of British goods, especially electrical equipment, at slightly above British prices (even though there was no VAT), but that meant way below Spanish prices for the ex-pats on the Costas. At times Spanish customs officials could get irksome when they found that tourists or foreign residents had filled their cars with British goodies. The unarmed, smart and helpful bobbies, who switched effortlessly from English to Spanish in mid-sentence, were a comforting contrast with the monoglot Spanish *Guardia*, often unshaven Tonton Macoutes with Ray Bans flashing and guns swinging on the hip.

For me the Rock was a friendly and efficient colonial relic, a welcome island of sanity when I edited a Spanish magazine there. I made a point of talking to the local political leaders. On my first visit in 1984 I was introduced to the luminaries by Henry Bautista, my favourite cameraman. His uncle was the equivalent of the Chancellor of the Exchequer. The chief minister was then Sir Joshua Hassan, the Jewish leader of an essentially Catholic electorate, who told me, 'Like the Welsh, small people have their rights, despite their size.' I wasn't sure whether he was being personal or philosophical.

Nearly all the population were fanatically pro-British. As the editor of one of the Rock's three weekly newspapers explained: 'We may not be English but we're certainly British.' His name was Campbell and he spoke with a heavy Spanish accent, yet he was sure London would not do a Hong Kong on him. Indeed, when the Iron Lady's empire struck back in the Falklands, jingoism of a positively nineteenth century flavour swept the Rock. Waving the flag was not just a phrase: Union Jacks were everywhere.

After years of conservative rule under Sir Joshua, in March 1988 Joe Bossano led his Socialist Labour Party to power in a colony which had its own parliament, flag and currency. Joe had his critics. To them he was the Joe Bananas who would disrupt the fragile economy with dogmatic socialism. He walked into two major international rows: the furore caused when the SAS killed three IRA members and the Barlow Clowes financial scandal. And always the eternal quarrel with Spain, the core of Gib politics.

I interviewed Joe – as everyone called him – several times, finding him a highly intelligent, approachable man, even though he did look like Groucho Marx on an off day. I asked about his relationship with his socialist counterparts, led by Felipe González, in Madrid.

'They still feel that Gibraltar is politically too hot a potato for them to start behaving as socialists and stop behaving as Spaniards. The national question transcends the ideological question... They still tend to look at Gibraltar as Spaniards, independently of whether they are fascists or communists.'

'So there's no relationship at all?'

'None.'

I recalled Henry's comment: 'Because of the siege, I didn't leave the Rock until I was 18. I saw my first cow then.' That insight inspired my continuing interest in Gib's staunch hostility to any take-over by Spain. In May 1991 González travelled to London, the first visit by a Spanish premier since the fascist era ended. He described Gib as an 'historical anachronism', which seemed a fair comment; then asked John Major to make an 'effort of imagination' over the future of the colony, which seemed to be asking a lot of this British PM.

Britain had maintained sovereignty of this tiny piece of real estate since 1713. The inhabitants had resisted regular Spanish attacks during

the eighteenth century, Italian naval assaults and Nazi conspiracies. But
the real enemy was Spain. Gibraltar might talk of UDI and conjure
Passport to Pimlico fantasies, but all the bravado relied upon British
military and diplomatic protection. I could hardly blame the Gibraltarians for developing a siege mentality. In 1969, after the colony was
granted full internal self-government, Franco imposed a blockade of the
Rock which lasted until 1985. At least there were no traffic jams.

Under the 1969 constitution, Britain said it would respect the wishes
of the Rock's inhabitants regarding any transfer of sovereignty. But in
referenda and elections, 95 per cent of Gibraltarians made it clear that
they wanted the *status quo.* I rang up Joe and asked him what he thought
of Felipe's pressure on London.

'Because of its special status in the EC, Gibraltar is essentially the
thirteenth member – with the fastest-growing economy,' he told me. 'If
Spain is seeking to use membership of the Community as a weapon in
order to take over Gibraltar, we consider that as a fundamental negation
of the very principle upon which the Community is based.' Despite his
comic appearance, Joe spoke with the gravitas of a butler at an orgy.

He pooh-poohed hints that Spain might ask for joint rule of the
colony, just as Andorra was administered by Spain and France. The King
of Spain and Queen of England would become Gib's dual heads of state.
The Rock's future, Joe insisted, rested upon tourism and its role as a
financial centre, developed according to Community and British, not
Spanish, rules. He attacked the Spanish for using bullying tactics to slow
down tourist and business traffic at the border, saying that Spanish
truculence over landing rights had caused a delay in sending vital
American equipment to US forces during the Gulf War.

González counter-argued that Gib was turning a blind eye to smuggling in the area, alleging that its financial centre had become a haven
for Spanish tax-dodgers and money-launderers. Spain, though, had to
tread carefully. It had two Gibraltar-sized, smuggling-prone colonies of its
own in Morocco – Ceuta and Melilla.

To the outsider, the squabbling seemed more than absurd because
local tourist and business interests dictated that Madrid and Gib should
co-operate. Despite its tiny beaches, nearly four million visitors squeezed
onto the Rock annually. It was the gateway to the Costa del Sol. But the
bitterness ran too deep. Joe, an affable visionary and workaholic, was
determined to build a rich mini-state, a second Monaco. His rocky
fiefdom's economy would be plastered with brass plates. He was an
ex-trade union leader heading a belated Thatcherite revolution.

But everything depended upon British steadfastness. 'Colonialism
isn't a word that stinks here. We want to remain a British colony,' a top

Gib civil servant said passionately. Gibraltarians swore by the Falklands factor. Britain had defended far fewer colonial dependants who also refused to be 'integrated' into their big neighbour. But Thatcher was forced to lay down her sword, and Britain was reducing its military subsidies and garrison to almost zero. The issue was no longer a strategic but a moral question.

Anglo-Spanish trade was becoming increasingly important. Joe's stone-walling relied ultimately upon Britannia keeping faith with her loyal colonists. Trust London? Sell that to the Chinese in Hong Kong. What alternatives? Ian Smith met Harold Wilson twice on gunships anchored off Gib. But UDI on the Rock? Despite the same ill-fitting suits, Joe Bossano didn't really look like Ian Smith.

10
Namibia – the South African Reich

Namibia

A Satanic cult manages to resurrect Hitler. They ask what changes he will make now he is back. 'This time,' he replies, 'no more Mr Nice Guy.'

South West Africa – now Namibia – was German in the late nineteenth century. After the Great War, the League of Nations asked the South Africans, who lived next door, to look after it for a while. This was rather like lending your lawnmower to a new neighbour who just happened to be a kleptomaniac. The South Africans refused to give it back. So there was a war. All the unrepentant ex-German Nazis in South West Africa could now comfortably switch Reichs.

The 90,000 whites appeared to be an endangered species there, so to make sure they didn't become extinct the people who ran the country (who just happened to be whites too) gave them a specially protected reservation which also happened to be nearly all the land with good grazing and water. The blacks had the deserts but the whites did not consider them an endangered species. The whites controlled what was under the land too – lots of minerals. Apartheid, itself a first cousin of Hitler's racist laws, was applied in South West Africa, although less rigorously than in the southern republic. What mattered was equal opportunity. Blacks, if they were bright enough, could get on. But the white 20 per cent of the school population got 80 per cent of the education budget. Blacks were largely taught in Afrikaans but many of the important exams were held in English or German. The blacks had a low pass rate, thus justifying the whites' low opinion of black abilities.

I sat in a cramped Hercules aircraft pondering these conundrums, surrounded by South African soldiers devouring comics. I had hitched a lift on an air force plane to Windhoek, the spotlessly clean capital of South West Africa. Then I cadged a ride in my favourite war-horse, the Dakota, which flew very low as it approached the Omega base. It was hot, hot, hot in the Caprivi strip. The suicide month of October. It was 1985, and the tangled mess of war between Angola, South Africa, the Cubans, Unita and various other hangers-on was in full swing. I wanted to travel along the length of the 960-mile Angolan/South West African border, sometimes accompanied by a film crew, sometimes by troops. When I could slip away from military escorts, I would snoop around on my own.

I had covered the war there on and off for years, but I was more interested in 'South West' for its angry, beautiful landscapes. It was the last great wilderness in southern Africa: the same size as France, Belgium and West Germany combined, with less than 1.5 million inhabitants, it boasted one of the world's lowest population densities. Much of the land was untouched desert. In some places no rain had fallen this century. Yet the wild symphony of harsh desert, lunar landscapes, pastoral serenity and almost unmolested wildlife was also the reluctant requiem for 25 years of bush war, most of it unreported.

South West was arguably the final unresolved legacy of the German defeat in 1918. If any metropolitan country – besides Belgium – deserved to lose its colonies it was the Second Reich. In the late nineteenth century Berlin sent out hard men to colonise in the furnace heat that blasted the burnt-out badlands. Namibia, like the Namib desert, implies 'the place where there is nothing'. The badlands, however, held lots of something – diamonds. The first commissioner, almost prophetically, was Dr H E Göring, father of the Nazi leader, who set about exterminating the local tribes, especially the Herero. In museums and old history books I came across early pictures of the few surviving Hereros. Beyond the minor difference of colour they were identical to the starved and enslaved inmates of Belsen.

After 1915 the South Africans did a bit of massacring, too, using bombs from aircraft. They started in 1922 and kept going until the late 1980s. The UN complained, to no avail. In 1958 the leading black nationalist, Herman Toivo ja Toivo, sent a recorded petition to the UN hidden in an old copy of *Treasure Island*. He also wrote to Queen Elizabeth and the Pope. There were even demands for the territory to be designated a US protectorate. Clearly, the nationalists were desperate.

South West became *de facto* a fifth province of South Africa, set to take the same route as its minder: both black and white nationalists talked past each other. The diminishing band of 'moderates' staggered in the middle of nowhere. Many Namibian nationalists had worked in South Africa alongside ANC activists. The same pattern emerged: petitions, passive disobedience, strikes and finally armed struggle. In 1961 Sam Nujoma and other leaders of the South West African People's Organisation (SWAPO) set up their HQ in Dar es Salaam, Africa's revolutionary oasis. Guerrillas began to infiltrate South West in 1965 to establish bases in Ovamboland along the central section of the border with Angola. The terrain was well suited to partisan warfare. With the exception of a small section in the northwest, along the Cunene River, the Angola/South West border was a straight cartographic line. In the centre the Ovamboland/ Angolan border ran for 270 miles, theoretically dividing the Angolan Ovambo people from their kinsfolk on the other side.

Ovamboland was exceptionally flat, covered in the west by often dense mopani bush and in the east by forest. In the subtropical climate, the rainy season (usually October to April) provided ample water and luxuriant foliage for guerrilla penetration. There were anthills every-where, all for some reason pointing north. Everywhere, too, were *Cuca* shops, tiny general stores with very little on sale but sporting grandiose titles such as 'California Inn', 'Los Angeles' and 'Country Club'. The

Ovambo were said to be born capitalists, 'black Jews', but most supported the Marxist-leaning SWAPO.

The war began properly in 1966 and became more acute after Portugal quit Angola in 1975. Pretoria always danced to two tunes – dealing with the UN over independence but simultaneously promoting a local UDI. Meanwhile, real power was gathered in the hands of the South African Defence Force, which initially regarded SWAPO more as a public nuisance than a military threat. South African intelligence agents stirred up the usual cocktail – tribal, ideological and personality clashes – to weaken SWAPO, which didn't need much prodding to tear itself apart. Then both SWAPO and South Africa became sucked into the Angolan civil war.

The result? A dirty little war in the last, almost forgotten colony became South Africa's very own Vietnam. It was a bizarre war in an almost surreal place, with images of the Tet offensive, old Rhodesia and the savage Congo of the sixties. To the north the South African military conducted brilliant conventional campaigns in Angola, and almost textbook counter-insurgency inside northern South West. But they lost the hearts and minds battles, the only ones that mattered. Meanwhile, in the south, almost quarantined, a kind of peace pervaded in the big farms, rich diamond mines and fishing fleets working out of picturesque ports.

South West made a profit, but then became a proverbial colonial millstone. It was not formally an Afrikaner colony, rather a territory illegally occupied. Pretoria not only kept a large army there, in contravention of the original League mandate, but also used it as a forward base to send legions into Angola, Zambia and Botswana. Originally South Africa planned to integrate the territory formally into the republic, then it decided to boost its local allies, centred around Dirk Mudge. In a free election SWAPO would win, so there followed ten years of chicanery, of Mudge-style Namibianisation as futile as America's Vietnamisation, because Pretoria adamantly rejected what it termed 'the red flag in Windhoek'. But the massive Angolan land battles in the late 1980s made even Pretoria realise that the game was up. South Africa would pull out of South West if the Cubans quit Angola. Pretoria was afraid of more sanctions, and wanted to denude South West's large deposits of uranium, diamonds, phosphates and other minerals. Hence the great filibuster. South African diplomats, often the clumsiest representatives of an unsaleable regime, became Machiavellian princes over Namibia.

Occasionally the puppets would roar; Mudge baulked at Pretoria's imperialism and tried to build up his own army. But after Mugabe won in Zimbabwe, the question was clear: how could Mudge, a white former National Party leader, do what Muzorewa, once an internationally accepted black nationalist, could not? The monotonous rhythm of South African diplomacy jangled the nerves: bash SWAPO, boost Mudge and then talk to the UN. Buying time, losing ground. It became a cliché of southern African politics: to avoid total sanctions, Pretoria would have to free either Mandela or Namibia. The scale of the battles in Angola would eventually force them to do both.

But in 1985, to the casual foreign visitor, the territory was a country that worked. Unusually for Africa, the roads were as good as the beer. Game parks were well run, as were the hotels, with their odd mixture of German efficiency, Afrikaner hospitality and African good manners. The clarity of the light made it a photographer's dream. An overwhelming sense of grandeur and space harmonised with the Moët et Chandon quality of the air. Because of the war and its isolation it was almost untouched by that great abomination of the twentieth century, packaged tourists. Below the narrow northern war zone, South West was usually the quintessence of primeval tranquillity. Enchanting classical German buildings looked as though they had been plucked from Rhenish forests and planted in the desert. Brechtian characters strolled along the sand-scoured, melancholic streets of quaint little towns such as Lüderitz and Swakopmund.

The Caprivi Strip, named after General Count Georg Leo von Caprivi di Caprara di Montecuccoli, Chancellor of Germany when the territory was acquired from Britain, was a finger of land which the Second Reich tried to stretch to touch German East Africa (Tanganyika). This strategic crossroads bordered on Angola and Zambia in the north and Botswana in the south, while Kasangula, at its extreme eastern tip, was the point where Zambia, Botswana and Zimbabwe intersected. This was perhaps the shortest border in the world: Botswana and Zambia touched for just 45 yards.

Omega was the HQ of 201 Battalion, made up of Bushmen troops officered by whites. I had been there on several occasions to interview SWAPO prisoners. Journalists were often given the PR treatment about South Africa preserving the ancient Bushman culture. I was fascinated by what remained of the sub-continent's oldest inhabitants. Like all those interested in military affairs, I marvelled at their almost supernatural field skills, especially their unerring tracking abilities. Their fathers had been hunted almost like beasts by southern Angolan tribes. Many regarded the South African military as their protectors and only source of employment.

Their officers confirmed their reliability under fire. Off-duty they could be a trifle erratic, explained the camp doctor, as he pointed to a corporal nursing a wound in his backside. 'He was shot with an arrow by a Bushman who refused to work after drinking too much.'

A discussion followed on the cultural survival of the San (Bushmen). A South African lieutenant, who could speak one of the 17 highly complex local San dialects, was defensive: 'The army is not turning the Bushmen into a war machine; it is preventing their extinction.'

Another officer added: 'We are not trying to Westernise the vulnerable Bushman culture. We just want to make him a better Bushman.' The army, he said, encouraged Bushman troops to spend a day each week with their children teaching them old customs and fieldcraft.

I wasn't sure an urban Afrikaner could show a Bushman much about bushcraft. And I wondered what would happen to these wonderful little people when South Africa pulled out. A good deal under SWAPO would be as likely as the Chinese communist party fêting the Gurkhas in Hong Kong.

In mine-proofed armoured vehicles we travelled to small army towns such as Oshivello and Ondangwa, where the white civilians and soldiers' families lived in stockaded areas with a trim little sand-bagged bomb-shelter in front of each bungalow. At the adjoining air bases, the odd artistic touch was evident. An Alouette gunship had 'I'm Noddy' painted on its Browning; 'Boswell Wilkie Circus' adorned the sides of a Buffel armoured personnel carrier. 'Road Runner' topped the logo list. Oshakati had the best collection of propaganda posters to inspire bored white troopies: 'Think: it might be a new experience'; 'Winners Never Quit'. Warnings about mines abounded, with good reason: SWAPO guerrillas were experts at mine warfare, but the majority of victims were black civilians. And everywhere the unofficial scrawl: *Min Dae,* indicating just a few days left of national service. But it was not *Apocalypse Now* revisited. There was no 'fragging' that I could discover. Morale was generally high. And, despite posters warning of the dangers of drugs, this army was not 'dropping out' in large numbers.

Ovamboland's flatness was monotonous. The rains, however, were beginning to brighten up the bush; the sandy soil smelt rich and fecund. I would call into *Cuca* shops to find a Coke. Often little was on sale except information. Some informers bought shops but were killed by SWAPO. The cleverer ones professed poverty and purchased property in Wind-hoek. A BMW might be parked outside some conspicuous shop-keeper's *Cuca.* The huts and villages were often poor and scruffy compared with the regimented tidiness of the army bases. On the bases the ordinary soldiers were suspicious of foreigners and had been told not to talk to journalists. But in the mess they would relax quickly over a beer or two with my Afrikaans-speaking film crew. The bored white conscripts moaned like young soldiers everywhere. The army didn't give them jobs that matched their skills, a comment echoed by many graduate soldiers.

The officers in the regular permanent force were also suspicious, but border duty was often boring for them, too. They liked meeting strangers, especially if the conversation was in Afrikaans. South African forces were officially bilingual but English was the language of formality, of reserve. Slangy Afrikaans was the language of combat, fear, orders, prayer and laughter. The talk was of war, sex and sport, the universal clichés of men at war. Above all, the war.

'SWAPO is good, so we have to be, too,' said a keen Citizen Force 'camper' (reservist).

More beers. A graduate officer admitted: 'We might be winning the war here but we are losing it at home.' Someone wore a T-shirt advertising *Koevoet* (Crowbar), an elite and ruthless police unit: 'Our business is killing and business is good.'

We filmed as we drove along the road that ran beside the 'cutline', the border with Angola. The troops rode up and down in Buffels like cowboys checking range fences. I went up in a Puma helicopter to get aerial shots. Dust was the real enemy of choppers, not SAM missiles. Then a change of pace: a motorbike patrol with hardy cross-country scramblers. The motor-cyclists acted as outriders for our small convoy. The enemy here was camel thorn – punctures, not mines.

Next a horseback patrol: 'SWAPO doesn't hear us coming until it's too late. The terrorists are dead scared of horses, you know.'

I always tried to avoid walking too far, especially with heavy film equipment, but we needed some foot patrols for the documentary. I disliked violating homes in kraals, although the soldiers were polite in front of a camera. There was shouting and two shots half a mile ahead. Four SWAPO insurgents had been captured with just a whisper of resistance. I thought it might be a set-up but I sat in on the interrogations. They were genuine. The guerrillas were not terrified. They were not mistreated (in front of me). They knew they were destined for a long captivity, unless they opted to be 'turned' and join Windhoek's army. They would have better training, food, proper pay – for the first time, medical attention, entertainment ... Why not? They could later say they were infiltrating the enemy to learn further skills before defecting back. Two of the captives, however, quietly explained that they were committed to SWAPO ideology and would never fight for 'the puppets in Windhoek'.

Ruacana was the furthest settlement on the western end of the border, overlooking a big hydro-electrical project on the Cunene River. Because of the war less than ten per cent of the potential electricity was being produced, even though the full amount was needed to boost attempts to cure chronic unemployment in the region. Perhaps 50 per cent of existing local jobs depended upon servicing the South African armed forces.

The commander of the Ruacana base drove me around in his pick-up truck. Elvis Presley blared from his on-board stereo. He chewed a pipe and addressed his wife as 'Corporal'. The main interest in Corporal's life was the new 'tourist wing' she'd had built near the tiny wooden hut that was the officers' mess. The 'tourist wing' was also a wooden hut with four rooms with bunk beds. There weren't any tourists in this military zone, a mile from the Angolan border, so she was glad to accommodate the film crew. We would christen the building. The commander moaned about the recent cease-fire. 'Now we have to wait for the bastards to come and hit us first.'

We were supposed to stay for two nights, but decided to go to another small base at the last minute. On the second night SWAPO obliged the commander with a stand-off bombardment, hitting the Ruacana base with 122mm rockets, mortars and a recoilless rifle. The new tourist wing was partially destroyed. Our room was demolished entirely and two officers in the next room were wounded. The commander was angry and embarrassed; Corporal was mortified, especially when we returned to film the damage they were trying to conceal. An angry reaction force pursued the attackers and claimed to have killed eight SWAPO guerrillas about ten miles across the border.

In the mess afterwards one of the officers in this retaliatory group admitted: 'I'm here in the operational area because this is the one place I can kill kaffirs legally.'

South West seemed like a surreal dream. Elsewhere, in dirt and muck – say in Afghanistan or Mozambique – there were highs and lows of fear, panic and exhilaration. That was the way with guerrillas. Here death was sanitised, casual, organised by a very professional army which had mess waiters, hot showers and air conditioning …

The next day the commander put on a powerful artillery display. Thirty high explosive shells rained down on Angola. It looked good on film but I wondered how many Angolans were killed.

We drove south in a Buffel to Opuwa, the midget capital of Kaokoland, stopping en route at a small Ovahimba village. Only a few thousand of these 'cattle people' had survived in the deserts of Kaokoland. They were a primitive, handsome tribe who daubed themselves in animal fat and ochre. The women plaited their hair and looked like red Bo Dereks. The soldiers gave them water and tobacco. The camera assistant had saved all his army ration packs and bargained some food for two carved bone bracelets. Most Ovahimba were almost untouched by civilisation, although a few less noble savage ladies were to be found drinking beer and smoking pipes outside a tiny store next to the army base.

At the Opuwa base I met a black major in the South West African Territory Force who wanted to show me the sights. We walked for a mile through flat, bare desert to a corrugated iron square. It belonged to the major's lady, Dorcas. Although the inside was immaculately tidy, the tiny metal hut had no windows. Over some beers, she explained slowly in broken Afrikaans: 'I want no windows. SWAPO come and shoot me otherwise.'

The discussion in the Opuwa officers' mess was hearty and sophisticated. More conservative officers spouted the 'Africans are generally happy here, we only need to kill the small amount of communist troublemakers' philosophy. But a law graduate from Stellenbosch led an opposing faction: 'You are talking about South West, but presumably the same applies to South Africa. If the blacks are so happy, why not give them the vote and let them happily vote for the National Party?'

The variety of opinion expressed – from brutal racism to liberal concern – suggested that this was not the brainwashed killing machine depicted by anti-apartheid activists. Morale seemed high. But coloured troops in the area had recently refused their home leave in the Cape, fearing reprisals in their own community because they were serving in the army.

In mid-1985 an appointed multiracial government was set up in Windhoek, the equivalent of the internal settlement in Rhodesia. Some blacks had voted for an earlier version of this government. This was the fundamental paradox of the war in South West: young white South African conscripts were fighting and dying to *defend* one sort of black majority rule in Namibia while fighting to *prevent* the same principle being applied at home. It made no sense. I didn't expect to find any answers when I sought out the leaders of the new government in Windhoek.

You can tell a lot about a country from its main airport. Particularly a developing country. Windhoek's main airport was clean, efficient and ultra-modern, with international signs ready for independence. Outside there were no armies of hustlers and hawkers, garishly painted broken-down buses, peeling paint or hand-painted signs saying 'Do not urinate here'. It was not Africa. But the airport was named after J G Strydom, the Afrikaner apostle of apartheid, a typical example of Pretoria's ham-fisted PR. Another misnomer was Windhoek's grandiloquently-titled Government of National Unity, which couldn't even agree on what to call the country. Whites wouldn't accept the hated word 'Namibia'. The new administration reeked of Muzorewa's defeat. Their rationale was to buy the time the bishop never had. The same white Rhodesian clichés permeated the conversations.

The new black ministers had a taste for blonde secretaries and black Mercedes. One, Moses Katjiuongua, 43, a former Maoist with a strong American accent, admitted: 'If things go wrong this time, we should blame ourselves, not Pretoria.' But Andreas Shipanga, the minister of nature conservation, mining, commerce and tourism, wanted to pass the buck: 'This country has become a pawn of superpower rivalries.' The ever-affable Shipanga had the shakes. The tough-talking white supremo, Dirk Mudge, outlined the changes made despite Pretoria's foot-dragging: 'As a result of these reforms we have relative peace. We have a war on our border but no women and children protesting in the streets.'

Many whites in Windhoek felt that their country was being used as a social laboratory, a litmus test for the faint-hearted in the south. A restaurateur who still refused, illegally, to serve blacks, said bluntly in Afrikaans: 'The *huigelaar* [two-faced] Botha clan is using South West as a playground to see if it [multi-racialism] works. If it doesn't they will shoot the kaffirs.' Social engineering clearly had its limits in Windhoek. So did fashion sense. I took false refuge in an *Oktoberfest*, full of fat local Germans in *lederhosen* guzzling quarts of beer.

A briefing by intelligence officers at the defence HQ was almost a relief. I was told that just before the rainy season offensive 'only 40 SWAPO terrorists are active in the operational area'. They conceded that the rains would make the numbers grow. Instinctively I looked through the barred windows to see if the rains and my exit were about to begin.

I asked what I thought was an intelligent question: 'Is it cost-effective to have such a massive and expensive military machine running around after 40 guerrillas on the northern border of South West, when South Africa itself is said to be infiltrated by hundreds of ANC insurgents?'

'No comment. I was not briefed to reply to such a question.' The cameraman and myself were escorted out quickly. Another glorious piece of Afrikaner diplomacy.

On a tour of Windhoek bars I bumped into one of the tough military escorts I had met on the border. He wore a beautiful pink silk shirt, a touch of rouge and a delicate gold earring. I politely declined his kind offer to take me to a gay club. Windhoek was seductive; solid colonial buildings injected grace into its dusty, small-town charm. The city centre was dominated by a German Lutheran church and a Teutonically well-preserved German fort. Surrounding hills were outlandishly adorned with imitation Rhenish castles. Some roofs were steeply tilted to stop the accumulation of desert snow.

The splendid architecture put me in a good mood and I was more inclined to be polite when I received an invitation to take afternoon tea with the Afrikaner governor-general. (South Africa wasn't quite that obvious; Louis Pienaar's real title was 'administrator-general'.) Louis and his wife treated me with an olde-worlde courtesy I had not encountered outside Jane Austen. 'South Africa,' he said, 'could leave like a thief in the night.' Pretoria was sick of the shenanigans of Windhoek politicians.

The feeling was reciprocated. Windhoek's most famous character, Johannes Martin Smith ('Smitty' to admirers), was venomous about the Boers. Smitty, a one-man slum who ran the *Windhoek Observer* almost single-handedly, was the scourge of the local establishment. People read his paper, sometimes banned for carrying nudes, for his column 'The People Hear'. My friend Denis Beckett, no mean scourger himself, dubbed Smitty's weekly diatribe 'one of the most libellous gossip columns of modern times'. Smitty might be called a South West nationalist in his dislike of Pretoria.

A highly articulate lawyer, Anton Lubowski, a more conventional, pro-SWAPO white nationalist, summed up his political views: 'Namibia is a land of internal exile where individual worth is colour-coded, law and order means a state of emergency, and Christianity is a mask for inhumanity.' Pretoria took Lubowski more seriously than Smitty. The lawyer was later assassinated.

After war and politics, I wanted to see South West's four-footed inhabitants. Windhoek was a good base from which to tour the country. To the north of the country was Etosha Pan nature reserve. Our camera assistant, overcome by the abundant wildlife, exclaimed: 'Christ, if you look hard enough you'll even see a smurf.' We saw everything but. I marvelled again at how giraffes always seem to move in slow motion. In Africa the best of the day is dawn and evening, when the game is most abundant. At the Namutoni fort I watched the thin sliver of the moon hang behind the battlements. Scops owls called, and in the distance I could hear the strangled war-cry of an hyena.

Swakopmund, on the coast, had a distinctly European air. The clean, cool oasis of palm trees and sturdy Teutonic buildings still dreamed of Kaiser Bill's Germany. With presumably unintended appropriateness, vehicle licence plates for the area bore the abbreviation SS (for South West Swakopmund). Local whites seemed to have trouble distinguishing apartheid from Nazism, although there was some contention as to whether the Kaiser's or Hitler's birthday was more important.

In the central Rehoboth region I encountered one of the distinct South West coloured communities. I was told they took great pride in being called 'bastards'. 'Coloured' was a tremendous insult, apparently. Actually the Rehoboth *Basters* were a mixed-race, mainly Afrikaans-speaking people originally from Namaqualand in the south. In a number of long conversations I managed to avoid the awkward nomenclature.

Keetmanshoop, to the south, the centre of the prosperous karakul farming region, maintained the South West tradition of good hotels with even better, if occasionally stodgy, food. The town was 90 minutes' drive from the Fish River Canyon, one of the natural wonders of Africa. Travelling west through Ai-Ais, a springs resort, I ventured into the Namib desert. As a travel writer I always tell people to carry water in desert regions; naturally I broke down without any spare water, having not seen another car for hours. Out of the heat haze emerged a police patrol car. The two policemen fixed my car and dispensed free cold beers. This was a long way from Soweto.

At the end of the desert road lay Lüderitz, a run-down port with heart-sick German buildings. I asked a black in English for directions to a hotel; he replied in perfect nineteenth-century high German. I explored some of the nearby ghosts towns such as Kolmanskop, villages besieged by sand and time. Much of the coastal region was *verboten* because vast tracts were owned by diamond concessionaires. Some of the coast was accessible. Sailors called it the Skeleton Coast because of many wrecks littering the area. To reach them required a four-wheel drive. The secret of driving through dune-fields was to let the tyres down until they were like squashed balloons. Then, once four-wheel drive was engaged, you could move fast. It was like hovercrafting across powdered snow. I was amazed to discover how slow the desert was to heal itself: tyre tracks could last for decades.

I left South West by train from Windhoek to Keetmanshoop. It took 13 hours. A goat joined the train; some AWOL soldiers, accompanied by military policemen, left. In the compartment was a scholarly South African colonel researching ethnology, who tried, unsuccessfully, to explain the differences between the many Namibian tribes.

South Africa had the power but SWAPO had the popular support. Battlefield attrition and the convergence of superpower self-interest in Angola eventually levered Pretoria out of Windhoek. On the first day of the UN-supervised transition – ominously 1 April 1989 – SWAPO started to invade, a stupid thing to do when they were about to win the forthcoming election. Whatever the reasons, with UN blessing the South African forces remobilised. There was also a world-class busybody to hand: Margaret Thatcher flew into Windhoek on the same day. The 'African Queen', as she was dubbed, was touring southern Africa. This was a replay of Soapy Soames's use of Rhodesian troops in January 1980 to counter guerrilla excesses. It was a strange twist of fate: South African troops hunting SWAPO guerrillas with UN consent. 'It feels strange to be in the right for once,' said a senior South African officer. 'I'm not sure we can handle it.'

In a week of savage fighting over 260 guerrillas were killed. Nonetheless Sam Nujoma won the most seats in the following elections and, in March 1990, South West Africa finally became Namibia. During the election campaign good ole' Sam was accused of some pretty nasty politicking. After independence a sticker on a Windhoek car bumper read: 'Fuck the [silhouette of a rhino], save the WHITES.' Maybe Sam had a solution for them, too. No more Mr Nice Guy.

11

Middle East – the Jerusalem Syndrome

Ever since God gave Charlton Heston the Ten Commandments Israel has been in the news. After 1948 too much in the news: 'We may be a chosen race but I wish God would choose someone else' was the gut feeling of many Israelis I met.

When I was a student I spent some time on various *kibbutzim*. On one in the Negev desert I was a lifeguard for six weeks, monitoring a quiet swimming pool, disturbed only by an occasional bikini. I sat and read in the sun. So I initially had a good impression, particularly of Israeli soldiers in their short skirts. I was interested in how the Hebrew language had been revived by Ben Yehuda in the 1870s. Ben said to his infant son: 'I am going to speak just Hebrew to you. You will be the first native-speaker of Hebrew for nearly 2,000 years.' I used to wonder how the kid ordered a pizza or bought a paper when nobody could understand him. But I studied some Hebrew, especially the rapid immersion method called Ulplan used by the waves of new immigrants to Israel. Along with other Welsh nationalists, I was keen to apply some of these lessons to the revival of Welsh. For a while, I was what you might call a Welsh nationalist Zionist. I shared some of the guilt by default of the previous generation which had caused or let the Holocaust happen. But I could see the obvious objections to the largely Muslim Palestinians paying for the guilt of the Christian West.

I spent a while at the Hebrew University, Jerusalem, studying the effects of the Yom Kippur War. I was stuck in a military hospital in England during that war, watching it on television, and was taken aback by Israel's unexpected fragility and the suddenness of the Arab attack in October 1973. In the words of one Israeli poet, 'When I heard the sirens of Yom Kippur, I heard the cries of Auschwitz'. My research was on the war's psychological and political aftermath. The scholarship was meagre so I lived in a cheap hotel in Jerusalem's Arab quarter. After making a few Arabs friends and being roughed up once by Israeli police when I was in Arab company, I began to see another side of Zionism.

The Middle East/Israel

In a series of articles, small books and pamphlets I poured out my views on solutions for the Middle East. I was an opinionated little sod; looking back now, I cringe. The beginning of a (thankfully) unpublished book called *The Small Leviathan* read: 'Israel is not just a nation but also a concept loaded with history, religion and passion.' I followed with 'Modern Israel was delivered by Caesarean operation after European surgery on the abdomen of Asia,' and went on to describe 'the hell-brew to end all hell-brews': a head-on collision between two nationalist crusades; a conflict between Western and oriental values; a dispute over border and historical rights compounded by highly distorted images of the adversary; a chronic arms race and superpower intrigue. It was my kind of place.

Perhaps the best way of summing up the Israeli–Palestinian dispute is to call it a confusing tale of two peoples with justice on each side in conflict over the same land. It was not a case of right and wrong but right versus right. Historically, I could see both sides of the argument. Emotionally, I empathised with the Jewish people but personally found most Israelis disgustingly arrogant, especially towards Arabs. I started sprinkling my work on Israel with phrases such as 'invisible bantustans' to describe the treatment of Arabs and 'conquistador attitudes' to label some Israelis, especially the occupying forces in the West Bank. I said that, from an Arab perspective, 'Zionism was an obnoxious mixture of Moses, Marx and Rousseau which had made Palestinians helots of a New Sparta in the Middle East'. I don't think the phrases were terribly original, so I wonder now why I bothered pinching such ugly little hybrids.

But no matter how much I disliked Israeli bigotry, I couldn't resolve the simple dilemma couched by Israel's most distinguished political scientist, Yehosefat Harkabi: 'Israel's problem is that with the best will in the world it cannot meet the Arabs' demand, because it is *unlimited* and cannot be satisfied as long as Israel exists.'

In Europe and southern Africa, I taught university courses on the Middle East and acted as an examiner. Levels of ignorance about the history of the region appalled me. Some students seemed stuck in the biblical era and never managed to reach the twentieth century. One said that Noah's wife was Joan of Arc, and that 'Solomon had 300 wives and 700 cucumbers'. I also liked 'The Mediterranean and the Red Sea are connected by the Sewage Canal' and 'After 1973 the oil slicks [sheikhs?] raised the price of oil'. And 'During the Final Solution Hitler tried to kill all the semantics, or Jews, in conservation camps'. 'The lost diatribes of Israel' lost me too. One student asserted that 'Rabies were Jewish priests who foamed at the mouth. They had to be shot. Hitler was good at this.'

These comments came from senior schoolchildren or history under-
graduates.

I'm not sure whether the Western media has done that much to
remedy popular ignorance about the growth of Islam, especially in the
Middle East. The pack journalism of the Gulf War or the parachute
hackery of the media stars have often enforced the stereotyping of the
region. The fall of the Shah was the classic example. The pruning of
foreign desks in major newspapers had almost destroyed the old
specialists, leaving only generalists, men with built-in universal bullshit-
detectors. But if you didn't speak the languages how could you tell what
was bullshit and what was not? Only one in 300 foreign hacks in Iran
spoke Persian. The comfort of the monoglot pack was too tempting. No
wonder the Shah's downfall came as such a shock to them, and their
editors. But then the Cold War was still in business. The opponents of the
Shah were dubbed, interestingly, 'Islamic Marxists'. Wasn't the Shah a
moderniser and all-popular, except for the few fanatics – beturbanned,
black-robed, self-flagellating ...? (At the time, I used to wonder why, if the
Shah was so damn popular, did he need such a large and viciously
omnipresent secret police.) Next door the same beturbanned weirdos
were on the right side in the holy war against communism. Afghan
fundamentalists were freedom-fighters, Muslim militiamen; at worst
noble savages and, at best, plucky anti-Soviet heroes.

TV depends upon pictures. No pictures, no story. The best stories
involve drama, action, and often bang-bang. That is the nature of the
beast. It is hard to record trends rather than events. But the decades-long
misreading of the Islamic revival, whether the *fatwa* on Salman Rushdie
or the slow destruction of Sarajevo, will have a very major impact on the
security and perhaps sanity of Western Europe. TV portrays many Islamic
groups as history's slow learners, anti-modern fanatics, and their terrorism as a form of madness without roots. Some are certainly nasty, vicious
primitives who would benefit from enforced lobotomies, but the majority
are not. TV images of heroes and villains are still conditioned by the
deceased Cold War: a mission to deliver foreigners from communism,
poverty or religious fanatics. Bill Clinton is finding much worse poverty
and fanaticism in the inner cities of America. I remember once confusing
two bits of film showing ruins in Sarajevo and Los Angeles.

On domestic news TV stations tend to play it down the middle. The
press councils and Joe Public have lots of ideas on what is fair in their own
backyard. Abroad, journalists like to act tough, but whether in the
Falklands or the Gulf the machismo usually toes the government line.
The press watchdog rarely leaves the kennel when it comes to challenging conventional wisdom on foreign policy

Precisely because nearly all Western journalists believe they are above and beyond ideology, they are most susceptible to its effects. I do not believe there was a wide-ranging media conspiracy to sanitise – to Americanise – the Gulf War, but many Western correspondents switched off their brains as they put on desert camouflage. From the numbers of Iraqi troops to the percentage of smart bombs, the official line was swallowed. It was later realised only seven per cent of the bombs were smart, laser-guided weapons; the vast majority were free-fall, old-fashioned gravity bombs. And they usually missed. The carnage of the Iraqi retreat was severely sanitised on Western screens. Gore footage and splatter shots had no place in TV spectaculars which looked more like arcade games than military massacres.

The American and British defence establishments learned from the Falklands and the invasions of Grenada and Panama: control of the media was paramount, especially in the initial stages of fighting. But satellites had become more powerful than politicians. The era of laptops, Marisat telephones and portable dishes left the blimps stumbling in the last decade. At great risk maverick journalists broke away from the defence pools to cross into Kuwait. The freelancers were part of the reason Stormin' Norman stopped short of advancing on Baghdad. President Bush did not want a second Vietnam live on cable. My old mate Tim was naturally among the mavericks, conning a US army uniform and official pass to escape the pools and escort officers. He had a tough war, although the problem was more working with prima donnas like Kate Adie than being bombed by Saddam Hussein.

I had a terrible war: I had to watch the build-up on TV. It took so long. And I thought Saddam would back down, not believing it would come to the crunch. When it did I tried to scramble out of my lecturing schedule at Cardiff University and persuade TV stations to buy my promised film in advance. Tim was already in Saudi Arabia, hired by a British network. And you needed big network muscle to get a TV team through the very restrictive Saudi authorities. J J Swart joined me on a plane to Israel; Tim said it might be possible to cross from Jordan into Saudi and come across the desert. The trouble was J J had a South African passport, not normally acceptable in Arab countries.

With my usual immaculate timing, I arrived in Jerusalem the day the war ended. To be fair, it lasted only 100 hours and I had moved fast. There was no point in trying to join the thousands of hacks in Kuwait. I had to do something different and I had to make some kind of film.

J J had organised for us to stay at the Tel Aviv Hilton – fortunately, because the Israelis had set up the major press centre there. Compared with the bribe-burdened, paranoid Arab states Israel's smooth PR made life easy for foreign journalists. The high literacy rate, an urbanised, multilingual population, often fluent in English, a democratic government and a vigorous press – plus the influence of the US Jewish lobby – had prompted many news organisations to set up bureaux in Israel.

At the press centre I bumped into a CNN cameraman who knew me from South Africa. He was friendly with the Israeli officials and told them I was a very distinguished journalist – it's nice when friends are prepared to lie for you. In less than 15 minutes we obtained our work permits: more than I got in three years in Spain.

Ramming my brain into overdrive, I checked into the hotel at 7pm, fixed up accreditation, attended and filmed a press conference, did a one-on-one TV interview with the charismatic deputy foreign minister, Bibi Netanyahu, and another with Ra'anan Gissin, the equally telegenic army spokesman. I sorted out editing facilities, did a brief voice report for the BBC, then walked around Tel Aviv for two hours to film the cease-fire celebrations. Most people were not sure that the war had ended but Israelis were jubilant that their greatest enemy, Saddam Hussein, had been defeated. Teenagers waving gas masks shouted 'Saddam is a maniac'. I had forgotten how scruffy Tel Aviv was; one suburb gave the impression of a seedy, oriental bazaar filled with dusky Israelis. As we filmed in (Ze'ev) Jabotinsky Square, I recalled the words of the old Zionist in the 1920s: 'We won't really be a country until we have Jewish policemen and Jewish prostitutes.' I saw lots of both.

J J and I returned to the hotel to attend a press party, where we bumped into more old friends. We also met a Dutch army captain manning a Patriot missile system. The Patriots hadn't knocked out any Scud missiles – or not more than one or two – but had played a vital part in the propaganda war. The captain said we could film the battery the next morning during the visit of Teddy Kollek, the celebrity mayor of Jerusalem. After viewing some of the footage on our monitor, we crawled into bed about 2.30am. We had done an awful lot in less than eight hours.

The next morning early we filmed the Patriots and did an interview with an irascible Kollek. He went straight into a tourist pitch with the ambiguous line: 'Why is it that every time someone gets killed in Jerusalem it's blamed on politics? There's a hell of a lot of "ordinary" crime.' Right on, Teddy, that's sure gonna make people rush out and buy an airline ticket to Jerusalem.

Then I nipped out to buy an Israeli bank. Actually all I wanted to do was cash a traveller's cheque, but the amount of papers I had to sign, phone calls that were made and close scrutiny of my passport by the manager and the office cat made me realise that Israel was the Middle

East, not a bit of Yankeeland in the Levant. In my naivety I had thought that Israel would welcome foreign exchange on principle, even if in practice it was just a few pounds.

We filmed some of the damage done by Scuds in Tel Aviv. The Israeli government claimed 20,000 homes damaged but this seemed a tremendous exaggeration. I bumped again into my CNN mate, who said that Shimon Peres, the leader of the opposition, was attending a wedding at our hotel. I had a soft spot for Shimon and risked the intrusion of grabbing him as he kissed the bride. The old pro gave me ten minutes of canned wisdom. I always liked his ponderous Kissinger-style delivery, oozing gravitas: 'History is like a galloping horse. When it passes near your home you must mount it or miss it. Now is the time to negotiate with the Palestinians.'

A military censor, ironically a colonel of Iraqi origin, came to check our pictures in the comfort of our own room. He was particularly keen to examine the Patriot stuff, explaining that a wide shot could give away the battery's position. 'We are protecting our allies, in this case the Dutch, not just Israelis.' He explained carefully and reasonably the security reasons for erasing certain sections. I could see the military rationale and wiped the offending shots in his presence.

We hired time in an editing suite and packaged some of the material we had collected after 24 hours in Israel. I did a short news item on the end-of-war celebrations and sent the Peres and Netanyahu interviews whole via satellite. Bibi Netanyahu was a good performer, looking good and sounding wise, despite his far-right position: 'It took 28 countries with armies and air forces much bigger than ours to control one Arab country. Living here on a sliver of land, on a pin-head, we have been fighting 20 Arab countries *alone.* Do they really expect us to reward the PLO with an Arab state in the West Bank which will be one mile from the *Knesset,* our parliament?'

I retired for a drink and bumped into an arms dealer from New York, who demanded: 'Where has the hardware Saddam bought gone? All those Stingers, those big artillery guns from South Africa, a million mines. It's all bullshit. Everybody believed Saddam's bluff.' He said the Israeli security men on duty at the Patriot batteries stopped the Americans from countering the Scuds, for deliberate political reasons. The Israelis, he insisted, wanted one or two Scuds to hit Israeli cities and the West Bank.

After one (soft) drink I had to do a live satellite interview to Johannesburg: one of the roof-top, skyline, potential-Scuds-in-the-background shots from a high building which became the vogue in the Gulf War. I struck up a rapport with Colonel Gissin – fortunately, as I had to reschedule the interview after confusing the times between local, UK, South African and GMT, forgetting that satellites operate on GMT. JJ was shouting on the phone to Jo'burg in Afrikaans while I tried to make sense of the Hebrew around me. I had an ear-piece to listen to the anchor in Jo'burg, and my mike to talk to them and the interviewee. When we started live – with no floor manager to tell me how I was doing – I realised my fly was open. I couldn't adjust my dress on air, and prayed that the camera went quickly into a medium close-up of my chest. The interview, in English, went well but was too long: thinking of angles, questions and my fly undermined my already severely limited capacity to count, so I ran way over time. But the anchor didn't say anything in my ear. Maybe she was transfixed by my dress sense.

I tried to get some sleep despite worrying about the interview: you feel self-conscious if millions of people watch you making a cock-up. There was a tremendous explosion and I rushed out onto the balcony: not a Scud, but a crack of lightning and a mighty storm. Shivering in my underwear, I sought the warmth of my bed, but somehow the balcony door had slammed and locked. It had not been a great evening; a night on a rain-swept balcony did not add to its appeal.

The next morning I was grumpy. Frustrated attempts to secure a visa to film in Jordan did not improve my mood. Then I did an interview in Afrikaans with the South African ambassador to Israel. I had not done any work for SATV for some years, partly because of my (late) conversion to sanctions. After Mandela's release I had sold documentaries and did a little work for them as a foreign correspondent: SATV paid quite well and promptly, unlike many other TV stations.

We hired a car and drove north. I planned a short documentary about the security position in Israel in the immediate aftermath of the war, which meant travelling around all the sensitive spots: the Lebanese border, the Golan Heights, the West Bank and Gaza. En route we would collect some pretty visuals which I could massage into a short tourism piece. What was lacking was bang-bang, especially if the war was really over. I had picked up a bit of gossip that Terry Waite and perhaps John McCarthy, two well-publicised British hostages, were being held in southern Lebanon. It was an extremely long shot but worth a go. I used one or two old Israeli military contacts to speed my access to the Lebanese badlands.

I visited some acquaintances in the north who lived in settlements next to Arab villages. 'Relations between Arab and Jew are on a knife's edge,' I was told. The Israelis were incensed by the Palestinians' passionate support of Saddam and stories of West Bank Arabs cheering from the rooftops as Scuds rocketed over them en route to Tel Aviv. 'There are two problems with the Russians: their Scuds and their immigrants.'

We stayed the night in Nahariya while I made arrangements with the Israeli army and UN peacekeepers to proceed into Lebanon. Leaving the car at the closed border crossing of Rosh Hanikra, we passed through army and police checks. At the end stood a white UN car manned by a black woman with a wonderful smile – Sarah, a Ugandan. Zig-zagging through big cement blocks Sarah and I discovered a mutual friend who had been in a convent school in Uganda. Ex-convent girls, I've found, can tend to treat the world as one huge pub, and thus sometimes make it big in journalism, although they are forever plagued with inbred, inescapable guilt. Actually our mutual friend didn't drink, but she was a bloody good journalist.

Sarah was immediately on-side and did her best to ease my way with the various UN contingents from whom I scrounged accommodation and armoured lifts. The main UN base was staffed with French troops, who had erected a mini Eiffel tower to make them feel at home. Sarah introduced me to her boss, a loquacious Indian, Timur Göksel. In his office a notice read: 'If you think you understand Lebanon, you've not been properly briefed.' After we had swapped Al J Venter stories and established other mutual contacts, he arranged UN passes for us.

Our first escorts were large Fijians driving Finnish armoured personnel carriers. J J had boundless energy. In Africa he would climb any tree or vantage point for his shots. In Lebanon we rode on top of the APCs, but he kept moving around to get travelling shots. I couldn't be in view, and spent bumpy hours clambering around trying to stay behind J J's camera. We passed through a series of road-blocks manned by the surly South Lebanese Army, who were in the pay of the Israelis. The countryside was initially dry bush and hilly country.

'Zia' (not his real name) was a burly Fijian lieutenant who soon befriended us. For some odd reason he thought that I was an expert on mercenaries; to become one was his main ambition in life. He sorted out our accommodation in the Fijian camp up in the hills. The Fijian army was sloppily based on the British model, but the officers mess was strictly dry. Zia said: 'Some people drink to socialise; we drink to get drunk.' These big, tough Fijians were very amiable when sober but I could see they would be handful on the grog, so the no-alcohol rule made sense. But life in the mess was boring. The food was awful and the only outlet was watching TV. After watching 'Bonanza' and 'Zorro' in Arabic I nagged Zia to take us on a tour of Palestinian camps.

We drove to a heavily armed PLO camp on the coast. On the outskirts two Palestinians invited me into the camp to 'take some tea'. I accepted out of curiosity but Zia pulled me aside and explained that the spot we

were in was exactly the one where an American, Colonel Higgins, had
been captured; he was later hanged. We moved on through territory
controlled by the Lebanese Army. Zia left the negotiations to my
fractured French, little knowing that letting me tell shaggy dog stories in
French to jumpy Lebanese soldiers was more dangerous than wandering
around a PLO camp. Still, we managed to talk our way through five road-
blocks on the pretext that I needed to speak to the Lebanese army
commander in Tyre. We were not supposed to film, but J J put the camera
on his side and let it roll.

Very few Western journalists had been into Tyre since the Israeli
invasion ten years before. I expected chaos but found instead a thriving
pirate economy. Mercedes proliferated, many apparently stolen in
Europe and smuggled into ports such as Tyre. Banks and shops operated
in the biblical but now high-rise city. Wrecked cars and houses littered the
landscape, although there were also new cars and buildings everywhere.
How the Lebanese economy had survived 16 years of civil war was a minor
miracle.

Lebanon was once called the 'Switzerland of the Middle East'. After
1975 the civil war killed at least 150,000 people. A quarter of its 3.5
million population had fled the country. It struck me as paradoxical that
the Lebanese, famed abroad as great fixers and organisers, had succumbed to domestic chaos. The origins of the war were so complex as to
almost defy classification. Internal religious rivalries (Muslim versus
Christian), allied with ideological and class hostilities and old tribal
feuds, had been exploited by outside powers. In this international
battlefield Syria, the PLO, Israel and Iran had been major contenders;
America, Saudi Arabia, Russia, France and Iraq also stirred the pot.

The Gulf War brought changes to Lebanon. First the Americans cosied
up to Syria, once called a 'terrorist state' by Washington. Next came the
termination of foreign subsidies to the numerous warlords, cutting off
the PLO from its Gulf funds. Supplies to Iraq's Christian allies were also
strangled. Even Iran, keen to rejoin the world community, was encouraged to rein in Islamic fundamentalists. And Syria, with its 40,000 troops
in Lebanon, could no longer rely upon a destitute Russia to bankroll its
military machine, which ran on Soviet technology shown to be very
inferior in the Gulf War.

Most important, though, was the utter war-weariness of the Lebanese.
As warlord Walid Jumblatt admitted: 'We are all just fed up with this war.'
Certainly ordinary Lebanese were sick of the militias and their Mafia-like
protection taxes. On the other hand, they did provide a rough and ready
sort of order in their military statelets. The Syrian army had helped the
weak Lebanese army recapture much of the country, although the

southern region was still a hotch-potch of UN troops, militias, PLO and Israeli-backed Lebanese proxies. It was a political mess.

The black market thrived, despite triple-figure inflation. Lebanese were starting to return from abroad. But those who had stayed, especially the drug smugglers, would suffer if the pirate economy was curbed. Nevertheless, Lebanon was allowing itself the luxury of hope. Some of the 5,000 UN contingent began to feel that in a few years they might be able to pack up and go home.

When we reached the Lebanese army HQ in Tyre I spoke to a deeply suspicious and very charming general who explained in immaculate French that we could not film. He was a civilised man who shared my interest in the Roman ruins in the area: provided our cameras did not leave our vehicle we could indulge in some sight-seeing. Urbanely, over mint tea, he gave us two hours to get out of town. We filmed discreetly from the vehicle and visited the market near the bustling harbour. I wanted to send some 'Wish you were here' postcards to Europe. There were lots of postcards but apparently stamps were unavailable. Since tourists were an endangered species, J J, a compulsive shopper, managed to haggle some real bargains – the only time and place in the Middle East where I saw a foreigner get the better of an Arab trader. This was about the most unpackaged tourism I could aspire to. I liked it. Zia didn't; he was keen to get us out of Tyre.

Zia became very shifty. We had switched from an armoured vehicle to a UN Land-Rover. He drove down some back streets, just the three of us, until we reached a small shop. He asked us to wait outside for him. 'Don't leave the UN vehicle. It's your only protection. I'll be back in an hour.' We wandered off to film, keeping the Land-Rover in sight. When Zia came back he confided that he had just visited the relative of a Lebanese Muslim widow, and told us a poignant love story.

He had seen her in a little shop. For months he visited on various pretexts, bringing flowers regularly. She had two children; her husband, a militiaman, had been killed two years after their marriage. Zia was a large black man, under strict military orders not to fraternise with local women. He was also already married. She was surrounded by fanatical Muslim extremists, who would happily take pot shots at any UN officer, let alone a black married Christian carrying on an adulterous relationship ... She told Zia: 'Our love will get us killed if we are caught.'

'I know. But I don't care.'

'Nor do I,' she replied, sealing their dangerous pact.

Zia wanted to take her to Cyprus and then France, where he planned to join the Foreign Legion. (This is a true story; not even Mills and Boon would mix a forbidden love with the Foreign Legion.) The plot was complicated by the fact that her relatives had whisked her off to Beirut where she was practically imprisoned. Zia told me how he planned to spring her. 'I will marry her,' he said, pulling out some of his poetry for me to read. I could see that he was desperate, completely crazy, and about to ask my advice and practical help.

But before I could become actively involved in his suicidal venture, J J and I decided to join some nearby Irish troops. The dry Fijian mess, and the mosque outside our bedroom which wailed us awake at 5am, were getting to us. We filmed the Fijians playing rugby, then Zia drove us to the Irish battalion. He had time, he said, to take us to an interesting place. J J was wary until Zia said it was a shopping trip.

About ten miles from Tyre, way up in the hills, was one of the world's greatest army surplus stores. The Lebanese owner had spent years amassing stolen weapons and equipment. J J was in seventh heaven, and we bought two UN caps. Suddenly Zia started shouting and raving, clutching a flak jacket with the name of a close friend on it, stolen a few weeks before from their HQ. This was a massive affront to the honour of his country, his army and himself. The shopkeeper said he could have it for $20. Zia said he would take it for free. It belonged to him. Zia drew his pistol; the shopkeeper, with great speed, pulled out a brand new AK 74, cocked it and aimed it at Zia's chest. In Lebanon the customer is not always right. While they cursed at each other J J took cover. I sneaked out to tell the Fijian private guarding the Land-Rover to get in there with his rifle.

The two Fijians, with rifle and pistol, faced the determined shopkeeper, who had been joined by another man armed with an AK 47. Four weapons a few feet apart and lots of angry words. What would all those shots going off do in a shop full of ammunition? I spotted an *Amal* militia officer sitting in a jeep across the road, and quickly explained the situation. He rushed in to defuse what was about to become, literally, an international incident. The guns were lowered and half an hour later Zia came out with the flak jacket. He didn't pay anything. He had made his point.

Unfortunately we were late for our rendezvous with the Irish troops. I had been dreaming of Guinness, but the Irish captain displayed a regard for punctuality which I had not before encountered in the Celtic personality. I tried hard to persuade him to accommodate us, applying my own Celtic charm, and attempting to evoke pity for the limp caused by a twisted knee ligament acquired when I had fallen off an APC while trying to hang on behind J J. But the captain didn't like journalists. 'Without UN escorts, you will have to quit Lebanon'.

I rang Göksel, who arranged for us to join the Finns. I had given up

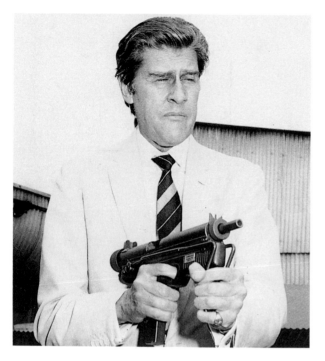

1. & 2. Ian Smith
(below) and his familiar,
P K van der Byl (left),
resolved to fight to the
bitter end. (Rhodesian
Ministry of Information)

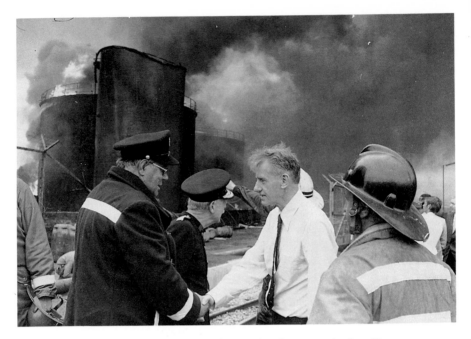

3. The Great Fire of Salisbury, December 1978. Ian Smith greets senior fire officers.

4. A poignant picture of war. An 18-year-old 'troopie' is about to go into action for the third time in a day. Mkoto, 1977/8, Rhodesia. (Chris Dehon)

5. *An unhappy follower of Bishop Muzorewa. These auxiliary units were supposed to be made up of ex-guerrillas but nearly all of them were unemployed thugs from the urban slums. (Allen Pizzey)*

6. *(Dave Anderson.* The Star, *Johannesburg)*

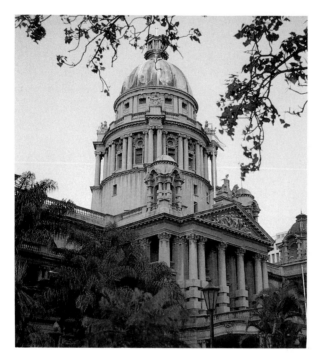

7. Durban's city hall.

8. Melville's first mardi gras. (1986)

9. Church square, Pretoria, statue of Paul Kruger, rebel leader during the Boer War.

10. Entrance to The Lost City, Transvaal.

11. On the edge of the Sahara.

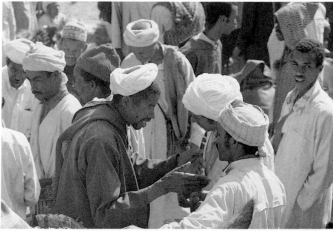

*12. Haggling in
the Zagora
market, Morocco.*

*13. Berber
girls seduced
by our
Polaroids.*

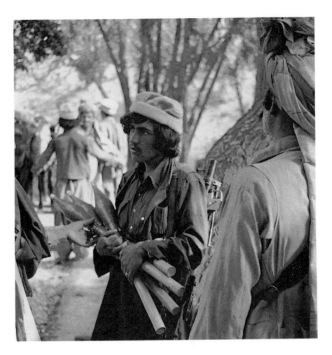

14. 'Donkey', the weapons 'expert' at Serracheena.

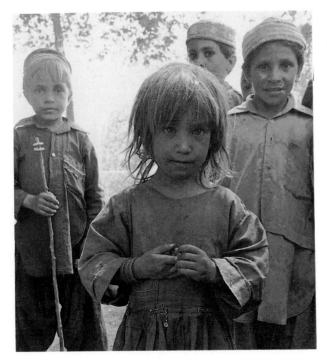

15. Suffer the little children: Afghan refugee camp in Pakistan.

16. The film crew arrives to find their host's house destroyed.

17. A barbecue at Serracheena. Tim (left), Doc (centre), Chris, Ian (kneeling), Joe (right).

18. 'Muj' at Serracheena.

19. A refugee amputee in Pakistan.

20. Film crew near Kabul. (Chris; centre, Ian; far right)

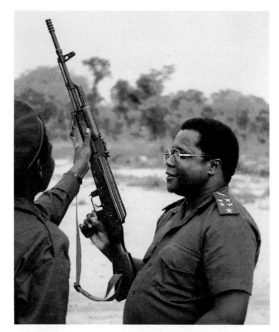

21. Too young to smoke, but carrying a gun. A UNITA soldier.
22. Afonso Dhlakama.
23. The mad general with Tim and me.

24. A Gaudí masterpiece in Barcelona.

25. The Rock from the Spanish side.

26. Lüderitz, German architecture in the desert.

27. Ovahimba women, Namibia.

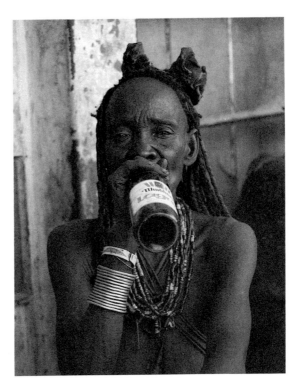

28. Ovahimba woman enjoying the joys of civilisation at a South African base.

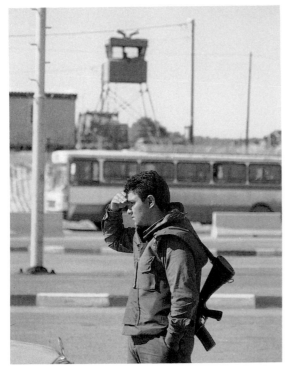

29. 'How do we get outta here?' Israeli soldier on guard at entrance to the Gaza strip.

30. *Fijian UN troops in southern Lebanon.*

31. *JJ with friends, Southern Lebanon.*

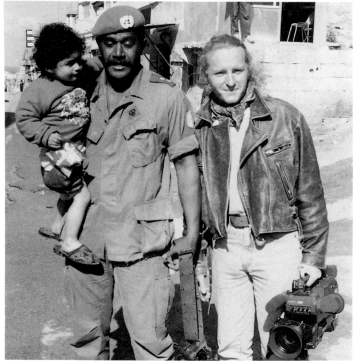

32. Young entrepreneur,
Elmina Castle, Ghana.

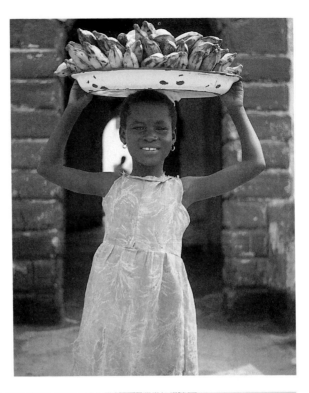

33. The ghosts of colonialism
and Marxism, Cacheu fort,
Guinea-Bissau.

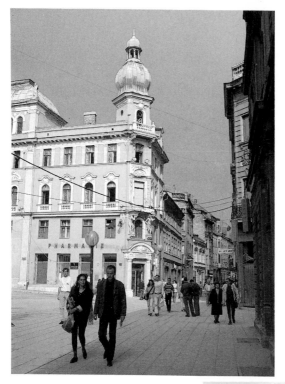

34. Between tall buildings in central Sarajevo it was possible to amble in relative safety from the sniper fire.

35. Nearly all Sarajevo's major buildings were destroyed or severely damaged. The Serbs targeted buildings of historical or commercial importance.

any idea of even asking about hostages. Southern Lebanon was one dangerous place. The Finns ran a luxurious mess compared with the Fijians: we wallowed in pizza, lager and saunas. This was a war for journalists. The officers, who spoke excellent English, treated us with great courtesy. In exchange we listened to endless bad jokes. The Finns must have learned a lot from their alliances with Germany. Their briefings were equally Teutonic: I took endless notes about the precise calibres of every rifle in the hands of the local militia. The frustrated PLO guerrillas, I was told, paid local Lebanese $100 per rocket to fire Katyushas into Israel.

The Finns gave us a lift back to the UN camp at the border, and we crossed back to Israel to pick up our hire car. Lebanon had depressed me; I wanted to find some gleam of hope in the promised land. I visited a few of the Israeli peaceniks to search for a good news story for a change. The war had polarised most Arabs and Jews in Israel, even those who were active in the peace movement. In Kfar Yassif, in Galilee, I came across a different story.

The Arab mayor, a communist leader called Nimur Murkus, had invited Tel Aviv Jews to stay in his village, an unlikely target for Saddam's Scuds. Mayor Murkus opposed Scud attacks on civilians. His invitation, ignored in the international media, was echoed by a number of other Israeli Arab mayors. We spent an enjoyable day with Murkus and his family, getting the perspective of 'moderate' Arabs who were Israeli citizens.

Later J J and I sought out the Jews who actually took up the offer. We contacted a wonderful 76-year-old lady from Tel Aviv, who spent some days in Kfar Yassif with her son and her dog while the rockets rained down on heavily-populated Tel Aviv. 'After 60 years of hatred, it was marvellous to stay with Arab people who treated me so kindly.'

Elsewhere, behind the scenes, tiny groups of Jews and Arabs were working together. I interviewed a rabbi who held small religious gatherings with Arab Muslims and Christians. The same rabbi organised trucks of food to be taken into the West Bank just after the 24-hour curfew was imposed at the beginning of the Gulf War.

J J and I drove north – it is easy to get around Israel, it's the same size as Wales – to stay the night at a *kibbutz* hotel at Kfar Blum. A number of South African Jews had settled there and I wanted to do a quick documentary on how they had gone through the war. We arrived late in the evening but a group of ten ex-South Africans and former Rhodesians were more than happy to be interviewed around a large table. They talked about the difficulties of adapting to gas masks and the special problems with children's protection. You always get somebody who wants to play the clown, so one did a brief chat through a mask. They complained that they had no masks for their pets. I did point out that initially the Palestinians in the West Bank had no masks at all. In the morning we filmed some visuals and cutaway shots around the *kibbutz*, a pleasant agricultural settlement in the shadow of the Golan Heights. The ex-South Africans joked about life without cars and maids: capitalist businessmen from Jo'burg and Cape Town, not without difficulties, had accepted the socialist ideals of the *kibbutz* movement. About three per cent of Israelis lived in *kibbutzim*.

Zionism was always a paradox. Jews in the affluent West were encouraged to give up their comfortable lifestyles to accept the bracing austerity of nationalism in Israel, while Palestinians in the West Bank were told to forget their national ideals in exchange for the economic advantages of the Israeli connection.

We left early to drive through the Golan to film Mount Hermon, shrouded in mist and rain, then cut back across the West Bank in late afternoon. The West Bank seemed empty, dry, dusty and run-down. In Israel there was crowded bustle, set amid a greening landscape. Over 190 million trees had been planted since 1948.

In Jerusalem we stayed at the American Colony, a beautiful hotel. It was the press watering hole and the best place to make contact with the PLO, while everybody was watched by alert Israeli intelligence men with bulges under their jackets and strong American accents. The old city was largely closed because of a strike called by the PLO but I found an Arab restaurant open and chatted to the locals. They all expressed support for Yasser Arafat and Saddam Hussein.

I made contact with the PLO and arranged for a guide to take us through the West Bank, even though it was still officially closed to journalists. Our guide, Suheir, was a brave and pretty 18-year-old student. We needed a hire car with Israeli plates to get through the Israeli army road-blocks, with our camera equipment stowed in the boot. Many journalists had had their cars stoned and burned by Palestinian youths, so we needed an official PLO guide in case we came to unofficial PLO road-blocks. When we saw a group of youths carrying stones, Suheir told us to put an Arab head-dress across the top of the dash. Around the next bend was an Israeli road-block, so she whipped it away.

We drove into a 40-year old refugee camp at Ramallah. The conditions were wretched. The camp's elders told me how thousands of new Soviet immigrants were taking Arab jobs: 'The curfews keep us at home and then they hand out our jobs to people who have been here a few weeks. We were born here.' They also complained about the Israeli army's practice of bulldozing and dynamiting the homes of activists. The older generation in the camp clearly supported Arafat and Saddam Hussein, although the younger elements were backers of *Hamas*, the fundamentalist opposition to the PLO.

As I was interviewing the camp elders, a messenger came to tell us that soldiers were looking for foreign journalists. Suddenly there were soldiers everywhere, partly because an Israeli woman had just been stabbed about a mile away. We drove the car into the large backyard of an old UN refugee building on the edge of the camp and sat tight. We might have our film confiscated and suffer deportation but Suheir told us that she would be jailed.

Six nervous young Israeli soldiers sauntered into the yard. The only way out was past them, so J J and I put on the UN caps we had bought in Lebanon. Our cameras were hidden in the back seat. I drove towards the soldiers, slowing down just enough to say quickly that we were UN workers. They shouted at us to stop and raised their rifles, but didn't open fire. We got out of the camp as rapidly as possible.

In Jericho, the biblical oasis 750 feet below sea level, I interviewed a prominent PLO official, Professor Sa'eb Erakat. He was one of the Palestinians negotiating with US Secretary of State James Baker, who was in Jerusalem at the time. We filmed the interview and J J surreptitiously shot some scenes from a roof. It was too risky to film openly. Six PLO guerrillas had just been killed in the West Bank and there was growing unrest in Gaza. The Israelis were unlikely to swallow our blue hat routine a second time.

Returning to Jerusalem we filmed secretly in an Arab hospital. We were allowed to interview young patients wounded, they said, by Israeli troops. The wounds were real but I had a problem with the boys' repetition that they were 'on their way to the mosque to pray', that they had not thrown any stones... Whatever the real reason for their injuries the tragedy of teenage paraplegics lay heavily on me. I would have liked to check each Arab claim with the Israeli authorities, but that was impossible. We weren't supposed to be filming in the West Bank at all. I had to rely upon my own balance when it came to editing the film.

We interviewed Major General Shlomo Gazit, the former head of military intelligence, who arrogantly derided the idea of a Palestinian homeland in the near future. Either he was not up on the latest intelligence or he wasn't sharing anything with us. But why should he?

We took a day off to film some of the old city of Jerusalem, which enchanted me no matter how often I visited it. You could see, smell, touch history here. Many shops were still closed and there were few tourists. Nonetheless storekeepers whispered to us to come in and buy behind closed shutters. Business was business, and J J was still a shopaholic. Again, he managed to beat down the best hagglers in the world. Israelis, it must be said, were not exactly backward when it came to business either. Jewish friends delighted in telling me stereotyping stories. I loved the one about the Jewish primary school:

Teacher: 'Hymie, what's two and two?'

Hymie: 'Are we buying or selling?'

We wandered for hours through narrow medieval streets, full of twisting lanes, oriental souks, steep stairways and dark, covered passages. We felt no threat, just wonderment. I could almost understand the Jerusalem Syndrome, which hospitalises 40 or 50 visitors each year. The spiritual overload of the old city causes people suddenly to think they are the Messiah or the Virgin Mary, with the odd sprinkling of John the Baptists and the occasional King David. Most of the nutters come from Europe or America, and they are usually Protestants, rather than Catholics or Jews. A local doctor told me that he once had two Jewish Messiahs in his care at the same time. Apparently they got on very well, even though they both said it was a pity they had to chat to an impostor. Most patients recover after four or five days and recall their crisis as a pleasant experience before flying off home to resume their normal lives. But going back to selling insurance or fixing radiators after being the Son of God must be tough.

Jerusalem must have affected J J and me because we ended up in the desert filming and visiting St George's Monastery. Both of us were attracted to the place and the long walk there. En route to Eilat we swam in the Dead Sea; I took the obligatory picture of J J sitting reading a paper in the superbuoyant salty water. At Eilat, a friend from Cape Town ran a diving school. We hired equipment and dived with the dolphins. On previous visits I had driven deep into the Sinai to visit Sharm El Sheikh and the intriguing St Catherine's Monastery. Now Sinai was in Egyptian hands.

After the rare, relaxing break at Eilat we headed north to film around Gaza, where the mood was very tense. You could reach out and touch the Palestinian anger. We also filmed in the picturesque port of Jaffa to beef up the short travel documentary I had in mind. In less than three weeks we had made a political documentary, sent off news footage by satellite and made a soft travel film plus some short pieces in Afrikaans. We had enough in the can. I went to defence HQ to buy some aerial library shots and used the opportunity to get customs security clearance. It would be more troublesome at the airport, where they might insist on viewing all the tapes.

We were interrogated by security personnel at the airport. Two men questioned us separately and in detail on our contacts with Palestinians, then swapped around to see if there were any discrepancies. They didn't check the already security-tagged film. We missed our plane but arrived back safely in London. The rudest people we met on the whole trip were the customs officials at Heathrow.

I left the Middle East feeling just a little optimistic. The proverbial window of opportunity was opening just a mite. The basic issue was still straightforward: land for peace. Jewish survival versus rights for the Palestinians. Cynics would say: swapping Jews for oil. Nevertheless, the Palestinians had lost everything, and had turned to Saddam Hussein in utter despair. Equally, the return of the possible death by gas traumatised the Israelis. Israel had a population of four million worriers, as well as four million would-be generals. But one of the main lessons of the war was that the old argument about strategic depth – the need for land to buy time in case of an Arab invasion – was seriously flawed in the missile age.

Once, Israel could rely on the almost unconditional support of Washington, but American public opinion was changing. The image of a tiny democratic state of brave Holocaust survivors has been tarnished by the arrogant military occupation of the West Bank and Gaza. The power of the once-mighty Jewish lobby has declined. With the collapse of the Soviet Union no longer was Israel seen as the only reliable ally in the region. Instead, it was a strategic liability costing the US $3 billion a year in military aid. In the longer term, utterly dependent on its American life-support machine, Israel's position must weaken.

Syria had lost its Soviet patron, Iraq was humbled, and America was top dog in the Middle East. The Arabs, cowed by American weapons' wizardry in the Gulf, had lost interest in fighting Israel. But in one sense Saddam won, by accident. He put the Palestinian uprising, the *intifada*, back on the centre of the world stage. The 1993 Israeli–Palestinian accords led to a Palestinian state, of sorts. As in South Africa, however, the liberator – Mandela or Arafat – might not be able to contain the radicals. The Middle East may become more unstable. Israel is still the only real democracy in the area; the Arab states are all more or less dictatorships. And, as the former Soviet empire further crumbles, 45 million ex-Soviet Muslims may be swept up by Islamic fervour.

And Jerusalem? How do you divide that ancient and holy citadel? Perhaps, just perhaps, the city should be shared under UN supervision. Jerusalem is the toughest nut to crack but nobody said a Middle East solution was going to be easy. Maybe Steven Spielberg could make a film called 'The Jerusalem Syndrome'. In it Charlton Heston would star as a deranged messiah who comes up with an answer to the city of three great world religions.

12

West Africa – forts and castles

West Africa is where the whites went to harvest blacks. But before the black gold, they hunted for yellow gold. For three centuries nine European states built, fought over and ransacked hundreds of forts and castles along the steamy, disease-ridden West African coast. The African continent has thousands of fascinating fortifications, ranging from the small Beau Geste forts of North Africa to the dry-stone masterpieces of Great Zimbabwe in the south. In the east Arab traders built Islamic citadels. West Africa, however, has the best collection of European-built fortresses.

The fortresses originated with the Portuguese, who started exploring this coastline in the late fifteenth century. Driven by favourable winds and currents, early explorers sought gold, glory, and a southern maritime route to the riches of the east. There was also a strategic impulse: Portugal wanted to find the legendary Christian kingdom of Prester John. Feeling threatened by advancing Muslim armies in south-eastern Europe, they thought a Christian thrust from the rear could undermine the march of Islam. Some of their castles were built with massive walls, similar to the great Crusader forts. Perhaps the Portuguese were mindful of the successful Muslim onslaught on the bastion of Constantinople. Instead, the African forts became prizes in a long series of colonial mini-wars waged mainly between the Portuguese, Dutch, British and French. Sometimes African armies would pitch in to tilt the local white balance of power.

West Africa was not my normal stamping ground, so when I received a phone call from Al J Venter about making a film in the region I was keen. It was early 1992 and I was bored and frustrated in my native Wales. Any adventure would do, even a crazy one arranged by Big Al. I liked Al so I had a very low learning curve about saying no to one of his 'missions'. He always worked a double, or even triple, agenda. You would be in some often disagreeable, sometimes dangerous place before you discovered what he wanted. Later, back in civilisation, you might find out what he was

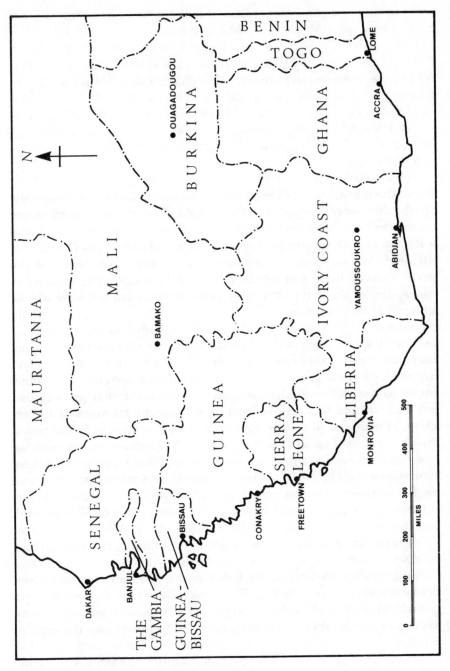

West Africa

really up to – sometimes years later. It took me six years to uncover his hidden agenda for Afghanistan, for example.

It started off in the usual way. Would I please take a large case to Lisbon? I sat in his hotel room in London and watched him pack it. The suitcase was extraordinarily heavy, although I'm sure he didn't put in any guns this time. In Lisbon Al explained that he was particularly interested in Christianborg castle in Ghana. I knew it was a wonderful building, but I also knew it was the heavily-guarded home of a rather paranoid generalissimo, Flight-Lieutenant Jerry Rawlings. He definitely didn't like unexpected guests.

'Dogs of war again, is it Al?'

He gave me one of his sly laughs. 'No, this is a straight film.' He showed me the dummy of a big picture book on African forts. The one printed chapter had some tremendous photos. He wanted the book to tie in with a 12-part TV series which he hoped to sell world-wide. I was to produce the pilot. As most of the castles were located in nasty dictatorships, no permission had been sought to film in any of the countries he wanted me to visit. We would do it with a small video-eight camera which we had to smuggle in. Here we go again.

Normally Al was noticeable by his absence in any of the places he asked me to visit. That suited me fine. He had an overbearing presence, despite his great charm. Most cameramen could take him only in small doses if he tried to play the great director. On this trip Al played the great white hunter and movie mogul. Two-man teams work well in war zones or tin-pot dictatorships. When we arrived in Abidjan, the capital of the Ivory Coast, I discovered Al was bringing his wife and two friends on our jaunt. He was paying so I couldn't really complain. But the cameraman, Tommy Doig, and I did our best to escape on our own. Tommy, in his early fifties, cynical, tough and experienced, was a veteran African film-maker whose work I admired. He was an old friend of Al's, and unlikely to be intimidated by his famous temper and constant changes of mind and mood.

We went to a restaurant in a seedy downtown area of Abijdan. Afterwards Al wanted to show his South African friends what a ghetto was like at night. Tommy and I knew better and went back to the hotel. Al's entourage arrived back half an hour later. 'Have a nice time?' I asked politely. Al did not know the meaning of sheepish grin, but he came as close as he could: 'Yeah, interesting. Brought the others back for security reasons.'

Tommy and I explored in daylight. Central Abidjan was swish, modern, very French. Many restaurants were expensive, as were the imported wines. It used to be an African success story. 'It's the one place on the continent where the numbers of whites increased after independence,' a French official told me. Foreign aid poured in and the profits poured out. Ivory Coast, or Côte D'Ivoire, played along with Western rules in the Cold War. Like next-door Ghana, it listened to the IMF. Urged on by aid donors, both countries boosted their mainstay, cocoa. (Coffee was also produced, but it was the awful instant stuff sold in big tins.) Then prices collapsed. The French settlers, originally 40,000 strong, began to drift away.

The wily and benevolent despot of the Ivory Coast, Félix Houphouët-Boigny – whom Tommy dubbed 'Humphrey Bogart' – started losing his grip, despite the presence of immaculately-dressed French troops. The French were growing tired of propping up their client states in Africa; paras were sent into Francophone Africa sparingly and reluctantly. Instead they advocated 'Paristroika' – usually French blueprints to conjure up 'national conferences' to end endemic dictatorships and establish multi-party democracies.

There were one or two half-successes – a few more or less free elections – before some sergeant or other grew bored in barracks on half-pay. But there had also been much backsliding. In remote states such as the Central African Republic and Burkina Faso the military paid mere lip service to reform. In many countries the national conferences had set southern, more urbanised tribes (who often had more to gain from 'democracy') against traditionally nomadic, often Muslim, northern tribes who tended to dominate the militaries.

Some West African states resisted foreign demands for multi-party systems. In French West Africa relying on France, however, had become a habit. The French had been more successful colonists than the British in the region because, as one journalist put it, 'All the colonisers stuffed up the locals, but at least the French called them "monsieur" while they did it.' Paris, as usual, was playing a double game. Despite Paristroika, France still sent troops and weapons to bolster autocrats. Cameroon was a recent example. The excuse was that Paris didn't want to support 'anarchy disguised as democracy' as Roland Dumas, the French foreign minister, declared. I don't think Brezhnev could have put it better.

West Africa was an important indicator of the continent's health. Its European connection with black Africa was old and complex. The Portuguese first ventured into the area in the 1440s. I wondered whether the 500-year connection had helped or hindered West Africa. The area was notorious for its virulent corruption: an indigenous trait or bad habits learned from centuries of encounters with the most rapacious of European traders and slavers? Whatever the cause many West African states were simply sinking into a morass of their own graft and venality.

In February 1992 Nigeria's election commission revealed the existence of some 20 million 'ghosts' – fictitious people who had dutifully registered to vote. The whole mess used to be blamed on shifty, greedy colonialists. But they left decades ago and the economies had deteriorated rapidly, with a few exceptions such as the Ivory Coast. Nigeria could have become an African superpower but it was heading for chaos.

The West was bored with Africa. Besides regular catastrophes only the occasional media circus grabbed attention. John Paul II and Michael Jackson had recently made (separate) papal tours of West Africa, for example. The West still officially showed some interest in 'good government' in Africa but it was a fleeting diplomatic flourish, for the simple reason that free-market economics and free politics do not necessarily go hand in hand, especially in Africa.

Ghana had frightened off investors but its slight economic recovery was praised by the World Bank and donors. Everyone ignored the strong-arm tactics of Flight-Lieutenant Rawlings, perhaps because he was not as obviously bonkers as some of his fellow dictators in uniform, or because he was practically the only African leader who deliberately avoided a personality cult. The fundamental question remained: can embryonic democracies take really tough economic decisions without slipping back into dictatorship? In West Africa the answer had usually been no.

Al gave me three days to fly to Ghana alone and get permission to film in Rawlings's castle. He and Tommy would drive down the coast and cross into Ghana by road, filming some of the coastal forts en route. But all the flights to Accra, Ghana's capital, were fully booked. I tried my luck with the manager of Ghana Airways, a large formidable woman. For once in West Africa a bribe just wouldn't work. I tried to pull rank, showing her a letter Al had received from the presidential palace about his book project. 'You are not Al J Venter and this letter is six months old.'

I decided to try the emotional approach. I had never been to Ghana before but I did have a female friend in Accra. I was looking forward to seeing her, although our relationship had been no more than the occasional lunch while she was studying in the UK. I apologised to the manager for trying to bribe and pressurise her. Everything I said was true, but I was trying to get to Accra quickly for *personal* reasons as well. I wanted to visit my friend, Mercy, for her birthday.

'Is she Ghanaian?'

'Yes.'

'That is good. Come back in ten minutes.'

She bumped an obnoxiously pompous white businessman off the plane. He made an awful fuss. I felt a bit guilty until he started racially abusing my benefactor. She gave him short shrift, summoned the airport security and winked at me. I liked her so I sent her a postcard from Ghana. I hate lying, but a successful journalist has to refuse to take no for an answer, especially in the third world. It contradicts all the rules of comfy Western journalism schools, but real life is different. Ethics are important in that you also say no, equally determinedly, when anyone tries to influence what you say. How you get the story is your business; what you say may be everybody's concern.

Accra airport was seedy, corrupt and chaotic: Anglophone West Africa, unlike the sleek, efficient, French-style airport at Abidjan. I fought my way, literally, through a host of would-be porters and crooks trying to grab my bag and ran for a car shared with a French businessman I had met on the plane. I wanted to find Mercy as soon as possible, so he dropped me at the hospital where she worked – the only address I had. They gave me her home address. I booked into a hotel and got a taxi to find her ramshackle house, at the back of an obscure market in a remote suburb. Her large family, intrigued by the white visitor from Britain, entertained me with beer.

Mercy seemed vaguely pleased to see me and reluctantly accepted my dinner invitation. My conscience demanded that I dine her as if it were really her birthday. I asked her advice on how to get into the dictator's castle, although I didn't put it that blandly. After she had told me – with cautious glances around the restaurant – about the political situation, and her father's imprisonment for political opposition, I felt I could trouble her no more with my quest. I had another angle: the dictator's brother-in-law, David, was a journalist I had met in Britain. David had also been imprisoned but his wife and Rawlings's spouse were close friends as well as sisters. His imprisonment had been brief. I arranged to meet Mercy again after contacting David.

The next day I left a message for David and explored Accra: wonderful, if you like cities where the traffic is one big stock-car race and the streets have open sewers. I spent the day looking for bookshops. Ghana once had an excellent educational system and a very high literacy rate, but I was curious as to what they read. It couldn't have been books. Even the university bookshop was rather like the Monty Python cheese emporium. After a day's hunt I found a book on Ghana's 60-odd castles and forts.

I also managed to contact the top civil servant in Christianborg castle. Al had written to him, and received a polite if wary reply. The fact that there had been a reply at all was very surprising and encouraging. More than half of government spending was on the civil service. One estimate put the number of civil servants as 22 times larger than the armed forces. That seemed a little unlikely in a state ruled by the military, so I didn't sully the information with any research. The castle official agreed to see me the next day, again such an unusual experience in Africa that I was extremely suspicious. I began to think of bills I hadn't paid, letters I hadn't written, friends I hadn't seen, the future of my dog without a master... I even tried to ring my mother-in-law.

David's jovial arrival pulled me out of my gloom. He was one of the most intelligent and energetic men I knew. David couldn't help me officially, but he said if I hung around for a while he might be able to fix up a social drink with Jerry. I said thank you but knew that I was lousy at small talk with dictators. David left early, but not before arranging for some of his friends to take me on a tour of the world's seediest bars and whore-houses, although they may have been the best on offer. Accra was full of very friendly women and a very high rate of AIDS. Besides, I was boringly obsessed with castles, especially Christianborg. I had one more day before Al arrived, and unless I had fixed things up the noise of Al's temper tantrum might conceal the gunfire from any number of local coups. I talked politics with the well-educated madam of a brothel with good beer. Really.

The next day I donned a suit, passed endless security checks, and waited around for two hours after the appointed time. I relaxed: this was the Africa I knew and loved. And I had wormed my way into the castle. I studied the architecture and worked out what to say. 'Have you seen the film *The Dogs of War,* sir? I have some nice well-behaved mercenary friends who want to come in and take pictures. Is that OK?'

When the time came I was ushered into a small office full of papers and the smell of booze. Again I felt more at home. After I had shown the senior official copies of the correspondence he became seriously aggrieved that Al had not responded to his letter of six months previously. I tried every tack possible. I couldn't mention video cameras because we had no permits to film, and asked merely to be allowed to take still pictures for Al's book. I got nowhere. Then I mentioned my contact with David. That went down like a lead balloon. On the point of giving up I tried the rustic touch. I started talking about Wales. The man's face lit up. By sheer coincidence he had been treated for a serious complaint in a hospital a mile from my home. The warmth and tenderness of the National Health Service in Cardiff had won his eternal affection. This might come as a surprise to 55 million Britons, but perhaps not many of them have been sick in Accra. He offered to see Al as soon as he arrived so I fixed up an appointment. I had been lucky.

Mercy's boss had lent me a car and driver to meet Al at Takoradi, a long way down the coast towards the Ivory Coast border. 'Uncle Boet', the driver, was late. He was a lovely old fellow so I didn't have the heart to tell him off. I would pay him handsomely and I knew the advantages of travelling in his government vehicle. We would sail through the road-blocks. The coast road was reasonable by African standards but the driving was genuinely terrifying. Cars drove straight for us, swerving away at the last minute. This was survivable in the day, perhaps, but suicidal at night. Many of the cars had religious inscriptions on them. I could understand why.

I was late. Al had endured endless harassment crossing road-blocks from the Ivory Coast border. (Since he was travelling in a car with Ivory Coast plates – Ghana and Ivory Coast were hostile to each other in the best Anglo-French colonial tradition – he should have expected hassles.) He also had a hangover and an embarrassing abscess in his crotch, and Ghana was not the best place to have a needle stuck in your nether regions. He bawled me out before I had a chance to tell him I had arranged everything. Tommy was embarrassed, but we set off to film some castles and with me doing stand-ups in front of them. I put Al's rudeness aside and concentrated on work.

St George's Castle, at Elmina, was built by the Portuguese in 1482 with dressed stone brought from Europe. It is perhaps the most important and certainly the oldest colonial edifice in sub-Saharan Africa. We approached it along a palm-fringed beach full of custom-painted, long-prowed pirogues. Decaying colonial buildings squatted around the castle. Parts of it were beginning to deteriorate but it was still imposing. In the morning mist it looked like an African Camelot. In the courtyard the Portuguese had built a Catholic church, which the Protestant Dutch turned into a mess hall and slave market. From the castle ramparts we filmed across the lagoon with its spectacular display of fishing boats. On the hill opposite stood Fort St Jago, another colonial monument built in the fifteenth century. Like several other Ghanaian forts, it had been transformed into a rest-house. When open, accommodation in the forts was usually basic. Very.

The marauding Europeans used these forts to seek ivory and peppers as well as gold before the coast became the centre for exporting over 20 million slaves to the Americas. Europeans bought the slaves, but local African chiefs sold them. By the end of the eighteenth century there were as many slaves inside Africa as outside. But that does not minimise the atrocious stain on European expansion. In African tradition slaves usually had some rights; in the hands of white Christians they had none. They had the same value as cattle and horses.

The wealth that slaves brought caused many wars between the slaving posts and later the colonial governments which took them over. Private traders and government troops fought each other, the indigenous peoples, the weather, pirates and disease. Malaria was the biggest killer. One sailor's warning went:

Beware and take care of the Bight of Benin
There's one comes out for every ten that goes in.

The castles were redolent of suffering, of both black slaves and the white overlords. Besides Elmina, Cape Coast Castle was the most accessible and impressive. It was founded by the Swedes, taken by the Danes, and eventually became the main base for British control of the Gold Coast, as Ghana was then known. It was extensively renovated in the nineteenth century. We walked and filmed through a maze of damp, claustrophobic dungeons where slaves were held before being transported. During the Ashanti wars of the nineteenth century three robust little forts were built on hills around the castle.

For tourist income some attempt had been made to keep the castles at the level of maintenance insisted upon by the British before they left. It appeared to be a losing battle. Locals had built slums around the castles, creating a poignant counterpoint between the colonial period and independence. We usually paid a small amount for permission to take still and video pictures in the castles. The smallness of the video camera made it look like normal tourist kit, although our radio mike and other extras would have betrayed us to a professional. But there were always hustlers who tried to charge us for filming anywhere, especially around the castles. Added to this was an appalling stench of open sewers. At Cape Castle Tommy had to stop filming while he retched.

We moved on to Fort Metal Cross, occupied by the English in 1691. It overlooked a lively fishing village and a circular bay. We walked down to the village and, after lengthy consultation, obtained permission to film an elaborate funeral ceremony. The chiefs, dressed in traditional regalia, carried ceremonial gold-coloured staves. Ghana offered much more inland away from the coast, especially in the Ashanti areas, but our job was to film coastal forts. We did travel 25 miles inland across dirt tracks to reach Gross Friedrichsburg, a fort at Princestown erected by the German Branderburgers in 1683 and restored since independence.

Back in Accra Al informed Tommy and me that we were to leave the next day for Senegal. I mentioned our appointment at Christianborg castle, for which I had sweated blood. But Al had changed his mind. It was his show. I did manage to leave a message for my new Welshophile friend that our appointment had been cancelled, and wrote a long apology to cover Al in case he changed his mind again. I am sure we could have taken at least still pics in the castle. The guy had seemed genuine. In nearly all other cases, the length of delays or prevarications by African bureaucrats usually signalled the size of bribe required. You learn to count the 'wells' or *Mais monsieurs* or *É impossíveis*, get a mental calculator out and make your offer.

Accra airport had become infamous for its corruption: bribes were demanded on a grand and highly organised scale. Al had seen a black American professor strip-searched and his anus examined for gold. Apparently the poor professor had just been searching for his roots, finding Mother Africa was not quite so maternal to her long-lost sons.

All six of our party arrived at the airport more than two hours before the flight, which had been confirmed the previous night. First we were told the plane had left; there was a plane-load of people waiting, so this seemed dubious. Then we were told it had to leave early and we did not have time to board – unless a few little presents were arranged. Our baggage might get lost if we did not take out insurance at $100 each. These threats were from officials, not hustlers. Al had already thumped two alleged porters who tried to grab our bags. We needed six of us to keep our luggage from disappearing in the throng. Al offered the baggage handler $50 to escort us through customs, another minefield. Once we were through Al gave him half, although he was angry enough to sabotage our luggage before it got to the plane. A favourite tactic, endured by some of my Ghanaian friends, was the simple removal of passports by customs officials. You had to buy it back or miss the flight. I should imagine that few tourists ever returned willingly.

I adamantly refused to use the airport again, sacrificing a ticket in doing so. Ghanaian airways replied to my complaints with a stream of polite evasions until I threatened to publish my experiences in detail. After lots of condescending letters they graciously sent me a cheque for £30 – not enough to cover my losses, let alone my discomfort. So beware all travellers to Accra airport; I wish I could print a health warning about it on this book. I was doing a tourist film which would have brought people to their beautiful castles, but by the time they clean up their act the castles will have disintegrated.

We flew to Dakar, the capital of Senegal. This ex-French colony sits in the middle of the belly of West Africa, swallowing the thin appendage of The Gambia (formerly British) like a greedy Pac-man. Dakar had touches of elegance, especially compared with run-down Ghana, and was almost Moroccan in flavour, a bit like Casablanca. To my ears the locals spoke excellent French.

The main purpose of our trip was to visit Gorée island, once a major slave *entrepôt*. The island was charming, full of eighteenth-century homes with wrought-iron balconies. It had a lovely beach with open air cafés. The centrepiece was the sombre Maison des Esclaves, where slaves were processed for three months or so while awaiting transport across the Atlantic. The curator told us how the slaves were stuffed into pens six by ten yards, inspected and valued as though they were cattle. Uppity slaves were chained to the walls and sea water piped into their cells to keep them partially submerged. The slaves fought for the scraps of food, the weaker ones died and were fed to the fish. Survivors were branded with the shipping company's insignia and packed like sardines into airless, rotten ship holds. American visitors, black and white, wept openly. Despite being on the *Roots* tour, Gorée was tragic and serene at the same time.

Al, Tommy and I left our fellow sightseers to continue with the more arduous part of our trip: trying to get into Guinea-Bissau, one of the world's most unwelcoming countries, not least to journalists. En route we stopped in The Gambia, where Al wanted us to film the main forts in a few hours the next morning. After arriving at Yundum airport we booked into a Butlins-type hotel in Banjul, the tiny capital. The state is not only named after a river; it *is* the river. The Gambia existed because the British wanted to exclude French access to West Africa's finest waterway. Except for the sea, the country's 700,000 people were surrounded on all sides by French territory. The narrow strip of land either side of the river was supposed to mark the maximum range of British naval guns. Everything was on a small scale; the capital's population was 50,000. This Islamic country was an exceptional paragon of political virtue in Africa: a democracy with no real army and no political prisoners. Even the minister of the interior had the friendly name of Mr M'Boob. The economy was based upon groundnuts and tourism.

The Gambia, to me, had lots of simple charm but the recent rapid growth of packaged tourists from Britain and Scandinavia (50,000 per annum in the late 1980s) disturbed me. Just like Germans on the Kenyan coast, Swedes were said to flock to Gambia for sexual safaris. There wasn't much else to do after a day on the beach, it must be admitted. But I would hate to see Africa turned into a giant bordello to work off European lusts, just as the sex industry has despoiled parts of South East Asia. Perhaps it was always so. The historian Ronald Hyam postulated that the principal impetus behind the British empire was the export of surplus sexual energy, not of surplus capital.

I didn't have any surplus energy in The Gambia. Tommy and I rushed to catch a ferry and hire a scrapheap to get to Juffure, the tiny village Alex Haley claimed as his ancestral home. An old lady, Binta Kinte, who purported to be a direct descendant of the *Roots* hero, demanded a little bit of compensation from each visitor for all the historical wrongs. Since a boat-load of Scandinavians, presumably full of surplus historical energy, were being led by the hand, and the nose, to Mrs Kinte we chose to ignore the rip-off. Haley was alleged to have written the Gambian bit of his book before he arrived in Africa, and since Juffure and Kinte are the region's equivalents of cross-roads, Jones and I thought avoidance the best strategy. But I couldn't blame the tourist board for making the most of a bit of fiction. The Gambia didn't have much else, except a fort.

Our taxi-driver helped us haggle for the hire of a very leaky long-boat which took us upstream to Fort James, built originally by a German aristocrat, the Duke of Courland, in 1651. In 1661 it became the first permanent British settlement in Africa. James Island had been severely eroded by the river and all that was left were romantic ruins and baobabs.

On the way back we took a quick look at the ruins of a French trading post established in 1681, just a few hundred yards from Kunte Kinte's alleged home. Poor old Kunte was surprised to find slavers in the area where he was caught and shipped off to American slavery. This showed either a singular lack of intelligence on his part or a serious deficiency in Haley's historical research. Still, it was a good story.

All this debunking made us late. I was glad about this because Al wanted us to fly to Guinea-Bissau on Air Mauritanie, which did not have the world's most impressive safety record. Al said our special visas for entering Guinea-Bissau were awaiting us at the capital's airport, and we now had to go by road. A taxi took us to The Gambian–Senegalese border, where hordes of Senegalese children demanded *cadeaux,* as did their parents. After some hard bargaining we persuaded a driver to take us south through the Casamance. Except for the occasional coastal resort, including one Club Med – which the locals called 'Club Merde' – the region was largely untouched by tourism. The spluttering of a local separatist insurgency was most helpful in this respect. We were forced to be travellers rather than tourists: living the day-to-day life of the country, foraging where we could rather than hiding away in hotel restaurants to avoid stomach upsets. Strangely, most tourists I met imagined they were great travellers. But the fact that I got the shits in more places than they had did not make me feel superior.

We found a real piece of France in a hotel in Zinguinchor, where I hugged the restaurant for its French cuisine and wines, and baguettes for breakfast. Before dinner Al and I set out to find the Guinea-Bissau consul to procure visas. Whenever I asked the way in West Africa I always found the village idiot. On this occasion he jumped in the taxi and gave us a guided tour of the town. We never did find the consul; we would have to bluff. Al liked to think that he was an expert on all things African, which he was. But he also fancied himself as a multilingual border expert, which he was not.

We left Senegal and entered no man's land before the Guinea-Bissau border. Suddenly, around a bend, we saw a rope across the road. Al said,

'I'll sort this out,' meaning: 'Let me show you how to do it.' He was very impressive for someone with only a few phrases in French and fewer words in Portuguese, although he did need to ask for one of the plastic half-bottles of whisky I kept for such occasions. It was a dramatic performance. After half an hour the man let down the rope, happily clutching his Scotch. Al seemed pleased with himself. I didn't like to tell him that, while he was giving a long speech about his personal friendship with the president of Guinea-Bissau, I had left the car to relieve myself in the bush and seen the border post half a mile down the road.

Al soon realised that the rope man was there just to slow down the one or two cars a day that passed through. Tommy was cruel enough to chuckle. Disheartened, Al said: 'You can handle this border post.' Guinea-Bissau was perhaps the least known and closed state in Africa, run by a paranoid military officer who didn't like strangers even when they came from the World Bank. The place had opened up a little recently, it was true, but we still didn't have visas. Al had landed a tough one in my lap.

I spent 45 minutes in reasonable French and broken Portuguese persuading the group of officials to let us in. I had finally reached the back office and was alone with the head honcho, about to seal the deal with a full bottle of whisky, when Al stormed in to ask why the fuck I was taking so long. He then left as abruptly as he came. I took a further 15 minutes to persuade the now jittery official that we were not escaped convicts or lunatics; we were tourists who liked unusual places. I gave him the whisky and he gave me the visas. Al said: 'Hell, I could have done it in half the time with just half a bottle of whisky.' There was no point in arguing.

We took ferries, taxis and buses, and eventually arrived in Bissau, the derelict capital. I couldn't believe the state of the harbour. Large ships had sunk at their moorings; some of the wrecks looked as though they had been stuck there since the Portuguese left in 1974. I wondered why they had stayed for 500 years – there was nothing much there except peanuts. Yet the country was unspoiled and beautiful, not that locals had much to eat except beautiful nuts. The interior was a vast plateau covered in almost impenetrable forest. The coast was flat, swampy and very unhealthy. Transportation was difficult because there were many rivers and few surviving bridges.

Tommy and I managed to hire a four-wheel drive, amazingly brand new. We drove for four hours through almost virgin Africa, sometimes along dirt roads with avenues of trees with pink blooms, to reach the fort at Cacheu. Sixty feet square and built in 1589, it contained a bizarre tableau of Africa's history. Statues of Portuguese colonial heroes such as

Vasco da Gama, dumped there after independence, had recently been joined by dethroned Marxist gods – Lenin and Stalin. On the way back we found some diesel, dispensed from a hand-pump made in the 1920s. Tommy insisted that I drive, even though we had to traverse broken bridges which necessitated balancing the jeep on two railway sleepers.

We got back to find Al in trouble with the police for refusing to pay a taxi fare. The manager of the hotel (a former Portuguese army barracks) eventually sorted it out, after Al agreed to pay half the 200,000 pesos demanded. The manager said his workers were paid only 150,000 pesos a month (roughly £30). In his arguments with the police Al went on about his special visit to the country to see the president, General João Vieira. This was partly true. Al had covered the colonial war in the country and wrote a book on the subject jointly dedicated to the generalissimo. He wanted to give him a copy in order to meet him. The little I knew of the leader suggested it was unwise dedicating even a limerick to him. In contrast, the founder of the revolution in Guinea-Bissau, Amilcar Cabral, was one of Africa's most influential thinkers … before he was assassinated.

After Al's cocktail do with the general we went straight to the airport. Although escorted by a presidential aide and the hotel manager, and although we had just left el supremo, we met a brick wall of red tape and aggressive demands for bribes from airport officials. We did have problems with visas: my efforts at the border had got us in but there was no permit to leave. Once it was firmly established that Al had just been a guest of the president the officials finally relented. We marched out of the airport cattle-shed and waited on the apron, Tommy heading for Johannesburg, Al and I for Lisbon.

Al and I started work in Lisbon, where I hired another cameraman to do visuals and stand-ups around historical buildings. On the final night Al took me to a *Fado* restaurant. The evocatively sad songs almost had me in tears. I am not sure whether it was entirely the music. Nor did I hear any more about the film.

13

South Africa – the new order

I was bored. Australia is a great place to raise kids but I don't know about adults. The stunning outback is dull and empty compared with the African bush. And even the grandest European cities are grey and lifeless when contrasted with the chaos, colour and vitality of Africa. I had to be there: the South African elections drew me back from the comforts and safety of Australia. The Australian federal government nominated me as a UN observer but at the last minute the UN vetoed me. A wise friend in South Africa said starkly: 'Someone must have known you in UN headquarters.' I am not one of nature's diplomats. Besides, I wanted to vote in, report on and share the elections. Diplomatic neutrality was not appropriate. The place, the people and, as a journalist, the story beckoned. Chris Munnion, the London *Telegraph* correspondent and doyen of old Africa hands, wrote: 'Every other bugger is trying to get out of here and into Oz and you want the reverse. Are you mad?' Yes.

It was April 1994. In the Jan Smuts customs hall a fat, middle-aged Afrikaner was grumpy about my papers. Same old South Africa. Although a resident, I had to have a special journalist visa. 'Don't you tell lies about us,' she warned. Once I explained that I was a returning resident, she spoke to me almost confidentially in Afrikaans: 'We're going to have a civil war here after the elections, you know.'

After hiring a car, which took ages, I drove into central Johannesburg. I had last been in South Africa six years before but the number of brash new buildings, especially in the largely white, elite areas, was astounding. So much for sanctions. Later I was told that many of the glass palatial offices were empty. I went straight to my old suburb, Melville, to pick up a few friends for lunch at Roma, a favourite haunt. Ornella and Enrico, the owners, refused to let me pay for the meal. 'It's great to have our best customer back.' South Africa was warming up for me. The friends took me back to their house, where I asked why the kitchen was stacked with tins of baked beans and dog food. 'Strange mixture.'

'Ja, the dogs are gonna eat and the humans are gonna fart the siege

*PWV = Pretoria – Witwatersrand – Vereeniging

*PWV = Pretoria – Witwatersrand – Vereeniging

The New South Africa

away.' The old defensiveness of white Johannesburgers. I recalled the open lawns in small-town America. Living in Australia I had almost forgotten about security. I had stopped locking my car; now I was told not to stop at traffic lights at night. Car muggings had become an epidemic. 'Armed response times' – the speed with which private security firms reacted – was a main staple of conversation. But my old white friends still seemed to live reasonably. They had servants – domestic workers now – although they were sometimes downright suspicious of them. Fewer workers lived on the premises, partly through cost and partly because of white insecurity. Even wealthier friends didn't have enough surplus rands to ask about doing a deal for US dollars. Maybe the black market had become more subtle.

Andy Gancewicz, my aggressive Polish friend, took me hunting on my second day back. After a year of political correctness at my university in Australia I was arming myself to go hunting defenceless animals. I hadn't held a gun since I was last in South Africa. It felt good. Driving through north-western Transvaal I noticed signs proclaiming a *Volkstaat* (Afrikaner people's state). In the shops of towns such as Ellisras, whites replied in Afrikaans when I addressed them in English. The old master–servant relationship between black and whites seemed to persist.

We saw lots of game. The 350 hunting farms had brought tourists and animals to a bush which 20 years before was almost bereft of wildlife. My rifle skills had not improved: I didn't shoot anything; I didn't really want to. I just walked in the sun and smelt the bush, and the familiar aroma of wood smoke on the tracker's clothes. Sunny Boy, the tracker, didn't say much; he just glided through the bush, with me clumping behind. I felt alive again, amid the serene sunsets and the perfume of the land when the first rains come. En route I spoke to some white farmers. 'Most of the others' would vote for the neo-Nazi AWB or the Conservative Party. I didn't feel it my place to tell them that neither party was participating in the imminent election.

Back in Johannesburg, I did the round of obligatory dinner parties. I was not invited for my repartee, but for my expertise on how to wheedle into Australia. I had missed lively dinner parties, full of the soul of survival politics. And in Oz you had to wash up yourself. I had missed the black humour, the cynical racism which infused white banter. 'There's good news and bad news about the new South Africa. The bad news is that the shit is going to hit the fan. And the good? The fan ain't gonna be working.'

The whites I met in Johannesburg were distinctly jittery in the days before the election. It was not surprising. Hordes of hacks streaming into the city all expected, and some hoped for, a blood bath. I sensed real fear in the white northern suburbs, huddled around shopping malls shifting ever northwards, away from the black town centre. You could almost squeeze the tension out of the air. The bombs didn't help, but I suppose they generated work for the ubiquitous security guards. The blacks I spoke to – especially those who lived in the townships – were also, frankly, shit-scared about the expected polling mayhem.

I was much more upbeat. When I had left, Mandela and the ANC were absolutely taboo. The secular saint now beamed at me from nearly every lamp-post. After being unpersons, the names of key black leaders were tossed around by even the most unwashed of whites. This was a refreshing change; the whites had been shaken out of their 'dreadful calm'. Everybody talked politics. The whites seemed resigned, weary, a few hopeful, a tiny minority euphoric. One white businessman said at a soirée: 'The whites have had an easy ride up until now. They must expect that the black man will have his day too. And the whites are going to pay. They shouldn't be surprised.'

South African television had changed. Some of the tongue-tied, brain-dead presenters were still preserved in aspic but some lively new black faces had arrived. True, some of it appeared to be tokenism but TV was better. The end of the Equity union ban on British programmes had made a difference: Basil Fawlty's walk was much more entertaining than P W Botha's finger-wagging. But I couldn't understand why the 8pm split between English and Afrikaans survived. I had never figured out why the Afrikaner overlords didn't allow at least English subtitles for the forced diet of Afrikaans. Some of the new experiments in bi- or tri-lingualism were laughable (especially as there were 11 language groups) but it was a stutter in the right direction, particularly in the brief interregnum of press freedom between Afrikaner and ANC authoritarianism. It was encouraging to see communist stalwarts such as Joe Slovo exchanging friendly televised banter with white Nazis.

Johannesburg's northern suburbs were always incestuous, a touch paranoid. I needed to get out. Buthelezi's impis were about to storm central Johannesburg; friends said I should stay for the action. It seemed more interesting to go to Zululand. So I was in kwa-Zulu when the mercurial chief finally decided to hop on board the electoral train. The sense of relief was almost tangible in the province. Whatever Buthelezi was promised – a fixed election victory in the local parliament? – it made the vital difference between ballot and bullet. I toasted the prospects of peace with Dave Willers, editor of the *Natal Witness*. Dave lived in Hilton, in the plummy white highlands. Here many whites prayed for the Zulu warrior's success, although Dave's white friends were ANC people. Dave and I celebrated till late, then I shared the euphoria by broadcasting on the radio to Australia. Switching from personal hopes for peace to detached observer, I had to do a live crossing by phone at 2am to fit in with the time difference. At breakfast I joked with Dave's father-in-law, a former Afrikaner diplomat, that while he was away from Pretoria it would be renamed Mamelodi (after the local black township). He laughed. I think he laughed inside as well. Times had indeed changed.

In Durban I listened to a tired Zach de Beer, leader of the liberal Democratic Party, singing the same old songs. What was different was the invitation to three 'former freedom fighters' to come on to the stage. They were from, it was said, the military wings of the ANC, the black consciousness movement and Inkatha. Two were painfully embarrassed by this outpouring of white liberal sympathy. The third was obviously a megalomanic psychotic – if there is such a condition. With eyes rolling insanely he shouted something about dying for the Democratic Party and 'Viva DP'. That's a bit like goose-stepping in a synagogue.

Natal and Transvaal were for politics; the Cape was for wine and architecture. On the Twee Jonge Gezellen wine estate, I was intrigued by the *kibbutz*-style living for the coloured workers. The white wines there were far superior, in my ignorant though extensively researched opinion, to their Australian equivalents.

Staying in excellent farmhouse accommodation, I fell into drinking and talking with the local farmers. I didn't mention that I understood Afrikaans (although only just after years away). In the most gentle of tones, one farmer admitted: 'I benefited from apartheid. I felt guilty but I made money. But I am glad it's over.' The contrition was tempered by a later outburst when he discovered some squatters had moved onto his land and were taking produce.

Tulbagh has one of the finest streets in South Africa. Each Cape Dutch building in Church Street is an architectural gem. It also has two excellent restaurants, where I drank with some sullen ex-Rhodesians who chided me about my reportage of their war. I nursed my hangover the next morning by chewing biltong, the thing I had missed most about South Africa. The dried meat strips are highly addictive.

In nearby Stellenbosch I enjoyed the bibulous hospitality of an ex-colonel who knew his way around *mampoer* as well as guns. He was an ardent admirer of General Constand Viljoen, leader of the right-wing Freedom Front, and told me the white call-up would have been five per cent without Viljoen, whose quiet intervention boosted the 'campers' (reservists) to about 65 per cent. 'He will save the election,' said the ex-colonel. Mandela's lavish praise of Viljoen seemed to confirm this opinion.

In Cape Town's refurbished harbour area, I had lunch with the coloured ex-girlfriend who had taught me so much about art, and apartheid, when we flouted so many of the hated laws in the 1970s. Now an ANC organiser, she bemoaned the fact that so many of her people would vote for their former oppressors, the National Party. She was right: the Western Cape voted to keep in the Nats and keep out the ANC. The Afrikaners had begun in the Cape; now the regional parliament was the last redoubt where they held a majority of seats.

For sentimental reasons I wanted to vote in Melville. I toured the bomb damage in downtown Jo'burg, right outside my former office. Whites were muttering about Lebanon revisited – the comparison was laughable. Central Johannesburg and Hillbrow, the night-life district, had changed dramatically. They had become African. It could be West Africa, except there were more goods on sale, the ghetto-blasters were marginally quieter and the streets were cleaner. Whites talked about the changes with disdain, whereas I considered the noise and colour much better than the stark glass and treeless desert I remembered.

In tense Sandton I met up with Marie Bruyns, once the top producer for SATV. She still had the brains and looks which once both irritated and charmed the dour apparatchiks in SATV headquarters. I told her that I – we – had been wrong to make programmes trying to side-swipe apartheid. I had thought I could work within the system; I had been wrong. We gave credibility to a propaganda monster. We had produced some powerful programmes that might have done some good but we were still wrong. She seemed more hurt than angry.

Come the first day of the elections, the queues were too long in Melville. But the multiracial community atmosphere boded well for the future. The bombs stopped, as did nearly all the killing. The voting process was chaotic but, except for kwa-Zulu, was a result of cock-ups, not conspiracy, or so it seemed to me. There were no voting rolls and no real idea of the size of the electorate. Chaos was inevitable.

I voted on the second day when the queues had diminished, choosing the liberal Democratic Party nationally and the right-wing Freedom Front in the regional parliament. Odd mix, any South African would say. I couldn't vote for the ANC simply because of its alliance with the communists. I had experienced the devastation in Eastern Europe. The Nats I could never forgive, no matter how much I might respect F W de Klerk's gutsiness. I never had much time for the upper-class twittery of the liberals, especially the Progs, but I admired Helen Suzman's courage. She might have been severely economical with her charm and have a voice like a dentist's drill, but she had stood alone in a racist parliament. I didn't agree with her anti-sanctions stance but whites like her, Helen Joseph, Bram Fischer and even Uncle Joe Slovo had done much to prevent black perceptions of a total racial chasm. That was vital for the future of all whites. I estimated that the DP would get about five per cent; I was slightly surprised by their poor showing but Zach was clearly yesterday's man. I voted, I guess, for Helen's bravery.

As for choosing Viljoen, he was honest, a good soldier and, above all, not a politician. All the clichés that justify coups. More personally, I had a paperback published in the month of the election which predicted Viljoen could lead a white homeland. I allied him with the ANC to crush the rejectionist crazies; his real soldiers wipe out the Nazi fat-guts. I was trying to be consistent rather than opportunistic; South Africa is probably an unworkable imperial creation. The Boers didn't much like the Union and Zulus and Xhosas weren't even consulted. Why should the country survive in its present form? It is a black Soviet Union. Nearly every other British federation, especially in Africa, collapsed; often in bloodshed like Nigeria and Rhodesia. I would prefer a non-tribal federation in South Africa but better a peaceful, tribal *con*federation than another Bosnia or Rwanda. Although I updated my book before the former key rejectionists – Buthelezi and Viljoen – had agreed to enter the elections, I still think there could be a white homeland. But don't ask me where.

On the eve of the elections Sue Ollemans, who owned a gallery in Rosebank, Johannesburg, told me merchants were removing valuables from their display windows. On the first day of liberation everybody expected looting – or 'affirmative shopping' as cynics called it. Her black partner suggested they should put some Africana, especially fetishes, in the window to deter thieves. Must have been powerful *muti* (medicine/magic). It worked – on a grand scale – for I heard of very little looting.

Buthelezi called the elections he had almost derailed 'a miracle'. Many of the 5,000 hacks who poured in expecting a replay of the Gulf War were clearly disappointed by Mandela's relatively peaceful triumph. CNN dismantled its huge replica of a NASA launch, and the correspondents drifted off to the genocide in Rwanda. I had seen enough tragedy in South Africa to hope fervently that the peace could lead to reconstruction. It was a hope, not an expectation.

On the first day of the new order, I went back to the citadel of Afrikanerdom, Pretoria, and said farewell to the Voortrekker Monument. The Afrikaner shrine was appropriately empty. The greater number of uniforms and fewer hawkers than in Jo'burg seemed to say: 'We Boers still run the show here.' I wanted to buy a doctoral gown from Pretoria's University of South Africa, even though I had graduated a long time before. A racist friend said: 'Better buy it now before it becomes feathers and skins.' It cost me R1,500 (£300), compared with the R400 it was on sale for in 1987. Sanctions had certainly helped to fuel inflation.

I spent my penultimate day at the ultimate metaphor of white society: The Lost City, two hours' drive north of Jo'burg. It is a spectacular piece of kitsch attached to the gambling and golf resort of Sun City. The Lost City is an almost surreal recreation of an ancient complex, a mix of Alan Quartermain, a high-as-a-kite Salvador Dalí and a set for an Indiana Jones movie. The central Palace is a brand new hotel with nearly 338 rooms and suites, boasting an artificial beach and the almost compulsory wave machine. Amusing myself on the near-empty water-slides, I wondered about the erstwhile emperor of the area, President Mangope, who ruled the former 'independent' homeland of Bophuthatswana. Nobody would or could tell where the dethroned and deranged Mangope was hiding.

Before I left I wanted to see the woman who had meant most to me in Africa: Latish. She was too beautiful in a too conventional way, having been Miss South Africa, runner-up in Miss Universe and a successful international model. We had been good friends, more brother and sister, and I never told her I was in love with her. My return to the dark continent had stirred my dark soul but I still didn't talk frankly when we lingered over wine in Sandman. She told me that she had queued for seven hours to vote. This, once the most apolitical of *meioses* (Afrikaner girls).

'I had been going to vote for the ANC but for seven hours the two guys in front of me said what they, the ANC, were going to do to us whites. In the end I voted Nat.' I don't think she was joking. After too much good wine, I took my leave. Sensing my unstated feelings, her last words were: 'Why did you always take the piss out of me?' I was going to say: 'What did you expect, voting for the Nats like that?' Instead I said: 'You were always surrounded by adoring men, what else could I do?' I wished her goodbye for another six years and her new family well.

Friends saw me off at the airport and we talked politics, of course. I thought but didn't say that in a few years time, as in Zimbabwe, local politics for whites would be like talking about the weather: interesting but nothing could be done about it. South Africa was a much better place in 1994 than in 1990; a morally comfortable perspective for foreign observers. It was, until the elections, a much more dangerous place for locals. Nearly 14,000 political murders were committed after Mandela was released. The killings receded after the ANC victory but the already chronic crime rates increased. Tourism would grow too, now South Africa was a politically correct place to visit. Like Eastern Europe after the fall of the Berlin wall, the republic was a novelty attraction. It had first-class hotels, roads, wines and game parks, often at third-world prices. There would be some investment, if there was much left over from bolstering Russia and her former empire. But there would never be enough to satisfy the 'liberation dividends' demanded by the feral youngsters in the townships. For four years of the odd-couple tango of F W and Mandela, the suits and *tsotsis* had been ripping off the country. Monsters such as Winnie Mandela could really jump on the gravy train before the wheels came off. The crisis of expectation – one person, one promise – was much more dangerous than the explosion of corruption. Whites would suffer reverse discrimination as blacks were 'artificially assisted' to top jobs. Whites with options would leave. Maybe, ten years on, affirmative action will insist that whites come back, like the Mozambicans begging their sleazy colonial masters to return and set up businesses again. Maybe the hardline Afrikaners will rebel to 'avoid the fate of the rest of Africa'.

It took me two hours of inefficient assistants and milling, cursing crowds to get my long-ordered cheque book from a Jo'burg bank; it would take two minutes in Australia. Some Oz banks pay you five dollars if you have to wait more than five minutes. But I had forgotten: I was in Africa. The sun shone. Nobody had been rude to me. I hadn't paid a bribe. I had stayed at world-class hotels at African prices (The Lost City excepted). Morally, I had committed myself by voting. I was glad I had been there to witness it all. I did not know, however, when I would return. South Africa now had a chance because I really did believe the election was a miracle. But I left with a disgruntled white's comments ringing in my ears: 'South Africa was a first-world dictatorship, now it's a third-world democracy ... for a while.'

Bill Clinton, Boris Yeltsin and Nelson Mandela were engaged in a long conversation with Jehovah. Clinton asks how long it will take for his country to solve its problems. 'Not in your administration,' says the Lord, 'but in the next one.' Yeltsin asks the same question. 'Not in your lifetime but in the lifetime of your children.' When Mandela asks, God sighs and replies: 'Not in my lifetime.'

14

The Balkans – Europe's wars

'For those who stand in the way of unity, a spit in the face, a sock in the jaw and, if necessary, a bullet in the head.' Enver Hoxha, the Albanian communist leader, didn't like anybody disagreeing with him. That's what Marxism was about in the Eastern bloc: if the people didn't like the government, change the people – or kill them if you were Stalin.

A trip to Romania made me think hard about the implosion of communism in Europe. Nicolae Ceauşescu had been one of the maddest and baddest of a very bad bunch. Once, the cold war was in the centre of Europe – in Berlin. For most of my reporting life it had shifted to the peripheries – wars in Asia, Africa and South America, proxy conventional wars in the Middle East. Pan-European history had frozen in the *glacis* of East–West confrontation. But with *glasnost* wars were springing up in the heart of Europe, most notably in the Balkans.

The collapse of the Soviet Union spelled the death of orthodox Marxist parties in China, Vietnam, North Korea and Cuba. Its world mission was the original *raison d'être* of Bolshevism. Destroying belief in the inevitable triumph of international socialism was bound to have a knock-on effect on electoral support for designer socialism in European democracies. Marxism had failed as a means of economic development and a model of government. Moscow's propaganda proclaimed its ideology would conquer the decadent West. Instead, the Soviet system created the starving and demoralised proletariat it was specifically designed to prevent. Above all, Marxism was judged a disaster because of the (now) obvious and extraordinary fragility of the former socialist regimes.

Marxism's downfall brought many changes, not least in language. From A to Z, from *apparatchik* to Zhivago, the 'evil empire' popularised numerous concepts and phrases. Big Brother and the gulag became less fearsome terms. Novelists had to invent alternatives to James Bond, moles and KGB honeytraps. The biggest change was that Marxists no longer set the intellectual agenda. John Torode, a British journalist, called Marxism

Romania

'a millennial cult disguised as the ultimate scientific philosophy'. It was a secular religion but history has pronounced its god dead. Scientific socialism has been proved as bogus as Nazi race theories.

Marxism had seduced generations of leading Western academics, writers, artists and poets. These fellow-travellers, dubbed 'useful idiots' by Lenin, never missed the chance to blame all evil on the US, while giving the USSR the benefit of every doubt. The murder of many millions by Stalin was deemed impossible in a 'worker's paradise'. In the social science faculties of Western universities it was a brave person who publicly defied the Marxist consensus. The intellectual frame of reference often began and ended with Bob Dylan's first album. Yet, after years of defending Marxist lies, very few, if any, dons recanted or apologised for misleading their students. There was a deafening silence.

The re-emergence of Eastern Europe seemed such a simple matter. Once the Wall was down, light would flood in. The Reds were gone or were going, and everyone would be free. Accustomed to seeing those behind the Wall as somehow uniform, uniformed, regimented, homogenous, there was an assumption that they would become uniformly free as well. But they haven't. Difference has become the antidote to the old failed ideology. Monolithic communism was easy to understand, hate, fear and fight. Today we have to wade through a fog of quasi-democrats, good old-fashioned fascists, born-again communists, bandoliered nationalists, mafiosi and Ruritanian warlords – stirring stuff for hacks, except that most of them liked taking pot-shots at journalists.

A friend of mine, Peter, was involved in sending aid to Romanian orphanages. In July 1991 he invited me to see what he was doing. We travelled to Bucharest on the same day. He was a charity-worker so he flew classy Swissair; I risked economy class on TAROM, the Romanian airline, which made even Pakistan's '*Inshallah* Airways' look upmarket. The only good part was the absence of cameras. Travelling the world with a video camera and gear is like running a marathon attached to a vacuum cleaner.

The plane, of obscure origins and past its sell-by date, looked likely to fall from the sky. When I met the passengers – a plane-load of Scottish football fans – I began to hope that it would. The airline food was seriously unrecognisable, with chunks of what I could see was meat but didn't risk tasting; normally, I will eat anything. Bucharest international airport was on a par with the food: poorly-lit, seedy, officious and studiously unwelcoming. It was a fair reflection of the whole country: post-revolutionary Romania was in the grip of an Orwellian nightmare. It didn't help getting stuck in the airport security control behind a Lebanese who even I thought was either a gun-runner or terrorist.

After queueing for an hour for my baggage, I was swamped by taxi-drivers drooling for payment in real currency. I found a man who looked and sounded like the idiot in Eco's *The Name of the Rose*. He spoke a smattering of all European languages in a way that suggested he had no native tongue. In a torrential downpour he had to find and attach his windscreen wipers – such capitalist trimmings were far too valuable to be left on a car. On our way through the flooded streets to the city centre I could see remnants – a few villas here and there – of the old grandeur of the 1930s. Bucharest was once called the 'Paris of the East'. Unfortunately most of it had been demolished by Ceauşescu and replaced by appalling concrete towers dedicated to the socialist utopia.

The great Romanian messiah, executed on Christmas Day 1989, decided to pull down much of the old picturesque Romania. I suppose he was also the sort of person who checked his desktop for bits of fluff. Ceauşescu destroyed villages wholesale, sometimes giving the peasants 48 hours to quit their homes. He levelled historic districts of his cowed capital to build egomaniacal monstrosities. In the very centre was a great citadel, the Casa Republicii, where he wanted to be buried. It dwarfed anything even Hitler or Franco had attempted. It is strange how often dictators try to mask their personal insecurities by building massively ugly monuments.

Ceauşescu had spared the old hotel I stayed in, but it had seen better days, maybe better centuries. My room was a decayed masterpiece of Art Deco. You could see it had been nice once but many of the important bits, like the shower head and light bulbs, were missing. Peter and his Romanian girlfriend, Diana, arrived to help me negotiate room service. It was just that: I had to go to a tiny room marked 'Service', discover what was available and then haggle on the price, amount of food and when. Prices were cheap. The £700 monthly rent on my house in Britain could have bought Diana's flat outright. She paid less than a pound a month for rental. I asked her about local politics, life and booze, but I could never get a straight answer on anything. Most Romanians were evasive on most topics ... except the possibility of getting out of Romania. Perhaps because they had spent a lifetime being threatened with jail for unauthorised conversations with foreigners.

Bucharest reflected a weird, shabby, sad, disorganised society. Take the lift in the hotel. In the day it was manned by an old woman who must have been in the Olympic wrestling team in her youth. At night it was driven by a striking peroxide blonde in very tight blue ski-pants. She spoke to me in broken Italian, so I never discovered whether she provided any extra night-time services.

I spent the next few days driving around Bucharest in a white coat in a brand-new ambulance donated by a British charity. It was sticky hot and we stopped to buy drinks from a roadside vendor. We wanted to take the bottles away with us. This was impossible, explained Diana. To do so we had to give the vendor the equivalent number of empty bottles of the same size. But how do you start off your bottle collection, if you are new to the country? We offered to pay extra for the privilege of taking a bottle plus drink; but no, we needed our own bottles. I began to understand why Romania had the world's highest suicide rate.

I was also beginning to comprehend Eastern Europe's transition to capitalism. The first advertising billboards had just appeared in the city – praising Panasonic and Xerox. You could get Coke in a few hotels. There was even imported beer if you paid in foreign currency. Diana led me into dark alleyways to meet shady characters who swapped me money at three times official rates. The city had a currency black market but very little in the shops. Once Eastern Europe had socialism without social justice, now it had capitalism with very little capital. I wondered which came first – political reform or economic development. In Romania the question seemed irrelevant: there was no chicken and no egg.

Romania was something of an odd man out in the Soviet empire. Romanians liked to think they were Latins, the French of Eastern Europe. During the Cold War the country reinforced the prejudices of both sides. To the East, its apparently enormous growth rate proved that communism worked. To the West the fact that it was still one of Europe's least developed countries proved that it didn't. Ceauşescu tried to be the de Gaulle of the Warsaw Pact. He was friendly with China, spoke to Israel and condemned the invasion of Czechoslovakia. For this he was fêted in the West. Actually, this was a clever bit of Moscow manipulation but that didn't stop even the House of Windsor showering royal accolades upon him. On their trips to the West, the Ceauşescus would strip every hotel room or noble house they stayed in and send all their loot back home.

Only in Romania was military force used extensively in an attempt to save the regime from the revolutionary fervour that swept Eastern Europe. The entirely out-of-touch Ceauşescu was overthrown by a combination of popular insurrection and a local communist party coup, encouraged by Moscow. The National Salvation Front, led by Ion Iliescu, won handsomely in the subsequent polls; elections that were judged 'flawed but not fraudulent' by international observers.

Iliescu was seen as the St George who slew the Ceauşescu dragon. Romanians have a disturbing history of flocking to support all-powerful leaders. Unfortunately the leadership of the National Salvation Front was largely made up of former communists, merely parading on the stage of democracy for the benefit of Western aid. Romania was an unfinished revolution.

The Salvation Front played upon traditional Romanian xenophobia, in particular discriminating against the large Hungarian minority in Transylvania. As one journalist put it, this had been the 'real bloodsucker of democracy' since the apparent revolution. Perhaps the best way to judge a country is by how it treats minorities. The government had not tried to stamp out lingering anti-Semitism, even though only 18,000 Jews had survived Nazism and communism. Defenders of the new government told me Romania was part of the typical Balkan culture where bouts of headbashing and corruption were inevitable, pointing out the horrendous legacy bequeathed by the worst dictatorship in the Soviet bloc.

Romania was the most backward state in Europe, except for Albania. The economy was pitiful. The workers and the population in general seemed utterly demoralised. There was little foreign investment – and for good reason. Elements in the government were paranoid about Romania being 'taken over' by foreigners. There had been 300 per cent price increases in key items such as petrol. Escalating unemployment prompted numerous wildcat strikes, but the general inertia made it difficult to judge whether Romanians were striking or working. They exemplified the classic Russian workers' joke: they pretend to pay us and we pretend to work.

As one foreign expert put it: 'Romanians will be happy to make do with half a capitalist loaf after having been denied the communist one.' Maybe. Life had been very hard under Ceauşescu: a seven-day working week, with lighting, hot water and heating severely rationed. He denuded the country in his (largely successful) attempt to pay off all foreign debt. I heard variations of other Russian jokes. 'What is five miles long and eats only potatoes? A Russian meat queue.' Few Romanians I met wanted the return of dictatorship, but the complaint 'at least things were cheaper under Ceauşescu' was very common.

Romanians, desperate to find out about the outside world, could now risk chatting to foreigners. Previously the dreaded secret police, the *securitate*, monitored nearly all contacts with outsiders, deploying a ruthless intelligence system where one in four Romanians was said to be an informer. On an individual basis Romanians, I found, could be very charming to foreigners but they still looked over their shoulders and talked cautiously until they got to know you. The government had reformed but not disbanded the *securitate*.

The atmosphere of fear and deprivation created a society with degraded values. Misha Glenny, the BBC's central European correspondent, used the phrase 'psychotic proletariat'. Hence the horror tales of dumping and trading in babies. Ceauşescu's rundown of the medical services had led to half Europe's child AIDS victims being in Romania, according to official figures. But Romania was also milking the AIDS and orphanage stories for all they were worth.

I wanted to find out whether Western aid was getting to the sick and abandoned children, or simply being siphoned off by desperate and greedy officials. After years bumbling around the third world – in which I definitely included Romania – I had become rather jaundiced about aid. I had met some saintly aid workers but my general impression was entirely negative. In Africa it destroyed local initiative, enriched the elites, and created armies of aid junkies. I was predisposed to expect the same in Romania. I was not disappointed.

I saw some aid enterprises in Bucharest but I wanted to get out into the country, away from PR exercises – not that Romanians were capable of understanding modern PR, but they had decades of training in public lying. Peter drove me to Slatina, about three and a half hours from the capital. I had heard of massive industrial pollution in Romania but I didn't see much evidence there, just drab peasant country with ribbon developments of roadside shacks. One or two shacks were elaborately decorated in the Eastern style; most were breeze-blocks, wooden or occasionally square mud huts. Donkey-carts were everywhere. So were soldiers. I wondered where the war was.

Slatina seemed more cheerful than grey, ill-lit Bucharest. It had a main street with recognisable shops. The orphanage had been given a few hours' notice of our visit. The children's home, in a normal apartment block, was also a home for senile adults. It stank of must and urine. Peopled with staring-eyed cripples and toothless dribbling crones, it was straight out of Dickens. We sat in various offices for a few hours where pot-bellied, unshaven admin types did nothing. Absolutely nothing. Nor did any of the male officials.

Then we had an inspection. Toys donated by British charities were taken out of a large box: the kids obviously hadn't seen them for a long time, if ever. The children went mad for an hour, but seemed more interested in the attention that Peter, Diana and I were giving them. They appeared utterly starved of affection. Although they didn't look unfed and were vaguely clean, they lived in stark, primitive surroundings. Their rooms – with open windows on the fourth floor – had just a few play-pens and dirty mattresses. There were no pictures and nothing else, once the toys were returned to the big box. All the children were mentally handicapped. One had just pulled his own eye out. As they clambered all over us, I had to leave with tears streaming down my face.

When I recovered I asked Diana why unskilled volunteers had to come all the way from England. Peter had brought four sixth-form vounteers to spend their summer helping in the orphanage. Why couldn't unemployed locals, who spoke the language, help out? I was treated to a classic piece of Romanian evasiveness.

Diana negotiated a hotel in Slatina for our volunteer do-gooders. It took less than half an hour. The place didn't have working toilets but it did have some food. The cabbage was OK and the rye bread and tomatoes were excellent. Tomatoes, I noticed, were always available in Romania. There was even beer and Coke. In the bar a group played a terrible mix of folk music and Turkish rock 'n' roll. It was like Nana Mouskouri played at very high speed. Peter commented: 'You've got me into some bad things but this is the worst.'

Then and there I decided to nip over the border to Yugoslavia. 'I'd prefer to get shot at than listen to this. I'm going to Yugoslavia tomorrow. At least it'll be quieter there.' Peter laughed. He understood my impulsiveness.

The next morning Diana took me to the railway station, where she spent an hour talking in Romanian. It seemed like a complicated deal to rent the place. She eventually emerged with a ticket, and spent an hour explaining how I would get to Serbia. There were so many possible vagaries that I just climbed on the next west-bound train. It was heading for Transylvania; that seemed interesting enough. The train was out of some World War Two movie, with carriage exteriors painted in metal grey, the colour of *Wehrmacht* trains in the early 1940s. I thought it would be an adventure to travel in an old Nazi caboose.

Clearly, nobody had done anything to the carriages since the Germans retreated. A peasant women boarded with a basket full of day-old chicks. People took their shoes off and lounged around. A young man opposite kept staring at me while he munched sunflower seeds. He picked bits out of his teeth with his tongue and blew them onto the floor. Various dark, swarthy men with droopy moustaches and 1940s clothes glowered at the obvious foreign intruder. There were lots of gypsies, real ones. It was like London's Northern Line. I felt at home.

The Sunflower Kid kept staring, and I began to wonder whether he was among the allegedly one in four Romanians moonlighting as informers. He stared, almost without blinking, for half an hour. I was determined not to be the first to break. I ignored him or gave him an occasional half-smile, one of those English work-place specialities when people see the same colleagues ten times a day. Eventually the starer spoke to me in very broken English. He wanted to live in England. I didn't meet a single Romanian in a country of fervent nationalists who wanted to stay at home. Luckily the Sunflower Kid had a reasonable mastery of the train timetable. He advised me to proceed via Craiova to Timisoara, the largely Hungarian-speaking town where the revolution had begun. Since

Romanian long-distance trains did not have buffets I ate enough sunflower seeds to germinate the whole of Wales.

Craiova station was like a large mausoleum, lit with a single bulb in the high-domed roof. I found someone who I thought might sell me a ticket. She was operating a large machine which was at least 50 years old. I spent 15 minutes trying to buy a ticket. I knew no Romanian but I did understand 15 minutes of no. Eventually a very beautiful young woman came to my rescue. She explained in French that if I gave her a wad of lei – just a few pounds – she would sort out my tickets. There was a train in four hours to the Serbian border via Timisoara. She said she would meet me later in the station bar. As I am always a sucker for a pretty face, I gave her the money and went in search of a beer.

The bar was in a large dowdy room. In the dim light I tried to attract the waiter. Once he skirted around me but thereafter ignored me. I had missed my chance: the only way I would get that much attention again was to marry his sister, or at least give him some cigarettes. I didn't smoke, but I always carried some good foreign cigarettes for such occasions. After I offered him one he rushed to bring me a beer. Soon my table was crowded with extras from the set of a Chicago gangster movie. Two self-proclaimed poets joined in the fray. To be fair, although I flashed the cigarettes they were happy to buy me beers. After an hour or so I remembered my promised ticket. I didn't expect to see the raven-haired beauty again and at about 10pm I started asking about accommodation. I was offered various private homes, whore-houses and possible hotels, but was saved from the agony of decision by the arrival of my ticket.

She shooed the Crazy Gang from the table and sat down to share a coffee. The train would be leaving in two hours, she said, handing me a ticket worth the exact amount of money I had given her. I cautiously offered her a few dollars for her trouble but she refused. She would be happy to sit and talk until my train left. That suited me fine.

Adela had worked for the railways for five years but was very frustrated with her menial job. She had worked in France and was very eager to return. Since my French was fairly basic she asked me basic questions. 'Are you married?' For the only time in my married life I almost said: '*Quelquefois*,' but refrained. She asked me to come back to visit her while I was in Romania. I told her I would write and that she was welcome to stay with me and my wife. After two hours of charming conversation with a striking 26-year-old woman, I was beginning to change my mind about Romania, even about going to Yugoslavia, but she put her arm in mine and led me to the train. She gave me a farewell which easily outclassed any kind of hospitality offered by any other railway official in the world. It was a pity I was standing on a platform with both hands full of luggage.

I wasn't stupid enough to think my boyish charm had won her over so quickly. That such a stunning female should be so desperate to get out of Romania was a tragic comment on her country.

Adela had organised the very best Romanian railways could offer, which wasn't much. I was booked into a 'first-class luxury sleeper', which translated as a doss-house on wheels. I shared a small compartment with an upper-class Romanian family: a 37-year-old woman and her two young children. She looked like Faye Dunaway and worked at the Romanian embassy in Belgrade. She spoke excellent French and a little English. Although it was 1.30am I played cards with the children. There was of course no restaurant car, so my new hosts shared their food and drink with me. Despite her diplomatic status and passport we endured constant rude interruptions by ticket inspectors and customs officials who had remembered all that the Gestapo had taught their old Romanian allies.

The Serb officials also combined the very best of Nazi and communist bureaucracy. I was glad to arrive in Belgrade's Hotel Moscow. Since the outbreak of the Yugoslav war tourists were thin on the ground and I haggled for a half-price room. There I sat down to enjoy the intermittent electricity and read a tourist booklet describing Yugoslavia as 'a land of contrasts'. For contrasts I had come to the right place at the right time.

Ex-Yugoslavia

Until the break-up of the Yugoslav federation newspaper editors tended to avoid political stories on the country because it was so bloody complicated. But in recent weeks the world's media was full of little lectures on and maps of Yugoslavia's six republics and two autonomous regions, as well as its different languages, religions and various isms. The contrasting cultures may have exacerbated the political strife but the great variety of language, cuisine, architecture and scenery attracted me. So did the fact that I could sample them all without enduring anyone wearing a 'kiss me quick' hat.

Straddling east and west, Yugoslavia once had everything; from picture-book Alpine villages, ancient Roman ruins and glorious coastline to reasonably efficient hotels, phones and transport. The abundance of splendid cathedrals, monasteries and mosques echoed the fact that although most Yugoslavs were Catholic or Orthodox Christians the federation had Europe's largest Muslim community. Scarcely larger than Britain, the country ranged in the north from Slovenia, a little Austria, to the Albanians in the south, one of the most backward regions of Europe. Many of the 24 million population spoke English, especially in

The Balkans

the main cities and on the hot, dry Adriatic.

Except for the destruction of the package tourist industry the war had done untold damage to the area. When I got there Slovenia had just seized independence after the deaths of only 20 people. Slovenia didn't matter much to the Serb communist politicians and generals who ran the old show. But Croatia was different. Lots of Serbs lived there. The fight to hold on to Croatia was just beginning. I had been involved in a number of Yugoslav war games while at Sandhurst, and knew something of the passions and the number of guns. I anticipated a long series of wars throughout the Balkans. First Croatia, then Bosnia, then Macedonia and, the most volatile of the lot, the Albanians in Kosovo province. I wanted to see something of the place before it all blew up in the faces of the smug Serb centralists trying to keep Tito's political corpse alive.

Belgrade was the federal capital and one of Europe's oldest cities. Because of its strategic position on the Danube it had been conquered and rebuilt 38 times. I wandered up to the much-restored Kalemegdan fortress right in the centre of old Belgrade, which offered a wonderful view over the city and river. Just outside the fortress stood the neo-baroque Orthodox cathedral, full of icons. The newer sections of the city were bustling, efficient, Western and expensive, but I had just left third-world Romania so perhaps my perspectives were a bit askew. By comparison Belgrade was a very cosmopolitan place where politicians wore dark suits and dark socks, often simultaneously.

I found the press club and made a few contacts, ending up in the Skadarlija district which my new friends likened to Montmartre in Paris. Like the Romanians, Serbs used France as their lodestone. I was happy to agree with their comparison. The cobbled streets, open-air restaurants, wandering musicians and hawkers were a pleasant backcloth to the excellent ethnic dishes. I spent most of the long meal being inducted into the arcane history of greater Serbia. Each person carefully explained that he or she was 'a moderate', not to be numbered among the crazy Serb nationalists. They were middle-class intellectuals who could see the wider picture. But when I touched on basic isssues, they were as chauvinist as the 'crazy nationalists' they purported to despise.

I asked: 'How can you expect to hold on to Kosovo, which is ten per cent Serb and 90 per cent Albanian, especially when you treat the majority like scum?' (My actual phraseology was slightly more diploma-tic.) This led to a long history lesson of battles in the Middle Ages. When I mentioned Croatia I got a blow-by-blow account of Croats bending over backwards to outdo the genocidal Germans during the Second World War, which seemed to tally with my own reading of Croat history. Nonetheless, despite the veneer of rationality, most Serbs I encountered glowed with an inner fire of intolerance.

Everyone I met felt that full-scale civil war was inevitable. Fighting talk was the rule, not the exception. Above all, the ancient hostilities between Serb and Croat fed off one another. For all their hatreds the Serbs and Croats spoke essentially the same language, albeit Serbs used Cyrillic script and Croats the Roman.

The EC was trying to maintain a ceasefire between Croatia and Serbia when I was there but no one was listening to Brussels. In central Belgrade numerous armed policemen relaxed in the summer heat. The federal army had called up its reserves. Were they preparing to fight for the dead federation or the new Greater Serbia? About ten million of the old federation were Serbs. Despite the apparent prosperity of the city Serbs complained about economic decline, massive hidden unemployment and inflation. Until recently inflation had been 2,500 per cent, but had dropped considerably. The more prosperous Croats and Slovenians claimed that the taxes they paid were being wasted by the bungling, bullying communist *apparatchiki* in Belgrade.

I asked a Serb lawyer why he wanted to fight when further conflict would destory the fragile economy. 'The English insist on hanging on to Northern Ireland. We feel the same about our people in Croatia.' About 600,000 Serbians lived in Croatia; some of the Serb-dominated areas had just declared themselves autonomous republics.

I caught a train from Belgrade to Zagreb, the capital of Croatia. The Serbs in my compartment warned me to stop talking politics when we reached the Croatian border. They were visibly angry but also tense when Croatia's new defence force stopped the train and demanded identity documents. An old Croat woman, dressed all in black, started to cry. 'All my family was killed in the fighting between Serbs and Croats during the Hitler war. I don't want it to happen all over again.' Once the Croat soldiers had left, a young Serb said: 'Those fascist Croats killed tens of thousands of Serbs in camps during the last war.' The bitterness ran deep…and the new war was only just beginning.

In Zagreb independence flags were as commonplace as the rumours that federal tanks were about to seize the city centre. Croatia seemed more efficient but not necessarily more democratic than Serbia. The country was ruled by a single party, the Croatian Democratic Union, which owed more than a few debts to its fascist predecessor. The break-up of Yugoslavia was not simply a question of brave little democracies challenging a communist centralism.

Inevitably the Balkans were unravelling the treaties imposed after the First World War. It was no coincidence that the two extremities of the old Ottoman empire, Slovenia and Kurdistan, should be demanding freedom at the same time. The general collapse of communism was another factor. Yugoslavia was more like the Soviet Union than the recently freed states of Eastern Europe. Both enforced federations were on the point of economic as well as political disintegration. That was why the EC was so reluctant to recognise the independence of Slovenia and Croatia, for fear of encouraging the premature collapse of the Soviet Union as well as separatist demands in other European countries, such as Czechoslovakia.

Germany, Croatia's old ally, was pushing for recognition; France, Serbia's traditional friend, was hostile. Political warfare embroiled the EC. In eastern Croatia real fighting between Serbian and Croatian irregulars was intensified by the intervention of regular Croatian and Serb forces. Hundreds had already been killed in this region. Because the overt invasion of Slovenia seemed to have failed, hardline communist generals in Serbia appeared to be adopting a policy of creeping annexation of parts of Croatia. Serbs controlled about a third of Croat territory.

If Serb tanks were going to rumble into Zagreb – which the local papers insisted they would – I wanted a good vantage point. I booked myself into a room with a view, the top floor of Hotel Dubrovnik overlooking the main square. I was excited; it was what I imagined Warsaw felt like in the early autumn of 1939. I had often done voice reports for BBC Wales news, phoning Cardiff reverse charge and doing ad-lib three-minute pieces live or recorded for later use. Looking out over the square I rang up the Beeb but none of my usual contacts were around. Some inane woman asked me whether Yugoslavia was an important story. She had the news sense of a butterfly. I tried to explain but she said she had to break off because there was an office party going on. It was some time before I bothered to report again for BBC Wales. Besides, they paid a pittance.

Since no tanks appeared I decided to explore Zagreb. It seemed a wonderful city, a little Vienna, clean and quiet except for the immaculate trams. In the plush piano bar of the best hotel in town I fell in with some foreign journalists. I wanted to go to Osijek, the scene of fierce fighting, so I needed some instant knowledge. If I had been filming I would have felt obliged to leave immediately for the front. But I was half on holiday so I decided to roam around Zagreb persuading myself that the tanks would come any minute. Frankly I didn't care. Without seeing it through the lens of a video camera it would not have seemed real to me.

The medieval part of town was dominated by the twin towers of the cathedral, first consecrated in 1217. Two other churches interested me: St Mark's, the roof of which displayed the coats of arms of Croatia and

Zagreb in enamel tiles; and St Catherine's, built by Jesuits in the seventeenth century. I was entranced by the baroque detail. Outside the main government building toytown soldiers paraded up and down in an amazing march, part goose-step and part ballet. Zagreb took its cultural role seriously, with numerous theatres and museums. The most famous museum was Muzej Mimara, which housed one of the world's great art collections. The town's classical architecture was well-proportioned, Austro-Hungarian style, rococo in parts but not over-dressy.

Zagreb was not all art, architecture and piety. I would argue that it *was* the best place in Europe to sample outdoor café life. Winding through the old town were streets full of open-air restaurants buzzing with vitality. Perhaps because visitors were thin on the ground, people came up to talk to me. An attactive art student asked if she could join my table; within five minutes she had volunteered to take me on a sight-seeing expedition. She was about to move to Vienna and was savouring Zagreb's delights before what she knew would be a long separation.

I hired a car to drive to Ljubljana, the capital of Slovenia, normally an hour's journey. It took me considerably longer because some roads were blocked or damaged by recent fighting. This was my good fortune because the side roads yielded scenery which was idyllic in its rustic charm: utterly tidy villages with spotlesss Alpine-style houses, perfect little guest-houses, and everywhere little churches with onion-domed spires. War in Europe seemed surreal, and even more preposterous in this setting.

Slovenia was the most advanced area of Yugoslavia, in economic terms the Sweden of the Balkans. Indeed, Slovenes always thought of themselves as European rather than Balkan. The prosperity of the little state of two million people seemed to justify their traditional smugness. They were also tense. In the capital, queues had formed outside a shop selling old Russian gas masks at exorbitant prices. The adjacent restaurants were full. With more hope than conviction Slovenes told me that perhaps Austrian or even Italian armies would help them if they were invaded again. This was the kind of talk which fuelled Serbian propaganda claims that Germany was trying to establish a 'Fourth Reich' by making Slovenia and Croatia economic satellites. But diplomatic recognition of Slovenia and Croatia was inevitable. After federal Yugoslav planes launched air raids on Slovenian cities – the first such incident in Europe since 1945 – Western support was bound to swing towards Slovenia.

I had seen the occasional burnt-out tank and armoured vehicle on the way into Ljubljana but the city itself seemed unscathed. The River Ljubljana ambled peacefully beneath an array of over-decorous little bridges. The small city was dominated by a twelfth-century castle and, below it, the cathedral next to a daily open market full of produce, flowers and people.

In spite of the war, I really liked ex-Yugoslavia. The occasional bursts of old-style communist bureaucracy aside, the mood of Oriental decadence, Balkan intrigue, ubiquitous courtesy and European sanitation appealed to me. In early 1991 it was obvious even to me that nobody could put Yugoslavia's Humpty-Dumpty together again. I wrote at the time that the problems of dividing up that Rubic Cube of mini-nationalities would probably not be accompanied without major population movements. I had not anticipated the future horrors of ethnic cleansing, and naively believed that the EC could be a peace-broker. The EC had immense clout: 53 per cent of federal trade was with the Community. I never accepted that Europe's borders were sacrosanct, preferring Balkanisation to Lebanonisation. Instead the EC proved to be totally inept; after years of slaughter it was left to the blue berets and NATO planes.

I was right on Austria's border; I could board a train to Paris. That was my first inclination, but I had promised to take Peter out for dinner in Bucharest and had left some of my kit there. Reluctantly, I would have to go back. I dreaded returning to Romania. On one of the last trains to run from Zagreb to Belgrade before Croats and Serbs started a major war which killed over 7,000 people, I found myself next to an apostle of peace: an Australian mystic called Marga. For the first hour he did not speak, meditating in the lotus position like some frozen Buddha with the odd audible mantra. Since there was no one else in the carriage I became bored and disrupted his trance. This was a mistake: for the next five hours I suffered a detailed description of his diet and bowel movements. He was a self-centred, health-obsessive neurotic who would drive anyone to murder not karma.

When I gratefully left him at Belgrade station I offered him my hand. Instead he cupped his hands together and gave an oriental bow. 'You're a nice bloke but I don't shake hands. Catch too many diseases.' I wondered what Mother Teresa would make of that, and prayed for divine help for a Croat sniper or Montenegrin bandit or Bosnian fundamentalist to zap this phoney Buddhist. Hopefully St Peter would extend his hand only to those who arrived at the pearly gates free of all isms.

Near Belgrade station I ate two meals on the trot and bought supplies for the desert of Romanian railways. As the train started off a young blonde medical student came into my compartment. She spoke excellent English – the long ride to Bucharest might not be so bad. After five minutes of animated conversation she abruptly walked out of the compartment. Did I have some dreadful disease of which the Buddhist and medical student had observed subtle symptoms? Hours later she came back to apologise, explaining she had to negotiate a money deal in foreign currency, the only way to survive in Romania. I would have given her good rates just for her company. Her place had been taken by a suspicious-looking Algerian with whom I chatted in French; he seemed a good sort. The notoriously xenophobic Romanians detested Arabs as well as gypsies, Jews, Hungarians...well, they didn't seem to like anyone except the French. I knew in my bones that the border would be trouble.

A very large Romanian customs official entered the compartment and demanded my passport. He looked at it and asked for what seemed a large amount of Romanian money. I am always confused by numbers in foreign languages. '*Je voudrais expliquer, monsieur ...*' He told me to shut up in very precise French and walked off with my passport. I had a second valid passport secreted in my bag but I wasn't going to let him bulldoze me. A soldier came into the compartment and pointed his rifle at me. It took me a while to realise that I was to get off the train. He indicated that he would guard my luggage. Two other soldiers frog-marched me into a room where the US dollar price of a visa (which I already had) kept escalating. I was torn between my desire to haggle and the possibility of the train going off with my gear. I could see other passengers being yanked off, including my new Algerian friend.

I was taken to another room to be interrogated, this time by a young woman who spoke good French and reasonable English. She asked me what I was doing in Romania. I explained the orphanage bit with heavy emphasis on the foreign donations and no mention of any journalism. I've never yet met an immigration or customs official who has shown me the slightest bit of warmth once they find out I am a hack. She noticed the 'Dr' on my passport and told the other security men in Romanian that I was engaged in vital medical work in Bucharest. I *think* that's what she said. It was the only time I have ever pretended my D Litt was an MD. But I paid a small fee and decided that silence was the better part of sound ethics.

The Algerian and I jumped on the train as it started to move. He could hardly comment on Romanian racism, having seen me given a hard time, and just said: 'All socialist states are the same. Too much bureaucracy.'

At Timisoara the compartment filled up with ethnic Hungarians. One nodded discreetly that I should follow him into the corridor. Always curious, I did so. He pulled out a bottle of Romania's famous plum brandy and shared it with me, along with his life story, explaining that he wouldn't talk to me in front of other people in the compartment. A schoolteacher, he made me his instant friend and pupil. He acted as guide and mentor during the constant surprise attacks by jack-booted ticket collectors. The whole compartment would be asleep with the lights out when officials would burst in, flicking on the lights to see if we had been digging escape tunnels. Waiting an hour for everyone to fall asleep again, they would launch another raid. Perhaps the Romanian tourist authorities ran a special charm school for them.

Back in my Bucharest hotel I had prepared a few Italian phrases for the voluptuous blonde lift operator. Unfortunately the all-in wrestler was doing night duty, undermining my theory about earlier approaches from the blonde. In a very short time in Romania I had received a surprisingly large number of offers from attractive young women. Ceauşescu had a lot to answer for.

After seeing Peter and debriefing the volunteers about their orphanage experiences, I flew out from Bucharest. Diana had spent the best part of a week working on the paperwork for my flight so there were none of the usual Romanian hassles. A young Romanian physics teacher sat next to me, on her way to Britain for the first time. She was obviously intelligent and spoke good English. 'I do not want communism in Romania but nor do I want capitalism.' She described modern Britain to me: Dickensian conditions which formed standard Eastern bloc propaganda. She had never heard of the National Health Service or free education. I didn't argue. If Russia was Upper Volta with rockets, Romania was just Upper Volta. Her first trip outside her own country would open her eyes.

I told her a little about my bad impressions of Romania. Like the society, much of the environment was ravaged. But how could ancient, mass-polluting industries be closed when there was already serious unemployment? Economic reform would mean ending government subsidies and even more price increases. Above all, it meant dealing with diabolical foreigners. Despite and because of its strong-arm methods Iliescu's government still feared another popular insurrection. The physics teacher supported the return of the king. Diana had said the same thing. Increasingly Romanians were hoping that King Michael, deposed in 1947, would return from exile. Perhaps they yearned once more for another 'great man' to save them. The royalist reverie was interrupted by our touchdown. I felt glad to be back in Heathrow. Things worked. Even the passport official smiled.

Bosnia

I felt ashamed to call myself a European after the genocide in Bosnia. I had lived too long in the shadow of Auschwitz to believe it could ever happen again. But it has. Forty-four per cent of Bosnia's former population – before the mass exodus and killings – were Muslim. Saddam Hussein rather cheekily complained about human rights' abuses in Los Angeles and, with more justice, of the Muslim plight in Bosnia. If it was morally right to attack Iraq to remove Saddam's occupying forces, why shouldn't foreign Islamic forces help liberate Bosnia after Serbia's (and Croatia's) invasion? Iran offered to send troops to do precisely this. Bosnia was recognised by the EC and the US. Then the country was subjected to foreign occupation, torture of civilians, *de facto* annexation of territory by force, and contempt and harassment of neutral representatives of the EC, UN and Red Cross. From the Bosnian Muslim perspective the question was clear: why didn't the overwhelmingly powerful Western European armies launch a Balkan version of Desert Storm? They didn't need massive airlifts; they could drive in from next door.

It can never be that simple in the Balkans. The battlefield *status quo* looks like being the basis of new frontiers. With minor territorial adjustments the Bosnian Muslims will be lucky to be left with a tiny state. The fighting in Sarajevo has been the heaviest in any European capital since 1945. To an outsider it seems so senseless, not least because the various communities there have lived together peacefully for decades. The peace movement was much stronger in Sarajevo than in jingoistic Zagreb and Belgrade.

The genocide in Bosnia will continue to have major repercussions on minorities throughout Europe and central Asia, not least among the Hungarians in Romania and the volatile Russian minorities on the fringes of the former Soviet empire. The Serbs and Croats originally denied that religion should define nationality. The Muslims were fellow Slavs who speak Serbo-Croat. But Muslim Bosnians argued that since religion was their main definition of nationhood it was that much more important to them.

It could be argued that it is in Western Europe's interest to see Bosnia carved up between Catholic Croats and Orthodox Serbs. What Western government wants a unified Muslim-dominated Bosnia, led by a 'mad mullah', right in the centre of Europe? There is already disquiet at the march of Islam in the Asian successor states of the Soviet Union, as well as the growing influence of Turkey. Bosnia could still be the first fully-fledged Islamic state in Europe. True, Albania is a country with a Muslim majority, but the trend there is towards a secular nationalism. In Bosnia Muslims do not distinguish themselves by any other factor than their religion.

Many Bosnian Muslims sympathised with Saddam Hussein in the Gulf

War. Arabs states have provided money and weapons for the Bosnian army. Although the Bosnian president, Alija Izetbegovic, is a deeply religious man, Bosnian Muslims have not formed a mullah-ridden society. The scenario of a militant Muslim state in Europe is not a likely one. But the Austrian, Italian and especially German outcry over the Serb treatment of Slovenia and Croatia took a long time to be extended to Bosnia, and only when the death toll reached fantastic proportions. Scores died in Slovenia; hundreds of thousands have died or been injured in Bosnia. Why? The sheer complexity of Balkan politics? Compassion fatigue? Or innate racism in a Europe increasingly fearful of being 'swamped' by immigrants, especially from Muslim states?

The crisis in the Balkans will not go away. In 1914 violence in Sarajevo led to the First World War. The massacres in modern Sarajevo are not likely – yet – to cause a pan-European conflict. But if the killings continue, the continent's major political problem – minorities threatening violent revision of state boundaries – will dash all hopes of European peace, let alone unity. After all, Bosnia's Muslims are also Europeans.

In Europe you don't expect to find people foraging for grass to eat. That's what it looked like in Sarajevo, although I was told the locals were hunting for 'wild lettuce'. Passers-by in smart-looking clothes ignored the scavengers. I sat drinking a cappuccino in an open-air café while snipers were blazing away a few hundred yards from the relaxed coffee set. It was September 1994. I needed to remind myself why one of the most cosmopolitan cities in southern Europe was tearing itself apart.

I travelled from Zagreb. Apart from the barely visible presence of tens of thousands of refugees, the Croatian capital appeared untouched by war. The cleaned-up Austro-Hungarian buildings and the green-domed churches were at their best in the late summer sunshine. The good company of a friend, Slavka, who spoke fluent Serbo-Croat, added to the holiday mood.

As journalists, we both had UN accreditation and could have flown, with our flak jackets and tin helmets, in a UN plane to Sarajevo … war permitting. Instead, we decided to go overland by bus. Before the war, the trip might have taken six or seven hours.

After 27 hours of road-blocks in a bus crammed with Bosnian peasants, refugees and food parcels, my holiday mood had dispersed. The shelled ruins of Mostar had depressed me. The sticky heat and smell of bodies were a minor problem compared with my concern at driving at night, without lights, in a large bus along hairpin bends on the tracks of Mount Igman, the only road access to the far outskirts of the Bosnian capital. The Serbs had largely stopped their shelling, but had tightened the siege by blocking all roads to the Bosnian government-held parts of the city.

Six miles short of Sarajevo, the bus was hit by cannon shells from a Serbian anti-aircraft position. The bus was overcrowded with mainly women and children. The first burst went through the windscreen. The bus stopped, a sitting target for the directional tracer bullets which kept up an intermittent fusillade for 15 minutes. In the confined space, the smell of shit, cordite, fear and sweat was overwhelming. There was little screaming or panic, while I tried to impress upon Slavka the need to translate loudly: 'Get the bloody door open.' I had been prepared enough to sit by the central door, with a quick 'grab bag' with my basics, passport and bribes.

Eventually, the door opened. I pulled Slavka out across the live, prone bodies jamming the aisle. After crawling on all fours through some undergrowth, and then bunny-hopping under fire, bizarrely leading Slavka, an old woman and a young Bosnian woman, in a game of follow my leader, we found an old trench. The granny prayed, the Bosnian girl was in deep shock, and I was trying to remember the Serbo-Croat word for minefield.

It took an hour to sneak to the bottom of the mountain into a Muslim area. I traded some whisky for a Bosnian army unit's agreement to allow us to join their attempt to get into the city. That failed and we were left with the only other route, a tunnel under the main minefield. It took 12 hours to queue and get permission; the locals were not keen on journalists using their precious tunnel.

By this stage the Bosnian girl, Vedrana, was in extreme shock and turning blue. The tunnel would be impossible for her. It was time to use my 'connections', the Bosnian way of doing business. A passing French armoured vehicle refused to take a local, no matter what state she was in. I finally persuaded a chivalrous British officer to break all the rules (and risk his career) by taking the three of us on board his UN vehicle and negotiate the French roadblocks, arguably more touchy than their Serb counterparts.

Slavka and I stayed at the ravaged Holiday Inn and joined the other hacks feeling their way around the pitch-black corridors. Vedrana's father, a local bigwig, insisted that we stay at his house on the sniper's front line. He wanted to thank us for getting his daughter into town. He insisted also on giving me long lectures by candlelight on 12th-century Bosnian history. I found his broken German, and the distinctly 20th-century rattle of constant small-arms fire in the street outside, rather distracting.

I needed a bath and a drink. Water was scarce, but the Sarajevo brewery was intact. Vedrana was a Slovene, her boyfriend, Tomo, a Serb, and their friends Muslims. After the rudeness of our initial welcome, I was treated to the most magnificent hospitaliy available in the old Muslim quarter of town. Because of the 10pm curfew, the drinking started very early and very earnestly. I could see why the Balkan tragedy was dubbed the 'slivovitz war'.

Every Sarajevan I met wanted to know why the world had betrayed them. 'All your Western armies defended the dictatorship in Kuwait. You could have just driven in and saved our democracy,' said one Muslim officer. 'Ah, but we have no oil,' said his friend. 'All the EC talks about is cantonisation. That's just a classy name for carving us up,' he added.

'Look at how we all get on – we're Serbs, Croats and Muslims drinking here together. It's the peasants in the countryside and outside propaganda that are destroying our city.'

Everyone I had ever encountered in the Balkans accused the other sides' leaders of being bedwetting psychopaths. Long ago I had come to the conclusion that Serbs and Croats were right about their politicians. The Muslims, the cement of Bosnia, were caught in the middle, and the shortest-lived state in modern Europe had been destroyed. Like rape victims, the Bosnian Muslims were obviously asking for trouble. Maybe it was because the Balkan names were too difficult for Western foreign ministries. To adapt P J O'Rourke, the unspellables were shooting the unpronounceables and committing unspeakable atrocities. UNPROFOR, the UN Protection Force, 'monitored' some of the wholesale rapes and massacres, but their mandate allowed them precious little room to do anything about them.

'This hell of a crazy war,' said Tomo in broken English. 'I commute front line in a tram. I think I have a nervous fall-down.' His Muslim friends were even crazier: they wanted to fight their only (unreliable) allies, the Croats, while the Serbs were strangling the city. This was *Passport to Pimlico* with lunacy and guns.

Like Romania, some of the besieged citizens asked me how to get out of their urban Hades, but most were surprisingly resigned to the day-to-day hazards. How do you cope with the drama? I asked one resident. 'Drama gets lost when you live it.' I talked to the assistant editor of the main newspaper who had somehow kept his paper alive throughout the two years of constant shelling. The children, he told me, had lost an average of 10 kilos in weight. One youngster explained how he had tried to prise open a 15-day-old loaf of bread with a hammer. Aid, a substitute for effective Western intervention, was now being flown regularly into the city. Water and electricity worked sometimes. Even the Pope was coming. When he didn't, the largely Muslim city felt let down once more by the world. Cynics said food aid just fattened them up to make easier targets for the snipers. It was a tough war for hacks, too. Nearly 40 had been killed by the end of 1994.

It was time to leave. I had run out of whisky and cigarettes. Avid foreign members of the anti-tobacco lobby became 'Sarajevo smokers' because of the strain, and cigarettes are an almost compulsory ice-breaker at road-blocks. It's hard for a man to kill you when you're doing your best to give him a Marlboro.

I did not intend to return by bus. I flew out on an RAF Hercules, the UN route dubbed 'Maybe Airlines'. The most difficult part of the journey back – luggage (temporarily) lost by BA and strike-bound British Rail which marooned me – was yet to come. Coming home was getting harder.